Religious Conversion in India

Religious Conversion in India

The Niyogi Committee Report of Madhya Pradesh in 1956 and Its Continuing Impact on National Unity

MANOHAR JAMES

FOREWORD BY
ROBERT ERIC FRYKENBERG

American Society of Missiology Scholarly Monograph Series 55

☙PICKWICK *Publications* · Eugene, Oregon

RELIGIOUS CONVERSION IN INDIA
The Niyogi Committee Report of Madhya Pradesh in 1956 and Its Continuing
Impact on National Unity

American Society of Missiology Scholarly Monograph Series 55

Pickwick Publications
An Imprint of Wipf and Stock Publishers
199 W. 8th Ave., Suite 3
Eugene, OR 97401

www.wipfandstock.com

PAPERBACK ISBN: 978-1-7252-9454-7
HARDCOVER ISBN: 978-1-7252-9455-4
EBOOK ISBN: 978-1-7252-9456-1

Cataloguing-in-Publication data:

Names: James, Manohar, author. | Frykenberg, Robert Eric, foreword.

Title: Religious conversion in India : the Niyogi Committee Report of Madhya
Pradesh in 1956 and its continuing impact on national unity / by Manohar
James ; foreword by Robert Eric Frykenberg.

Description: Eugene, OR: Pickwick Publications, 2022 | American Society of
Missiology Scholarly Monograph Series 55 | Includes bibliographical references
and index.

Identifiers: ISBN 978-1-7252-9454-7 (paperback) | ISBN 978-1-7252-9455-4
(hardcover) | ISBN 978-1-7252-9456-1 (ebook)

Subjects: LCSH: Missions—India—Madhya Pradesh. | Hinduism—Relations—
Christianity. | Christianity and other religions—Hinduism | Christianity—
India—Madhya Pradesh. | Freedom of religion—India—Madhya Pradesh. |
Nationalism—India—History.

Classification: BV3280.M23 J36 2022 (print) | BV3280.M23 (ebook)

03/03/22

To

All my Indian brothers and sisters

and to

All who love India, despite its shortcomings

*. . . Every man going out of the Hindu pale is not only
a man less, but an enemy the more.*

—Swami Vivekananda

Contents

Illustrations

Foreword

ON THE FIFTH OF August 2020, a momentous and pivotal event took place in India's history. At a ceremonial puja linked to the official laying of the cornerstone for the Ram Janmabhoomi Mandir, an event presided over by Prime Minister Narendra Modi, India became a de facto Hindu nation. This action was taken in stark defiance of India's avowed secular Constitution. This deed was done on the very site in Ayodhya where, on the sixth of December 1992, violent mobs belonging to the Vishva Hindu Parishad had demolished the Babri Masjid. In the ensuing communal riots and violence that followed, many thousands of people lost their lives. Barely a decade later, in February of 2002, was a massive Gujarat pogrom perpetrated against Muslims. That state was then being governed by none other than the Chief Minister Narendra Modi. Thousands more lost their lives. What this all means is this: The Republic of India today has abandoned any pretence of abiding by the avowedly secular Constitution which guaranteed rights to its many ethnic and religious minorities. Instead, what has come into being is a blatantly "Hindu Rashtra" where claims of majoritarian rule have turned into a system of majority tyranny resulting in oppression and persecution, if not outright destruction and death, for people not belonging to the "Hindu nation."

What took place on August fifth, 2020, however blatantly it violated India's Constitution, was no sudden, or surprising, or shocking event. Rather, it can be seen as the culmination of a process that had been developing for nearly two centuries, ever since India as a single political system covering the entire subcontinent came into being. Indeed, the very concepts of "India" (or "Indian") and "Hindu" (or "Hinduism") can be seen as twins that entered the modern vocabulary of a newly emerging country at almost the very same time—beginning in the 1770s when the Government of India first came into existence and gained momentum. Simultaneously, a new consciousness and self-realization of forming an Indian public also began to come into existence. While initially synonymous, meaning anything that was "native" to all cultures and peoples within the Indic subcontinent, meanings of the two terms gradually diverged. The term "Hindu" was increasingly applied, and applied more particularly, to religious phenomena; and the new term "Hinduism" (initially spelled "Hindooism")[1] was coined specifically to describe religious cultures, systems, ideologies, and traditions within the subcontinent. Subjected to rigorous analysis in more recent times, the term "Hinduism" was found to be so amorphous, complex, and confusing, if not contradictory, that Professor Romila Thapar coined the concept of "Syndicated Hinduism" to denote a single over-arching system of organized religious institutions and traditions.[2]

At about the same time that these two processes, one political and the other religious, were coming into being, a third set of movements also emerged and then started to proliferate throughout India. This process began in 1799, in the Tirunelveli area of Tamil Country, not far from Kanya Kumari, near the southern tip of the continent. A mass movement of radical conversion to Christianity was led by local Tamil evangelists who had been trained by German missionaries in Thanjavur who had come from Tranquebar (aka Tarangbadi). The Tranquebar Mission, begun in 1706, and led by Bartholomäus Ziegenbalg, had imported two explosive ideas from Halle in Germany: (1) that every man, woman, and child on earth should possess the Word of God in that person's own mother tongue; (2) that basic literacy (as well as numeracy) should be provided to every human being, regardless of class or caste. Thus it was that institutionalized renditions of these two explosive ideas prompted gifted and highly trained Tamil preachers to enter into the villages of Tirunelveli. As a result, a mass movement

---

1. The origin of this concept has been traced to 1780s. Charles Grant, an official of the East India Company, was probably the first to use the term "Hindooism": cf. Oddie, *Imagined Hinduism*, 71; but the term was codified by William Ward, of the Serampore Trio of British Baptist missionaries, in his *View of the History, Literature and Religion of the Hindoos*.

2. Challenges in historiography concerning the term "Hindu" and "Hinduism" have been advanced for nearly fifty years. In Sontheimer and Kulke, *Hinduism Reconsidered*, see "The Emergence of Modern 'Hinduism' As a Concept and As an Institution: A Reappraisal with Special Reference to South India," by Robert Eric Frykenberg, 1–29 (or 74–109). Perhaps the most recent studies are found in Sweetman and Malik, *Hinduism in India: Modern and Contemporary Movements*; in this volume, also see "The Sacred in Modern Hindu Politics: Historical Processes Underlying Hinduism and Hindutva, by Robert Eric Frykenberg, 95–122.

occurred that eventually led to village temples being turned into chapel-schools. Increasing literacy enabled local Christians, most of them Shanars (aka Nadars), to read the Tamil Bible in their own mother tongue. Indeed, the fact that the Bible had been translated and published in earlier decades of the 18th century, making it available to all classes of Tamil people, had itself been a revolutionary event. The social revolution resulting from this mass movement upset the agrarian order and, in turn, provoked violent reactions. Local lords of the land and other elites who benefitted from the old order brought gangs of "clubmen" from the Ramnad to quell conversions and to restore the old order. Christian chapels and schools were demolished, and local believers beaten, deprived of their belongings, and sent into the jungle to suffer or die. Due to the persecutions they suffered, many of these Christian converts formed new settlements—sanctuary "villages of refuge" for fleeing and homeless Christian families. As numbers of Christians doubled and tripled, multiplying in the decades that followed, and as Christian institutions proliferated, with schools and churches multiplying, so also movements of opposition increased in size and ferocity. One of the earliest anti-conversion movements, known as the Vibuthi Sangam (or "Ashes Society"), arose in Tirunelvelli during the 1820s. This movement for the forcible reconversion of Christians soon allied itself to the Salay Street Society of Madras. Similar movements also sprang up in Bengal, and in other parts of northern and western India.

This brings us to the remarkable book by Manohar James. His work is a splendid and thorough study of the influence of Niyogi Committee Report of Madhya Pradesh as a pivotal turning point in the expression of rising Hindu Nationalism and of radical resistance to the presence of Christianity in India. At that time, fierce reactions against Adivasi (aboriginal) peoples of Central India who had converted to Christianity had recently arisen. Hundreds had been massacred. Despite the fact that most conversion movements in the area had been led by Indian missionaries, Christian conversions were blamed on what were called "foreign" missionaries. Insidious "colonial" intrusions from abroad were seen as exploiting and taking advantage of the "backward," and therefore gullible and simple-minded "tribals." Such influences needed to be eradicated.

The significance of this work by James lies in its focus upon the first break away from the legal tenets of even-handed secular safeguards of religious toleration and multicultural diversity guaranteed by India's Constitution. While the author traces earlier influences leading to this development into the early nineteenth century, and while he also shows that India under the British Raj had benefitted from a legal system that protected religious liberty and social diversity, it was the official action of the State of

Madhya Pradesh that first brought forward formal measures to contravene provisions of India's Constitution. These provisions had been painstakingly laid down by Dr. Bhimrao Ramji (or "Babasaheb") Ambedkar, India's inspired jurist, economist, and social reformer. It was he who, as India's first law minister and prime architect of India's Constitution, had done his best to protect minorities and despised ("untouchable") communities from discrimination and oppression.

In light of such an historical background and context, this perceptive and thorough study by Manohar James can be seen and appreciated. The India of Ambedkar and Nehru existing when the Niyogi Commission Report was written can be seen as suffering the first important official challenge to the secularism enshrined in its Constitution. The fact that this violation of the Constitution was allowed to go unchallenged, and hence, was tacitly unopposed by authorities of India, is significant. This basic contradiction, or self-deception, had been inherent within the nationalist movement from its very first inception in the nineteenth century. This contradiction was partially due to the fact that it had been allowed, or engendered, from the outset, by inclusion of two parallel, and often conflicting, forces or processes then developing within India. On one side, India's nationalism was being fuelled by what came to be known as the "Hindu" religious revivalist movements. These movements had been reactions to what some would later label the "conversion bogey" of under-classes and lower-castes turning Christian and/or Muslim—or eventually, under the inspiration of Ambedkar, of conversions to Neo-Buddhist, and other faith communities. On the other side was the rise of a modern and secular middle class, with many of its leaders emerging from universities and law schools of the United Kingdom, as also from growing numbers of modern colleges and universities in Mumbai, Kolkata, Chennai, and throughout the land.

These two processes which were blended within the Indian National Congress from when it first formed in 1885, continued to exist until India's Independence in 1947. It was this inherent contradiction with the INC, along with fears of being overwhelmed by Hindu majoritarianism, that led Muslims who felt threatened to pull away and form the All-India Muslim League in 1906. It was also this contradiction that prompted Mohammed Ali Jinnah to abandon the Indian National Congress and become the leader of the separatist Muslim League during the 1920s. On the opposite side, it was also this same contradiction that engendered M. K. Gandhi's Satyagraha campaigns of non-violent resistance to the Raj while, at the same time, ritually invoking blessings of Hindu deities and imagery—all of this being in defiance of Nehru's vision of a secular India. Thus, simultaneous membership within the Indian National Congress, enabled militant campaigns of the Hindu Mahasabha, founded and led by V. D. Savarkar, and the Rashtriya Swayamsevak Sangh (RSS), founded and led by K. B. Hedgewar, to pursue communalist goals while, simultaneously, remaining under the inclusivist umbrella of the INC.

Thus, all these exclusive elements of "Syndicated Hinduism" and inclusive elements of secular nationalism, blended within the Indian National Congress, enabled continuous, as well as sporadic, outbreaks of communal violence against Muslims and Christians but never provoked Congress outrage sufficient for official actions of prevention. Indeed, Gandhi himself opposed mass movements of conversion to Christianity, even reprimanding Bishop V. S. Azariah of Dornakal for leading such a movement; moreover, Gandhi engaged in "fast to death," forcing Ambedkar to abandon his demand for separate electorates as safeguards for Untouchables. This fundamental contradiction in actions, beliefs, and policies pursued by Gandhi himself—between the astutely inclusive, modern, and non-violent politician who called outcaste Untouchables *"Harijans"* ("Children of God [Krishna]"), on one hand, and the exclusively Hindu politician who strongly defended caste and opposed all conversions of outcaste peoples and their attempts to gain protections and self-respect—betrayed a flaw in the socio-political life of India that remains to this day.

It is this contradiction, in the wake of the Partition when millions were massacred, that led to the assassination of Gandhi in 1948 by Nathuram Godse. While this RSS disciple of Savarkar was hanged, the RSS itself was never eradicated but allowed to survive, and eventually, to thrive. Out of this RSS has come the Bharatiya Janata Party (BJP) that now rules India. Again, it was this fundamental contradiction within leadership of the weakened Congress Party, nominally under the sway of Sonia Gandhi, that Prime Minister P. V. Narasimha Rao (the aging Niyogi Brahman from Karimnagar, Telangana), let the Government of India sit on its hands and do nothing on the 6th December 2002, while many thousands of violent *karsevaks* tore down the five-century old Babri Masjid. That event, occurring upon the very site claimed as "Lord Rama's" supposed birth-place in Ayodhya, is exactly where the cornerstone for the great new Ram Mandir has now been dedicated (August 5, 2020). Narendra Modi, as the current Prime Minister of India, has just laid this cornerstone. This is hardly surprising since it was same person who, as Chief Minister of Gujarat, sat idle while RSS mobs massacred as many as ten thousand Muslims throughout that state.

It should not be surprising, therefore, that what has been alluded to above provides but a small glimpse of the context of historical circumstances for understanding the significance of the Niyogi Commission Report of Madhya Pradesh. The very same forces that had produced the militant Hindu nationalism of the past two centuries lay behind this event. James' penetrating and thorough study explores various remarkable elements of these twin processes that cannot be explained without understanding how it represents the study of a nexus of two parallel political cultures that have grown in India during the past two centuries. Not surprisingly, shortly after the Government of Madhya Pradesh officially accepted the Niyogi Report, laws prohibiting religious conversion began to proliferate out of local governments throughout India. Yet, anyone who knew how Gandhi himself had taken actions against the mass conversion movements in Dornakal being led by Bishop V. S. Azariah would not have been surprised. The contradiction persists to this day.

Finally, the scholarship exhibited by Dr. James within this volume can be seen as a display of the nexus between faith and learning. That a serious scholar has produced such a careful study reflects a willingness to challenge those points where rational analysis and religious belief meet. This kind of commitment was vividly displayed years ago by Ambassador Charles Habib Malik. In his *The Two Tasks* (1980), and his A *Christian Critique of the University*, published the following year (1981),[3] Malik discussed the nexus of his two lifelong tasks, namely, his commitment to the frontiers of historical learning and his commitment to the challenges of theological belief both intersection; and how these two tasks interrogated each other. The resulting convergence, as well as synthesis, of his understandings led to a deepening and a strengthening, both of his faith and of his learning.[4] It is in the light of just such convergence that the rigorous scholarship and robust faith of this work by Manohar James can be viewed.

Robert Eric Frykenberg
Professor Emeritus of History & South Asian Studies
The University of Wisconsin—Madison (U.S.A.)
16th November 2020

---

3. Crossway Books, 38pp. "The Two Tasks," first published in the *Journal of the Evangelical Theological Society* 23 (1980) 289–96, was based on a lecture delivered at the Billy Graham Center of Wheaton College in Illinois.

4. Many years earlier, conflicts within the world of secular learning between scientific and humanistic disciplines had been addressed by C. P. Snow. In his 1959 Rede Lecture at Cambridge University, this Cambridge scholar who was both a writer and a physical chemist lamented the intellectual gulf that existed between the worlds of science and literature. His *The Two Cultures*, the slim volume published at that time, has been in print ever since.

Preface

THIS WORK GREW OUT of my personal experience and doctoral research.[1]
An old Arabian adage goes like this:

> He who knows not, and knows not that he knows not, is a fool;
> shun him.

> He who knows not, and knows that he knows not, is a student;
> teach him.

> He who knows, and knows not that he knows, is asleep;
> wake him.

> He who knows, and knows that he knows, is wise; follow him.

In my journey of learning and growing, I was in each of these life
stages where I was ignorant or did not know much, or I did not know that
I did not know. Through education and life experiences, I continue to be a
learner. As I progress in learning, I realize how little I know.

Over the past three decades, I traveled across India and worked as a
cross-cultural missionary and seminary professor. I am proud of Indians
because they are mostly hospitable and live in harmony regardless of differences. However, one cannot disregard how Hindutvavadis, in an urge
to make India a Hindu nation, are becoming intolerant of religious others
over the last few decades. It is hard to overlook the rising anti-Christian

---

1. *The Influence of the Niyogi Committee Report of Madhya Pradesh on Hindu Na-
tionalism and Its Resistance to Christian Missions in Independent India*, A Dissertation
Presented to the Faculty of Asbury Theological Seminary Wilmore, Kentucky, USA in
Partial Fulfillment of the Requirements for the Degree Doctor of Philosophy; Disserta-
tion Committee: Dr. Lalsangkima Pachuau, Mentor; Dr. Timothy C. Tennent, Reader;
B. Manohar James, June 2016.

incidents in many parts of India. It surprises me how in an age of globalization, education, modernization, and technology Hindu Nationalists are becoming ethnocentric and religiocentric to the extent of justifying their prejudices and propaganda against their fellow citizens who are different from their religious beliefs and ideology. By underscoring the cultural, economic, and political motivations behind Christian conversions, Hindu right-wing activists seek to create a negative consensus against Christianity, stereotyping it as a hostile, foreign, and anti-national religion which poses a threat to Hindu society and national security. Such widespread anti-Christian propaganda contributes to the ongoing Hindu-Christian disharmony, communal tensions, and violence against Christians in various parts of India.

While teaching at Mission India Theological Seminary in India in the first decade of this millennium, I dreamed of conducting unbiased academic research on the growing gap between Hindu Nationalism and Christian mission in India. I wanted to study why Hindu Nationalists saw Christianity differently than I did. When I enrolled in the PhD program at Asbury Theological Seminary in 2009, I chose to conduct research into the Hindu Nationalist anti-Christian rhetoric—its origins and continuity.

Under the guidance of Professor Lalsangkima Pachuau, I investigated the 66-year-old Niyogi Committee Report, which Hindu Nationalists use as a manual for anti-Christian rhetoric. Because of my personal experience of persecution, he cautioned me not to be prescriptive in my work. In the process, he provided me valuable guidance, though it was painful at times. Therefore, this work has become a descriptive and informative perspective rather than a prescriptive one.

The Hindu Nationalist opposition to Christian missions is often justified by an anti-conversion perspective built on the contentious argument that most Christian conversions are the result of irreligious and unethical missionary methods (such as "force, coercion, fraud or inducement") and have been politically motivated by the western missionary enterprise for imperialistic purposes. Although several historical dynamics, such as the contexts of colonization, certain foreign missionary behaviors and the rise of Hindutva ideology, have also contributed to the present-day Hindu extremist reactions to Christianity, this study shows that the controversial "Christian Missionary Activities Enquiry Committee Report" of Madhya Pradesh, published by the state government in the mid-1950s, has played a significant role in the anti-Christian rhetoric and antagonistic attitudes of Sangh Parivar and has considerably influenced the aforementioned view against Christian missions in post-independent India.

This study also demonstrates how the advocates of Hindu National-ism, particularly the RSS, VHP, and BJP, have been utilizing the frame-work, conclusions, and recommendations of the Report to justify their anti-Christian propaganda, their activism, and their attempts to stymie the Christian missionary enterprise across the nation. Today, the effects of the Niyogi Committee Report are not limited to the Madhya Pradesh region alone, but have also had a nationwide impact on socioreligious de-velopments in India.

This research experience has been an invaluable journey for me as I was able to gain emic and etic views of Hindu Nationalist opposition to Christian mission in India. I believe this book will help the readers understand the underlying causes of the anti-Christian propaganda and the Hindu Nationalist perspective of Christian mission in India. It is my prayer that Indian Christians as well as Hindu Nationalists will learn what they do not know, so that they might lay aside their prejudices and live at peace with one another.

Manohar James
November 20, 2021

Acknowledgments

LOOKING BACK ON MY research journey, I find that a project such as this would not have been possible without the help of many sponsors, friends, and professors who have spared their valuable time for me and shared their invaluable resources with me. From the beginning God, who led me to Asbury Theological Seminary (ATS), KY, USA, has been faithful to my family and me with His provision and protection so that we did not lack anything in this exciting and exhausting academic voyage.

My heartfelt gratitude goes to my mentor Dr. Lalsangkima Pachuau, Dean of Advanced Research Programs, for his time, insight, guidance, and supervision. I am likewise thankful to my reader, Dr. Timothy C. Tennent, President of Asbury Theological Seminary, for his invaluable suggestions and encouragement, and especially for sparing his precious time for me. I want to express my appreciation to my examiner, Dr. Arthur G. McPhee, who has been a great encouragement to my family and me throughout my stay in Wilmore.

I am indebted to Libby Bergstrom, who patiently read my chapters and sacrificially provided me with proofreading and editing assistance throughout this writing project free of cost. I am also thankful to Sally Graham, Fran Diederich, and Megan Tatreau for helping me with quick proofreads whenever I was in need. I am grateful to Dr. Saji K. Lukos, President of Reaching Indians International Ministries, Chicago, for being instrumental in my higher education in the United States. I highly appreciate the help of Rev. Nicola Gibson, Dave Dawson, and others for their love, encouragement, and financial support during the years of my studies. I sincerely thank Lynn Haven United Methodist Church in Florida, Johnson Scholarship, and ScholarLeaders International for providing me with scholarship assistance, without which my doctoral education in the USA would not have been possible.

Without the cooperation, prayers, and support of my beloved wife Jasmine S. Manohar, this dissertation project would not have been accomplished. I am immensely thankful to her. I cannot ignore thanking my two-year-old son, Jason Abhishek James, whose cute smiles rejuvenated my spirit and eased my mind in times of stress. I am grateful to all my family members in India, especially my parents and my brother George's family, whose earnest prayers and timely encouragements sustained me in my studies.

Abbreviations

ABHM	Akhil Bharatiya Hindu Mahasabha
ABS	Abhinav Bharat Society
AIKP	All India Khilafat Parishad
BD	Bajrang Dal
BJP	Bharatiya Janata Party
BJS	Bharatiya Jana Sangh
CAB	Catholic Association of Bombay
CBCI	Catholic Bishops Conference of India
CMAEC	Christian Missionary Activities Enquiry Committee
DJS	Dharm Jagran Samiti
EIC	East India Company
FCRA	Foreign Contribution Regulation Act
HJS	Hindu Janajagruti Samiti
HVK	Hindu Vivek Kendra
INC	Indian National Congress
LSD	Lok Sewak Dal
M.P.	Madhya Pradesh
MLA	Member of Legislative Assembly
MP	Member of Parliament

MPDSA	Madhya Pradesh Dharma Swatantrya Adhiniyam
NCCR	The National Christian Council Review
NCCI	National Christian Council of India
NGO	Non-governmental organization
RSS	Rashtriya Swayamsevak Sangh
SMP	Saptahik Madhya Pradesh
SVD	Samyukta Vidhayak Dal
UDHR	Universal Declaration of Human Rights
VHP	Vishva Hindu Parishad
VKA	Vanvasi Kalyan Ashram
VKM	Vanvasi Kalyan Manch

Introduction

GROWING UP AS A pastor's kid in southern India, I accompanied my parents whenever they visited nearby villages to share the gospel with non-Christians and pray for people. During those years, I personally witnessed hundreds of people turning to Jesus by the conviction of the Holy Spirit and through the miracles God had performed. I have seen true transformation in the lives of people who embraced Christ.

On the other hand, I have also seen up close how people opposed my parents when they preached in public, heckling them with foul language. At times, anti-Christians snatched Christian literature from their hands and pushed and slapped them. Since I grew up seeing such incidents from my childhood, I thought it was normal for Christians to be opposed or to get beaten up for preaching the gospel. This was my unbiased, irrational, and non-theological mindset. However, even from my childhood, one thing stood out for me: I couldn't understand why those persecutors hated Christians. They saw Christians as a threat to their culture, society, and religion. Why? I wanted to know where their biases came from, but I didn't have an easy way to finding answers to my questions. My learning resources were limited. Google or Wikipedia were not available.

Years later, in the mid-1990s, after completing a three-year seminary education in south India, I went to a place in a northern state of India to preach the gospel. As a young man I was excited to share about Jesus to people who did not know Him. I chose this career not as a job to make money or a good living, but because I love to see people's lives transformed through the gospel of Jesus Christ.

After going there, I found out that the people I was trying to reach were respectful, kind, and peaceful. I could not have been happier! I even enjoyed the love and hospitality of people who showed interest in knowing about Jesus. I never expected any sort of opposition in that place because of the way people lavished their love on me. With the seminary education, I also felt I could use all the contextual methods I had learned in seminary to possibly avoid any opposition and persecution from the people. This all changed when I encountered a group of people on the road who questioned me about my whereabouts and my work. After I answered all their questions truthfully and respectfully, they mocked me, snatched the gospel tracts from my hands, and told me to stop distributing the tracts and preaching Christianity in that place. They pushed me down, screaming at me to go back to where I belong. I thought they were yelling at me to go back to my home in the south. But in their language, they were saying I should leave the country, since India does not belong to Christians. They also shouted that Christianity is a foreign religion and it has no place in India. They stalked me all the way to my house, hollering at me that I was destroying their culture, traditions, and beliefs by preaching about Jesus. They took away my literature and sent me off with a warning to not be found again in the streets with the gospel tracts or preaching about Jesus.

When I came back to my room, I reviewed the incident and tried to understand whether they hated me personally because I came from the south or if they hated Christianity. After a while, I dismissed my questions about why they hated Christianity as they distracted me from my dedication and work. I continued my ministry with a renewed commitment to love people for the sake of Jesus even if they opposed me.

A few months later, another mob caught me while I was distributing gospel tracts at a bus stand. This mob, while kicking and beating me in front of many people, shouted that Christianity is a dangerous western religion that has entered India to destroy its old religious beliefs and culture. Christians, they screamed, are the agents of the west, trying to take the country away from people and aiming to destroy Hindu religion through conversions. They also yelled other things at me that I did not understand.

A year later, I attended a three-day pastors' conference in a place 200 kilometers away in the state of Haryana. About 300 leaders (pastors, native missionaries, evangelists, and some with families) gathered for a spiritual retreat. No white people were present in the meeting. It was organized by a local Christian organization at a rented campus. The first day felt like heaven with praise and worship, the powerful Word, and the revival the Holy Spirit had brought among the servants of God. In the evening of second day, while lively worship was going on, a mob of young people entered the meeting hall by jumping the compound wall, interrupting the worship service to physically attack those who gathered there. Within a few minutes, the meeting hall was in darkness as the mob had cut the electricity in the campus, and they began to beat everyone with the metal chairs. Some participants were scattered across the campus away from their family members in silence, while others cried uncontrollably in pitch black darkness. I found a spot in the corner of a wall and sat there until the police arrived at midnight, two hours after the incident.

In the dead silence of that dreadful night, all we heard were anti-Christian slogans that the mob had shouted against us while frantically beating us before leaving the scene. The hate speech against Christians I heard in some parts of the south was not so different from what I heard in the north, thousands of miles away across India. A few days later, when I returned to my home, I began to connect the dots to the phenomenon of orchestrated opposition to the Christian mission. I know India is divided by sub-cultures, religious beliefs, castes, and a thousand dialects. Yet, I realized opposition across India uses the same, anti-Christian slogans despite language and cultural differences.

In subsequent years, especially after the brutal killing (burning alive) of Australian missionary Graham Staines and his two sons in Orissa by a Hindu fundamentalist group in 1999, it has come to light that anti-Christian sentiment is being actively spread across India to strategically hinder the spread of Christianity. Until that time, not many anti-Christian incidents were reported by the media. (Only 38 incidents were recorded in 32-year span following 1964). Since the mid-90s, the news media has begun to report (although selectively) an exponential increase in instances where Christians were harassed or attacked; nuns raped; priests and pastors beaten; believers ostracized, threatened, beaten brutally, and murdered. In many parts of India, church buildings have been demolished or burned, mission hospitals vandalized, Bibles destroyed, and Christian orphanages closed. On top of this, foreign funding has been stopped, and legal licenses to run philanthropic Christians institutions have been canceled.

The last quarter of the twentieth century witnessed the beginning of coordinated propaganda against and opposition to Christian mission by Hindu nationalists. The reason for the sudden rise in orchestrated opposition was perhaps caused by the panic among Hindu nationalists that India might become a Christian nation by AD 2000. This fear was probably sparked by the Global Consultation on World Evangelization Movement (The AD2000 & Beyond Movement) which held a series of global consultation meetings in the last quarter of the 20th century in the Philippines, Thailand, South Africa, Singapore, South Korea, and other parts of the world to consider strategic issues of reaching the unreached by the end of the millennium. Those meetings were attended by thousands of key Christian leaders, representing hundreds of nations, who met to formulate evangelism plans to reach the world with the gospel by AD 2000. India was one of the targets for evangelization by the end of the millennium as it falls in the 10/40 window where 95 percent of the world's least-evangelized people are found. Close to the turn of the twentieth century, many Christian organizations in India and abroad optimistically declared India for Christ by AD 2000 and encouraged the local church to be more missional. Many mission organizations and churches openly articulated their vision and goals for AD 2000 through literature and social media, while others in some parts of India wrote on the street walls with block letters, INDIA FOR JESUS BY 2000. It is hard to deny that such optimism had provoked Hindu nationalists to plan against the progress of Christian mission in India.

The intellectual Hindu nationalists were early in the game to not allow the progress of evangelization of India. As adult literacy had steadily increased since the last quarter of the 20th century, they felt the need to influence the young Hindu minds to safeguard Hindus from religious conversions and revere their own religion with utter reverence and dignity. In 1982, Hindu thinkers Ram Swarup and Sita Ram Goel established Voice of India publishing house to provide a platform to express Hindutva viewpoints, revive Hinduism and encourage Hindu nationalism through apologetical writings. By this time, they had already published several books and articles supporting Hinduism and opposing Christianity and Islam. The Voice of India publication has welcomed numerous journalists, historians, social commentators, and academicians such as Arun Shourie, David Frawley, Shrikant Talageri, Francois Gautier, Harsh Narain, Subhash Kak, Koenraad Elst, and N. S. Rajaram to inform Hindu society about its own great heritage, and the dangers it faces from other religious groups especially Islam and Christianity. It also prints out-of-print Hindutva materials and makes them available to people at an affordable price, or for free.

In 1998, Voice of India reprinted the Report of the Christian Missionary Activities Enquiry Committee 1956 under the title, Vindicated By Time: The Niyogi Committee Report on Christian Missionary Activities, with a preface and an introductory chapter by Sita Ram Goel. This republished version provides the language for Hindu Nationalist propaganda against Christians and their work in India. It is now freely available on www. voiceofdharma.org and a dozen Hindu websites, not to mention the availability of excerpts and redactions on social media. The Niyogi Committee Report has become an anti-Christian manual to the Hindu Nationalists who rely on it to brainwash themselves into blindly opposing Christians and their mission. It has been used by them time and again to caricature Christianity as a Western religion and to portray Christians as outsiders.

This indoctrination contributes to the ongoing hatred against everything Christian mission did and does.

In this book I explore how Hindu intolerance has contributed to anti-Christian propaganda over the centuries, how such intolerance has informed the conclusions of the Niyogi Committee Report, and how the Report's ongoing publications, redactions, and recensions have intensified anti-Christian rhetoric in India over the last six decades.

1

Overview of the Research

CHRISTIANS IN INDIA RELISHED a culture of religious tolerance and non-violence for centuries. However, the notion of Hindu tolerance, which was once thought of as a national identity, a hallmark of multi-religious harmony and an integral part of India's tradition, appears endangered by radical Hindutva[1] movements. While portraying themselves as self-dedicated, culturally patriotic, and guardians of national integrity, these movements tend to ethnicize religious categories, politicize identities, and demonize "the religious others."

Prominent Hindu leaders like Vivekananda and Gandhi often boasted about the Hindu dynamic of tolerance which they said was absent in other religions. Historically, Hindus were believed to never have launched a religious war against other nations. On the other hand, Peter van der Veer contends that the popular notion of Hindu tolerance is a misconception and a byproduct of orientalist discourse. It was categorically attributed to Hindus to differentiate them from fanatic Muslims who were religiously and politically aggressive and it has gradually come to dominate the Hindu discourse on Hinduism.[2] Building on the same premise, Thomas B. Hansen notes that Hindu reformers codified this imaginary cultural category to show that it is a key characteristic of Hindu faith.[3]

---

1. Hindutva (Hinduness) is an ideology of ethnic nationalism which was crystallized by Hindu nationalists in the first and second quarters of the twentieth century. V. D. Savarkar, one of the pioneers of Hindu nationalism, envisioned and advocated for uniting people in India under "one nation, one race and one culture mediated by one language."

2. Veer, *Religious Nationalism*, 67.

3. Hansen, *Saffron Wave*, 60.

It is true that Christians throughout history faced obstacles, opposition, and even persecution from local Rajas and religious leaders. However, such conflicts rarely turned into the widespread antagonism seen today.[4]

Since the last quarter of the twentieth century, Christians and their conversion activities have begun to come under the strict surveillance of the radical Hindu nationalism of the Sangh Parivar, that is, Hindu nationalist organizations which operate under the ideological guidance of Rashtriya Swayamsevak Sangh (RSS). Conversions, which have met with strong criticism since the explosion of mass conversions in the pre-independent era, are systematically problematized by the exigencies of Hindu nationalist politics in post-independent India. By underscoring the cultural, economic, and political motivations behind Christian conversions, Hindu right-wing activists seek to create a consensus against Christianity, stereotyping it as a hostile, foreign, and anti-national religion which poses a serious threat to Hindu society and national security. Such widespread anti-Christian propaganda contributes to the ongoing Hindu-Christian disharmony, communal tensions, and violence in various parts of India. Since the last decade of the twentieth century, Christians in many parts of India have undergone persecution, killings, burning of churches, destruction of institutions, and displacement of families.[5]

Historical Setting

There are several historical dynamics that have contributed to the present-day Hindu extremist reactions to Christianity. They can be traced to the contexts of colonization, certain foreign missionary deeds, and the rise of Hindutva[6] ideology.

With the arrival of Muslim conquerors, India witnessed serious political upheavals from the eighth century onwards. Political invasions which often came hand in glove with the religion of the invaders affronted and affected Hindu society and Hinduism. In the process, conquerors destroyed several Hindu temples, idols, and local shrines, and converted many Hindus to Islam.[7] Ever since, religious conversions have become repugnant in the eyes of Hindu fundamentalists.

---

4. Mattam, *In the Shadow of the Cross*, 36.

5. Esteves, *Freedom to Build*, 253–88; Lobo, *Globalisation*, 56; Raj, *Divide to Rule*, 53.

6. See "Definitions of Key Terms" for its etymology and rhetoric.

7. Elst, *Negationism in India*, 36, 49, 89; Swarup, *Hindu View*, 46, 84; Seshadri, *RSS*, 7; Elst, *Decolonizing the Hindu Mind*, 174, 201, 294, 325.

Just as Hindus resisted religious conversions associated with Islamic invasions, they similarly responded to the conversions sought and wrought by Europeans, as it was apparent to them that the comportment and the strategies employed by these colonizers and convert-seeking missionaries were not so different from that of their former Muslim aggressors. Historian T. R. De Souza mentions Sasetti, who was in India from 1578 to 1588. De Souza argues, "The fathers of the Church forbade the Hindus under terrible penalties the use of their own sacred books, and prevented them from all exercise of their religion. They destroyed their temples, and so harassed and interfered with the people that they abandoned the cities in large numbers, refusing to remain any longer in a place where they had no liberty, and were liable to imprisonment, torture and death if they worshipped after their own fashion the gods of their fathers."[8] While British colonization and western ideals gave rise to the spirit of nationalism among Indians, various aspects of the modern missionary movement challenged some intellectual Hindus in the nineteenth century to stand up to missionaries and their ways of religious propagation.[9] Historian K. M. Panikkar observes that as educated Hindus came in contact with missionaries, they began to see concurrently the need for social reform of religion and the need for defense against the Christian attacks on Hinduism.[10] Raja Ram Mohan Roy, the father of the Hindu Reformation and the prophet of Indian nationalism, was the first Indian influenced by western liberal thought who attempted to reform Hindu religion and society. He also critiqued the religious attitudes of European Protestant missionaries who sought conversions by force of argument and the preaching of the superiority of Christianity over Hinduism.[11]

The mid-nineteenth century also saw the rise of Hindu revivalists like Vishnubawa Brahmachari, Arumuga Navalar Pillai, Swami Dayananda Saraswati, and others, who were consterned by the advance of the Protestant missionary enterprise under the legal provisions of the British[12] and who attempted to defend Hindu *dharma* from missionary onslaughts. They confronted missionaries through inter-religious debates and taught their followers how to face the religious challenges posed by missionaries. Brahmachari was a Maharashtrian Brahmin who was a precursor of Dayananda Saraswati. He confronted missionaries and raised opposition to their

8. De Souza, "Goa Inquisition."

9. Ambrois, "Hindutva's Real Agenda," 13–14.

10. Panikkar, *Asia and Western Dominance*, 241.

11. Roy, "Brahmunical Magazine," 10, 146.

12. The East India Company's Charter Act of 1813 allowed missionaries to freely propagate their religious faith and the Charter Revision of 1833 legally permitted the entry of missionaries in British India.

missionary work in Maharashtra before the mid-nineteenth century.[13] Pillai belonged to Jaffna in Sri Lanka. He defended Shaivism against the attacks of British Christian missionaries and wrote anti-Christian literature in Tamil. Events in Jaffna against missionaries had their effect in Madras, India, where a *Samaj* was formed in defense against Christian onslaughts. He traveled to India often to encourage Hindus against Christian missionaries.[14]

Dayananda Saraswati was also very unsympathetic to other faiths, sparking antipathy toward every non-Hindu religion, especially to Christianity and Islam. In 1875, Dayananda Saraswati founded Arya Samaj with the objective of countering British colonialism and Christian missions.[15] He worked hard to revitalize Hinduism and attempted to reform the social practices as carried out by Ram Mohan Roy. He mobilized Hindus to unite against political and religious threats, so that "ethnic pride inherent in Arya Samajist ideology was combined with an open stigmatization of the Others."[16] He and his followers propagated the idea that Christianity "is a western religion and as everything that comes from the West is to be discarded, Christianity must also be discarded."[17]

Crystallization of Hindu Nationalism

Arya Samaj injected in the minds of people a politicized Hindu consciousness and a spirit of nationalism.[18] However, the idea of Hindu nationalism was not crystalized until conservative nationalists[19] within the Indian National Congress (INC) became apprehensive of internal threats such as the Khilafat movement and set up Hindu masses to stand up to the challenges of Islamic movements.[20] In 1909, Arya Samajists in Punjab initiated Hindu Sabha "when the pro-Muslim bias of the British administration, which was anxious to assure itself of support among the minorities, was gradually translated into the granting of various important concessions, one of which was the setting-up of separate electorates in 1909."[21] Some members of Arya Samaj showed a radical form of an inferiority complex and began

---

13. Conlon, "Polemic Process," 5–26.

14. Hudson, "Arumuga Navalar," 27–51.

15. Jaffrelot, *Hindu Nationalist Movement*, 11.

16. Jaffrelot, *Hindu Nationalist Movement*, 16.

17. Gandhi, *Hindu Dharma*, 269.

18. Arya, *Religion and Politics in India*, 68, 278.

19. Lal Bal Pal trio (Lala Lajpat Rai, Bal Gangadhar Tilak and Bipin Chandra Pal) and Sir Aurabindo.

20. Devadas, *Ideologies of Political Parties*, 18.

21. Jaffrelot, *Hindu Nationalist Movement*, 18.

to display proto-Hindu nationalism by declaring themselves "Hindus," not "Aryas."[22] Lal Chand, who headed the educational institution of Arya Samaj, emphasized that "patriotism ought to be communal and not merely geographical,"[23] adding a new dimension to the stigmatization of "threatening Others." In 1919, when the Government of India Act accorded communal representation to Muslims, Sikhs, Europeans, Anglo-Indians and Indian Christians,[24] the Hindu Mahasabha, which moved to acquire a more Hindu nationalist orientation, began to attribute territorial and ethnic significance to its nationalism. They began to categorize people as Hindu or non-Hindu (the threatening others) in their struggle for unity and hegemony.

The booklet, "Hindutva: Who is a Hindu?," which V. D. Savarkar wrote in response to the Khilafat movement, became a foundational text for the Hindu nationalist ideology of "one nation, one race and one culture."[25] It was Rashtriya Swayamsevak Sangh (RSS), founded by K. Baliram Hedgewar in 1925, which put flesh on Savarkar's ideology. In order to consolidate Hindu unity, several strategies were proposed by likeminded nationalists. For example, Swami Shraddananda, an Arya Samajist, proposed in his work, *Hindu Sanghatan-Saviour of the Dying Race,* that huge temples with a capacity of 20,000 people should be built so that Hindu scriptures could be recited daily.[26] In order to advance Hindu numbers, he also proposed that the *Shuddhi* movement should be revised and directed more toward "Untouchables" to purify and integrate them into Hindu society, which seemed a realistic response to Muslim militancy at that time.[27] In promoting the notion of *Hindu Rashtra*, RSS streamlined its ideology away from the ideals of Indian nationalism. M. S. Golwalkar, the second chief of RSS, popularly known as Guruji, gave the movement a more radical and militant outlook. Historian Ramachandra Guha calls him "the Guru of hate."[28]

Independence and Hindu Nationalist Anxiety

The RSS, which believed that "the hostile elements within the country pose a far greater menace to national security than aggressors from outside,"[29]

22. Jaffrelot, *Hindu Nationalist Movement*, 18.

23. Lal Chand, *Self-abnegation in Politics*, 101.

24. Smith, *India as a Secular State*, 86.

25. Savarkar, *Hindutva*, 110–11. In the beginning, this book was anonymously published as "A Maratha," which means, A Maharastrian.

26. Sanyasi, *Hindu Sanghatan*, 140–41.

27. Jaffrelot, *Hindu Nationalism*, 13–14.

28. Guha, "Guru of Hate."

29. Golwalkar, *Bunch of Thoughts*, 177.

emerged as a force to consolidate Hindus against three major internal threats: Muslims, Christians, and communists. Until independence, the Hindu Mahasabha and RSS had focused mostly on Muslims. After independence, the advocates of Hindu nationalism imagined a threat of internal subversion of national freedom by the influx of foreign missionaries into the country. Hence, RSS and its allied organizations became watchful of the missionary enterprise in free India to avoid intimidation of the majority community and began to suspect Christians as early as the 1950s.

The constitution, which officially came into effect on January 26, 1950, played a role in the anti-missionary attitudes in Hindu nationalists because it provided a broadly lawful "Liberty of thought, expression, belief, faith and worship." It was a boon for foreign missionaries.[30] At a time when foreign missionaries were expected to leave India along with British colonialists, they had not only decided to remain in the country under the shadow of constitutional rights, but they doubled their missionary presence in the first few years of independence, raising anxiety among Hindu nationalists. Although many foreign missionaries supported India's movement for independence from British rule, their presence in independent India fell under suspicion because many Indians associated missionaries with the memory of British imperialism.[31]

The question of foreign missionaries was not viewed from a religious point of view, but from a political and social perspective.[32] In the central provinces, especially in the adivasi (tribal) regions of Madhya Pradesh, where foreign missionaries gained a strong foothold for the propagation of Christianity through medical services, schools, and other philanthropic works, it was alleged that some missionaries were involved in provoking local Christians to fight for a separate Christian state.[33] At times, *The Hindu Outlook* of Hindu Mahasabha also attempted to mobilize Hindu support for its opinion that, "converts to Christianity in a large majority of cases have been changing not only their religion but even their nationality. Their allegiance to India became doubtful."[34]

---

30. The Niyogi Report underlines that the missionaries were encouraged by the promulgation of the Indian Constitution which set up a secular State with liberty to propagate any religion in the country. See *Report on the Christian Missionary Activity Enquiry Committee, Volume 1*, 16, 43, 54, 60. Hereafter, it will be cited as Niyogi Report.

31. Bauman, "Postcolonial Anxiety," 4.

32. *The Hindu Outlook*, May 30, 1954, 4.

33. Some Christians even pondered naming their region Christiansthan or Kristusthan. See "Christian Missionaries Active in Chhattisgarh," *The Hitavada*, January 23, 1954, 5.

34. *The Hindu Outlook*, May 30, 1954, 4.

A few months before the passing of Deputy Prime Minister Sardar Vallabhbhai Patel in December 1950, M. S. Golwalkar visited him and discussed various things. During their talk, according to RSS biographer C. P. Bhishikar, Sardar Patel referred to "the increasing of Christian missionary activities in the country and emphasized the need to augment the assimilative power of the Hindu society."[35] Bhishikar mentions that Patel had a deep regard for the Sangh.[36] When Patel passed away, Golwalkar wrote in his condolence message that, "Shri Vallabhbhai Patel . . . had great affection for our work. It is our duty to rescue the country from internal strife and external aggression by making it strong and invincible. Such a pledge alone would be our true homage to him."[37]

The Hindu Nationalist Challenge to Missions in Madhya Pradesh[38]

Madhya Pradesh (M. P.) is one of the bigger states in the central region of India where foreign missionaries initiated their educational, philanthropic, and conversion activities among adivasis during the last quarter of the nineteenth century. However, during the second quarter of the twentieth century, missionary activities among adivasis were restricted by local Rajas in some princely states. After India's independence, especially after the promulgation of the liberal constitution, missionaries freely entered the restricted regions to carry on developmental as well as evangelistic activities among adivasis. As missionaries and their socioreligious activities began to gain wider acceptance among the backward communities, non-Christians began to allege that foreign money was being poured in for the work of mass conversions of poor and ignorant communities. There were also allegations that missionaries converted the backward people by force, fraud, or inducements.[39] In this context, Hindu extremists began to fear that the constitutional freedom, which provided impetus for the influx of foreign missionaries, would allow some sort of colonialism in the country again.[40] With an aggravated attitude, Hindu nationalist advocates began

35. Bhishikar, *Shri Guruji*, 79.

36. Bhishikar, *Shri Guruji*, 88.

37. Bhishikar, *Shri Guruji*, 88.

38. The state of Madhya Pradesh on a contemporary map of India does not correspond to the map of Madhya Pradesh in the early 1950s which includes Chhattisgarh, part of Maharashtra, and several pre-merged princely states in the central province. See Appendix–A for maps of M.P. and India.

39. Niyogi, *Report*, 1:1.

40. Fey, "Report Urges Ban on Missionaries," 892.

to mobilize like-minded Hindus against missionaries and their activities in Madhya Pradesn.

While the representatives of RSS and Vanvasi Kalyan Ashram (VKA) were involved in inciting non-Christians to complain to the government against foreign missionaries, the Akhil Bharatiya Hindu Mahasabha (ABHM) was involved in publishing provocative articles against them in its weekly publication, *The Hindu Outlook*. For example, on March 28, 1954, *The Hindu Outlook* published an article with the headline, "10,000 Hindus Taken Away from Hinduism Every Day: Call to Mahants to Save Country." Another issue dated July 18, 1954, carried a headline which said, "Change of Religion Connotes Change of Nationality." ABHM also led anti-missionary *morchas* (campaigns), calling upon foreign Christian missionaries to quit India. One such campaign was organized and led by Dr. N. B. Khare, vice president of the Akhil Bharatiya Hindu Mahasabha, on July 25, 1954.[41]

In the milieu of the mixed feelings of achieved independence and continued anxiety over constitutional religious freedom which allowed an increase of foreign missionaries in independent India, Bharatiya Jana Sangh (Indian People's Union or BJS), the Hindu nationalist political party, the political arm of the Rashtriya Swayamsevak Sangh movement, founded in 1951 by Syama Prasad Mukherjee, which existed until 1977, launched an anti-foreign missionary week in April 1954 to challenge missionary proselytism in the state.[42] BJP is the direct successor of Bharatiya Jana Sangh.

The Christian Missionary Activities Enquiry Committee and the Controversial Report

In the wake of alarming Hindu-Christian conflicts and complaints against each other in Madhya Pradesh, where the presence of Hindu nationalist organizations Rashtriya Swayamsevak Sangh, Hindu Mahasabha, and Bharatiya Jana Sangh was strong, the state government (of the Congress Party) appointed an independent enquiry committee on April 14, 1954, to probe the allegations made against missionaries. The committee was called "The Christian Missionary Activities Enquiry Committee," popularly known as The Niyogi Committee.

During its two-year investigation period, the committee visited 77 Christian centers in fourteen regions of Madhya Pradesh, including institutions such as hospitals, schools, churches, leper homes, and hostels operated by various foreign missions. It took notes at each center and

---

41. *Hitavada*, July 22, 1954.
42. Jaffrelot, *Hindu Nationalist Movement*, 164.

received 375 written statements. The committee also interviewed 11,360 people, both Christians (missionaries and tribal converts) and Hindus. It collected statements from the representatives of various communities in 700 villages. In addition to its field investigations, the committee made an extensive review of literature on the missionary expansion in India and its religious and political connections abroad. It collected information from various government records on sociopolitical conflicts and religious tensions caused by missionaries in the past and gathered statistics about the inflow of foreign money for conversion activities. It thoroughly cross-examined the Christian and secular critiques of missionary activities from historical, academic, and missionary documents. After carefully analyzing the data, the committee interpreted its findings, organized the missionary issues thematically, and compiled a 939-page report, which was submitted to the Madhya Pradesh government in 1956.

By tracing missionary activities in India since the arrival of Portuguese colonizers, the controversial report exposed[43] the evil side of conversion activities. Drawing inferences from historical as well as field findings, it concluded that since the promulgation of India's secular constitution, missionary presence had increased and caused socio-religious and political conflicts in adivasi regions of Madhya Pradesh. Christian institutions such as hospitals, schools, hostels, and orphanages had been used as centers of proselytization. Most conversions were advanced by the use of foreign money under the influence of force, fraud, or material attractions, not by spiritual motives. The poor and illiterate were the targets of aggressive evangelization and had been de-nationalized after their conversions. Evangelism in India, which appeared to reestablish western supremacy, disrupted the solidarity of non-Christian societies. Christian missions were a danger to the security of the state as missionaries in some regions served extra religious ends.

Furnishing these reasons, the committee proposed recommendations in its report to the government to legally restrict conversions sought by force, fraud, or inducements. The Report was published by the state government in two volumes and was made available to the public in 1956 as an investigative report on missionary activities.

Volume I is the main report. It consists of a history of missionary activities, interpretations, conclusions, and recommendations, and it contains four parts. Part I deals with the circumstance of the appointment of the committee and the background of Madhya Pradesh. Part II narrates the history of missions in Madhya Pradesh and India and the problems thereof.

43. Niyogi, *Report*, 1:131–32.

Part III elaborates on religious liberty in other countries and the Indian constitution. Part IV is the recommendations and conclusion.

Volume II consists of the details of the inquiry, survey tours, questionnaires, and written statements. It contains the field notes, questionnaires and narration of oral testimonials. It has two parts, A and B. Part A has tour programs of the committee, explanatory tour notes and petitions from 12 regions as well as 18 replies to the questionnaire. Part B contains the correspondence of Catholics with the Committee, the state government and the central government, as well as transcribed statements and extracts on the activities of Christian missions in the northeast.

Although the government of Madhya Pradesh did not immediately act on the recommendations of the Report against missionary activities, and the Report seemed to have no impact initially, it is the contention of this study that the advocates of Hindutva ideology find in this prescriptive Report the rationale for their contempt and opposition to Christian missions in India. RSS and its allied organizations played a major role in the outcome of the document and have been using the document as authentic evidence to oppose Christianity even today.[44]

PURPOSE STATEMENT

The purpose of this study is to trace the influence of the Niyogi Committee Report on Hindu nationalism and its resistance to Christian missions in independent India. The study will examine the significance and impact of the Report on Hindu nationalism by tracing how Hindu nationalists reread the Report and utilize it to augment their anti-conversion arguments, justify their stereotyping of Christian missions, and perpetuate anti-Christian propaganda in India.

THE RESEARCH PROBLEM

The post-independent Hindu nationalist opposition to Christian missions in India is often justified by an anti-conversion perspective which is built on the contentious argument that Christianity is a hostile, foreign, anti-cultural, anti-national, and anti-Hindu religion that poses a serious threat to Hindu society and national security.[45] The Hindu resentment to conversion is not limited to a group of fundamentalists, but is widely shared by

44. Seshadri, *RSS*, 74–75.

45. Golwalkar, *Bunch of Thoughts*, 188–94; Sudarshan, "Speech in RSS-Christian Perspective Meet," 18–38; Goel, *History of Hindu-Christian Encounters*, 323–57; Shourie, *Missionaries in India*, 113–14.

a majority of Hindus today because[46] the Sangh Parivar blanketed India with anti-Christian propaganda. The propaganda stated that most Christian conversions from the past to the present are the result of irreligious and unethical missionary methods such as "force, coercion, fraud or inducement" and have been politically motivated by the western missionary enterprise for imperialistic purposes.[47] Since its publication Hindutva organizations have been utilizing the Report as a significant source of historical and social support against Christian conversions in India. For example, the most well-known RSS chief M. S. Golwalkar, who regarded the Report to be an impartial verdict on Christian conversions, often referred to the Niyogi Report in his public speeches to emphasize that Christian activities are "not merely irreligious, they are also anti-national."[48] The widespread distribution of the aforementioned anti-Christian propaganda by Hindu nationalist activists has posed a huge challenge to the continuation of Christian missions in many parts of India today and incites interreligious tensions to the extent of violence against Christians.

The thesis of this study is that the Niyogi Report has considerably influenced Hindutva advocates' views of Christianity and has shaped their perspectives against Christian missions, providing impetus to justify their anti-conversion and anti-missionary positions. These advocates also redacted, reinterpreted, and disseminated the Report to promote their anti-Christian agenda. By researching the Report and its use and promotion by Hindu nationalists, especially the RSS, the VHP, and the BJP, in the years following its 1956 publication, this work will show how the Report has influenced the modern-day Hindu nationalist ideology, perceptions and attitudes against Christianity in India.

The Niyogi Report's portrayal of Christian missions and its rational proposal to the government of Madhya Pradesh to oppose, resist and control Christian missionary activities in India have caused great anxiety among Christians. During the first decade of India's independence, the Report stirred discussions on foreign missionary personnel working in various parts of India and affected India's foreign missionary visa policies. Arguably, the recommendations of the Report have prompted Hindu nationalist politicians within and outside Congress to make a case against Christian conversions and propose religious freedom laws in the Center and state legislative assemblies in the subsequent years.[49]

---

46. Kim, *In Search of Identity*, 182.

47. In addition to the sources cited above, see also Eshwar, *Paravartan*, 26–27.

48. Golwalkar, *Bunch of Thoughts*, 182.

49. Kim, *In Search of Identity*, 73; Seshadri, *RSS*, 75.

Although the Report played an undercover role until the last quarter of the twentieth century, it regained momentum in India when the Bharatiya Janata Party (BJP) burst into prominence in the 1980s. The conversion debates held by Sangh Parivar thinkers at the turn of twenty-first century thoroughly reflected verbiage and the rationale of the Niyogi Report against missionary enterprises. The Report, which gave a new impetus to the nationalist prospect against conversions in the late twentieth century and early part of the twenty-first century, still produces strenuous resistance to Christian missions today.

RESEARCH QUESTION

What is the role of the Niyogi Report in the history of Hindu nationalists' perceptions of Christianity and their opposition to Christian missions in independent India?

RATIONALE, SCOPE, AND SIGNIFICANCE
OF RESEARCH

The Niyogi Report, which extensively dealt with the Christian missionary enterprise in India, particularly foreign missionary operations in Madhya Pradesh, has played a significant role in the Hindu nationalist view of Christian missions. The Sangh Parivar and its thinkers continue to display the Niyogi Report as corroborative evidence against Christian missions to defend their anti-Christian stand and to use its framework to stymie Christian work across the nation. Today, its effects are not limited to the Madhya Pradesh region alone, but have a nation-wide impact.

Many research articles and books have been written on the issue of Hindu violence against Christians and their institutions. The majority of these works have highlighted the issues of conversion, nationalism, and Hindu extremism and the ways in which they have affected religious tolerance and the church's mission in independent India. A few Christian scholars have indicated that the Niyogi Committee Report has been instrumental in shaping the Hindu nationalist ideology against Christian missions.[50]

The Report has become a matter of political and religious interest to many Hindu nationalists. Except for some theological scholars and a few churchmen, most of the Christians in India do not know that there is such a document as the "Niyogi Committee Report." Considering present-day anti-conversion sentiments, anti-missionary allegations, and violence

---

50. Kim, *In Search of Identity*, 72; Vedhamanickam, "Serving under the Saffron Shadow," 195; Bauman, "Postcolonial Anxiety," 181–213; and others.

against Christians in India, it is important that Christians become aware of the Niyogi Report.

There has been no in-depth research conducted on the impact and implications of the document so far. This research is an attempt to survey the historical significance of the Report so that Christians may gain from this work a clear understanding of the Hindu nationalist perspective of Christian missions and their objections to it.

THEORETICAL FRAMEWORK

This study investigates how Hindu nationalists utilize the Niyogi Report as one of their authentic sources for their propaganda against Christianity. In order to understand the backdrop of the Niyogi Report's argument of missionary enterprise as a western political strategy to revive and re-establish Christendom worldwide, [51] and to see how such understanding contributed to the Hindu reactions to Christian missionary work in India since the nineteenth century, leading up to the current phenomenon of Hindu nationalist resentment to Christianity in general and the conversion activity of the missionary enterprise in particular, it is helpful to look at the theories of colonialism, revitalization, and ethnonationalism.

Colonialism-Conflation

In the last quarter of the nineteenth century, when Arya Samaj was trying to politicize Hindu consciousness and raise a spirit of nationalism to counter British imperialism, it saw Christianity as a colonial enterprise and began to propagate that it was a western religion that had to be overthrown along with the British. Such an understanding had a profound impact on Gandhi,[52] the Niyogi Report and the Hindu nationalist thinkers of independent India such as M. S. Golwalkar,[53] Sita Ram Goel, Arun Shourie,[54] and others who conflate imperialism and Christianity as partners in the destruction of national interests. Golwalkar called Christians "agents of world strategy." Referring to missionaries, he said, they reside in India "to demolish not only the religious and social fabric of our life but also to establish political dominion in various pockets and if possible all over the land."[55]

---

51. Niyogi, *Report,* 1:65, 69, 131–32.
52. Gandhi, *Hindu Dharma,* 269.
53. Golwalkar, *Bunch of Thoughts,* 192–93.
54. Shourie, *Missionaries in India,* 41–109.
55. Gandhi, *Hindu Dharma,* 269.

To substantiate the argument that Christianity shares in colonial kinship, the Niyogi Committee Report stated that, "The Christians under the British rule in India enjoyed a privileged position . . . Legislation protected the rights of the converts. The decision of the High Courts enabled converts to blackmail their wives to follow them into the fold of their new religion. The Government also encouraged the Missionaries to work among the backward tribes."[56] As George Smith pointed out, since the time of Francis Xavier, there has been a perception that, "Colonization is the habitual, perhaps the indispensable, forerunner of the gospel among barbarians or half-civilized tribes."[57] Krishna Prasad De also showed that, "under British rule, India had an ecclesiastical department maintained out of State-funds."[58] The suspicion and anxiety which the Niyogi Report showed against missionary activities, especially their political and de-nationalizing aspects, perpetuated an attitude among nationalists that makes them unwilling to perceive the difference between colonizers and missionaries.

On the other hand, Christian scholars like Felix Alfred Plattner, Robert E. Frykenberg, and others disagree with the Hindu nationalist contentions regarding the conflation of missions with colonialism.[59] On various occasions, Rajendra Prasad and Pandit Jawaharlal Nehru, prominent leaders of India, acknowledged in their speeches and writings that Christianity was brought to India by St. Thomas in the very first century,[60] implying that Christianity reached India many centuries before colonialists or western missionaries arrived. Plattner argued that, "after annexing newly conquered territories the Company [EIC] took over all temple property, paid priests and temple prostitutes, encouraged temple worship and pilgrimages, which netted them huge profits in pilgrim taxes, they even went to the extent of restoring pagan temples. Christianity meant nothing to such business-minded people."[61] As Frykenberg rightly noted, "One of the most lingering, persistent, and stubborn misperceptions, both in India and in the West, is the notion that Christianity is essentially European and the European religion has traditionally

---

56. Niyogi, *Report*, 1:68–69. To understand how such perceptions were shaped, see Frykenberg, *Christians and Missionaries in India*, 11, 307–10.

57. Smith, *Conversion of India*, 57.

58. Prasad De, *Religious Freedom*, 120.

59. Plattner, *Catholic Church in India*, 23.

60. *Hitavada*, December 16, 1952; *The Christian Century*, January 14, 1953, 54–59; Speech in Lok Sabha, December 3, 1955; Nehru's letter to Archbishop of Uppasala, Sweden, dated August 22, 1953; Gopal, *Selected Works*, 733–34.

61. Plattner, *Catholic Church in India*, 23–24.

been Christian. Of course, neither of these notions is true,"[62] although they have been used or misused to stereotype Christianity.

In the Indian context, "colonialism" generally denotes "oppression by an alien and foreign forces or rulers (again, especially and often specifically by Western: European and American oppressors)."[63] The term colonialism in the minds of Hindus, according to Frykenberg, is "more of a rhetorical device" used "for denigrating, shaming and shunning."[64] His "colonialism-conflation theory" best describes the Hindu ascription of Christian mission as colonial.

> While especially applicable for demonizing all things "British," the terms have also been extended so as to include things American and European (or Western). In relation to Christianity, Christian mission or even to all things Christian, the term has been useful for categorically demonizing or epitomizing evil and exploitation, for assigning the guilt, or for categorizing anything deemed to be "anti-national." Christian "colonialism" in other words, is a manifest form of oppression of the weak (East and South) by the strong (West and North). Its essence is to be found in charges of forced conversion and proselytization.[65]

Frykenberg gives an example with Mahatma Gandhi. When Bishop V. S. Azariah, an Indian Christian leader, attempted to evangelize outcast groups of Malas and Madigas of Dornakal in Andhra Pradesh, Gandhi called his action, "anti-national." The term has been used "to implicate Indian Christians as being alien, anti-national, and unpatriotic, or subject to forces from outside of India."[66]

Revitalization

The religious others which have so complicated the socio-religious structures of India for centuries, have challenged Hinduism in such numerous ways that the last decades of the nineteenth century and the beginning of the twentieth century saw the emergence of various Hindu revivalist movements.[67] According to Anthony Wallace's theory of revitalization,[68] when traditional

---

62. Frykenberg, *Christians and Missionaries in India*, 5.

63. Frykenberg, *Christians and Missionaries in India*, 6.

64. Frykenberg, *Christians and Missionaries in India*, 7.

65. Frykenberg, *Christians and Missionaries in India*, 7.

66. Frykenberg, *Christians and Missionaries in India*, 7–8.

67. Gould, *Religion and Conflict*, 161.

68. Wallace, "Revitalization Movements," 264–68.

worldviews are threatened by external changes, revitalization movements inevitably evolve within the cultural and social contexts. He defines a revitalization movement as "a deliberate, organized, conscious effort by members of a society to construct a more satisfying culture."[69]

Appropriating Wallace's theory, Paul Hiebert says neo-Hinduism is "the result of India's encounter with Enlightenment and Christian thought."[70] The Christian critique of Hinduism, missionary portrayals of Hindu society, and the Christian doctrines of exclusivism and methods of conversion were the key botherations which stirred some fundamental Hindus to combat religious otherness in Christians. Hindu organizations like Brahmo Samaj, Arya Samaj, Hindu Mahasabha, and others have emerged to safeguard Hinduism from non-Hindu attackers.[71] According to Sita Ram Goel, a prominent Hindu nationalist scholar, those movements were "the earliest expressions of this Hindu spirit of resistance."[72] It is, therefore, crucial to understand the historical dimensions of Hindu revival movements and how they entered into conflict with religious others in search of political, religious, and cultural freedom and how they attempted to revitalize Hinduism.

Ethnonationalism

According to Walker Connor, who first coined the term, ethnonationalism is much more than its static interpretation of nationalism. For him, ethnonationalism is a self-defined "nation-consciousness," which cannot be understood in the way "nationalism" is defined in its pristine sense. He said, "Nationalism connotes identification with and loyalty to one's nation as just defined."[73] The essence of ethnonationalism, for Connor, is "the driving force behind expressions of nationalist feeling. It has also become known as the primordial view of nationalism."[74] Ethnonationalism deals with conflicts, old and new, that involve socio-religious, linguistic, and cultural aspects in ethnonational political mobilization.[75]

Nation-state is another crucial aspect of ethnonationalist thinking. Connor differentiates "nation-state" from nationalism in that it "is designed to describe a territorial-political unit (a state) whose borders coincided with

69. Wallace, "Revitalization Movements," 265.

70. Hiebert, "Missiological Issues," 51.

71. Ambrois, "Hindutva's Real Agenda," 14.

72. Goel, *Hindu Society Under Siege*.

73. Connor, *Ethnonationalism*, xi.

74. Comier, "Ethnonationalism in the Contemporary World," 1.

75. Baruah, *Critical Issues in Indian Ethnonationalism*, 1.

territorial distribution of a national group,"[76] and it is used to describe varied contexts in which a nation has its own state.[77] Ethnonationalist theory helps one understand the Hindu nationalist ideological framework.

As mentioned in the introduction, the rise of ethnonationalist consciousness, particularly Hindu nationalism in India, is the due outcome of the socioreligious and political contexts of the past, which burgeoned into movements such as Brahmo Samaj, Arya Samaj, Akhil Baratiya Hindu Mahasabha, Rashtriya Swayamsevak Sangh, Vishva Hindu Parishad and other sister socio-political institutions. Since these movements want to maintain ethnocentric hegemony in their ideology, they keep Hindu nationalism alive by suppressing the threatening others, especially Muslims and Christians.

Hindu nationalism is understood as the product "of a collective Hindu consciousness inhibited not only by the extreme social and religious differentiation within Hinduism but also by a tendency to discount the importance of the other."[78] According to Frykenberg, "If anything can undermine and destroy the unity of India, as so painstakingly constructed under the current constitution of India, Hindutva is its name."[79] Indicating the relationship between anti-Christian aggression and the gradually grown ideology of Hindutva which "is profoundly political, profoundly religious, and profoundly nationalist," Frykenberg argues that the Hindu fundamentalist blend of religious and national aggression has spawned fear among non-Hindu communities.[80] Thus, it is essential to understand the history of Hindu nationalism, which throws light on more hidden dots that eventually render connections to opposition phenomena.

METHODOLOGICAL APPROACH

This research is intended to be a narrative and interpretive history of the Hindu antagonism to Christian mission in India, particularly the Niyogi Report's role in Hindu nationalist resentment towards Christian conversion in independent India. It is a historical-descriptive study.

In identifying and gathering relevant data pertinent to my research problem, I read the two volumes of the Niyogi Report and extracted the themes and issues that have been in proportion to the prevalent anti-Christian propaganda of the advocates of Hindu nationalism. After reading the

76. Baruah, *Critical Issues in Indian Ethnonationalism*, 96.

77. For epistemological understanding of ethnonationalism, see Pachuau, "Nationhood in Conflict," 55.

78. Jaffrelot, *Hindu Nationalist Movement in India*, 2.

79. Frykenberg, "Hindutva and the Aftermath of Ajodhya," 27.

80. Frykenberg, "Hindutva and the Aftermath of Ajodhya," 17.

Report, I realized that the Niyogi Report was a meticulous compilation of historical and contemporary evidences of Hindu objections and allegations against the Christian missionary enterprise, particularly conversion activity in India until the 1950s. Therefore, to grasp the historical roots of Hindu animosity to Western missionary expansion in India and to examine how bygone sociopolitical contexts have been depended upon by the Niyogi Report to make a case against missionary activities in Madhya Pradesh, I considered the scholarly works of Christian and Hindu critics of European mission history in India and missionary activities in Madhya Pradesh.

Secondly, as I read the field notes, surveys, statements and replies in Volume II of the Report, I realized that the Niyogi Committee gave special weight to the statements and replies submitted by the representatives of RSS, BJS and VKA to show ample references against missionary work in Madhya Pradesh and to conclude that missionary activities have been dangerous to Hindu society and threatening to the national security. Therefore, I chose to go deeper to understand the history of Hindu nationalism and its relation to non-religious adherents in India and how the circumstances of independence and a liberal constitution prompted Hindu nationalist leaders to create a situation needing the appointment of the Niyogi Committee.

Third, in order to investigate the impact of the Niyogi report on religious and political events in India and to show how Hindu nationalist ideology, perceptions, and attitudes were shaped by the Report in the subsequent years, I chronologically traced the repercussions of the Report on Hindu nationalist organizations, particularly RSS, VHP and BJP. I also considered the scholarly writings and debates of Hindutva thinkers like Sita Ram Goel, Arun Shourie, H. V. Seshadri (or Sheshadri), Ashok V. Chowgule, and others whose anti-conversion rhetoric falls under the shadow of the Niyogi Report's anti-Christian rationalization.

I used historical analysis as a method for my study, meaning that I had a specific set of queries surrounding my key research question to probe in the historical records. A history is an account of some past event or combination of events. Historical analysis is, therefore, a method of discovering, from records and accounts, what happened in the past. In historical analysis, researchers consider various sources of historical data such as historical texts, newspaper reports, diaries, and maps. The method is commonly used by historians to gain insight into social phenomena.[81] Therefore, in this study, I considered primary and secondary materials, both published and unpublished works, and reviewed relevant literature to discover how historical influences have shaped Hindu perceptions toward

81. Sengers, "Historical Analysis," 35–49.

Christian missions since colonial times, how they contributed to the ascent of contemplated opposition, and how those historical factors figured into the making of the Niyogi Report.

I mainly delved into Hindu nationalist literature to obtain the needed data to resolve the key research question rather than repeating Christian scholars' assessments of Hindu opposition. In addition to locating relevant information on the websites of Hindu nationalist organizations, I found some useful materials from the offices and libraries of RSS, VHP, and BJP in Nagpur and Bhopal, and gathered data from their tracts, books and booklets relevant to my research enquiry. I also located some valuable materials such as news articles, reports, and socio-political discussions on the Niyogi Committee and the subsequent religious debates from Nehru Memorial Museum and Library and National Archives of India, New Delhi and the archives of Asbury Theological Seminary, Wilmore, USA, and the University of Kentucky, Lexington, USA.

LIMITATIONS AND DELIMITATIONS

The scope of this research is limited to the historical study of Hindu challenges to Christians with a special reference to the influence of the Niyogi Report on Hindu nationalist perceptions of and reactions to Christian missions in India. It intends to demonstrate how the Niyogi Report has served as a resource document for Hindutvavadis, particularly to the members of RSS, VHP, and BJP to maintain opposition to conversions in independent India. In doing so, I analyze significant themes which emerge from the Niyogi Report to appropriate them to the historical context to understand the opposition phenomenon.

This is not a study on Hindu faith or Indian mission history, though various aspects of these subjects will be consulted and referenced, and the nature of Christian missionary practices will be included and addressed in the process. Although this research focuses on the influence of the Niyogi Committee on Christian missions in Madhya Pradesh, its overarching impact has a nationwide scope.

I do not claim to deduce that the Niyogi Report is the only stimulus of Hindu hostility toward Christian mission in free India. Since the claims of the Report were contested by Christians soon after it was published, I neither hermeneutically deal with the text of the Report nor attempt to verify how authentic the committee's investigation process was. I only intend to trace the repercussions of the Report on the sociopolitical events in independent India and its influence on the Hindu nationalist view of Christian missions.

In finding answers to my research problem, I gave more attention to Hindu scholarly writings, articles, and views than to Christian works on the issue.

DEFINITIONS OF KEY TERMS

Some terms, such as Hindu, hindutva, proselytization, saffron, missionary, evangelization, and conversion are complex themes to understand, as they are derived from the distinct context of the socio-political and religious situation of India. While most of these terms are helpful to cognitively understand the underlying rationale of the issues in the Niyogi Report, others also have been used in a broad spectrum of Hindu nationalist ideology in order to throw light on the logical sequence of the argument and to maintain the line of thought as intended and described.

Hindu

The term "Hindu" has been defined in at least five different ways.[82] First, when Turkish, Persian, and Arab Muslim invaders arrived in India, they used the Persian words *Sindhu, Hind* or *Hindu* in a territorial sense to identify the people living beyond the Indus River. Second, it is used in the socioreligious context of "Brahmanical Hinduism," which refers to the religious order rooted in the caste-system that emerged in the 10th century BC. The third definition of Hindu is the western or oriental depiction of Indian civilization. As Edward Said pointed out, Hindu is "depicted as mysterious, exotic, sensual, despotic, traditional, and irrational in their fervent religiosity."[83] The fourth definition evolves from a political aspect where Hindu refers to a category of people who are differentiated from Christians, Muslims, Buddhists, Sikhs, Jains, and others within India. Fifth, the Hindu term is used in a religious sense, sometimes referred to as Neo-Hinduism.[84]

Adivasi

The word, "adivasi," which comes from Sanskrit (also Nepali, Hindi, and other Indian languages), literally means "ancient-dweller or original inhabitants." It was coined by political activists in the 1930s and is used to broadly describe the aboriginal or indigenous population in India, especially the tribal, ethnic, and forest-dweller groups.[85] Other synonyms include "girijan," "vanavai" and so on. The Sangh Parivar prefers to use the

---

82. Hiebert, "Missiological Issues," 48–49.

83. Hiebert, "Missiological Issues," 49.

84. Hiebert, "Missiological Issues," 49.

85. Barnes, *Indigenous People of Asia*, 105.

word vanavai, which means forest-dweller, because, the term adivasi "runs counter to its own claim that the Aryans, who brought Vedic civilization to the country, are the original inhabitants of the land."[86]

Hindutva

The term "Hindutva" means "Hinduness" or "Hinduhood."[87] It was a late nineteenth century construct of Indian thought, specifying "a mode of being of the possessor of the property 'Hinduness,' without carrying ontological implications about the property itself."[88] In the last quarter of the nineteenth century, Brahmabandhav Upadyay (1861–1907), an influential Indian Christian thinker and a passionate nationalist who was culturally chauvinist and virulently anti-British, sought to indigenize his Christian faith. He utilized the concept of "Hindu" or "Hindutva" to promote indigenous expressions of Christianity.[89] For him, there was no such thing as Hindu religion and therefore, he adopted the term Hindutva, which refers to the sociocultural aspects of the people of India, to unite the people of India.[90] He believed that irrespective of religious affiliations, every Indian remains a Hindu until death.[91] Until Hindu nationalists, especially RSS and its allied organizations, have complexly attributed various socio-religious and political overtones to the concept of Hindutva, it had a different usage in the history of Christian contextualization in India.

In the twentieth century, and especially in contemporary times, the Hindu nationalist idea of Hindutva became a complex, convoluted, debatable ideology rather than a term to define. It was the brainchild of V. D. Savarkar, the founder of the modern-day Hindutva movement, who coined the term in his small booklet, "Hindutva," published anonymously in 1923. Because of its deep-rooted philosophy, the connotation of the term has been ingrained into culture, nationality, Indian religion, and ethnic pride beyond its simplest meaning, Hindu-ness. The enigmatic word Hindutva is somewhat explicit only if it is viewed in the way the word "Hindu" is defined by Savarkar and the modern Hindu nationalists. For Savarkar it "is not a word but a history"[92] that signifies national identity (geographical unity, racial features, and a

86. Outlook India, "Adivasi vs Vanvasi."

87. Lipner, "On 'Hindutva,'" 1.

88. Lipner, "On 'Hindutva,'" 2.

89. Tennent, *Building Christianity on Indian Foundations*, 304.

90. Tennent, *Building Christianity on Indian Foundations*, 302–3.

91. Tennent, *Building Christianity on Indian Foundations*, 304.

92. Savarkar, *Hindutva*, 3.

common culture) rather than mere religious identity.[93] Hindutva, therefore, "embraces all the departments of thought and activity of the whole being of . . . Hindu race," "uniting people under one nation *(rastra)*, one race *(jati)*, one culture mediated by one language *(samskrata)*."[94]

The ideology built around Hindutva is now "profoundly political, profoundly religious, and profoundly nationalist."[95] Modern day Hindutva can be identified with a form of fundamentalism which is "proselytizing and political in character, chauvinistic and imperialistic in demand, and defensively aggressive and militant in attitude, it claims to 'represent' *all* the 'noble' and 'pure' peoples of India; and it calls for the subordination and the subjugation of *all* defiling or non-pure people of India."[96] Hindutva as coercive is an "ideology of violence and not merely a movement that happens to employ violence."[97] According to Melanchthon, an ideology of violence "needs a hate-object to keep itself alive and must express itself through aggression and violence."[98]

In independent India, the usage of Hindutva in an election speech or an appeal to vote for Hindutva is considered a corrupt practice, because an appeal to vote on the grounds of religion amounts to election malpractice, according to Section 123 of the Representation of People Act, 1951. On various occasions, such practices have been challenged in courts. In the cases of Sastri Yajnapurushdasji in 1966 and Sridharan in 1976, the Supreme Court held that "Hinduism was no religion but a way of life and therefore any appeal to vote for Hinduism would not by itself constitute an appeal in the name of religion which is a corrupt practice under the Section of 123 of the Representation of People Act."[99] Again on December 11, 1995, the Supreme Court's three-judge bench said that "Ordinarily, Hindutva is understood as a way of life or a state of mind and is not to be equated with or understood as religious Hindu fundamentalism. . .it is a fallacy and an error of law to proceed on the assumption. . .that the use of words Hindutva or Hinduism per se depicts an attitude hostile to all persons practicing any religion other than the Hindu religion. . ."[100]

93. Savarkar, *Hindutva*, 3; Jaffrelot, *Hindu Nationalism*, 86.

94. Savarkar, *Hindutva*, 110–11.

95. Frykenberg, "Hindutva and the Aftermath," 3.

96. Frykenberg, "Hindutva and the Aftermath," 13–14.

97. Melanchthon, "Persecution of Indian Christians," 106; Stanislaus, "Christian Response to Hindutva," 184.

98. Melanchthon, "Persecution of Indian Christian," 106.

99. Jois, *Supreme Court Judgement on "Hindutva,"* 62.

100. Jethmalani, "Hindutva is a Secular Way of Life."

Saffron

"Saffron" has been regarded as an auspicious color in Hinduism from ancient times and has various significances in Hindu religious ceremonies. It is also a general dress code of Hindu *Babas* (god-men) and sanyasis.[101] At the time of India's independence, RSS desired and demanded that India should adopt a saffron colored pennant as its national flag to represent Hindu society. Its request was denied by the Congress party. Instead, the Congress adopted a tri-color national flag to represent the harmony of different religions, multi-social systems and cultures in India.

Since the tri-color symbolizes the secularism of the state, which is contrary to Hindutva ideology, the RSS does not salute the tri-colored Indian flag.[102] Therefore, RSS adopted the single colored saffron flag called "bhagwa dhwaj" as the representation of Hindutva or *Hindu Rashtra* to which they pay homage.[103] Since the last quarter of the twentieth century, scholars have widely used the term *Saffron* as an alternate blanket word to refer to the Hindutva movement.

Missionary

The term "mission" comes from the Latin word, *missio,* which means, "act of sending"[104] and has been mostly understood as a Christian ecclesiastical term in a religious sense.[105] Until the mid-nineteenth century, "mission," "missions," "missionary," "mission field," or "missiology" denoted the idea of geographical expansion as it was considered to be an activity that proceeds in one direction: from the West to other parts of the world.[106]

The Hindu nationalist view of a missionary is similar to the traditional understanding that, "A missionary is an agent of evangelical expansion and a mission field is any area outside the West where this activity is being done."[107] According to C. V. Mathew, "Perhaps, due to its association, alleged or real, with colonialism, both within the 'guilty' Western Churches and the 'defensive' churches in the former colonies, 'mission,' originally a

101. There are four age-based life stages discussed in ancient and medieval Hindu texts called *asramas*. The four asramas are Brahmacharya (student), Grihastha (householder), Vanaprastha (retired), and Sansaya (renunciation).

102. Basu, *Khaki Shorts and Saffron Flags*, 39.

103. For more information, see Singh, "Bhagwa Dwaj"; Vishva Hindu Parishad, "Who is a Hindu? "

104. Etymonline, "Mission."

105. Mathew, *Saffron Mission*, 17.

106. Mathew, *Saffron Mission*, 17; Goheen, *Light to the Nations*, 4.

107. Goheen, *Light to the Nations*, 4.

Christian concept, today does not seem to have a pleasant connotation"[108] in the eyes of Hindu nationalists. On this narrow view, the Niyogi Committee expounded much, saying that the church in India is not independent, rather it is tied to the West in every manner, especially in its political and religious aspects. Therefore, the Niyogi Report portrays missionaries as "the limbs of national imperialism."[109]

Proselytization

Proselytization is an act of proselytizing. The word proselytize is derived from the Greek term προσήλυτος, which means "to come toward" or "a new comer." According to the Oxford dictionary, proselyte means "a person who has converted from one opinion, religion or party to another."[110] Biblically, it refers to "those who cross over from non-Jewish to Jewish society affirming Jewish monotheism."[111]

Tad Stahnke defines proselytization as "expressive conduct undertaken with the purpose of trying to change the religious beliefs, affiliation, or identity of another."[112] Under the rubric of proselytism, various methods of expressions and activities have been employed such as "religious discussions; preaching; teaching; the publication, distribution or sale of printed or electronic works; broadcasting; solicitation of funds; or provision of humanitarian or social services"[113] with an intention to convert others. Unfortunately, the word proselytization has acquired negative undertones in due course and "in some form is usually perceived as an inalienable aspect of Christian identity"[114] because in the non-Christian Indian context, proselytism and conversion have been viewed synonymously.[115]

The Niyogi Committee's understanding of proselytization is "the advertisement of one's beliefs and the winning over of people by unscrupulous methods, as if the end justified the means. Conversions brought about by force, fraud, undue influence, or material inducements are held to be the distinctive marks of proselytism."[116] The Niyogi Committee Report has such mentions of proselytization throughout Volume I and II. The Committee

---

108. Mathew, *Saffron Mission*, 17.

109. Niyogi, *Report*, 1:31.

110. www.oxforddictionaries.com.

111. Pachuau, "Ecumenical Church," 196.

112. Stahnke, "Right to Engage in Religious Persuasion," 262.

113. Stahnke, "Right to Engage in Religious Persuasion," 262.

114. Sharma, "Christian Proselytization," 425.

115. Pachuau, "Ecumenical Church and Religious Conversion," 196.

116. See Niyogi, *Report*, 1:48, 73, 157, 175.

also portrays proselytization as anti-national. Borrowing ideas from Marcus Ward's understanding of proselytization, the Niyogi Report asserts that, "to proselytize means to induce an individual or a group, by various motives, high and low, to change the outward allegiance, the religious label."[117] Anti-Christian Hindus often prefer to use the term proselytism to refer to Christian conversions in India because "proselytism is not just seen as a way of spreading religious ideas: it is often perceived as an attempt to extend ideological influence and political dominance" over the other.[118]

Conversion

Religious conversion has been referred to as involving the "process of self-transformation and commitment," "a radical reorganization of identity, meaning, [and] life," "the process of changing a sense of root reality [and] one's sense of grounding;" and "a total transformation of the person [that strikes] to the root of the human predicament."[119] According to Peter Stromberg, "a religious conversion is often understood as an event which alters the self and thereby transforms character."[120] A. Soares argues that Christian conversion is "an act of individual will, moved thereto by the grace of God which has touched his heart. It is not something imposed from outside. It is something which moves from inside. It is the response of the human heart to the attraction of Christ, his life, his works, his teachings and his death."[121]

Christian conversion and proselytization are the two major discussions in the Niyogi Report. The Report acknowledges the Christian point of view that "conversion is an act of God and is not a simple matter,"[122] but questions conversion methods adopted by missionaries. According to the Report,

> The word conversion may be viewed in different aspects. Spiritually, conversion marks the first step, and it is followed by Purification, Illumination and Union. Intellectually, it means assent by conviction—ethically, the spontaneous feeling of reverence for a true saint. All this is as far apart from the Missionary conversions as anything can be. As stated by Everett Cattell, most men come with a need, social, physical, economic or the like,

---

117. Niyogi, *Report*, 1:157.

118. Jean-Francois, "Conflicts Over Proselytism," 40.

119. Stromberg, *Language and Self-Transformation*, ix quoted in Young, *Asia in the Making of Christianity*, 419.

120. Stromberg, *Language and Self-Transformation*, 31.

121. Soares, "Conversion—Means and Ends," 1.

122. Niyogi, *Report*, 1:128 also see 52–53.

and an awakened faith that Christ could meet that need. (P. 17. Ways of Evangelism). The Missionary, as the representative of Christ, meets such material needs and thereby obtains influence on the person helped. It is this influence, which brings about the change of religion. Is this conversion or proselytism? . . . . The schools and medical institutions facilitate this accomplishment of the change of allegiance.[123]

Lalsangkima Pachuau writes, "While proselytizing aims at bringing people to one's community, conversion is process of turning to or renewing oneself in God."[124] Indian Christians have maintained the distinction between conversion and proselytization, but the non-Christian communities do not necessarily see the difference between proselytization and conversion because conversions generally result in social changes.

Religious Propaganda

Garth Jowett and Victoria O'Donnell's concise and workable definition of the term "propaganda" is "the deliberate, systematic attempt to shape perceptions, manipulate cognitions, and direct behavior to achieve a response that furthers the desired intent of the propagandist."[125] Richard Alan Nelson's comprehensive description of the word "propaganda" is neutrally defined as "a systematic form of purposeful persuasion that attempts to influence the emotions, attitudes, opinions, and actions of specified target audiences for ideological, political or commercial purposes through the controlled transmission of one-sided messages (which may or may not be factual) via mass and direct media channels."[126]

The Niyogi Report argues that Christian "attacks on Hindu religion, its gods and deities, are an important and integral plank of Christian propaganda, and are being indulged in, in a concerted manner deliberately in all parts of the State and by all sorts of preachers and are occasionally sought to be justified by authoritative organizations as a mere explanation of one of the Commandments."[127] On the other hand, Hindutva is also viewed as propaganda by some as its advocates marginalize and stereotype religious others, particularly Muslims and Christians, as threatening and dangerous to the culture and national security. For example, the Hindu nationalist portrayal

---

123. Niyogi, *Report,* 1:157.
124. Pachuau, "Ecumenical Church and Religious Conversion," 197.
125. Jowett, *Propaganda and Persuasion,* 7.
126. Nelson, *Chronology and Glossary of Propaganda in the United States,* 232.
127. Niyogi, *Report,* 1:128.

of Christian converts as de-nationalized is propaganda against Christians to incite public opinion against Christian conversions.

Evangelization

The term "evangelism" comes from Greek word, εὐαγγέλιον (transliterated as "euagelion"), which means, *good news* or *gospel.* Evangelism is "the preaching of the Christian gospel or a particular interpretation of it to (a group or area) in the hope of making people converts."[128]

The Niyogi Report's understanding of evangelization in India is that it is "a uniform world policy to revive Christendom for reestablishing western supremacy and is not promoted by spiritual motives. The objective is apparently to create Christian minority pockets with a view to disrupt the solidarity of the non-Christian society and the mass conversion of a considerable section of adivasis with this ulterior motive is fraught with danger to the security of the State."[129]

Religious Liberty vs Freedom of Religion Acts

"Freedom of religion" or "religious liberty" is a fundamental right of the people of India guaranteed by the Indian Constitution which came into existence in independent India on November 26, 1949. Under the "Fundamental Rights" section, Article 25 of the Indian constitution delineates religious freedom as "Subject to public order, morality and health and to the other provisions of this part, all persons are equally entitled to freedom of conscience and the right freely to profess, practice and propagate religion."[130] However, it is circumscribed by the suffix that, "nothing in this article shall affect the operation of any existing law or prevent the State from making any law regulating or restricting any economic, financial, political or other secular activity which may be associated with religious practice."[131]

Interestingly, what were introduced as "Freedom of Religion Acts" in Orissa, Madhya Pradesh, Arunachal Pradesh, Chhattisgarh, Gujarat, Himachal Pradesh, Rajasthan, Jharkhand, and Uttarakhand were alleged to be against Christian religious liberty. Though each state's Religious Freedom Act slightly differs from the others, the laws generally stipulate that, "No person shall convert or attempt to convert, either directly or otherwise, any person from one religious faith to another by the use of force or by

128. Collins Dictionary, "Evangelism."

129. Niyogi, *Report,* 1:160.

130. Religious freedom is explained at length in Articles 25, 26, 30 (1, 2); 31 (2) of the Indian Constitution: http://india.gov.in/my-government/constitution-india.

131. Indian Constitution, Article 25–2(a).

inducement or by any fraudulent means nor shall any person abet any such conversion."[132] Anti-conversion bills have been proposed in over a dozen states so far: Orissa (1967), Madhya Pradesh (1968), Chhattisgarh (1968, 2006), Arunachal Pradesh (1978), Maharashtra (1996, 2005, 2012), Gujarat (2002, 2003, 2007), Tamil Nadu (2003), Jharkhand (2005), Himachal Pradesh (2006), Rajasthan (2006), Uttarakhand (2007), Karnataka (2009), and Uttar Pradesh (2020). They have been passed and are currently active in nine states: Orissa, Madhya Pradesh, Chhattisgarh, Gujarat, Jharkhand, Himachal Pradesh, Uttarakhand, Karnataka, and Arunachal Pradesh.[133]

When these laws were first enacted in Orissa and Madhya Pradesh in 1968, a few Catholic leaders were arrested and prosecuted on the charges of fraudulent conversions under the guidelines of these Acts. Christian leaders felt that these laws would provide "a way of identifying and exposing converts for harassment,"[134] and therefore they appealed to the Supreme Court to challenge that these laws violated constitutional freedom of religion. Discussions continued for almost five years until the Supreme Court gave a final ruling in 1977 that "there is no fundamental right to convert another person to one's own religion."[135]

The Hindu nationalists do not see religious freedom in the same way "freedom of religion" was defined by the Universal Declaration of Human Rights (UDHR) in 1948. According to Article 18 of the United Nations' Universal Declaration of Human Rights, religious freedom is that "Everyone has the right to freedom of thought, conscience and religion; this right includes freedom to change his religion or belief, and freedom, either alone or in community with others and in public or private, to manifest his religion or belief in teaching, practice, worship and observance."[136] But Hindu nationalists contend that it is the fundamental right to protect and promote ethnosocial and ethnoreligious identity as opposed to the secular understanding of freedom to choose.[137] According to William Inboden, religious freedom is defined in self-assessed cultural and ethnic settings.

> Religious liberty has both an individual and a communal component, as the obligations of a particular confession apply to

132. See Appendix–G for the text of conversion laws in various states of India.

133. See Panadan, "Anti-Conversion Laws," 132.

134. Pachuau, "Ecumenical Church and Religious Conversion," 191.

135. Saldanha, *Conversion and Indian Civil Law*, 166.

136. United Nations, "Universal Declaration of Human Rights." See also Grim, *Price of Freedom Denied*, 26.

137. For an analysis of formal restrictions on religious minorities, see Grim, *Price of Freedom Denied*, 147–49.

individual and corporate body alike. Related to this, religion is often a determining feature of ethnic or national identity, whether Tibetan Buddhism, Hindu nationalism in India, Judaism in Israel, Russian Orthodoxy, or Turkish Islam. Just as it often correlates with ethno-nationalism, religion also connects with the eternal. Its eschatological dimension is often most compelling for believers yet most inscrutable for nonbelievers.[138]

138. Inboden, "Religious Freedom and National Security."

2

The Historical Antecedents of Anti-Missionary Attitudes and Hindu Awakening

THIS CHAPTER PRESENTS THE historical context for the development of anti-missionary attitudes and the evolution of Hindu consciousness against religious conversions by showing how bygone conditions, especially the Portuguese Christianization, colonialism, and Western missionary expansion, served as the framework for the upsurge of modern Hindu reactionary attitudes, the nationalist consciousness, and the organized Hindu resurgence against the Christian missionary enterprise in the nineteenth and twentieth centuries.

Ainslie T. Embree, an Indologist and historian, notes, "In the nineteenth century, after the British established their political hegemony throughout the subcontinent, many Hindu intellectuals began to reassess and reinterpret Indian history and culture and its relation to the present. A primary result of this reassessment was the articulation of a nationalism that was deeply colored by a nostalgia for the Hindu past."[1] Hindus who critically view the conversion activities of Christianity based on India's political and religious past emphasize the need for "reawakened Hinduism" to consolidate unity for the defense of Hinduism and to resist the conversion of Hindus into other faiths. Ram Swarup Agarwal, a Hindu thinker of the twentieth century, stressed that, "The most important role that a reawakened Hinduism has to play is that of helping the world to understand its religious past."[2] He believed that if the people began to realize that once they had belonged to a different spiritual culture and that religious impositions had been placed on

1. Embree, *Utopias in Conflict*, 16.
2. Swarup, *Hindu View of Christianity and Islam*, 114–15.

them, they could "break from their present confines and . . . recover their lost identity."[3] As Martha C. Nussbaum points out, "History is important to people's sense of their selfhood and their attempts to construct national identity. History was important to Savarkar and Golwalkar, and it is important today to the Hindu right, because a historical narrative makes a powerful statement about the identity and unity of the nation."[4] To rightly comprehend the anti-missionary and anti-Christian appeals of the Hindu fundamentalists and Hindu rightists of the day, it is crucial to explore the historical Hindu-Christian encounters from the Hindu point of view.

Sita Ram Goel, a prominent Hindu scholar and historian, painstakingly traces the unpleasant acts of Christian missionaries in his scholarly works, *History of Hindu-Christian Encounters (AD 304 to 1996), Jesus Christ: Artifice for Aggression, Pseudo-Secularism, Christian Missions and Hindu Resistance, Papacy and History,* and *Hindu Society under Siege,* in an attempt to show that the opposition to Christianity in India is a spontaneous response of Hindus to the bitter history of Western Christianity's intolerance and ill portrayal of Hindu beliefs, social customs, and traditions. He points out that as early as AD 304, when St. Gregory attempted to destroy the images in the temples of a Hindu colony in Taron on the upper Euphrates, Hindus stood in opposition, but were defeated.[5] He indicates that it was after the arrival of the Portuguese that Hindus began to view Christianity critically and oppose the Christianizing efforts of the West in India.[6] According to Arun Shourie, a well-known economist, politician, and Hindu thinker, Hindu animosity can be understood against the context of Christian conversion activities and their repercussions on socioreligious aspects.[7] He said, "To convert us, missionaries have worked for five hundred years to undermine our reverence for our gods and scriptures. Till the early 1950s the denunciation used to be open, shrill, abusive."[8] He argues that conversion causes grave disruption and tensions in the families of converts and their communities.[9] As Koenraad Elst, a Belgian scholar, pointed out, "missionary Christianity brought by the colonizers is strongly disliked by Hindu activists . . . because of its *rejection of Hinduism's Otherness.*"[10]

---

3. Swarup, *Hindu View of Christianity and Islam*, 10.

4. Nussbaum, *Clash Within*, 213.

5. Goel, *History of Hindu-Christian Encounters*, 2.

6. Goel, *Pseudo-Secularism*, 1.

7. Shourie, *Harvesting Our Souls*, 1–2.

8. Shourie, *Harvesting Our Souls*, 3.

9. Shourie, *Harvesting Our Souls*, 1.

10. Elst, *Decolonizing the Hindu Mind*, 45.

Sita Ram Goel argued that, "Hindus from early seventeenth century Pandits of Tamil Nadu to Arun Shourie in the closing years of the twentieth, have spent no end of ink and breath to demolish the dogma of Christianity and denounce missionary methods."[11] Arguably, his contention has been supported by some Hindu as well as Christian scholars. Dennis Hudson, a Christian scholar of Indian religions, reasoned that Hindus in Tamil Nadu "opposed the Christian missions from the earliest days they were establishing among the Tamils; literary evidence for it is indirect, largely because the printing press was not available to Tamil ownership until 1835."[12] Arthur Mayhew, an educationist in British India, also argued that Hindus displayed signs of antipathy to Christianity when they began to observe Portuguese colonizers' coercive and alluring attempts to Christianize Hindus. In his work, he examined how Christian forces were at work in the administration of India and how the British government and Christian missions entered a mutual relationship which lasted from 1600–1920.[13]

When the British arrived in India, being sensitive to the religious sentiments of Hindus against Christian conversions, the East India Company (EIC) in Bombay (now called Mumbai) gave orders in 1662, that "There shall be no compulsory conversion, no interference with native habits, and no cow-killing in Hindu quarters."[14] Until 1813, the EIC maintained this policy throughout India, actively discouraging the spread of Christianity in the country. It was William Wilberforce, Member of Parliament, who attempted to influence the British Parliament in 1793 with a proposal to make it obligatory on the part of the company to send missionaries to India. His proposal was not accepted until 1813.[15]

The Protestant work which began in India in the early 1700s continued at a slow pace outside British colonies until the arrival of William Carey, the father of the modern missionary movement, who brought a revolution in missions through his unbridled passion to reach the heathens with the gospel by means of preaching, education, literacy works, philanthropic works, and advocacy for social reformation. The works of missionaries, especially the educational efforts, played a significant role in

---

11. Goel, *Pseudo-Secularism*, 1.

12. Hudson, "Arumuga Navalar and the Hindu Renaissance," 28.

13. Mayhew, *Christianity and the Government of India*, 30–38.

14. Smith, *India as a Secular State*, 66.

15. For a detailed parliamentary discussion, see Pearson, *Memoirs*, 269–307. Sita Ram Goel argued that Wilberforce and others wrongly influenced the British parliament to permit missionaries in India by overstating the horrible customs of the Hindus such as sati, infanticide, throwing children into the Ganga, religious suicides, and above all, idolatry.

the Bengal Renaissance, which set the pace for change throughout India.[16] While missionary works of development were received with thankfulness, their zeal and methods for seeking conversions came under criticism from various people beginning with Raja Ram Mohan Roy.

THE HINDU CRITIQUE OF CHRISTIANIZATION
UNDER THE PORTUGUESE

The arrival of Portuguese explorer Vasco da Gama in South India in 1498 brought not only the discovery of a sea route for wider trade between the East and the West, but also a great turning point in the history of Christianity in India. According to the Report of the Christian Missionary Activities Enquiry Committee of Madhya Pradesh, "the aggressive missionary era" began at this time.[17]

Missionary Zeal and Methods of Conversion

When the natives asked Vasco da Gama what brought him to India, he replied that they had come "to seek Christians and spices."[18] As argued by Fernando and Gispert-Sauch, this statement was often misunderstood or misinterpreted as if the Portugal adventure in Asia was primarily to make converts. "Actually, they came to *find* Christians, rather than to *make* Christians"[19] as was shown in a letter written by the king of Portugal to his peers in Spain in 1599. The program of Christianizing India was not in their initial agenda, although religion played a vital role in the success of the enterprise.[20] During the time of King Emmanuel I, the policy of conversion was not dictated by missionary zeal, but in the time of King João III, evangelization became one of the main objects of the political agenda, as he was very anxious to spread Christianity around the world.[21] However, it was not until half a century later, when Jesuit missionary Francis Xavier came to India, that the idea of making converts became part of the imperial ideology.[22] In the process, as John Chethimattam writes, "The zealous missionaries who accompanied

16. Tennent, *Building Christianity on Indian Foundations*, 46–47.

17. Niyogi, *Report*, 1:35.

18. Fernando, *Christianity in India*, 72.

19. Fernando, *Christianity in India*, 73.

20. Moffett, *History of Christianity in Asia*, 3.

21. Panikkar, *Malabar and the Portuguese*, 186.

22. Fernando, *Christianity in India*, 73; Firth, *Introduction to Indian Church History*, 51–52. See also Koschorke, *History of Christianity in Asia*, 8, 9; Panikkar, *Malabar and the Portuguese*, 183, Moffett, *History of Christianity in Asia*, 5; Panikkar, *Asia and Western Dominance*, 280.

the sailors were often forced to be instruments and agents of the ambitious political power."[23] With Christianization becoming a state enterprise,[24] Portuguese rulers were believed to have destroyed temples and mosques and forbidden public worship by Hindus and Muslims in the areas that came under their authority. They passed orders which "prohibited the open observation of all Hindu religious rites and rituals"[25] in their enclaves. Anant Priolkar notes in his work, *The Terrible Tribunal for the East: The Goa Inquisition,* that "heated efforts were made to destroy Hinduism."[26] In his view, the Portuguese's anti-Hindu laws, banishment of Hindus from Christianized regions, and public humiliation of Hindus were all for the encouragement of conversions.[27] At times the Portuguese took advantage of the condition of parentless Hindu children for forced conversion as they were taken into Catholic schools to be baptized, educated, and indoctrinated into the priesthood for the spread of Christianity.[28] In this endeavor, "even children whose mother and grandparents were living were being snatched away from their families for being baptized." In view of these forceful proselytizing efforts, the Portuguese entry into India was "the eighth crusade"[29] as Panikkar calls it, which Moffett dismisses by saying it couldn't be the repetition of a crusade; rather it was a trade war, not even a holy war.[30]

The Mission of Francis Xavier and Hindu Responses

The Christian Missionary Activities Enquiry Committee (CMAEC), which was involved in the investigation of anti-missionary allegations in Madhya Pradesh during 1954–1956, argued in its report that the "aims and objects of missionary activity in some parts of Madhya Pradesh can best be understood against the background of [missions] history."[31] The Report highlighted some portions from that history to indicate that the proselytizing activities of missionaries were advanced by colonial zeal and meddled with the Hindu religious system. For example,

23. Chethimattam, *Dialogue in Indian Tradition,* 134.

24. Panikkar, *Asia and Western Dominance,* 280.

25. Savarkar, *Hindutva,* 54.

26. Priolkar, *Terrible Tribunal for the East,* 25.

27. Priolkar, *Terrible Tribunal for the East,* 114–49.

28. Priolkar, *Terrible Tribunal for the East,* 127.

29. Panikkar, *Asia and Western Dominance,* 313.

30. Moffett, *History of Christianity in Asia,* 3.

31. Niyogi, *Report,* 1:34.

The King of Portugal, dissatisfied with the small progress made, applied to Ignatius Loyola to send the entire Jesuit Order to India. . . Loyola could not grant the request; but in 1541 Francis Xavier, the greatest of all Jesuits, was sent to the East . . . He only spent about four and a half years in the country, but in that brief space of time he is said to have baptised about 60,000 people, nearly all from the fisherman castes, living on the South-West and South-East coasts of India . . . This mass movement work of the Jesuits was in fact an appeal to material interests . . . . The impatient Xavier, still dissatisfied with the result of his labour wrote to the King of Portugal that the only hope of increasing the number of Christians was by the use of the secular power of the State. As a result of this note, the King issued orders that in Goa and other Portuguese settlements, "all idols shall be sought out and destroyed, and severe penalties shall be laid upon all such as shall dare to make an idol or shall shelter or hide a Brahman . . . " He also ordered that special privileges should be granted to Christians in order that the natives may be inclined to submit themselves to the yoke of Christianity.[32]

It is argued that conversion during the Portuguese period was more from strong inducement than from compulsion or the preaching of the gospel because converts usually came under the protection and provision of a powerful foreign government.[33] An example was the conversion of the Paravas, a caste-group of pearl fishers in the southernmost part of Tamil Nadu,[34] who requested priests to baptize them, motivated by hidden desires for employment in secular business or protection from the exploitation of their Hindu masters. Under such circumstances, between 1535 and 1537 the entire caste of about 20,000 people was baptized.[35] After baptism, each member "received a palm-leaf strip on which *kanakapuka* (accountant) had written his new Portuguese name in Tamil"[36] and was declared Christian. Since only Catholic Christians could hold public offices and enjoy the same privileges as the Portuguese, some Thomas Christians also desired to become Catholic Christians.[37] According to John Rutherfurd, in order to

32. Niyogi, *Report*, 1:36.

33. Koschorke, *History of Christianity in Asia*, 24–25; Priolkar, *Terrible Tribunal for the East*, 55, 58.

34. Travancore and Thoothukudi or Tuticorin.

35. Neill, *History of Christianity in India*, 142.

36. Ponnumuthan, *Spirituality of Basic Ecclesial Communities*, 130. See also Schurhammer, *Francis Xavier*, 262, 295.

37. Panikkar, *Malabar and the Portuguese*, 170; Niyogi, *Report*, 1:66; Chethimattam, *Dialogue in Indian Tradition*, 134.

increase the Christian population, the Portuguese also bought a great many poor people as slaves and baptized them without so much as asking them one question about the substance of these transactions.[38] At this time in history, Christianity was identified with "changing over to Portuguese names and dress, beef eating, wine drinking, and loose living."[39]

When Francis Xavier, the Apostle of the Indies, came to India, he touched the poor, the needy, and the low-caste people in Travancore with his philanthropic services and attracted many into Christian faith.[40] He devoted himself to reaching marginalized communities with the gospel and to reforming the worldly Portuguese Christians in Goa. It was Xavier who, in 1546, asked the king of Portugal to set up the Inquisition against Christian heretics in Goa. Xavier's intention in inviting the Inquisition (also known as the Holy Office) to Goa was to purge evil characters from the church of the Portuguese in Goa and other parts of Malabar regions. According to Monfieur Dillon, it was never intended to be implemented against Hindus for conversion.[41] He wrote, "The Inquisition, which punishes apostate Christians with death, never sentences to that penalty those who have not been baptized."[42] However, Hindu scholars such as A. K. Priolkar, Ram Swarup, Sita Ram Goel, and others often relate Portuguese political cruelty with the office of Inquisition and argue that it was under a zealous conversion plan that thousands of Hindus were killed and hundreds of temples were destroyed.[43]

In one of his letters, Xavier wrote, "When all are baptized I order all the temples of their false gods to be destroyed and all the idols to be broken into pieces. I can give you no idea of the joy I feel in seeing this done, witnessing the destruction of the idols by the very people who but lately adored them."[44] Along with Christian doctrines, school boys were taught of his passion against idols, and they often showed that "their greatest delight of all was to assist at the demolition of the idols in the heathen temples."[45]

---

38. Rutherfurd, *Missionary Pioneers in India*, 27.

39. Thomas, "Christian Missions in the Pluralistic Context of India," 92.

40. Lilly, *India and its Problems*, 156; Panikkar, *Malabar and the Portuguese*, 195.

41. Dellon, *Account of the Inquisition at Goa*, 83.

42. Dellon, *Account of the Inquisition at Goa*, 83.

43. Priolkar, *Terrible Tribunal for the East*, 115; Swarup, *Hindu View of Christianity and Islam*, 84. Goel, *History of Hindu-Christian Encounters*, 4; De Souza, "Portuguese in Asia," 11–29.

44. Coleridge, *Life and Letters of St. Francis Xavier*, 281. Xavier wrote this letter from Cochin on January 22, 1545 to the Society at Rome. For whole content of the letter, see 279–84.

45. Coleridge, *Life and Letters of St. Francis Xavier*, 175.

To some, Xavier's mission appears counter-cultural since he encouraged his converts to detach from their old religious practices and destroy temples and images after their baptisms.[46]

Xavier's efforts at converting the poor and the Portuguese strategies of Christianizing Hindus bred hatred of Christianity in Brahmans.[47] Looking back at the whole scenario of conversion strategies under the Portuguese regime, Hindu activist Sita Ram Goel, portrays Xavier as "the pioneer of anti-Brahmanism" and "a rapacious pirate dressed up as a priest."[48] He argued that, "Christian iconoclasm pioneered by Xavier was no less ferocious and predatory . . . no less criminal in its inspiration."[49] He contended that "The school of Francis Xavier was all for augmenting the degree of force used in the advancement of the mission."[50] He blames Xavier for enlightening the poor Christians, educating and emancipating them from their ignorance and social depravity.[51]

Hindu Critique of Robert De Nobili's Adaptation

The characteristic feature of Jesuit missionary zeal in India was their intolerance of non-Christian traditions and cultures, which meant that their mission received no attention by high caste Hindus until Robert De Nobili arrived. Nobili perceived that Christianity would have but little success in India if the West refused to understand the minds and the thoughts of the people of the country.[52] Following the example of Paul from 1 Corinthians 9:22, Nobili said to himself, "I will become as a Hindoo to save these Hindoos."[53] As envisioned, he ended up in Madurai, Tamil Nadu, in 1606, and took the form of a Brahman, adapting their socio-religious and cultural patterns in doing mission. The Brahman and higher caste converts were allowed to keep their symbols of social ranking such as cord, hair-tuft, sandal paste, and forms of clothing, but must give up the Hindu ceremonies and mantras connected with them.[54]

46. Schurhammer, *Francis Xavier*, 470.

47. Schurhammer, *Francis Xavier*, 159, 175; Kaye, *Christianity in India*, 267; Priolkar, *Terrible Tribunal for the East*, 56.

48. Goel, *History of Hindu-Christian Christian Encounters*, 11.

49. Goel, *History of Hindu-Christian Christian Encounters*, 2.

50. Goel, *History of Hindu-Christian Christian Encounters*, 18.

51. Goel, *History of Hindu-Christian Christian Encounters*, 4

52. Panikkar, *Asia and Western Dominance*, 281.

53. According to Strickland's account Nobili and his associate baptized 100,000 idolaters. Strickland, *Jesuit in India*, 39.

54. Firth, *Introduction to Indian Church History*, 116.

In his endeavors to reach Brahman communities with the gospel through an adaption model, he called himself a "Brahman from Rome" and built a place of worship which he called "Kovil," which means "temple" in Tamil. He called the gospel *the fifth Veda,* Yeshurveda.[55] While some appreciated Nobili's stringent determination and sacrifice to denounce his Portuguese sociocultural aspects to become like one of the Brahmans to win them for Christ, others criticized him, saying that by assimilating himself into a particular caste, he promoted the caste system, which has oppressive characteristics.[56] Arguably, he won many converts,[57] but his success among Brahmans was believed to not have been so remarkable. Stephen Neill mentions that in 37 years Nobili baptized about 600 persons of higher castes, most of whom did not remain faithful.[58]

Nobili's mission was met with opposition from some Brahmans who were believed to have brought charges against him on account of his lying, saying that he was a "Brahman from Rome" and misleading people into Christianity.[59] The Niyogi Report remarks that Nobili "showed documentary evidence to prove that he belonged to a clan of the parent stock that had migrated from ancient Aryavrat and assured the members of the high castes that by becoming a Christian one did not renounce one's caste, nobility or usage."[60] Julius Richter writes that, "He [Nobili] mollified the opposition of influential Brahmans by means of bribes."[61] John William Kaye records an allegation that, when Nobili's followers did not achieve significant conversions by Nobili's method, they went down to the villages of *Pariahs* and baptized all the dying children on the pretext of administering medicine to them.[62] There was also an allegation that Nobili and his associates "turned aside from the practice of no deceit; from the exercise of no hypocrisy. They lied in word, and they lied in action. They called themselves western Brahmans; and in the disguise of Brahmans they mixed themselves with the people, talking their language, following their customs, and countenancing

55. Niyogi, *Report,* 1:37.

56. Schmidlin, *Catholic Mission History,* 481.

57. Strickland, *Jesuit in India,* 39.

58. Neill, *History of Christian Missions,* 159.

59. Kaye, *Christianity in India,* 287.

60. Niyogi, *Report,* 1:37.

61. Richter, *History of Missions in India,* 63.

62. Richter, *History of Missions in India,* 32.

their superstitions."[63] The Niyogi Report includes these aspects as background to the Hindu-missionary problems in India.[64]

In the context of the aforementioned charges there was opposition and persecution of Nobili's followers in 1686 in Ramnad and Pudukottah of Tamil Nadu.[65] Arun Shourie and Sita Ram Goel and other Hindu thinkers called Nobili a forger who had smuggled notions from Hinduism to inveigle people into Christianity.[66] Shourie writes, "To deceive people into conversion, de Nobili not only altered his own appearance, he disguised rites such as baptism, the service, etc. And he asked his disciples as well as the new converts to retain Indian appearances."[67] Hindu critics fail to sympathize with Nobili's aim of freeing Christianity from the reproach of foreignness, while even in the twenty-first century, they continue to indict Christianity as a slave of foreign culture.[68]

Decline of Catholic Missionary Expansion and the Arrival of Protestants

As the seventeenth century dawned, Jesuit missionaries became more fervent in reaching non-Christians. A stream of missionaries from Goa went in all directions to evangelize India.[69] John William Kaye records that when they approached the northern regions where the Ganges flows, they were so strongly repulsed by Hindus that they became disheartened and finally abandoned their work in despair.[70] Panikkar notes that the Portuguese Christians' "intolerance of other religions and their arrogant attitude toward the exponents of other faiths were unwelcome . . . "[71] With the entry of other European nations, especially the Dutch, French and British in the seventeenth century, Portuguese power in Asia was greatly challenged and began to decline.[72] Since the Dutch were Protestant, as soon as they captured places, they attempted to drive away all the Catholic clergy, whether Italian

63. Kaye, *Christianity in India,* 31.

64. Niyogi, *Report,* 1:34, 37.

65. Firth, *Introduction to Indian Church History,* 121.

66. Shourie, "Roman Brahmin."

67. Shourie, "Roman Brahmin."

68. Swarup, *Hindu View of Christianity,* 112; Bhishikar, *Shri Guruji,* 55, 100–101.

69. Kaye, *Christianity in India,* 30.

70. Kaye, *Christianity in India,* 30.

71. Panikkar, *Asia and Western Dominance,* 281.

72. Dutch dispossessed Portuguese in Java (1595), Malacca (1641), Ceylon (1638–1658), Quilon (1661), Cranganore (1662), and Cochin (1663).

or Portuguese.[73] Though the Dutch and the British disliked each other, they were in agreement with one another about detesting Roman Catholics. Since Dutch and English people did not follow aggressive methods like the Portuguese, they did not arouse hostility from the locals.[74]

In the early eighteenth century, while some Jesuit missionaries were still carrying on their work in Tamil Nadu, the first Protestant missionaries from the German Pietistic Movement, Bartholomäus Ziegenbalg and Heinrich Plütschau, arrived in Tamil Nadu at the invitation of King Frederick IV of Denmark. Their missionary work was opposed both by Hindus and Danish authorities. Ziegenbalg attempted to convert Brahmans through dialogue. He was involved in literary works such as the translation of the Bible and the composition of dictionaries, school textbooks, catechisms, and so on in the local vernacular, Tamil. He established "charity schools to give a Christian training to the rising generation and prepare workers for the church."[75] By using a compare-contrast model, he appealed to the intellectuals of Tamil Nadu and wrote a number of tracts for dissemination among Hindus which emphasized the monotheist core of Hindu belief and praised the subtlety of Hindu philosophical thought about the divine.[76] According to Will Sweetman, Ziegenbalg stressed "the high moral standards of the Hindus, which he invariably contrasts with the degenerate lifestyle of the supposedly Christian Europeans in Tranquebar, which causes the greatest resistance to conversion on the part of the Hindus."[77] Ziegenbalg's works, *Malabar Heathendom* (1711) and *Genealogy of the South-Indian Gods* (1713), received counter reactions from the Brahmans of his day.[78] These books, which demonstrated the beginning of what would become a major movement in the 19th century, caused a stir in the missionary community as well. According to John Rutherfurd, Ziegenbalg's converts, at times, were opposed and persecuted by their family members.[79]

73. Panikkar, *Malabar and the Portuguese*, 148–56; Neill, *History of Christian Missions*, 173.

74. Neill, *History of Christianity in India*, 272.

75. Firth, *Introduction to Indian Church History*, 135.

76. Sweetman, "Prehistory of Orientalism," 19.

77. Sweetman, "Prehistory of Orientalism," 19.

78. Goel, *History of Hindu-Christian Encounters*, 25.

79. Rutherfurd, *Missionary Pioneers in India*, 22–23.

THE IMPACT OF BRITISH COLONIALISM AND
THE MODERN MISSIONARY MOVEMENT ON INDIA

As J. N. Farquhar noted in his writings, the trading Europeans, who began to flock into the Indian subcontinent as early as the 1500s, produced no remarkable repercussions in the nation until the opening of the nineteenth century when the British, who initially came to India for trade purposes, began to show their ambitions in political and socio-religious reforms.[80] "The new techniques—the railway train, the printing press, other machinery, more efficient ways of warfare—could not be ignored, and these came up against old methods of thought almost unawares, by indirect approaches, creating a conflict in the mind of India. The most obvious and far-reaching change was the break-up of the agrarian system and the introduction of conceptions of private property and landlordism."[81] All these changes influenced Indian minds and gave rise to "modern" consciousness to the extent that intellectual Hindus began to self-assess their socioeconomic and religious situation and question European imperialism and the Christian missionary enterprise.

Historian R. C. Majumdar notes that the first evil of magnitude of the British rule was observed in the economic exploitation of the country.[82] The impact of colonialism was observed not only on the economic and political conditions of India but also on the socio-religious, health, and cultural aspects of Hindu society. The European voyages of exploration and settlements resulted in the exchange of animals, diseases, and plants. While some of the European exchanges contributed to development and globalization, others had catastrophic consequences on the colonized indigenous people.[83] India's political awakening, religious reformation, and revitalization were the result of three crucial Western influences: the British government, Protestant missions, and the work of Orientalists.[84]

80. Farquhar, *Modern Religious Movements in India*, 2. See also Morris, *Heaven's Command*, 71–72; Nandy, *Intimate Enemy*, 6.

81. Nehru, *Discovery of India*, 314.

82. Majumdar, *History of the Freedom Movement in India*, 89.

83. Page, *Colonialism*, 190.

84. The educational mission of Scottish missionary Alexander Duff and Baptist missionaries Carey, Marshman, and Ward enlightened the minds of elite Hindu intellectuals to gain emic perspective on the significance of their own religious heritage and traditions and eventually to turn against the forces that gave them self-esteem. Farquhar, *Modern Religious Movements in India*, 8. Also, Hedlund, "Hindus and Christians for 2000 years."

Britain's Religious Neutrality and Missionary Policies

The present-day Hindu nationalist view of Christianity as the "religious arm of colonialism" can be viewed against Britain's indecisive policies that transitioned from supporting Hindu socio-religious customs to encouraging the work of missionaries who were against them. The Christian character of the British in India appeared complex from its inception. In winning the confidence of the elite Hindus for successful trade relations, the British government initially invested a large sum of money in strengthening Hinduism. Until the renewal of the Charter of EIC in 1813, the British had been actively involved in the traditional and religious welfare of Hindus by repairing and rebuilding their temples, paying salaries to temple pujaris, making financial grants for festivals, and supporting their sacrifices. Farquhar mentions that, "Even the cruel and immoral rites, such as hook-swinging . . . , [and] the burning of widows, were carried out under British supervision."[85] At times the British Army even paid respect to Indian gods and goddesses.[86] George Smith showed in his account that the British also supported social traditions such as *sati* so that from "1757 to 1829, three-quarters of a century, Christian England was responsible, at first indirectly and then most directly, for the known immolation of at least 70,000 Hindoo widows."[87] They actively refused the incoming of foreign missionaries, discouraged native Christians from entering military or civil services, and enforced rigorous laws against those who Christianized Hindus. In Frykenberg's words, it was no less significant that "the imperial state became the guardian of all 'Hindu' endowments, temples, places of pilgrimage, sectarian academies (*mutths*), ceremonies and festivals . . . The Indian Empire became, for all practical purposes, a de facto 'Hindu' Raj."[88]

It was by an Act of Parliament in 1813 that the British changed their stringent policies against Christian missionaries and officials began to show neutrality to missionaries and support them when necessary. Although the Charter of 1813 extended freedom to British missionaries to settle and work in India, the directors of EIC continued to disfavor missionary enterprise and passively supported the Hindu religious system until 1862.[89] Nevertheless, the missionaries from Europe and the United States of America have plunged into India in large numbers since 1813.

---

85. Farquhar, *Modern Religious Movements in India*, 9.

86. Nandy, *Intimate Enemy*, 5.

87. Smith, *Life of William Carey*, 285.

88. Frykenberg, "Hindutva and the Aftermath of Ayodhya," 7.

89. Farquhar, *Modern Religious Movements in India*, 9.

A complex collaboration between the government and missions began to take place as the British could not undermine the innovative capabilities of missionaries with whom they could advance government projects of education, health, and other liaison works.

Education, which was pushed aside for centuries by Islamic political convulsions, was largely made possible with the help of William Carey, Joshua Marshman, and William Ward (the Serampore Trio), Scottish missionary Alexander Duff, and many others. These men opened boarding schools, orphanages, and medical clinics to help develop modern skills in Indians, not only to advance their welfare but also to evangelize them.[90] They proposed and were strenuously involved in reforms to abolish social evils associated with socio-religious traditions such as *Sati* (widow-burning), *Devadasi* (temple prostitution), child-marriages, infanticide, torture and human sacrifices, caste-oppression, and obscenity in the streets.

The Impact of Orientalists' Literary Works on Hindu Self-realization

The goodwill of Warren Hastings to educate Europeans on the Hindu religious and cultural system and acquaint them with Sanskrit bore much fruit for the revitalization of Hinduism itself. At the order of Hastings, the code of Hindu law was compiled and translated into English in 1776.[91] Hastings commissioned Sir Charles Wilkins to study Sanskrit, which he mastered. Wilkins also became well-versed in Persian and Bengali. Wilkins created a font for *Devanagari* which helped advance literary works in Bengal. Wilkins was also involved in the translation of the Hindu epic *Mahabharata,* of which he completed the portion of *Bhagavad Gita,* published in 1785. In 1808, his work *The Grammar of the Sanskrita Language* was published, which brought him greater honor.

Sir William Jones, a judge of the British EIC's high court, was another prominent Orientalist scholar who identified the interconnectedness between Sanskrit, Greek, and Latin, and was probably the first to propose the theory of an Aryan invasion in India.[92] The Aryan invasion theory has been strongly contested by many scholars, particularly by contemporary Hindu nationalist writers, who claim that it was "a propagated myth," used against Hindus. David Frawley, an Indologist and supporter of Hindu nationalist principles, argues that, " .... Christian and Islamic missionaries have used

90. Tennent, *Building Christianity on Indian Foundations*, 47.

91. Zachariah, *Modern Religious and Secular Movements in India* , 10.

92. Wolpert, *New History of India*, 25; Bates, "Race, Caste and Tribes in Central India," 14; Nehru, *Discovery of India*, 156.

the theory to denigrate the Hindu religion as a product of barbaric invaders and promote their efforts to convert Hindus."[93]

William Jones' passionate interest in oriental culture led him to establish The Asiatic Society in 1784, which made a vital contribution to the cultural revivalism and Indian nationalism of the late nineteenth century.[94] He completed the translation of *Sakuntala* and first published it in Calcutta in 1789 as *Sacontala; or, The Fatal Ring: An Indian Drama.*[95]

The British government, the educational enterprises of missionaries, and the literary contribution of Orientalists not only awakened Indians from their long psychological slumber, but also gave them self-esteem and equipped them with the intellectual skills to counterattack "whiteman's" masquerading impulses.[96] When European Christian scholars were exploring the Hindu scriptures to understand the depth of the Hindu worldview so that they could enable their missionary enterprises to appropriate the gospel to the followers of Hinduism in an effective way, they never imagined that through their literary works they were equally enabling Hindus to defend their faith and fight back against Christian values. W. S. Hooton argued that Europeans, together with Indian religious intellectuals, praised the Vedantist philosophy to such an extent that it became one of the causes of an increasing opposition by Hindus to the Gospel.[97] Sir Monier-Williams, who extensively studied Hindu literature, stressed that the *advaita Vedanta* represented the "highest way to salvation" in Hinduism.[98] Although he later admitted that he was misled by Hinduism's philosophical attractiveness, his earlier praise of truth in Hinduism enabled Hindus to either see their religion on equal terms with Christianity or place their religion above Christianity. At times, newspapers and magazines even remarked that, "We are glad to see that the people of England are waking up to see that Christianity has far more to learn from Hinduism than we from Christianity."[99]

Recent Hindu thinkers such as Girilal Jain, Ram Swarup, and others both appreciate Orientalists and Anglicists for exposing Hinduism to the world through their literary works and equally criticize them for misunderstanding and misrepresenting India in every conceivable way.[100]

93. Frawley, *Myth of Aryan Invasion of India*, 3.

94. Copley, *Religions in Conflict*, 31.

95. Farquhar, *Modern Religious Movements in India*, 8.

96. Veer, *Religious Nationalism*, 56.

97. Hooton, *Missionary Campaign*, 38–39.

98. Hooton, *Missionary Campaign*, 42–44.

99. Hooton, *Missionary Campaign*, 46.

100. Jain, *Hindu Phenomenon*, 37–40; Swarup, *Hindu View of Christianity and*

According to Jain, the European discovery of Hindu culture and traditions is an "imperialist perversion,"[101] while Swarup contended that their scholarly works, which had missionary motivations, undermined the significance of the Hindu system.[102]

The Influence of the Modern Missionary Movement

A new phase of missions dawned in India with the arrival of William Carey in Calcutta in November 1793. According to George Smith, "for three centuries, from Columbus to Carey, foreign missions were identified with the intolerant and sacramentarian form of Christianity."[103] It was the missionary zeal and toil of Carey and his colleagues which roused first Britain and then America and the other European nations to a sense of their duty to the non-Christian peoples of the world.[104] Before coming to India, self-taught Carey had conscientiously managed to be a part-time cobbler and a village teacher alongside being a country pastor. Although he was not a descendant of the elite class of England, his determination and evangelical passion lit a fire among his fellow ministers. He had eventually become a leading spirit in the formation of the Baptist Mission Society. It would take another book to write on the influence and missionary contributions of William Carey.

Carey believed that in order to meet intellectual Hindus on their own ground, education was an essential tool. As Brian Stanley points out, "The literary undertakings of the Serampore missionaries were motivated by a confidence that the spread of general knowledge throughout India would loosen the bonds of Hindu 'superstition' and thus promote the advance of the Christian gospel. Education was therefore a proper part of the missionary's work, for Hinduism had imprisoned Indian minds as well as Indian souls."[105] On January 10, 1800, Carey, in partnership with Joshua Marshman (a schoolmaster) and William Ward (a printer), began the Serampore Mission which primarily focused on literary works and educational establishments. According to George Smith, "Carey and Marshman were the first educational missionaries, not only because they were men of culture and foresight, missionary statesmen who must adapt their means so as to make all subservient to their divine end, but because they sought at once the

---

Islam, 12–56.

101. Jain, *Hindu Phenomenon*, 38.

102. Swarup, *Hindu View of Christianity and Islam*, 26.

103. Smith, *Conversion of India*, 44.

104. Farquhar, *Modern Religious Movements in India*, 6.

105. Stanley, "Winning the World."

conversion to Christ of the born leaders of the people, and the creation of an educated indigenous ministry."[106]

Alexander Duff, a Scottish missionary who later joined Carey in the educational enterprise, proposed making English the medium of instruction in the educational system to attract the children of affluent and high caste communities so that the propagation of the Christian faith could be achieved. Since Duff held "a superior West—inferior East attitude," he believed that "English medium education was the key to the disintegration of Hinduism."[107] He opened a school where modern scientific knowledge, including Biblical knowledge, was taught in English.[108] Duff also interacted with the students of a Hindu college which was established by Raja Ram Mohan Roy. Roy, who had a keen interest in learning English, came in contact with Carey, Duff, and the other Serampore missionaries and was gradually influenced by modern thought and Christian ideals, which played a role in his awakening against Western imperialism, missionary criticisms of Hinduism, and social reformation.

While Anglicists believed that the propagation of the gospel in India was possible through the diffusion of English education to the high-caste communities, Carey and his associates were committed to the dissemination of scientific and historical knowledge in the vernacular. They were involved in translation works and contributed to the preservation of local cultures and languages. The missionary developmental and educational efforts, which provided stimuli to Indians for the re-discovery of India's past, played a role in the Indian desire for nationalism.[109] Carey thoroughly studied the languages, cultures, manners, and customs of the land to effectively articulate the gospel to locals. Unlike Robert De Nobili in the south, Carey allowed no caste distinction among converts of high and low castes. At the Eucharist service, Carey's first Brahman convert Krishna Prasad was believed to have gladly "received the cup after the Sudra Krishna Pal had drunk from it, and when he was married, his bride was Krishna Pal's daughter."[110] The caste convergence stimulated by the ideals of Christianity received serious reactions from Brahmans. Carey and his associates also saw the need to purge Hindu society of traditional practices such as the caste system and human sacrifices, throwing children

106. Smith, *Conversion of India*, 134.

107. Tennent, *Building Christianity on Indian Foundations*, 49.

108. Firth, *Introduction to Indian Church History*, 182.

109. Tennent, *Building Christianity on Indian Foundations*, 51.

110. Smith, *Life of William Carey*, 141, 145; Firth, *Introduction to Indian Church History*, 149.

into the Ganges as offerings to gods, burning widows alive on the funeral pyre of their husbands, and so on. His campaigns against these practices and his attempts to reform social structures appeared to some Hindus as if he waged war against Hinduism and its culture.

The missionaries and Orientalist scholars who were curious to learn more about Hindu religion, practices, customs, and traditions took up the study of Hinduism with the assumption that Christianity was superior to all other religious systems.[111] According to Geoffrey A. Oddie, one view of the motives of missionaries' study of non-Christian religions was that they wanted to undermine and destroy the defense of Hinduism and conquer it.[112] Some missionaries were suspicious of the Brahman accounts of stories and symbolism associated with the worship of Shiva and Parvati and thought that it would be a waste of time to listen to their mythical stories,[113] while others, as Majumdar records, regarded Indians almost as barbarians.

In their literary works, European missionaries largely portrayed Hindus as dull, naked, ignorant, poor, and inimical to progress. In order to inform and enhance mission partnerships in the West, most missionaries pictured India as uncivilized and pathetic in a manner offensive to Hindus.[114] European depictions of Hindus as heathens, their gods as demons and devils, and their social customs, traditions, and ceremonies as inherently evil, were a humiliation upon them and their religion. Hindus looked critically at Carey's methods of proselytization, which hung on the essential conviction that Hinduism was a religion of darkness and only Christianity could dispel it.[115] Antony Copley points out that the years between 1830 and 1880 marked a distinctive phase in the Protestant mission history of India when "no other foreign agency came into such close, if confrontational, contact with Indian society as did British Protestant missionaries in this period."[116] The religious convictions of missionaries, as well as their views and depictions of the Hindu socio-religious system eventually challenged Hindus to defend their insulted religion intellectually, to combat

---

111. Oddie, *Imagined Hinduism*, 33.

112. Oddie, *Imagined Hinduism*, 34.

113. Oddie, *Imagined Hinduism*, 33.

114. There are a few examples of missionary descriptions of Hinduism including: Ward, *View of the History, Literature and Religion of the Hindoos*; Dubois, *Description of the Character, Manners and Customs*; Duff, *India and India Missions* (ch. 3); and Campbell, *British India*.

115. Copley, *Religions in Conflict*, 34; Kopf, *Brahmo Sama*, 34; Stanley, *History of Baptist Missionary Society*, 47.

116. Copley, *Religions in Conflict*, 3.

the missionary onslaught on Hinduism and to strengthen it through reformation and revitalization.[117]

J. N. Farquhar, a renowned educational missionary, arrived in India
at the beginning of the twentieth century, when religious and political nationalism was on the rise. Unlike other missionaries who viewed Hinduism and its traditions negatively, Farquhar realized "the need for an irenic
approach that would remove cultural hindrances to the favourable reception of the Christian faith in India."[118] Ivan Satyavrata writes, "Farquhar's
sympathetic sensitivity toward Hinduism was matched by a strong sense of
optimism regarding the future of Christianity in India, which bordered on
triumphalism."[119] In his notable work, *The Crown of Hinduism* (1913), by
acknowledging that "the greatness of Hinduism" offers philosophical justification for Hinduism as a religion, Farquhar offered the way in which Christianity would become the one religion of India without destroying India's
national, cultural, and religious heritage.[120] He emphasized the fulfillment
approach in connecting Christianity with Hinduism.[121] It was his apologetic
attempt to not only make the gospel relevant to the Hindu mind, but also to
"remove the misconception that the Christian gospel was anti-national and
destructive of the Indian religious cultural heritage."[122]

THE MODERN REFORMATION AND HINDU
REVITALIZATION

With the commencement of the modern missionary movement and by the
effects of European missional and linguistic contacts with the socioreligious
dynamics of Indian culture, the Hindu perspective of Christianity and the
Christian perception of Hinduism have significantly changed as well as challenged each other.[123] Europeans identified the Hindu religion with the social
customs of the community and believed that religious conversion should
bring about change in the latter. In the process, the missionary methods that
have been employed in securing neophytes were seen as ways of proselytization and aroused all the powers of the Hindus in defense of their religious
and social traditions; they attempted to reorganize and strengthen Hindu

---

117. Majumdar, *History of the Freedom Movement in India*, 93, 114.

118. Satyavrata, *God Has Not Left Himself Without Witness*, 51.

119. Satyavrata, *God Has Not Left Himself Without Witness*, 54.

120. Farquhar, *Crown of Hinduism*, 451–52.

121. Farquhar, *Crown of Hinduism*, 3.

122. Satyavrata, *God Has Not Left Himself Without Witness*, 59.

123. Cornille, "Missionary Views of Hinduism," 1; Oddie, *Imagined Hinduism*, 15;
Misra, "Missionary Position," 369.

society.[124] S. Radhakrishnan noted that, "The Hindu religious revival is partly the result of Western research, partly reaction against Western dominance and partly the revolt against Christian missionary propaganda."[125]

Since the beginning of the nineteenth century, Christianity in India has received a variety of responses from learned Hindus, especially the urban middle-classes, who interacted with the modern ideas and ideals of the West. During this time, the *bhakti* movement, which saw various resemblances between Hinduism and Christianity, played a pivotal role in the revitalization of Hinduism and contributed to the proliferation of cults and sects within Hinduism.[126] Although the reaction of some Hindus such as Sri Ramakrishna was indifferent to Western thought, understanding the response of other intellectual Hindus to everything of the West, including Christianity, is crucial. Those responses can be broadly categorized as philosophical, conservative,[127] and socialist.

Raja Ram Mohan Roy, K. C. Sen, Swami Vivekananda, the Tagore family, Gopal Krishna Gokhale, M. G. Ranade, M. K. Gandhi, and several others were among the Indian philosophical responders who rejected the evils of old traditions and were inclined to learn from Western values, including those of Christianity,[128] for the sake of transforming the Hindu traditions that determined social life and for the sake of securing Indian nationalism. The response of these individuals, who held varied and contrasting views on Christianity and its missionary passions, was both critical and selectively affirming regarding the things of the West. For example, Gandhi, who held a non-exclusivist Hindu philosophy, utilized religious terminology to explain the objectives of the nationalist movement. Although at times his leadership of the INC gave a Hinduized appearance, his advocacy for the unity of socio-political and religious communities helped lay the foundation for the secular state.[129]

The second group was the conservative responders or extremists, who favored outright and hostile rejection of the values of the West, including Christianity. Some argue that the Mutiny of 1857 was a result of such reactionary attitudes. This classification covers individuals of the mid-nineteenth century such as Vishnubawa Brahmachari, Dayananda Saraswati, Arumuga

---

124. Panikkar, *Hinduism and the Modern World*, 4.

125. Radhakrishnan, *East and West*, 108.

126. Embree, *Hindu Tradition*, 275.

127. Some conservatives were Hindu fundamentalists while others were both fundamentalists and communalists.

128. Embree, *Hindu Tradition*, 276,

129. Smith, *India as a Secular State*, 92.

Navalar, Bal Gangadhar Tilak, Bipin Chandra Pal, Lala Lajpat Rai, Aurobindo Ghose,[130] Lal Chand, and others. The attitude of conservatives was that "the Hindu tradition needed no support from the findings of identities, real or fancied, with Christianity."[131] In the twentieth century, it was V. D. Savarkar, another conservative, who outlined the vision for *Hindu Rashtra*. This vision was taken up by K. B. Hedgewar and M. S. Golwalkar of RSS, and Pandit Prem Nath Dogra and Syama Prasad Mukherjee of Hindu Mahasabha and others who geared the ideology more toward the militant path of marginalizing religious others, especially Muslims and Christians in India. The Hindu nationalist organizations (known as Sangh Parivar), which burgeoned after independence, inclined more toward the ideological framework prescribed by Golwalkar and sought to isolate religious others from mainstream society for their socio-religious and political advantages.

The third category was socialist responders, who were neither against Western developments, nor against the presence, practice, and propagation of other religions in India. They struck a neutral balance on socio-religious issues for the promotion of secularism and religious harmony. Jawaharlal Nehru, Subash Chandra Bose and some other leaders of the INC were among those who subscribed to the teachings of Marx and Laski for promoting secular nationalism and who relegated religious matters entirely to the individuals' consciences.[132] Together with others, they helped to form the Indian understanding of secularism. Nehru defined the secular state as "a state which protects all religions but does not favor one at the expense of others, and does not establish any religion as the official creed."[133] Although Nehru did not personally appreciate attempts at proselytization, he believed that there must be full freedom to offer and accept different beliefs on all subjects.[134]

The Emergence of Sociopolitical and Religious Awakening

With the abolition of the EIC's monopoly in 1813, missionary activities were radically augmented by the influx of Protestant missionaries from England, America and other European nations. The reformative policy of the British had a profound impact on Indian society and Hinduism as missionaries and Christian educators were actively involved in philanthropic and

130. Aurobindo was both a philosophical and conservative responder.

131. Embree, *Hindu Tradition*, 299.

132. Smith, *India as a Secular State*, 92.

133. Smith, *India as a Secular State*, 155.

134. Smith, *India as a Secular State*, 175.

humanitarian activities as well as evangelizing.[135] Orthodox Hindus feared that through social legislation the British were attempting to destroy Hindu religion and culture as it was believed that the legislation was undertaken to aid missionaries in their quest for evangelization.[136]

The social reformation advocated through the missionary adventures of the Serampore Trio and Duff's strategy of converting high caste Hindus ignited the passion of Brahmanism to reform Hinduism in Bengal and contributed to a social renaissance with religious reformation.[137] Around 1870, a great Hindu spirit began to be manifest in the evolution of religious reform movements, which led to a rediscovery of a glorious Hindu religious past. Farquhar calls it "the great Awakening." The great Awakening was the result of the cooperation of two forces, the British government in India and Protestant missions together with the works of the Orientalists.[138] K. M. Panikkar refers to it as "the great Recovery."[139] C. F. Andrews, D. S. Sarma, and others call it as "the new or modern Renaissance."[140] Andrews believed that English literature and Western science played a vital role in the new renaissance.[141]

Beginning with Raja Ram Mohan Roy, the leading reformer of Hinduism, Dayananda Saraswati, Sri Ramakrishna, Swami Vivekananda, Annie Besant, Mahatma Gandhi, Rabindranath Tagore, Sri Aurobindo and S. Radhakrishnan, who were among the heroes of all-India fame, hoped that with religious reformation and the gaining of political freedom the achievement of national integration would be completed. Their task was fourfold. First, "to make its [Hindu philosophy] more and more adequate as more and more experience is gained." Therefore, the schools of Vedanta began to consider the scientific knowledge of the modern age to make their philosophy adequate and more appealing. For example, to free themselves from the notions of pseudo-science, mythical or legendary aspects of religious beliefs, the modern schools of religious philosophy attempted to assimilate the findings of radio astronomy and nuclear physics into the religious concepts of Samkhya and Yoga. The second task was "to make its rituals more expressive and significant and its moral teachings more effective and fruitful." A great deal of work has been accomplished to strengthen and purify

135. Mathew, *Saffron Mission*, 24.

136. Chandra, *India's Struggle for Independence*, 37.

137. Andrews, *Renaissance in India*, 10.

138. Farquhar, *Modern Religious Movements in India*, 5–13.

139. Panikkar, *Survey of Indian History*, 207.

140. Panikkar, *Survey of Indian History*, 10; Sarma, *Renascent Hinduism*, 3.

141. Andrews, *Renaissance in India*, 10.

sections of Hinduism by catering to the religious needs of communities in accordance with their language, culture, and tradition. Attempts have also been made to balance religion and morality through the performance of rites and ceremonies. The third was "to make the knowledge of it more widespread, precise and accurate." In this endeavor, various traditional means such as Hari Katha, Kalakshepam, and folklore have been employed to spread the teachings of Hinduism, particularly to promote Hindu epics and puranas. The fourth task was "to eradicate the evil customs and practices which hinder its progress." The socioreligious Hindu reformers strove hard to eradicate the primitive customs, superstitions, and beliefs long embedded in the Hindu system such as slavery, *sati* (widow-burning), animal and human sacrifices, body-piercing by hooks, enforced widowhood, child marriage, untouchability etc.[142]

Raja Ram Mohan Roy and the Brahmo Samaj

Roy was one of the earliest native leaders to respond to the changes and anxieties brought about in India by the British rulers and Western missionaries. His association with missionaries, especially the Serampore Trio and Alexander Duff, played a significant role in the formation of the Brahmo Samaj,[143] one of the most prominent and earliest social reform movements in India. The Brahmo Samaj focused on reforming the socio-religious and traditional structures and practices of Hindu society, such as idolatry, sati, child-marriages, etc. Roy was "the first to speak of an authentic Hinduism which was to be separated from the spurious, the false, and the popular mode of its existence."[144] He was optimistic about the European endeavors of education and technology and the missionaries' thrust to improve India by freeing natives from traditional bondages. However, he keenly observed the flip-side of the imperial nature of the British and questioned their economic exploitation and religious exclusivism.[145]

While protesting the idolatry and cruel practices within the Hindu system, Roy criticized missionary attacks on the Hindu gods and the arrogant attitudes of missionaries toward people of other faiths. He observed that missionaries followed three strategies in their attempts to convert Hindus to Christianity. "The first way is that of publishing and distributing among the natives various books, large and small, reviling both religions, and abusing and ridiculing the gods and saints of the former: the second way is that of

142. Sarma, *Renascent Hinduism*, 5.

143. "Brahmo Sabha" or "Brahma Sabha" means "Society of Brahma."

144. Basu, *Religious Revivalism*, 14.

145. Parekh, *Brahma Samaj*, viii.

standing in front of the doors of the natives or in the public roads to preach the excellency of their own religion and the debasedness of that of others, the third way is that if any natives of low origin become Christians from the desire of gain or from any other motives, these gentlemen employ and maintain as a necessary encouragement to others to follow their example."[146]

In order to fight the evil practices in Hindu society and to revitalize Hindu spiritual ideals, he initiated Atmiya Sabha in 1815, which attracted the attention of many Baptist missionaries. He entered into debates with missionaries on the subjects of God, incarnation, and Unitarian and Trinitarian concepts. He became instrumental in establishing the Hindu College in Calcutta in 1817 to give liberal education to the children of the members of the Hindu community. He published magazines and other literary works to reform Hindu society, to strengthen Hinduism, and to dialogue with missionaries on religious doctrines.[147]

The Brahmo Samaj, which Ram Mohan Roy and his friends founded in Bengal on August 20, 1828, was a quasi-Protestant, theistic movement within Hinduism and a product of European rather than of Hindu thought.[148] During the first half of the eighteenth century, Bengal was perhaps the most economically flourishing province in the whole of India.[149] However, at the time of the birth of this movement, "The whole country, and especially the province of Bengal, was steeped in the most debasing forms of idolatry. The moral and spiritual aspects of religion and its elevating influence upon character had long been lost sight of, and in their place the grossest superstitions had taken hold of the national mind" and, "the corruption and degeneracy of the priesthood was great."[150] With the help of Dwarkanath Tagore, who believed that "the happiness of India is best secured by her connection with England,"[151] Roy held worship services for Hindus in patterns similar to Christianity.[152] Through this movement, Roy represented the new spirit of rational inquiry into the basis of religion and society. He attempted to give a new dimension to the worldviews of

146. Roy, "Brahmunical Magazine," 10.

147. Roy published the Vedanta (1815), Ishopanishad (1816), Kathopanishad (1817), Moonduk Upanishad (1819), The Precepts of Jesus—Guide to Peace and Happiness (1820), Sambad Kaumudi—a Bengali newspaper (1821), Mirat-ul-Akbar—Persian journal (1822), Bengali Grammar (1826), Brahmapasona (1828), Brahmasangeet (1829) and The Universal Religion (1829).

148. Mazoomdar, *Faith and Progress of the Brahmo Somaj*, 11.

149. Majumdar, *History of the Freedom Movement in India*, 27.

150. Sastri, *History of the Brahmo Samaj*, 2–4.

151. Majumdar, *History of the Freedom Movement in India*, 49.

152. Zachariah, *Modern Religious and Secular Movements in India*, 19.

Brahmanism, Hindu theology, and moral and religious practices, and he endeavored to purify Hinduism with precepts and ceremonies borrowed from Buddhism, Islam, and mostly from Christianity.

With the coming of Debendranath Tagore in 1842, the Brahmo Samaj entered a new phase. In this phase, Debendranath introduced new forms of worship called Brahmopasana or Brahmo-dharma, in which the religious aspects of the Samaj were enriched, but no Christian thought was entertained as had been done by its founder. However, when Keshub Chandra Sen, who was influenced by Christian ideals like Roy and who attempted to incorporate Christian theology within the framework of Hindu thought, joined the Brahmo Samaj for a few years, starting in 1857, further attempts were made to disregard everything that was heathen and idolatrous. He insisted that the people of higher castes should give up their sacred thread as a sign of renouncing caste.[153] Keshub also initiated informal theological training for the Samajis and started Prarthana Samaj. The Brahmo Samaj, which became more oriented toward Christianity under the leadership of Keshub, also influenced the thought and theology of several Indian Christian thinkers like Upadyay,[154] as well as serving as a channel for theological discussions and religious interactions between Hindu intellectuals and missionaries. Although the Brahmo Samaj gave new impetus to the rejuvenation of socio-religious practices in the Hindu system and attempted to prevent Hindus from slipping into other faiths, it became moribund because of its eclectic philosophy and by the emergence of similar movements after the death of its founder.[155]

Vishnubawa Brahmachari and Missionaries

In the mid-nineteenth century, Hindu society in Bombay was invigorated by a series of religious discourses delivered by a "new champion of Hinduism," Vishnu Bhikaji Gokhale (popularly known as Vishnubawa Brahmachari), a thirty-one year old Brahman who believed that "the best strategy for the defense of his faith was to go on the attack against Hinduism's missionary antagonists."[156] This was at the time when Christian missionaries were converting people in various ways and abusing Indian religious and social systems through preaching and print media. Brahmachari felt called to meet

---

153. Zachariah, *Modern Religious and Secular Movements in India*, 19–22.

154. Tennent, *Building Christianity on Indian Foundations*, 374; Aleaz, "Theological Writings of Brahmabandhav Upadhyaya Re-Examined," 55.

155. Mazoomdar, *Will the Brahmo Somaj Last?*, 6.

156. Conlon, "Polemic Process," 5.

the danger and rescue Vedic religion from the onslaughts of Christianity.[157] He had a keen mind, sharp wit, and clear vision to "protect, preserve and promote the ancestral Hindu *dharma*."[158] According to S. V. Puntambekar, with his 15 year frontal attacks on Christian religion, Brahmachari not only defeated Christian missionaries by way of argument, but also "stopped the overpowering wave of conversion in Maharashtra."[159]

Arumuga Navalar's Defense against Missionaries

Arumuga Navalar was one of the early revivalists of Hindu Tamil traditions in Sri Lanka and India. He studied in a missionary school. After his studies, he was employed in the same school to teach Tamil and English. He was also invited to assist in the translation of the Bible and Christian prayers into Tamil. During this time, he took a keen interest in improving his knowledge of his mother tongue and ancestral religion, and he acquainted himself with the Bible and Christian doctrine. He mastered Shaiva Siddhanta including *Agamas* and left his job under the missionaries to take up the task of preaching Shaiva Siddhanata. During his time, anti-Christian polemic was being churned out by the Hindu Tamils as a response to the intensified Christian missionary attacks on Hinduism. Navalar began writing letters to *The Morning Star*, a Christian magazine published by missionaries, defending the Shaiva position against missionary attacks.[160] He found that "a large number of his countrymen were embracing Christianity not on conviction, but owing to certain undesirable influences brought to bear on them. Fully equipped as he was for his self-imposed task, he set his heart on preventing people from converting to Christianity based on insufficient knowledge."[161] He founded "Shaivaprakasa Vidyasala," School of Shaiva Splendor, through which he trained Hindu people to defend and promote Hinduism. He also published educational materials and tracts refuting Christian views against Hinduism.

157. Puntambekar, "Vishnu Bawa Brahmachari," 156, 157; Malhotra, *Reform, Reaction and Nationalism*, 7.

158. Conlon, "Polemic Process," 5.

159. Puntambekar, "Vishnu Bawa Brahmachari," 157.

160. Hudson, "Arumuga Navalar," 31.

161. Pillay, "Life History of Arumuga Navalar."

DAYANANDA SARASWATI AND THE ARYA SAMAJ

Lala Lajpat Rai, a member and biographer of *Arya Samaj*, described Swami Dayananda Saraswati,[162] the founder of Arya Samaj, as "the World-Apostle of Hinduism," who "opened the sealed gate of Hinduism to the rest of mankind."[163] Saraswati's followers called him, "Maharshi," "the regenerator of Aryavrata," "the Luther of India," the savior of Hinduism and so on.[164] Saraswati came into contact with Ramakrishna and Keshub in December 1872 and was received by the Brahmo Samaj. But he was reluctant to join hands with Hindu philosophers who were imbued with Western ideas.[165] Even though he was obliged to reckon with European science and civilization, he actively scorned European thought, philosophy, and especially its religious advocacy.[166] With a dream of bringing a national awakening in multifarious fields, he founded Arya Samaj, a dynamic socio-religious-political movement, in Bombay in 1875, which aimed to purge the evil traditions within the Hindu system, secure the nation, and protect Vedic culture from the grab of religious others. He campaigned against corrupt social practices such as the caste system, *Sati*, polygamy, child marriage, dowry and idol worship; he supported widow-remarriages and equal opportunity between men and women. He also fought against the hegemonic system of Orthodox Brahmanism, which had regulated ceremonial practices and the code of law for non-Brahmans for centuries.[167]

Arya Samaj had both religious and nationalist agendas. Its influence was measured by the escalation of its membership. In 1891 its membership was 40,000 which rose to 101,000 in 1901 and grew to 458,000 in 1921. Many Hindu personalities, politicians, and Maharajas were part of this membership.[168] To Saraswati, Hinduism was superior over other faiths and all the non-Vedic religions were false. He believed in the superiority of Vedas, accepted Shastras, the Upanishads, the Brahman Granthas, the Vedangas, and the Smritis only if they were in consonance with Vedas and greatly differed with orthodox Hinduism. He did not believe in the incarnation of God or

---

162. His real name was Mulshankar or Mula Shankara. Saraswati was the surname of his guru which he adopted for himself.

163. Rai, *Arya Samaj*, 79.

164. *The Guardian*, "The Nazis or Hinduism"; Mathew, *Saffron Mission*, 69.

165. Rolland, *Dayananda and Arya Samaj*, 8.

166. Robson, *Hinduism and Its Relations to Christianity*, vi.

167. For brief information on Saraswati's initiatives and Arya Samaj's socioreligious achievements, see *Aryan Voice*, "What is Arya Samaj?" 6–9.

168. Rolland, *Dayananada and Arya Samaj*, 10.

astrology.[169] He called the followers of non-Hindu religions, "hypocrites, rascals, rogues, scoundrels, imposters, quacks, defrauders, and trickers."[170] In the revised version of his magnum opus, *Satyartha Prakash* (which literally means "Exposition of the Truth"), he ruthlessly criticized and expressed his hostile spirit toward every religion known to him other than Hinduism.[171] He condemned Christianity as a "barbarous religion and a false religion believed only by fools and by people in a state of Barbarism."[172] M. K. Gandhi expressed his disappointment in *Satyartha Prakash* and commented that Dayananda "has unconsciously misrepresented Jainism, Islam, Christianity and Hinduism itself."[173] In Gandhi's view, Dayananda Saraswati also "made his Hinduism narrow."[174]

Political independence was one of the objectives of Dayananda Saraswati. It was he who coined the concepts of *Swaraj* and *Swadeshi* long before Gandhi arrived at the thought; he wanted to rebuild the nation by uniting Hindus and patronizing *swadeshi* products. Arya Samaj also established orphanages and opened homes for widows and destitute women in service of the country.[175] In Dayananada's understanding, the weakness of the Hindu race lies in its division and disunity, which can be regenerated by the development of an indigenous education system in which Vedic philosophy and culture are taught.[176] Even though RSS, BJS, VHP, and other Sangh Parivar affiliates are not members of Arya Samaj, they owe much to Arya Samaj for its stimulus in nation building by unifying the Hindu race in defense of Hinduism and in securing back converts through reconversion programs.

SWAMI VIVEKANANDA AND RAMAKRISHNA MISSION

Vivekananda, who was discipled by Ramakrishna,[177] played a key role in introducing the Hindu philosophies of Vedanta and yoga to the Western

---

169. See Meera, "Arya Samaj and Caste System," 69.

170. Panicker, *Gandhi on Pluralism and Communalism*, 39.

171. Sharma, *Hinduism as a Missionary Religion*, 37.

172. Panicker, *Gandhi on Pluralism and Communalism*, 39.

173. Gandhi, *Hindu Dharma*, 15.

174. Gandhi, *Hindu Dharma*, 15.

175. Rai, *Arya Samaj*, 211–18; *Aryan Voice*, May 2010, 7.

176. Rai, *Arya Samaj*, xiv.

177. Ramakrishna or Gadadhar Chattopadhyay (1836–1886) was a poor Brahman pujari of Kali Temple at Dakshineswari in Bengal, who represented a religious spirit of India and later came to be known as Ramakrishna Paramahansa. He was also known as the nineteenth century doyen of Hindu revivalism. He had many disciples who learned Tantra, Vedanta, yoga, and Vaishnavism under him.

world. Vivekananda's original name was Narendra Nath Datta. He was born in Calcutta, Bengal, in British India. Like previous reformers, he condemned superstitions, rigid rituals, and evil practices within the Hindu system and favored the oneness of all religions.

With his impressive presentation in the Parliament of Religions in Chicago in 1893, Vivekananda became the leading advocate for neo-Hindu nationalism that aroused a sense of national unity through Hinduism.[178] He became known to the West as a symbol of the religious awakening of India.[179] Vivekananda, who looked upon and was proud of Hinduism as a non-missionary religion and who often questioned the value of the missionary enterprise on anyone's part, actively promoted Vedanta and yoga in the West, which duly reflected neo-Hinduism's missionary character.[180] After his persuasive speech, in which he articulated the greatness of Hindu spirituality and subtly critiqued Christian missionary endeavors in India, the New York Herald wrote, "After hearing him, we feel how foolish it is to send missionaries to his learned nation."[181]

Vivekananda admired Christ but criticized missionary practices. In Gerald Studdert-Kennedy's words, Vivekananda "was a theological inclusivist with a vengeance, boldly assimilating Jesus as one, but only one, manifestation of the principle of Christhood within endless cycle of worlds such as ours. All are held within the manifestation of the power of *maya*, from which man is to be liberated only through the knowledge of his own identity with God."[182] Vivekananda founded Ramakrishna Mission in 1897, which grew to serve humanity in the fields of education, medical care, rural development, and social welfare.[183] There are about twenty-three mission centers[184] outside India, which conduct religious classes, discourses, prayers, worship, and philanthropic services and which promote the cultural work and the teachings of Vivekananda.[185]

178. Basu, *Religious Revivalism as Nationalist Discourse*, 8.

179. Panicker, *Gandhi on Pluralism and Communalism*, 7, 23.

180. Sharma, *Hinduism as a Missionary Religion*, 48.

181. Zachariah, *Modern Religious and Secular Movements in India*, 78.

182. Studdert-Kennedy, *British Christians, Indian Nationalists and the Raj*, 75.

183. For more details on the services of Ramakrishna Mission, see The Report of 100th Annual General Meeting of Rama Krishna Mission, December 20, 2009.

184. The major centers of Ramakrishna Mission are in Bangladesh, Fiji, France, Malaysia, Mauritius, Singapore, South Africa, Sri Lanka, and Switzerland.

185. See the Report of 100th Annual General Meeting of Rama Krishna Mission, December 20, 2009, 33.

ANNIE BESANT AND THE THEOSOPHICAL SOCIETY

Annie Besant was an English woman who made India her home and considered it her real motherland. She went so far as to believe that in her previous life she was a Hindu. She adopted a Hindu way of life and became a devotee of Sri Krishna. Annie Besant, together with Russian spiritualist H. P. Blavatsky and an American Col. H. S. Olcott, founded the Theosophical Society in 1875 in the USA, which played an important role in the promotion of Hinduism and Indian culture. She introduced the society to India in 1879 and strove to strengthen the ancient religions such as Hinduism and Buddhism. She established Hindu educational centers and worked for emancipating women from their traditional bondages. Although she believed in the universal brotherhood of men, she developed a national spirit in Indians and worked for the progress of the Hindu religion through her lectures and social action.[186]

The Rise of Nationalist Consciousness and Mass Movements

The concept of nationhood has found a dominant place in modern history. According to Benedict Anderson's theory of nationalism, nation-ness or nationalist consciousness arises from the creation of "cultural artefacts of a particular kind," "the spontaneous distillation of complex 'crossing' of discrete historical forces."[187] Anthony D. Smith clarifies the notion of 'nationhood' as "a consciousness of belonging to the nation, together with sentiments and aspirations for its security and prosperity," along with "an ideology, including cultural doctrines."[188]

The Indian Mutiny of 1857 began as a rebellion of Indian sepoys from the East India Company's army in the cantonment of Meerut against Britain's insensitivity toward the economic conditions and religious sentiments of Indians. It soon grew into a civil rebellion and spread to present-day Uttar Pradesh, Madhya Pradesh, Bihar, and Delhi. The Indian civil rebellion and mutiny were believed to have been chiefly instigated by religious Brahmins whose religion the British had threatened to undermine.[189] Prior to the 1857 Mutiny, there were several instances of regional resistance movements against EIC's hegemony in southern India beginning in the last quarter of eighteenth century. The earliest is said to have been by Puli Thavan in 1757

186. Zachariah, *Modern Religious and Secular Movements in India*, 78.

187. Anderson, *Imagined Communities*, 4.

188. Smith, *National Identity*, 72.

189. Oddie, *Imagined Hinduism*, 342.

in the Madras presidency; the other mobilized by Pazhassi Raja in Malabar, Kerala, was known as the Cotiote War (1774–1805). The Vellore sepoy mutiny took place in 1806. There was also a rebellion against British forces in Pipili, Orissa, initiated by Jayee Rajguru, the chief of Army of Kalinga, in 1804 and 1817, known as the Paika Rebellion.

While the Indian rebellion of 1857 against the East India Company prepared the British to be more circumspect regarding the aspirations of Indians for independence, the British Raj's policies and sociopolitical reforms laid the foundation for the emergence of nationalist movements such as the East India Association in 1867, the Indian National Association in 1876, and the Indian nationalism of the last quarter of the nineteenth century. The Hindu reform movements, which were symbolic of socioreligious and cultural revival and change, both reflected and contributed to the rise of nationalist spirit.

INDIAN NATIONAL CONGRESS

Charismatic Hindu thinkers and religious reformers from West Bengal provided the impetus for the independence movement which surfaced regionally and nationally in the forms of political criticisms, campaigns and agitations. From 1877 on, there were attempts to form an all-India political organization to strengthen the nationalist spirit among Indians.[190] In this disposition, the Indian political workers and British members of the Theosophical Society founded the Indian National Congress (INC) in 1885 with an aim to promote the presence of educated Indians in the government, to represent the country's political and civil issues, and to transact justice and freedom for India in economic, sociopolitical, and religious spheres. It was the first organized expression of nationalism by Indians on an all-India scale. The first period (1885–1905) of the Indian national movement held a liberal approach, which espoused secular aspects within the plural traditions of India, as advocated by Justice Mahadev Govind Ranade, Dadabhai Naoroji, and Gopal Krishna Gokhale. This phase of INC, which was organized on a democratic basis and was opposed to communalism, was moderate in its approach to the political liberty of India, so that radical leaders like Bal Gangadhar Tilak, Lala Lajpat Rai, and others thought the freedom of India would not be possible with secular ideals or peaceful negotiations.[191]

190. Chandra, *India's Struggle for Independence*, 73.
191. Chandra, *India's Struggle for Independence*, 62.

SWADESHI MOVEMENT

Some British officials never believed that India would become a nation based on its religious, social, and cultural diversity and its varied anthropological identities. Therefore, radical nationalists within INC felt that it would take a radical approach to overthrow British hegemony in India, and for that to happen, Hindu unity was essential. The second phase of the independence movement (1905–1919) witnessed the rise of charismatic Hindu national leaders like Bal Gangadhar Tilak, Gopal Ganesh Agarkar, Lala Lajpat Rai Vishnubawa Brahmachari, Bipin Chandra Pal, Sri Aurobindo Ghose, and Chidambaram Pillai, who changed the political discourse of the movement, flavoring their efforts with Hindu dimensions to gain the majority nationalist voice through Hindu unity.[192] In advocating for the *Swadeshi* movement, they boycotted the use of all imported goods and promoted the use of Indian-made products to render support for the idea of self-reliance and self-sufficiency. As D. D. Pattanaik points out, the early *Swadeshi* movement constituted "a great stride in the annals of modern history so much so that it was the cumulative effect of an indigenous Indian nationalist thought-structure or what may be called, the genuine Indian variant of nationalism."[193] Jawaharlal Nehru remarked that the radicals "looked too much to the past and thought in terms of reviving it"[194] and ignored the reality of new outlooks, new techniques, and modern thought altogether. They could not lead a successful movement until Gandhi arrived on the scene.

The third phase of the Swadeshi movement (1919–1947) was headed by M. K. Gandhi, who dreamt of a nation of *sarva dharma samabhava* (equality of all religions) and secularism. He believed that political freedom was possible only through *Satyagraha* and non-violent civil disobedience (passive resistance) and not on the basis of the religious unity of a particular group. He admired the New Testament, especially the Sermon on the Mount, and adapted the Christian principles of non-violence in his political agitation against the British. In the 1920s and 1930s he had close interactions with Christian leaders of world fame: C. F. Andrews, Waskom Pickett, E. Stanley Jones, and others. Although he admired Christ, he detested Christian zeal for conversions and strongly criticized the Europeanizing of Indian converts to Christianity.

192. Majumdar, *History of the Freedom Movement,* 299.
193. Pattanaik, "Swadeshi Movement," 9.
194. Nehru, *Discovery of India,* 133.

Manifestation of Cultural Nationalism

Bal Gangadhar Tilak (aka Keshav Gangadhar Tilak or Lokmanya Tilak), who believed in *Swaraj* (self-rule) as the destiny of the nation, deeply opposed the British system of education that ignored and defamed India's culture, history, and values. His watchword, "Swaraj is my birthright, and I shall have it!", echoed in the lives of the people of India from 1896 on.[195] He was "the pacesetter of religious nationalism"[196] in India. He used religious symbols to arouse the spirit of Hindu nationalism to unite Hindus to fight against British domination.[197] Bipin Chandra Pal's view of *Swaraj* was "supremacy and dominion of the self over the not-self" and to him, the term *Swaraj* belongs to an ancient category of Hindu spiritual order.[198] The idea of *Swaraj* was later espoused by Mahatma Gandhi, who became a strong voice for the *Swadeshi* movement with secular ideals. The immediate impact of the *Swadeshi* movement, which was marked by a cultural compass, not only led to the rejection of anything foreign (burning of imported goods, for instance), but was also manifested in the construction of an imagined nationhood that was reliant on the Indian sociocultural and religious ethos.[199] Rabindranath Tagore (1861–1941), the winner of the Nobel Prize in 1913, who related himself to the nationalist movement, also emphasized the universality of the Hindu tradition over its ethnicity. [200]

The Spirit of Religious Nationalism

Religion shares many of the physiognomies of nationalism in India.[201] As Peter van der Veer indicates, "from its very beginning in the nineteenth century nationalism in India has fed upon religious identifications," and "nation building is directly dependent on religious antagonism."[202] According to Ainslie T. Embree, "Religion understood in terms of both its role in the life of the individual and its function in society has many points of correspondence with nationalism . . . .Religion and nationalism have very often combined to produce social and political conflict because in certain historical situations they reinforce each other in terms of providing

195. Athalye, *Life of Lokamanya Tilak*, 304; Pattanaik, "Swadeshi Movement," 10.

196. Cherian, *Hindutva Agenda*, 314.

197. Cherian, *Hindutva Agenda*, 314.

198. Pal, *Brahmo Samaj*, 2.

199. Kinnvall, "Globalization and Religious Nationalism," 758.

200. Sharma, *Hinduism as a Missionary Religion*, 48.

201. Sharma, *Hinduism as a Missionary Religion*, 48.

202. Veer, *Religious Nationalism*, 2.

leadership, formulating ideologies that make change possible and desirable, and developing utopian visions of a good society."[203]

R. C. Majumdar notes that prior to the rise of the so-called Hindu reform movements, there was a multi-religious uprising called "The Sanyasi Rebellion," which rose against the British at the very beginning of their rule in Bengal.[204] The rebellion, which was initiated by two different religious groups, Hindu Sanyasis and Muslim Fakirs, in 1763, turned into a great upsurge along the country belt from Rangpur to Dacca by the end of 1772.[205] To the Muslims, the appeal was made in the name of their religion. Hindus mobilized their members in the name of Hindu *dharma* by pointing to how the British government defiled Hinduism by introducing the abolition movement. John William Kaye gives an example of how one of the native rulers appealed to local Rajas against the British in the name of religion. "Their design for destroying your religion, O Rajas, is manifest . . . Be it known to all of you, that if these English are permitted to remain in India, they will butcher you all and put an end to your religion."[206] Surendra Nath Sen observes that the 1857 Mutiny was initially a fight for religion rather than a fight for political freedom, for he writes, "What began as a fight for religion ended up as a war of independence . . . "[207]

Muslim leaders Sir Syed Ahmad Khan and Sultan Muhammad Shah dreamt of a separate state for Muslims within India. In about 1820, Syed Ahmad of Rae Bareilly of Uttar Pradesh began to preach doctrines of religious reforms in Islam similar to the Wahabi movement in Arabia.[208] The Anjuman-i-Himayat-i-Islam, founded in Lahore in 1884, also played a vital role in creating a political platform for Indian Muslims. The Khilafat movement (1919–1924), which sought British protection of the Ottoman Empire, on the other hand, appeared to be threatening to some Hindus. Other nineteenth century non-Hindu reform movements which were backed by religious frenzy and led to anti-British outbreaks include Sikh's Kula movement and the Birsa movement of the tribes of Kols and Santals.[209]

The notion of *Swaraj*, which was political rhetoric in its initial sense, gradually grew as a bifurcated-thought within the ideology of Indian

203. Embree, *Utopias in Conflict*, 6, 7.

204. Majumdar, *History of the Freedom Movement*, 116.

205. Majumdar, *History of the Freedom Movement*, 117.

206. Majumdar, *History of the Freedom Movement*, 221; For a comprehensive history of the Mutiny of 1857, refer to Kaye, *History of Indian Mutiny*.

207. Sen, *Eighteen Fifty-Seven*, 411.

208. Majumdar, *History of the Freedom Movement*, 119, 247.

209. Majumdar, *History of the Freedom Movement*, 253–55.

nationalism as it was deciphered more along the lines of Hindu culture, tradition, and religion by the charismatic Hindu thinkers. Saraswati dreamt of a nationalism, which would be built on the primal rock of self-respect, "to rear it thereon in the true spirit of swajati and swadharma."[210] D. D. Pattanaik points out that, although Arya Samaj made headway into religious nationalism, "the Hindu identity of Indian nationalism was carried aloft by a number of religio-reformatory organizations like *Hindu Mela* of Nabagopal Mitra and Rajnarain Bose (1867–1880), *Prarthana Sabha* of Atmaram Pandurang in 1867, one *Patit Pawan Samaj* in 1880, *Arya Mahila Samaj* of Pandita Ramabai, one *Gayan Samaj* at Poone in 1874, Society for Protection of Hindu Religion by the Chapekar brothers in the 1890s, *Mitra Mela* (later *Abhinav Bharat*) of the Savarkar brothers at Nasik in 1899, and the like."[211] Bipin Chandra Pal imagined that the movement of *Swaraj* was "a movement of protest against the bondage of medieval religion and social and sacerdotal laws and institutions."[212] Similarly, Aurabindo saw "Swaraj as the fulfillment of the ancient life of India under modern conditions, the return of the *satyayuga* of national greatness, the resumption by her great role of teacher and guide, self-liberation of the people for the final fulfillment of the Vedantic ideals in politics."[213]

Religion grew as a powerful platform in the politics of nationalism in the twentieth century "as religious revelations [were] turned into national shrines, religious miracles [became] national feasts, and holy scriptures [were] reinterpreted as national epics. Hence, by turning history into a chosen trauma or a chosen glory, it becomes a 'naturalized' past of an identity group's definition of self and other."[214] Thus, as Van Der Veer puts it, "the radical version of Indian nationalism takes one religion as the basis of national identity, thereby relegating adherents of other religions to a secondary, inferior status."[215]

THE HINDU VIEW OF CHRISTIANITY AND ANTI-MISSIONARY ATTITUDES

Christianity is viewed by some as the vanguard of Western imperialism because the history of missionary ventures generally appears as though either

210. Rai, *Arya Samaj*, 259.

211. Pattanaik, "Swadeshi Movement," 9.

212. Pal, *Brahmo Samaj*, 3–4.

213. Aurobindo Ghosh, *Bande Mataram*, May 1, 1908 quoted in Basu, *Religious Revivalism*, 34.

214. Kinnvall, "Globalization and Religious Nationalism," 756.

215. Veer, *Religious Nationalism*, 23.

European political and economic power was succored in Christianizing heathens in their dire conditions or Christianization helped sustain the political foothold of European nations. Over the past four centuries, Christian missionaries have bred contempt in the minds of Hindus through their commercial, political, and religious partnerships, so much so that Christianity is now patently discredited as an alien and anti-Hindu religion. It is also referred to as "the white man's religion" or pejoratively called Christian colonialism.[216] According to R. G. Tiedemann, the motives behind conversions in China are viewed in three broad categories: "(1) material incentives; (2) socio-political incentives; (3) spiritual incentives."[217] These are true in the context of India as well.

There were at least four indelible marks left by foreign missionaries on Hindus, which led them to see Christianity as an enemy of the land. First was the Portuguese intolerance of religious others, particularly their aggressive political and religious actions against Hindus and their religious images, temples, and lands in Goa and other places. Second was the forceful mass conversion of people. Historian T. R. De Souza mentions that Hindus viewed the "mass baptisms" practiced by Jesuits and Franciscans in Goa as a grave abuse of Hindus. On every January 25, the day of the feast of the conversion of St. Paul, the Jesuits staged mass conversions to secure as many as possible as neophytes. "A few days before the ceremony the Jesuits would go through the streets of the Hindu quarters in pairs, accompanied by their Negro slaves, whom they would urge to seize the Hindus. When the blacks caught up with a fugitive, they would smear his lips with a piece of beef, making him an 'untouchable' among his people. Conversion to Christianity was then his only option."[218] R. C. Majumdar argued that "the conversion of Hindus to Christianity—by force or fraud as the Hindus thought—embittered the relations, sometimes almost to breaking point."[219] By imagining how missionaries in their conversion-seeking zeal had damaged the bridge between Hindus and Christians, Rutherfurd asserted that, "it would be infinitely better if never any Christian had been among 'em, for then their mind would be less prepossessed against Christianity."[220]

---

216. In the last fifty years, the term "colonialism" has been used as rhetoric for denigrating, shaming, or shunning. It has been categorically used to express an oppressive nature over the weak and demonizing or epitomizing evil. See Frykenberg, *Christians and Missionaries in India*, 7.

217. Tiedemann, "Indigenous Agency," 232.

218. De Sousa, "Portuguese in Asia," 17.

219. Majumdar, *History of the Freedom*, 93.

220. Rutherfurd, *Missionary Pioneers in India*, 22.

The third aspect was the campaign of Protestant missionaries' and their participation in the reformation of Hindu social structures and traditional religious practices. For example, William Carey constantly campaigned against socio-religious practices such as caste, *sati,* human sacrifices, idolatry, and so on.[221] The fourth aspect of missionary nature was the preposterous portrayal and mockery of the Indo-religious and social system in the missionaries' literary works, religious propaganda, and in their schools. For example, when Father Odoric of Pordenone lived in South India from A.D. 1316 to 1318, he gave a description of how Hindu idols looked, attributing to them the features of the devil. Another Italian traveler Ludovico di Varthema from Bologna, who traveled to India between A.D. 1503 and 1508, described in his work regarding Raja of Calicut and his god that he "paid respect to a devil known as Deumo."[222] The Protestant missionaries in the eighteenth and nineteenth centuries also made similar depictions in their writings. According to Dwarka Prasad Mishra, some Christian educators were involved in the mockery of Hindu deities and Hindu traditions in the schools. For example, on January 19, 1895, a British educator by the name of Evans "spoke to the students of Hislop College in Nagpur and indulged in some ridicule of the Hindu gods, Rama and Krishna." Mishra contends that, "They [the British] were shrewd enough to realize that the most fertile ground for their work of proselytization was the young adolescent mind. Therefore, they set up schools and colleges in the large cities aided by the encouragement of the Government. It is probable that the policy of the British was to create in the country a class of educated people moulded by Christian missionary teachers, divorced from their own native fountains of religion and culture, looking to the British for guidance and preferment."[223] In such contexts, it appeared to some Hindus as if missionaries were against Hinduism and the Hindu sociocultural system.

As Anthony Copley pointed out, there was a popular Hindu perception that conversion to Christianity was also conversion to Western culture.[224] After studying mass movements, J. Waskom Pickett found that there is a tendency among converts to abandon their social "patterns and customs for those of their Western conferrers in religion."[225] He added,

---

221. It was not only missionaries who were involved in campaigns against social evils in the Hindu system, but also leaders like Raja Ram Mohan Roy and a host of Hindus who led the fight for the abolition of sati and other immoral practices.

222. To understand more on how derogatively Europeans portrayed Hindu gods in their works, see Mitter, *Much Maligned Monsters,* 9–14.

223. Mishra, *History of Freedom Movement,* 155.

224. Copley, *Religions in Conflict,* 180.

225. Pickett, *Christian Mass Movements in India,* 332.

"This tendency has been a menace to the welfare of the church and of the nation because of influences it has exerted upon many converts and upon the attitudes of non-Christians toward Christianity."[226] Charles Kraft finds it unfortunate that Western missionaries gave too little or no attention at all to cultural dynamics in their cross-cultural missionary endeavors. If "Western Christianity is (ideally) God in Christ made relevant to members of western culture, which is characterized by familiar forms of worship, music, organization, philosophy (theology), moral standards,"[227] it was certainly Western theological blindness and political cravings to win converts that led to their stomping indigenous cultures.

In the process of reaching Hindus with the gospel, European and American missionaries in the eighteenth and nineteenth centuries used print media, education, religious dialogue, and other intellectual methods to convince Indians about the Christian faith, not knowing that these very methods would be used by Hindus against them.[228] Hindus established new educational institutions and undertook a whole variety of social reform initiatives. Religious presses were established; tract societies set up; newspapers and magazines published.[229] Hindu activists like R. Sivasankara Pandia from Madras began publishing religious propaganda magazines and anti-Christian pamphlets condemning the missionary tactics of securing conversions.[230] As Rutherfurd remarked, Hindus have "abundance of subterfuges whereby they endeavor to vindicate themselves and to frustrate the design of a missionary. If Christians find one error in the doctrine of the heathens, these will find ten in the life of the Christians."[231]

By the closing years of the nineteenth century, Christian missionary work in India found its place in the midst of various criticisms. According to Edwin Munsell Bliss, "reference has been made to three classes of people in mission fields: those easily attracted to Christianity; those bitterly opposed to it, and those—the great majority—indifferent, yet easily excited to hostility when they see their cherished customs endangered . . . As, however, the number of Christians has become larger and seemed likely to prove a serious disturbing element, the indifferentism of the great mass has not infrequently become active opposition."[232]

---

226. Pickett, *Christian Mass Movements in India*, 332.

227. Kraft, *Culture, Communication and Christianity*, 398–99.

228. Shaw, "Initiative that Backfired."

229. Shaw, "Initiative that Backfired."

230. Shaw, "Initiative that Backfired."

231. Rutherfurd, *Missionary Pioneers in India*, 21, 22.

232. Bliss, *Missionary Enterprise*, 181.

Anti-Christian Hindus often see Christianity as an enemy of the land because of its Western ties. Lalsangkima Pachuau observes that, "Because the modern Christian missionary movement—through which the majority of India's Christians embraced Christianity—was concerned primarily with conversion, and because the movement came to pass in India under the protective umbrella of colonialism, the majority of Indians relate religious conversion *vis-à-vis* Christianity closely to the colonial realities of the past."[233]

With the commencement of mass conversions[234] of lower caste groups and *Dalits* between the 1870s and the 1930s, which became the greatest opportunity for missionaries in various parts of India, the Christian population quadrupled and appeared to be threatening the Hindu majority. Although the mass conversions raised serious questions in the minds of some critical Hindus, theologians, and missionary-thinkers regarding the credibility of the motives of converts and their spiritual vitality in the context of transformation,[235] many European missionaries confidently expressed glee in their literary works over their successful missions and the decline of Hinduism.[236] Hindu activists, who imagined this dramatic rise of the Christian population could not have been possible without Western economic and political power and religious zeal, argued that in making conversions possible, missionaries took advantage of (or rather exploited) the socioeconomic conditions of the poor and lower sections of society. This process caused anxiety among the upper caste people, who worried about the blurring of caste distinctions that went with conversion to Christianity.[237]

Critiquing the mass conversion of Shudras and Dalits, the *Singh Sahai* wrote in 1893, " . . . the Christian Missionaries are doing a great deal of harm to the country by converting sweepers and *Charmars,* as after their conversion these people cease to work as sweepers. If the missionaries think that the progress of their religion depends on the conversion of sweepers, let them continue to convert them, but they should not try to make them

---

233. Pachuau, "Ecumenical Church and Religious Conversion." See also Raj, *Confusion Called Conversion,* 2–10; Aghamkar, *Insights into Openness,* 37–48.

234. For a comprehensive understanding of the interpretations of the impact of mass movements in central India, see Picket, *Christian Missions in Mid India.*

235. Not every Western missionary agency was so quick to baptize all the ignorant and illiterate in India. For example, the Presbyterians were careful not to rush to baptizing others until the seeker's motives were scrutinized. For a scholarly analysis of the perception of mass movements, see Pachuau, "Clash of Mass Movements," 157–74.

236. Read William Campbell, *British India in its Relation to the Decline of Hindooism and the Progress of Christianity,* 1839.

237. Webster, *Christian Community and Change,* 146; Jones, *Arya Dharma,* 12.

civilized, and induce them to give up their occupations."[238] Upper class Hindus were consternated that Christianity would become a threat to the traditional social order as missionaries working among depressed classes would endeavor to improve their lot.[239] Therefore, since the late nineteenth century, *Sat Dharm Pracharak* has urged Hindus to reclaim as many out-castes as possible back to Hinduism.[240] According to Heike Leibau, mass protests against new converts took place as early as the beginning of the nineteenth century in the Tirunelveli region of Tamil Nadu.[241] She mentions that, "the Hindus not only resorted to physical violence, they also began a widespread campaign against Christians . . . "[242]

Through anti-conversion propaganda and reconversion drives, Hindu activists campaign against Christian conversions and call upon Hindus and new converts to actively reject Christianity and faithfully return to their former religious belief.[243]

238. Webster, *Christian Community and Change*, 146.

239. Brown, "Who is an Indian?" 114.

240. Webster, *Christian Community and Change*, 146.

241. Liebau, *Cultural Encounters in India*, 275.

242. Liebau, *Cultural Encounters in India*, 275.

243. Misra, "Missionary Position," 369.

3

The Advance of Hindu Nationalism
and Religious Antagonism

THE RELIGIOUS OPPOSITION AND violence Christianity faces from Hindu communities in post independent India is often ascribed to the orchestration and strategy of a group of Hindu nationalist movements commonly known as the Sangh Parivar, whose rhetoric demonizes the religious other with its pervasive religious binaries.[1] In their urge to promote the Hindutva agenda, the advocates of Hindu nationalism have been actively engaged in blanketing the nation with obnoxious propaganda against religious minorities, especially Muslims and Christians. They often allege that Christians aim to fragment the nation, its traditional values and Hindu culture through religious fermentation endowed by the economic power and political interests of Western countries.[2] Sangh Parivar's continued politicization of religious identities and marginalization of religious minorities, for the sake of the promotion of Hindu nationalism, indicates the crisis of Indian secularism.

Ainslie T. Embree defines nationalism as a "deliberate construct" and "a manufactured ideology . . . 'a work of time and a work of art' . . . an attitude of mind and a pattern of attention and desires."[3] Hindu nationalism, which is the byproduct of both the religious zeal and the political construct

1. Malik, "Voices of Hindutva."

2. Raj, *Confusion Called Conversion*, 2–3. For a comprehensive understanding of how India's Christianity is portrayed by some Hindus, see Niyogi, *Report*, 1:6.

3. Embree, *Utopias in Conflict*, 7. Embree borrows these ideas from Benjamin Disraeli and Karl Deutsch. He quoted from Deutsch, *Politics and Government*, 80.

of nineteenth century renascent India, grew as a complex and vague,[4] yet definable ideology known as *Hindutva* in the twentieth century with a vision of nation-freeing, nation-building, and nation-leading in terms of ancient Hindu culture and religious settings.

Hindu nationalism in India, according to Dibyesh Anand, "is a chauvinist and majoritarian nationalism that conjures up the image of a peaceful Hindu Self vis-à-vis the threatening minority Other."[5] He adds, it "normalizes a politics of fear and hatred by representing it as a defensive reaction to the threats"[6] posed by those non-Hindu religious others. It is the taproot of religious antagonism in India.

For a comprehensive understanding of how Hindu nationalist ideology is edged with a view which intensifies intolerance towards religious minorities and how it affects Christianity in India, it is crucial to determine the ideological premises in which this movement evolved. Therefore, this chapter presents the evolution of Hindu nationalist ideology, how it is aligned to safeguard Hindu traditions from the attacks and proselytization efforts of religious others, and how it attempts to decolonize India through the reestablishment of the Hindu race, subjugating every religious other to the Hindutva organism. This chapter hints at how Hindu nationalist ideology provided the impetus to the formation and perspectives of the Niyogi Committee Report against Christian Missions, which will be covered in the next chapter.

THE PRECURSORS OF THE HINDU NATIONALIST VISION

Since the mid-nineteenth century, religion and nationalism in India have reinforced each other "to promote the national feeling, sense of patriotism and a spirit of self-help among the Hindus."[7] In this disposition, the ideological framework of Hindu nationalism gradually surfaced during the period between the 1870s and the 1920s and doctrinally crystallized after the 1920s.[8]

Society for the Promotion of Nationalist Feeling

Rajnarain Bose (Rajnarayan Basu) was perhaps the earliest to give his country people a complete picture of nationalism by establishing a "Society for the Promotion of Nationalist Feeling among the educated Natives

4. Oommen, "Religious Nationalism and Democratic Polity," 458.
5. Anand, *Hindu Nationalism*, 1.
6. Anand, *Hindu Nationalism*, 1.
7. Majumdar, *History of the Freedom Movement in India*, 294.
8. Jaffrelot, *Nationalist Movement in India*, 11.

of Bengal" in 1866. This society purposed "to resist the powerful tendency of imitating the West by reviving the old idea, traditions and customs in every walk of life."[9] Majumdar mentions that it was this society which gave Rabindranath and his older brother the inspiration to free India from the yoke of the British.[10]

Bose, who initially eschewed politics and religion from the purview of this society, later moved to base his "nationalism on the Hindu religion." Through lectures and writings, he audaciously proclaimed "the superiority of Hindu religion and culture over European and Christian theology and civilization."[11] He was one of the earliest Hindu leaders to politically envision India as a rejuvenated Hindu nation, illuminating the world with her pride of knowledge, spirituality, and culture. Regarding Bose's passion and influence, Bankim Chandra Chatterji, who fostered the ideas of Hindu nationalism in his own writings, said that Bose's "clarion call rallied around his banner a large number of Hindus who accepted his views with enthusiasm, and probably without argument or discussion."[12]

The Hindu Mela

Long before Hindu Mahasabha was constituted, Nabagopal Mitra, who embraced the ideals preached by Bose, started an annual gathering of Hindus known as the Hindu Mela through which he attempted to unite Hindus against the Western modernization of society, economy, and religion. Held in 1867, this Mela included lectures, patriotic songs, poems, and a detailed review of socioeconomic, political, and religious conditions in India, as well as the performance of indigenous forms of physical exercises and feats of physical strength.[13] Mitra led fourteen Hindu Mela gatherings between 1867 and 1881. At the fourth session of Mela an association which was purely for the promotion of nationalist feeling among Hindus was formed under the banner of "National Society." In his various writings, Mitra maintained that "the basis of national unity in India has been the Hindu religion,"[14] adding that, "Hindu nationality is not confined to Bengal. It embraces all of Hindu name and Hindu faith throughout the length and breadth of Hindustan;

---

9. Majumdar, *History of the Freedom Movement in India*, 293; See also Louis, *Emerging Hindutva Force*, 42.

10. Majumdar, *History of the Freedom Movement in India*, 293.

11. Majumdar, *History of the Freedom Movement in India*, 295.

12. Majumdar, *History of the Freedom Movement in India*, 296.

13. Majumdar, *History of the Freedom Movement in India*, 294.

14. Majumdar, *History of the Freedom Movement in India*, 295.

neither geographical position, nor the language is counted a disability. The Hindus are destined to be a religious nation."[15]

The Impulse of Arya Samaj

Arya Samaj, which arose from a new generation of Hindu activists in Punjab, served as a driving force for Hindu nationalist thought and soon gained influence among Hindus throughout India, with the exception of some southern parts of India.[16] C. V. Mathew lays down four reasons why this movement gained momentum in Punjab.[17] First, the Hindus in Punjab province were a minority greatly overwhelmed by the imposing and active presence of the majority Muslims. Second, in seeking independent identity, Sikhism, Hinduism's offshoot religion, witnessed self-purification and revivalist movements such as the Akali and Nirankari and the Singh Sabha movements in the mid-nineteenth century. Third, the extension and success of Christian missionary work in Punjab since 1851 made Hindus feel more insecure. Four, in the light of growing religious others, Hindus felt a great need to be defensive as well as competitive to retain a dignified survival. In Lajpat Rai's words, "Hinduism in Northern India cannot be thought of without the Arya Samaj. It is not only a source of strength to Hinduism and Hindus, but is the principal effective agency, always and everywhere present, to defend them, to save them, and to serve them."[18] Dayananda Saraswati's work, *Satyartha Prakash,* became the Bible of Arya Samaj and a powerful defensive weapon for Samajis. It not only aided Hindus in repudiating claims of the superiority of Christianity and Islam over their national religion, but also shaped the modern Hindu mind to stereotype non-Hindu religious others as inherently evil, inferior, and treacherous to the Hindu race.[19] To counter proselytizing missionary activities, Araya Samaj imitated many of their organization skills and techniques.[20]

RECLAMATION RITUALS

In his intolerance of non-Hindu religions, Dayananda Saraswati initiated two movements within Arya Samaj which not only fostered apologetic unanimity among Hindus, but also impinged upon religious others,

---

15. Majumdar, *History of the Freedom Movement in India,* 295.

16. Louis, *Emerging Hindutva Force,* 44.

17. Mathew, *Saffron Mission,* 63–64.

18. Rai, *Arya Samaj,* 229.

19. Majumdar, *History of the Freedom Movement in India,* 297.

20. Anderson, *Brotherhood of Saffron,* 18.

particularly converts. First was the *shuddhi* program, which is known today as *ghar wapsi* (homecoming), through which Arya Samajis actively promoted and were involved in the reconversion of converts to Islam and Christianity back to the Vedic faith.[21] The *Shuddhi* movement, which acquired a particular meaning in the last two decades of the nineteenth century, created interreligious tensions in Punjab through these reconversion programs and active proselytization.[22] Second was the *Go Rakshini Sabha* (Cow Protection Association), which stirred the feelings of Hindus against beef-eating Christians and Muslims.[23]

THE UNITED HINDU RACE

While people in large numbers began to respond positively to Christian missionary efforts, the first British census in 1872 revealed a significant Muslim population in India. It raised the eyebrows of the guardians of Hinduism and caused them to think seriously of regenerating the Hindu race against Moors and Christians by uniting Indians into Hindu culture, reclaiming converts, and assimilating minorities such as Buddhists, Sikhs, and Jains under the Hindu religious umbrella.[24] Arya Samaj was a militant sect from its very inception.[25] Through the *sanghatan* (union) program, Arya Samaj united Hindus against religious others, cultivating in them a militant spirit to defend Hinduism and oppose conversions of Hindus into other religions. While emphasizing Hindu unity, Saraswati advocated for the replacement of Urdu by Hindi in the *Devanagari* script, in addition to bringing the movement of cow protection to the forefront. These aspects further worsened communal relations in north India during the last two decades of nineteenth century.[26]

Until the outcastes were called into the Hindu fold by charismatic thinkers and reformers, especially by the Arya Samaj and Gandhi's popularization of the term *harijan*,[27] so-called Hindus were conscious of and were consternated at their own status against the Muslim population of

21. Panicker, *Gandhi on Pluralism and Communalism*, 6. See also Hedlund, "Hindus and Christians for 2000 Years," 4.

22. Thursby, *Hindu-Muslim Relations in British India*, 136.

23. Zachariah, *Modern Religious and Secular Movements in India*, 59, 63.

24. Jaffrelot, *Hindu Nationalism*, 5.

25. Majumdar, *History of the Freedom Movement in India*, 298.

26. Basu, *Khaki Shorts and Saffron Flags*, 8.

27. Since masses of outcastes had been relegated to the outside of "pure" Hindu society for centuries, Gandhi worked a strategy of strengthening the Hindu majority by labeling the outcastes *harijan* and including them in the Hindu system. See Frykenberg, "Concept of 'Majority,'" 267–74.

India.[28] In Lajpat Rai's words, "The Arya Samajists reclaim these depressed classes by admitting them to the privileges of the *Dwijas*. They administer *Gayatri* to a select number, invest them with the sacred thread, confer on them the privilege of performing *Homa*, and start inter-dining and in a few cases even inter-marriage with them."[29]

OPPOSITION TO CHRISTIAN CONVERSIONS

Arya Samaj was perhaps the earliest group to propagate the idea that "Christianity is a Western religion, and as everything that *comes from* the West is to be discarded, Christianity must also be discarded."[30] Gandhi had profound respect for Dayanada Saraswati, the founder of Arya Samaj. While copying Christians in their propaganda, Arya Samajists have not only opposed Christian conversions, but have also been actively involved in reconversion schemes through the *shuddhi* movement. They placed spies in mission schools to report if students showed any interest in Christianity so that they could take precautions to prevent them from being converted to Christianity. For example, when two Hindu boys at Foreman College in Lahore converted to Christianity in 1894, Arya Samaj organized a mass campaign against the school which affected the enrollment of students in the following years.[31] Because of the pressure of Arya Samaj, some new converts were seen apostatizing.

THE HINDU NATIONALIST MOVEMENT

Bal Gangadhar Tilak was "the first man to combine Hindu revivalism with active political agitation," inspiring "an era of religious fanaticism and political violence which lasted until Gandhi introduced other methods in the early 1920s."[32] By 1920, before his death that year, he lit such a fire in everyone's heart with the dream of achieving independence that various schools of political thought emerged, from communalism to the formation of the Hindu Mahasabha, the Muslim League, and RSS, whose members could all be found working under the umbrella of Indian National Congress initially.[33] The basic thought of the Indian Nationalist Movement advocated by Dadabhai Naoroji, Gopal Krishna Gokhale, Surendra Nath Benerjee, and

28. Veer, *Religious Nationalism*, 26.

29. Rai, *Arya Samaj*, 230.

30. Gandhi, *Hindu Dharma*, 269.

31. Webster, *Christian Community and Change*, 142.

32. Edwardes, *Last Years of British India*, 25.

33. Kelkar, *Lost Years of the RSS*, 3.

others was anti-colonial, a nationhood of economic development coupled with a secular, democratic, civil-libertarian, and republican political structure.[34] However, since the first quarter of the twentieth century, India witnessed a dramatic rise of national leaders within Indian nationalism who were strongly convinced of the need for independence more along ethnoreligious and cultural lines.[35] Prominent among the leaders who relentlessly endeavored to mobilize Hindu masses through regional and national campaigns, efforts, and agitations, and who proposed a militant approach toward political independence were Lala Lajpat Rai, Bal Gangadhar Tilak, Bipin Chandra Pal, and Aurobindo Ghose. Their ideals were inspired by Hindu culture and Hindu *dharma* as anticipated by their precursors.

Trajectory of Hindu Identity

R. C. Majumdar points out that, "Every historical incident in the past which reflected glory upon the one was a humiliating memory to the other."[36] "The triumphs of Muhammad ibn Qasim, Sultan Mahmud of Ghazni and Muhammad Ghuri which swelled the pride of Muslims as a great conquering nation of the world, only evoked painful memories of national degradation and humiliation in the minds of Hindus."[37] When people in great numbers joined the freedom movement with the goal of ousting the British from India, the Muslim leaders of the Wahabi movement and the leaders of Hindu revivalism chose diametrically opposite ways. Although it was the work of Christian missionaries and Orientalists which evidently wounded the pride of Hindus in their traditions and culture and which bred Hindu intolerance toward religious intruders, a strong spirit of Hindu nationalism was not felt until the Muslim nationalism represented by the Wahabis.[38] Thus, "the strength and diffusion of Hindu nationalist identity were predicated on the perception of a threatening Other."[39]

After the partition of Bengal in 1905, the nationalist leaders Gangadhar Tilak, Aurobindo, Lajpat Rai, and Bipin Chandra Pal had a religious extremist tinge in their approach to nationalism. They promoted unity among Hindus by popularizing the Hindu religious festivals, Hindu gods, and the notion of

34. Louis, *Emerging Hindutva Force*, 47.

35. Zavos, *Emergence of Hindu Nationalism*, 9.

36. Majumdar, *History of the Freedom Movement in India*, 300.

37. Majumdar, *History of the Freedom Movement in India*, 300.

38. Majumdar, *History of the Freedom Movement in India*, 299. Mujumdar does not say that Hindu nationalism arose as a counterpart or rival movement to Muslim nationalism.

39. Jaffrelot, *Hindu Nationalist Movement in India*, 8.

mother India.[40] C. V. Mathew mentions that Gangadhar Tilak, who believed that Hinduism is capable of serving as a powerful force of regeneration and union, played a remarkable role in making nationalism a mass program and reconstructing Hindu society on *swadharma*.[41] Tilak admired violent acts motivated by the patriotic spirit and contributed to the rise of secret societies which were involved in terrorist activities.[42]

Aurobindo Ghose, on the other hand, whose passion for the liberation of India surfaced from joining a secret society called the "Lotus and Dagger" formed by Indian students in England,[43] extolled the virtues of muscular Hinduism, calling for Hindus to unite against the British, Christians, and Muslims.[44] He saw *Sanatana dharma* as nationalism[45] and stressed that the "Hindu nation was born with the Sanatana Dharma; with it, it moves, and with it, it grows . . . The Sanatana Dharma, that is nationalism."[46] He was thoroughly influenced by the teaching and philosophy of his maternal grandfather Rajnarain Bose and shared in his fire for a militant form of Hindu nationalism. In 1902, Aurobindo helped form *Anushilan Samaiti* (Self-culture Association), a secret armed anti-British revolutionary organization, which was involved in making bombs, arms training, and the assassination of British officials.[47] It was banned by the British in 1909. Aurobindo was one of the strongest proponents of militant nationalism at the time and encouraged armed youth clubs under this society.

The Hindu nationalist movement entered a significant phase under its grand theorists V. D. Savarkar, Swami Shraddhananda, and Lajpat Rai, who were known as the architects of Hindu nationalism.[48] Shraddhananda and Lajpat Rai were devout followers and leaders of Arya Samaj who brought the ideas and aggressive spirit of Dayananda into strategic action.

40. While Tilak popularized *Ganapati Utsav* (festivals) and Shivaji Jayanthi in Maharashtra, the Hindu fundamentalists in Bengal popularized the worship of Kali (Durga). Louis, *Emerging Hindutva Force*, 47–48.

41. Mathew, *Saffron Mission*, 150.

42. Chopra, *Comprehensive History of Modern India*, 205.

43. Sharma, *Hindutva*, 47. See also Samadder, "Marxist: History of Armed Revolution."

44. Vedhamanickam, "Serving Under the Saffron Shadow," 43.

45. For a comprehensive understanding of Aurobindo's Hindu nationalist philosophy, see Varma, *Political Philosophy of Sri Aurobindo*, 206–14.

46. On May 30, 1909 Sri Aurobindo gave this *Uttarapara* speech, quoted in Chitkara, *Hindutva Parivar*, 18; also in Varma, *Political Philosophy of Sri Aurobindo,* 206. Aurobindo's full speech is available at http://intyoga.online.fr/uttaspch.htm.

47. Chopra, *Comprehensive History of Modern India*, 206–7; Majumdar, *History of the Freedom Movement in India*, 250.

48. Zavos, *Emergence of Hindu Nationalism in India*, 9.

In the 1920s, to tackle the mass Christian conversions of lower caste people, Shraddhananda, who had a fair share of Danyananda's spirit,[49] sought
to contextualize *shuddhi* for untouchables and attempted to include them
in the Hindu mainstream. In 1926, he published a pamphlet called *Hindu
Sangathan: Saviour of a Dying Race* in which he alleged that Hindus were
at risk of extinction due to conversions, provoking Hindus against non-
Hindu religious others.

Savarkar and Hindu Rashtra

Hindu nationalist thought was shaped and strengthened by V. D. Savarkar
(1883–1966), who is known as the father of Hindu nationalism. From his
childhood, Savarkar was proud of Hindu religion, customs, and culture,
and was revolutionary in his patriotic thoughts and activities. According to Matthew Lederle, during his high school years, Savarkar and two
of his friends founded a secret society called *Rastrabhakta Samuha* (the
Group of Patriots) in 1899 and from 1900 on he was involved in discussion
groups of insurrection called *Mitramela* (the Gathering of Friends).[50] In
1904, he founded Abhinav Bharat Society (ABS), a revolutionary organization, and in the following year he organized a public bonfire of foreign
clothes in Pune against the British.[51] After the announcement of the partition of Bengal in July 1905 by the Viceroy of India, Lord Curzon, ABS and
Anushilan Samiti intensified their revolutionary activities and sought the
support of Hindus to foment a national uprising.[52]

In his writings, Savarkar laid down definitions for the key concepts
of Hindu nationalist thought and formulated the notion of *Hindu Rashtra*
along ethnoreligious lines. *The Indian War of Independence (1908)*, *Hindutva
(1923)*, *Hindu Pad Padshahi (1942)*, and *Hindu Rashtra Darshan (1949)* are
among dozens of his literary works and speeches which underline the ideology of Hindu nationalism. With Savarkar, the center of gravity of Hindu nationalism shifts from Punjab and the United Provinces, where Arya Samaj
had previously stirred Hindus against non-Hindu others, to Maharashtra
where Gangadhar Tilak prepared the ground for a wider scope.[53]

---

49. Gandhi, *Hindu Dharma*, 15.

50. Lederle, *Philosophical Trends in Modern Maharashtra*, 279, quoted in Mathew,
Saffron Mission, 165.

51. Chopra, *Comprehensive History of India*, 205. For chronology of Savarkar's life
events, see "Swatantryaveer Savarkar Smarak." http://www.savarkarsmarak.com/chro-
nology.php.

52. Andersen, *Brotherhood of Saffron*, 17.

53. Jaffrelot, *Hindu Nationalism*, 85.

Hindu Mahasabha

In 1907, a year after the All India Muslim League was formed, Savarkar organized the Hindu Mahasabha (the great gathering of Hindus) as a sociocultural body (*sanghatan*) in Punjab with the aim of representing and safeguarding the interests of Hindu communities in British India. In 1910, an All India Hindu Conference was convened in Allahabad to unite Hindus in response to the rise of Muslim leagues. As C. V. Mathew postulates, the Hindu Mahasabha was born out of a "fear complex and helplessness of the majority community" to tackle the rapid growth of Christianity and Islam.[54] In 1915, Madan Mohan Malaviya and Lajpat Rai formed Akhil Bharat Hindu Mahasabha (ABHM) as a Hindu nationalist political party, whose activities by the 1920s were increasingly directed against Muslim communities. ABHM worked as a pressure group within Congress Party until it was expelled in 1937. It became a forerunner of *Sangh Parivar,* providing an ideological base for the Hindu unification movement. Among the programs enunciated by the president of Mahasabha, Lajpat Rai, the following illuminate the grand plans of Hindu union against religious others.[55]

1. To organize Hindu Sabhas throughout the country

2. To provide relief to Hindus who need help on account of communal riots

3. To reconvert Hindus who had been forcibly converted to Islam

4. To celebrate Hindu festivals

5. To represent the communal interests of Hindus in all political controversies.

The exigencies of the time brought together Bharatiya Hindu Shuddhi Sabha and the ABHM, which provided a common platform for the Hindu agenda against the interests of religious minorities.[56] In 1937 (after spending 27 years in jail from 1910 to 1937), when Savarkar became the president,[57] ABHM's attention was turned more against the Congress and Muslims as "he constantly harped on the theme of Muslims being anti-Hindu, anti-Indian and harboring Pan-Islamic ambitions."[58] Although the Hindu Mahasabha did not secure any important position in the political affairs of independent

54. Mathew, *Saffron Mission,* 163.

55. Louis, *Emerging Hindutva Force,* 49.

56. Mathew, *Saffron Mission,* 69.

57. Jaffrelot, *Hindu Nationalism,* 85.

58. Sharma, *Hindutva,* 141.

India, it nurtured antagonism against the religious others, particularly toward Muslims and Christians. Savarkar saw an inseparable connection between "swadharma and swarajya" and said, "Swaraj without Swadharma is despicable and Swadharma without Swarajya is powerless."[59] According to him, the sword of *swarajya* must always be ready to defend Swadharma. This is the command of God. He often stressed what Swami Ramdas underscored, "Die for your Dharma, kill the enemies of your Dharma while you are dying; in this way fight and kill, and take back your kingdom!"[60]

HINDUTVA

The central theme of Hindu nationalism is Hindutva, the brainchild of V. D. Savarkar. During the time he was in prison in 1922, Savarkar wrote *Hindutva,* a tract which was reproduced by hand and distributed among Maharashtrian nationalists.[61] In 1923, it was published as an anonymous tract, *Essentials of Hindutva,*[62] which gained popularity among Indians, particularly among Hindus who sought a dignified religious identity and freedom from the British. It was reprinted in 1928 as *Hindutva: Who is a Hindu?* According to Jaffrelot, "This book is the real character of Hindu nationalism, the ideology which has become precisely equated with the word, 'Hindutva.'"[63] After coming in contact with Khilafatists, Savarkar began to see Muslims as the prime enemies of India and not the British. Therefore, with an assumption that Hindus were weak compared to Muslims, Savarkar penned this booklet to provide an ideological framework for the unity of differentiated Hindus under the nationhood of Hindu pride.[64]

Savarkar's notion of *Hindu Rashtra* was based on the theme of Hindutva. For him, "Hindutva" is not a word or a religious dogma; it is a history.[65] It "embraces all the departments of thought and activity of the whole Being of our Hindu race,"[66] making Hindus a nation by default. "Hinduism is only a derivative, a fraction, a part of Hindutva."[67] Savarkar argued that his ambi-

59. An Indian Nationalist. Savarkar, *Indian War of Independence of 1857,* 9–10.

60. Savarkar, *Indian War of Independence of 1857,* 10.

61. Andersen, *Saffron Brotherhood,* 60.

62. The publisher of the second edition mentions that it was published in 1923 by Advocate V.V. Kelkar under the "non-de-plume" "*A Maratha*" as Savarkar was still in prison. See Savarkar, *Hindutva,* vi. See also Savarkar.org, "Essentials of Hindutva."

63. Jaffrelot, *Hindu Nationalism,* 85.

64. Keer, *Veer Savarkar,* 161, quoted in Jaffrelot, *Hindu Nationalism,* 89.

65. Savarkar, *Hindutva,* 3.

66. Savarkar, *Hindutva,* 4.

67. Savarkar, *Hindutva,* 4.

tion for *Hindu Rashtra* did not evolve in a vacuum, but was the reaffirmation and reclamation of the ancient name *Sindhu rashtra* in fulfilment of the wishes of the Vedic forefathers who made that choice.[68]

In constructing the idea of Hindutva, Savarkar assigned multiple perspectives and implications to the word "Hindu" beyond its religious or geographical outlook. In Savarkar's understanding, "A Hindu is primarily a citizen either in himself or through his forefathers of *Hindustan* and claims the land as his mother-land."[69] However, he expressed fear of calling a Mohammedan a Hindu based on citizenship status.[70] When he said that all the inhabitants of the Indian subcontinent are considered *Bharati Santati*[71] or Hindus irrespective of their caste, language, culture, and sectarian traditions, his inclusive language only comprises "Sanatanists, Satnamis, Sikhs, Aryas, Anaryas, Marathas and Madrasis, Brahmins and Panchamas,"[72] not Muslims and Christians. For Savarkar, the three essentials of Hindutva are "a common nation (*Rashtra*), a common race (*Jati*) and a common civilization (*sanskriti*). All these essentials could best be summed up by stating in brief that he was a Hindu to whom *Sindhusthan* is not only a *Pitrubhu* (Fatherland) but also a *Punyabhu* (Holy land)."[73] "A Hindu then is he who feels attachment to the land . . . .of his forefathers—as his Fatherland . . . ; and who has inherited . . . the Hindu Sanskriti, the Hindu civilization, as represented in a common history, common heroes, a common literature, common art, a common law and a common jurisprudence, common fairs and festivals, rites and rituals, ceremonies and sacraments."[74]

Two of the most essential requisites of Hindutva, according to Savarkar, were "incorporation and adaptation," by which one inherits the blood of the Hindu race.[75] He said that anyone who "has not adopted our (*Hindu*) culture, and our history, inherited our blood and has come to look upon our land not only as the land of his love but even of his worship, he cannot get himself incorporated into the Hindu fold."[76] In this way, Savarkar deliberately placed Indian Christians and Indian Muslims outside the Hindu fold because of their non-Hindu religious status. He added, "Christian and

68. Savarkar, *Hindutva*, 14.

69. Savarkar, *Hindutva*, 72.

70. Savarkar, *Hindutva*, 72.

71. Savarkar, *Hindutva*, 34.

72. Savarkar, *Hindutva*, 39.

73. Savarkar, *Hindutva*, 100–103.

74. Savarkar, *Hindutva*, 87–88.

75. Savarkar, *Hindutva*, 79.

76. Savarkar, *Hindutva*, 73.

Mohammedan communities, who, were but very recently Hindus and in a majority of cases had been at least in their first generation most unwilling denizens of their new fold, claim though they might have a common Fatherland, and an almost pure Hindu blood and parentage with us, cannot be recognized as Hindus; as since their adoption of the new cult they had ceased to own Hindu civilization (Sanskriti) as a whole."[77]

THE HINDU RASHTRA

From the time Savarkar became the president of ABHM, he vehemently campaigned and fought for national freedom in defense of Hindudom and Hindusthan.[78] In his presidential address at the 19th session of ABHM, Savarkar stressed that Hindus should be "indissolubly bound together by the enduring ties of blood and religion and country."[79] In political spheres, the ABHM remained a Pan-Hindu organization with the aim of shaping the destiny of the Hindu nation in all its social, political, and cultural aspects.[80] However, Savarkar's vision of *Swaraj* was quite different from Gandhi's. Savarkar emphasized that, "Our country is endeared to us because it has been the abode of our race, our people . . . The independence of India means, therefore, the independence of our people, our race, our nation. Therefore, 'Indian swarajya or Indian Swatantrya' means, as far as the Hindu Nation is concerned, the political independence of the Hindus, the freedom which would enable them to grow to their full height."[81]

Savarkar further clarified that, "The real meaning of *swarajya* then, is not merely the geographical independence of the bit of earth called India. To the Hindus independence of Hindusthan can only be worth having if that ensures their Hindutva—their religious, racial and cultural identity."[82] Although Savarkar acknowledged the lesser degree of involvement of non-Hindu minorities in the freedom movement, he argued that Indian freedom was achieved largely by the efforts and sacrifices of Hindus for a united Indian state, which therefore should be a Hindu nation.[83] Regarding Christians, Savarkar said, "Only in religion they differ from us and are a proselytizing church. So in that matter alone the Hindus must be on their

---

77. Savarkar, *Hindutva*, 88.
78. Savarkar, *Hindu Rashtra Darshan*, 1.
79. Savarkar, *Hindu Rashtra Darshan*, 4
80. Savarkar, *Hindu Rashtra Darshan*, 9.
81. Savarkar, *Hindu Rashtra Darshan*, 15.
82. Savarkar, *Hindu Rashtra Darshan*, 17.
83. Savarkar, *Hindu Rashtra Darshan*, 17.

guard and give the missionaries no blind latitude to carry on their activities beyond voluntary and legitimate bases."[84]

In his campaigns, Savarkar predicated how in his prospective liberated nation, Hindu nationalism ensures the religious freedom of minorities. He said, "We shall ever guarantee protection to the religion, culture and language of the minorities for themselves, but we shall no longer tolerate any aggression on their part on the equal liberty of the Hindus to guard their religion, culture and language as well. If the non-Hindu minorities are to be protected, then surely the Hindu majority also must be protected against any aggressive minority in India!"[85] He envisaged a dominant and militant Hindudom in post-British India. His oft sung mantra was, "militarize Hindudom and Hinduise politics." N. B. Khare popularized this slogan through his editorial work at *The Hindu Outlook*, the mouthpiece of Hindu Mahasabha. According to Khare, it was this watchword which inspired Subash Chandra Bose to dream of building a powerful, militant Indian army.[86]

Rashtriya Swayamsevak Sangh (RSS)

On Vijayadasami Day, 27 September 1925, in Nagpur, Keshav Baliram Hedgewar (1889–1940), a Telugu Brahmin, founded the RSS, the National Volunteer Organization as a sociocultural supremacist Hindu organization to articulate Hindu revivalism, and to promote unity among Hindus to counter British colonialism and Muslim separatism.[87] Karandikar mentions that Hedgewar chose this particular day in order to boost RSS members with a religious sentiment (collective psyche of the society) and motivation. According to religious traditions of Hinduism, on this day Lord Rama killed Ravana, the evil king of Lanka, which symbolizes victory, bravery and a fight against injustice.[88] However, according to Sanjeev Kelkar, a long-time associate of RSS, "the anger towards the growing Muslim atrocities and arrogance in the early 1920s, coupled with the Gandhi way of dealing with them, contributed to the formation of the RSS in 1925."[89] Its main objective was to establish India as a *Hindu Rashtra*.[90]

While Hedgewar was studying medicine in Bengal, he was attracted to and influenced by the *Anushilan Samiti*, a secret society of martial arts

84. Savarkar, *Hindu Rashtra Darshan*, 69.

85. Savarkar, *Hindu Rashtra Darshan*, 28.

86. *The Hindu Outlook*, November 8, 1953, 7.

87. Chitkara, *Sangh Pariwar*, 42.

88. Karandikar, *Architects of RSS*, 5.

89. Kelkar, *Lost Years of the RSS*, 14.

90. Chitkara, *Sangh Pariwar*, 42.

involving tooth and nail in fighting the British.[91] His interest in revolutionary acts overwhelmed his passion for studies so that, according to Seshadri, "he set out to Calcutta more to delve into the intricacies of the revolutionary movement than to study medicine."[92] It was Krishna Shivram Munje, a medical doctor and militant Hindu nationalist from Hindu Mahasaba, who influenced Hedgewar's life with his anti-British revolutionary spirit and encouraged him to go for medicine in Calcutta.[93] Meanwhile, he read Savarkar's handwritten manuscript, *Hindutva*, which greatly influenced and advanced his thinking on the thesis that Hindus were a nation. It had given him intellectual justification for the Hindu nation, but it did not provide a method of how to go about uniting Hindu communities to that end. Hedgewar's strategy to implement the vision of a Hindu nation was to emulate the practices of *Anushilan Samiti* and establish a paramilitary that would multiply itself by inviting and training others.[94] With that backdrop, at the founding meeting of the RSS, Hedgewar said to his fellow like-minded revolutionists, "We have trained ourselves physically, militarily and politically and we will train others."[95] The RSS spread so much within the year it was founded that wrestling rings and gymnasia were seen all over Maharashtra. Every Hindu youth who was influenced by the ideology of RSS saw in himself a representation of *Hanumant*, the Hindu deity of physical strength. Every RSS gymnasium had an idol of Hanumant and prayers were offered to him prior to their physical exercises, mostly push-ups, sit-ups, and wrestling.[96] In the same year, RSS acquired a large open area in Nagpur for the military training of young boys and recruited Martandra Jog, a former officer in the army of Maharaja of Gwalior, as the head of the military section of RSS.[97] They chose the bhagwa dhwaj (a saffron-colored flag) as their official symbol of Dharma. Prayers to motherland were incorporated, and they sang verses from Ramdas during drills to arouse revolutionary fervor among the young.

In articulating the vision of *Hindu Rashtra*, the RSS showed varied faces through various phases and dramatically transitioned from being a revivalist sociocultural movement to a fascist, militant, multi-faceted sociocultural Hindu nationalist organization. During its early years, the

---

91. Jaffrelot, *Sangh Parivar*, 56.
92. Seshadri, *RSS*, 1.
93. Andersen, *Saffron Brotherhood*, 31.
94. Andersen, *Saffron Brotherhood*, 33, 34, 60.
95. Quoted in Karandikar, *Architects of RSS*, 7.
96. Karandikar, *Architects of RSS*, 7.
97. Andersen, *Saffron Brotherhood*, 35–36.

RSS felt an ideological tension to draw clear lines between the "Hindu" and the "non-Hindu" to prove its conceptual premise and to revolutionize its vision. Although Hedgewar followed the sociopolitical framework of Savarkar and Hindu Mahasabha in order to consolidate Hindus on the grounds of the Hindutva framework, his initial view of "non-Hindus" as "near-Hindus" led him to participate in the non-Cooperation movement.[98] When M. S. Golwalkar assumed leadership of RSS after the death of Hedgewar, the organization entered a militant phase because he looked upon "non-Hindus" as "non-citizens" of *Hindu Rashtra*. He demanded that in order for non-Hindus to be accepted into the mainstream Hindu fold, Muslims, Christians, and minority religious others were required to look upon Ram as their hero.[99] This majoritarian attitude of Hindu nationalism, according to Dibyesh Anand, "is typically sprung from masculinized memory, masculinized humiliation and masculinized hope."[100]

While influential leaders like Rama Jois, Arun Shourie, Narendra Modi, and a host of others praise the contribution of the RSS in nation building, Ashis Nandy calls RSS "'an illegitimate child of modern India, not of Hindu traditions.'"[101] In spite of scholarly criticisms, the anti-RSS protests of religious minorities, and the government's occasional efforts to suppress the movement, the RSS has emerged as the largest voluntary non-governmental Hindu organization in the world today.[102]

MUSLIMS AS INSIDE ENEMIES

Until Savarkar was released from jail in 1937, Hedgewar led the RSS in cooperation with the Congress and believed that as a political arm, the Congress would help him achieve his goal of an independent India.[103] When Hedgewar realized that it was the "disorganized and weak Hindu Society" which allowed Islamic conquerors and colonizers to surmount India, he followed the path of Savarkar and the ideology of ABHM to organize Hindus into a force to show enemies their *parakram* (valor). The RSS could not sync with, but rather opposed Gandhi's refrain that "unless all Muslims joined the struggle for independence with the Congress, independence could not be achieved."[104] The RSS suspected that Gandhi's

---

98. Baxter, *Jana Sangh*, 34.

99. *The Organiser*, June 20, 1971, quoted in Basu, *Khaki Shorts and Saffron Flags*, 12.

100. Anand, *Hindu Nationalism in India*, 152.

101. Nandy, "Fear of Gandhi,"

102. Chitkara, *Rashtriya Swayamsevak Sangh*, 362.

103. Kelkar, *Lost Years of the RSS*, 2.

104. Kelkar, *Lost Years of the RSS*, 5.

support of All India Khilafat Parishad (AIKP) helped Khilafat committees spring up all over and strengthened the idea of separatism.[105] This was the point of departure for the RSS to remain militant in their approach, as they did not want to give a part of India to Muslims, who had browbeaten Hindus over the centuries, if India achieved freedom.

SHORT-TERM GOAL AND LONG-TERM VISION

Hedgewar's short-term goal in founding the RSS was to oust the British, which was necessary "to protect the Hindu society, Hindu Dharma and Hindu culture"[106] from Western influences. This was the vow of RSS in the pre-independence period.[107] Their long-term vision, however, was to provide the impetus for the restoration of *Hindu Rashtra* by keeping India united and by drawing Muslims into the Hindu mainstream "at all costs,"[108] not because of their love for Muslims, but because of their bitterness against them.

For the RSS, "*Hindu Rashtra* is the largest inclusive concept, incorporating Hindu, Hindutva and Hindu Dharma, as well as much more."[109] Like Savarkar, Hedgewar and Golwalkar fundamentally believed that *Hindu Rashtra* had existed for many thousands of years,[110] Hindutva being its basis. They argued that "Hindutva has been latent force which has given uniqueness and continuity to this land variously known as Bharat, Hindustan and India."[111] Therefore, the claim of the RSS is that "India is culturally one nation, even if the name 'Hindu' is recent."[112] Its definition of nationalism is beyond the Gandhian and Nehruvian understanding of territorial nationalism. Territorial nationalism, according to the RSS, has to be imbued with historical and cultural nationalism.

In the early period of the RSS, some in the movement favored the political concept of Hindutva as emphasized and endorsed by Hindu Mahasabha, but it was never the official view of the RSS.[113] For the RSS, "the concept of Hindutva is cultural and not political . . . The Hindutva of the RSS does not aim at creating a theocratic Hindu state, but wants to consolidate the

105. Kelkar, *Lost Years of the RSS*, 5.

106. Kelkar, *Lost Years of the RSS*, 8–9.

107. Malkani, *RSS Story*, 200.

108. Kelkar, *Lost Years of the RSS*, 14.

109. Kelkar, *Lost Years of the RSS*, 25.

110. Kelkar, *Lost Years of the RSS*, 26.

111. Chitkara, *Hindutva Parivar*, xviii.

112. Chitkara, *Hindutva Parivar*, 29.

113. Chitkara, *Hindutva Parivar*, 1.

culturally-based Hindu Nation."[114] Their demand is that all religious others should recognize Hindutva as the basic cultural unifying factor while maintaining their separate identities as Hindu, Muslim, Christian, etc . . . [115] Religious others are like separate branches of a common tree.

However, after the partition of India, even when Indian Muslims are a much-reduced minority and appear to share a common cultural life with Hindus, the Hindu-Muslim conflict does not seem to end. Hindu nationalists reverberate an animus attitude toward them by contending that "Muslims came to India as invaders, first to loot, and then to rule and convert. They still retain this mindset of the victor. They have neither respected this country's traditions nor this land as the sustaining principle of their life. Their loyalty does not lie here. Therefore, they cannot be included in the concept of the nation."[116] Similarly, they seek ways and means to scapegoat Christians as anti-national and disloyal to the culture, which contributes to the escalation of religious bigotry and Hindu antagonism in post independent India.

M. S. GOLWALKAR AND HINDU NATIONALISM

When Madhavrao Sadhasiv Golwalkar, popularly called "Guriji," came in contact with Hedgewar in 1931, he immediately bought into the philosophy of the RSS. Since Golwalkar was a native of Ramtek which is close to Nagpur, he was regularly and passionately involved in RSS activities. In 1934, he was appointed as secretary of the main branch and rose to the supreme leadership at the demise of Hedgewar. V. R. Karandikar mentions that, "Dr. Hedgewar founded the Sangh and took it to all parts of Maharashtra, while Guruji took it to all parts of India."[117] According to Kelkar, even when public sympathy for the RSS died down at its ban, Golwalkar still formed a huge, intensive network for the RSS, right down to village level.[118]

Delineating his perspective on "nation" and "nationhood," Golwalkar wrote a controversial book in 1939 titled *We or Our Nationhood Defined*, which substantially drew upon the framework of *Rashtra Meemamsa*[119] written by Babarao Savarkar, the elder brother of V. D. Savarkar. According to Ram Punyani, this book has been considered the "Gita" of the Sangh[120] or

114. Chitkara, *Hindutva Parivar*, 1.

115. Chitkara, *Hindutva Parivar*, 2.

116. Chitkara, *Hindutva Parivar*, 30.

117. Karandikar, *Architects of RSS*, xix.

118. Kelkar, *Lost Years of the RSS*, 94.

119. Kelkar, *Lost Years of the RSS*, 34.

120. Puniyani, "M.S. Golwalkar: Conceptualizing Hindutva Fascism,"

"the Bible of RSS" until 1960, when Golwalkar's *Bunch of Thought* became available.[121] In this work, Golwalkar emphasized that "for the Nation concept to exist and be manifest, it must have as its indissoluble component parts the famous five unities, 'Geographical (Country), Racial (Race), Religions (Religion), Cultural (Culture) and Linguistic (Language)' that the loss or destruction of any one of these means the end of the Nation as a Nation."[122] While speaking at a meeting in Bangalore in 1960, Golwalkar referred to the minority communities as "guests" and "not the children of this soil."[123]

We or Our Nationhood Defined shows how Golwalkar was profoundly influenced by Italian fascists and German Nazis in verbalizing the thought of Hindu nationalism. To reject the idea of Indian nationhood and to scaffold an appealing framework for *Hindu Rashtra,* Golwalkar clung to Mazzini's definition of nationalism and espoused Johan Kaspar and Bluntschli's ideals of cultural nationalism; he harped on Hitler's way of implementing the vision. For Golwalkar, Germany afforded a very striking example of how to achieve his vision.[124] He said, "German pride in their Fatherland for a definite home country, for which the race has certain traditional attachments as a necessary concomitant of the true Nation concept, awoke and ran the risk of starting a fresh world-conflagration, in order to establish one, unparalleled, undisputed German Empire over all this 'hereditary territory.'"[125] He added, "To keep up the purity of the race and its culture, Germany shocked the world by her purging the country of the Semitic Races—the Jews. Race pride at its highest has been manifested here. Germany has also shown how well-nigh impossible it is for races and cultures, having differences going to the root, to be assimilated into one united whole, a good lesson for us in Hindusthan to learn and profit by."[126]

Golwalkar demanded that, "The non-Hindu peoples in Hindustan must either adopt Hindu culture and language, must learn to respect and hold in reverence the Hindu religion, must entertain no ideas but those of glorification of the Hindu race and culture, or may stay in the country wholly subordinate to the Hindu nation, claiming nothing, deserving no privileges, far less preferential treatment—not even citizenship rights . . . In this country, Hindus alone are the nationals and the Moslems and others, if

121. Kelkar, *Lost Years of the RSS*, 35.
122. Golwalkar, *We or Our Nationhood Defined*, 83–84.
123. Golwalkar, *Why Hindu Rashtra?* 8.
124. Golwalkar, *Why Hindu Rashtra?* 86.
125. Golwalkar, *Why Hindu Rashtra?* 87.
126. Golwalkar, *Why Hindu Rashtra?* 87–88.

not actually anti-national, are at least outside the body of nation."[127] Since the 1940s, the RSS has gone through an aggressive phase and was violently active during the 1946–47 communal riots, truly reflecting the militancy articulated in *We or Our Nationhood Defined*.[128]

Since this book has fetched the RSS and Golwalkar a lot of criticism for their racist tendencies, Golwalkar himself disowned authorship of the work, saying that it was a mere paraphrasing of *Rashtra Meemamsa*.[129] The original publication of the book in 1939 was altered many times thereafter and thus, there are four different versions available today. In 2006, for the first time, the RSS officially disowned this book saying, it was "neither representing the views of the grown Guruji nor of the RSS."[130] According to Kelkar, over time Guruji abandoned some of the aggressive views recorded in *We or Our Nationhood Defined*.[131] However, Vedhamanickam argues that Golwalkar philosophically subscribed to the views represented in the book whether he authored it or not, and those views were emulated by the Sangh under his 33 years of leadership. So, it is unfair for him to disclaim his authorship or the views of the book at a later point in time.[132]

Golwalkar claimed the superiority of Hinduism over Christianity because Hinduism does not accord with modern knowledge nor dogmatically force itself down the throats of others.[133] He popularized calisthenics, weapons training, and worship of Mother India, while adulating and replicating the bravery of Shivaji to secure the highest place for Hindutva ideology. During his leadership, the RSS was banned by the Indian government for the first time on charges of anti-social and anti-governmental militant activities, especially for its alleged involvement in Gandhi's murder. Savarkar and Golwalkar were arrested and put in jail for about 15 months in the murder conspiracy. The RSS was also banned during 1975–78 and in 1992.

After the death of Golwalkar, accelerated activism was furthered by the later chiefs of the RSS, Madhukar Dattatraya Deoras, popularly known as Balasaheb Deoras (chief. 1973–1993) and K. S. Sudarshan (chief. 2000–2009). Under the leadership of Deoras, RSS core membership reached 2.5

127. M. S. Golwalkar's words, quoted in Devanandan, *Gospel and Renascent Hinduism*, 31.

128. Basu, *Khaki Shorts*, 25.

129. Kelkar, *Lost Years of the RSS*, 34.

130. Mukul, "RSS Officially Disowns Golwalkar's Book."

131. Kelkar, *Lost Years of the RSS*, 35.

132. Vedhamanickam, "Serving Under the Saffron Shadow," 99.

133. Gier, *Origins of Religious Violence*, 36.

million.[134] Deoras was the first among the *Sarsanghchalaks* who was active in politics. He took dynamic steps to popularize the ideology of the RSS through simplified forms of literature such as comic books, posters, post-cards, inland letter cards, etc.[135] When K. S. Sudarshan assumed leadership, he simplified the catholicity of Hindu nationalism with analogies such as "many flowers, one garland; many rivers, one nation"[136] and emphasized that "the country can have only one culture . . . and so all must accept Ram—if not as divine, at least as the nation's hero."[137] He also stressed that all foreign churches and missionaries should be expelled and that India should have a state-controlled indigenous church.[138]

The RSS's Multi-face Vicissitudes

The RSS, which was formed as a sociocultural organization to consolidate Hindus culturally, which eschewed politics in its early stages, over the course of time became what I. K. Shukla calls the "hydra-headed RSS"[139] with versatile standards, attitudes, principles, programs, and political agendas. It was started as a non-religious, non-Brahmanical, and non-political movement with only one aim—to build Hindutva within sociocultural parameters, not as the way Hindu Mahasabha conceived the idea.[140] On the contrary, M. G. Chitkara remarks that, "The Hindutva of the RSS does not aim at creating a theocratic Hindu state," and its ideology "shows equal respect to all religions and as such is secular."[141] The RSS initially believed that the basic culture of all communities of India—Hindu, Muslim, Christian, etc.—is Hindu.[142] The RSS also admitted volunteers from all strata of society as it did not believe in caste-discrimination or suppression.[143] Contrarily, the RSS secret circulars[144] clearly indicate that since the last quarter of twentieth century, the RSS has followed the path of hatred for religious others and suppression of untouchables.

134. Hasan, *Forging Identities*, 189.

135. Hasan, *Forging Identities*, 206.

136. Basu, *Khaki Shorts*, 6.

137. Basu, *Khaki Shorts*, 7.

138. Atkins, *Encyclopedia of Modern Worldwide Extremists*, 264.

139. Shukla, *Hindutva*, 14.

140. Chitkara, *Hindutva Parivar*, 1.

141. Chitkara, *Hindutva Parivar*, xviii, 1.

142. Chitkara, *Hindutva Parivar*, xviii, 1.

143. Kelkar, *Lost Years of the RSS*, 86.

144. See Appendix D for RSS secret circular, minutes and hate-speeches.

In the 1940s, the RSS entered a strategic phase to implement its vision in both its theoretical and practical fields.[145] On October 9, 1943, Golwalkar advised "the secret enrolment of reliable and honest young Government servants, particularly teachers and clerks so as to spread the influence of the Sangh presumably in official circles."[146] On August 8, 1943, in a private meeting held at Chand, he advised Hindus not to allow any religious others to dominate them in any area of their lives and stressed that they should prepare themselves physically, morally, and politically to face those situations.[147] In another secret meeting in Jabalpur in May 1944, he commanded his followers to regard RSS's flag bhagwa as a religious symbol and not as a "mentor" or "guru."[148]

The RSS experienced a paradigm shift in its organizational maneuvers and ideology when it went from the hands of Hedgewar into the hands of Golwalkar and then to Balasaheb Deoras. After the RSS was banned by the government in 1948, there was also an internal conflict between Guruji and Deoras in the areas of implementing policies and managing finances. While the leadership of Golwalkar was spiritual, saintly, and ritualistically oriented, Deoras was a strongly mission-minded man.[149] In these differentiated passions, the slogans of the RSS were slightly altered, its banner christened itself as the Ram Sewak Sangh,[150] and its ideology moved from protecting "Hindu Dharma" to protecting "Hinduism" in order to "set Hinduism on a progressive path or turn it inward upon itself in a self-satisfied growing exclusiveness."[151] In the process of its growth and progression of its vision, it has become hydra-headed, giving rise to multi-faceted Hindutva movements which have received varied receptions and reactions.

Sanjeev Kelkar, who was brought up in a diehard RSS family in Nagpur and who worked closely with the RSS for forty-three years, admits in his well-narrated first-hand account, *The Lost Years of the RSS,* that the RSS has drastically moved from its earliest vision, ideals, and passion, which made him leave the RSS.[152] The prayer which was composed in 1939 by

145. Basu, *Khaki Shorts,* 25.

146. Government of Madhya Pradesh, *State History Committee,* note on Volunteer Organization in C.P., 3.

147. Government of Madhya Pradesh, *State History Committee,* note on Volunteer Organization in C.P., 3.

148. Government of Madhya Pradesh, *State History Committee,* note on Volunteer Organization in C.P., 3.

149. Joshi, "Shraddheya," 34.

150. Shukla, *Hindutva,* 14.

151. Kelkar, *Lost Years of the RSS,* 149–50.

152. Kelkar, *Lost Years of the RSS,* 32.

the RSS and was recited for six decades by its members doesn't talk about freeing the country from the British or the enemies of the nation or killing them.[153] Hedgewar's vision of the RSS was simple in that he wanted to see a "Common Civic Nationalist Character" in Hindus for the welfare of society and never intended "aggression as a habit or article of faith."[154] According to Kelkar, the RSS became a Hindu sect and has drastically compromised its ethics and principles and is no longer concerned about the fundamental needs of the nation.[155]

The Sangh Parivar

The Sangh Parivar refers to the family of Hindu nationalist organizations, whose archetypes are aligned with or fully subscribed to the philosophical framework of Hindutva delineated by the RSS. There are dozens of institutions in India and abroad allied with the RSS which operate autonomously with varied sociocultural, political, and charitable activities. Their ideological affiliation keeps them under the umbrella of the RSS although they differ in their shades of saffron beliefs. The core belief and the common agenda of all these institutions is "the supremacy of Hindutva in the Indian scheme of things"[156] and the cultural rejuvenation of India. Sangh has covered all spheres of life with its pervasive ideology of Hindutva, including the political, professional, economic, social, religious, educational, ecological, cultural, and academic areas of the Indian social fabric.[157] This section deals with only the three organizations of Sangh Parivar of national importance—RSS, Vishva Hindu Parishad, and the Bharatiya Janata Party—because they together have "the unique power of defining what being a Hindu means"[158] and are in the forefront of diplomatically suppressing religious others in the nation.

Vishva Hindu Parishad (VHP) and its Nationalist Activism

VHP was founded in Mumbai on August 29, 1964, at the instigation of Golwalkar and Shivram Shankar Apte to consolidate Hindu society and

---

153. Kelkar, *Lost Years of the RSS*, 10.

154. Kelkar, *Lost Years of the RSS*, 11.

155. Kelkar, *Lost Years of the RSS*, 32.

156. Chitkara, *Hindutva Parivar*, xiv.

157. See Appendix E for the list of Sangh Parivar organizations.

158. Basu, *Khaki Shorts*, 57.

to serve and protect the Hindu Dharma in India and beyond.[159] According to VHP, during the millenniums of serfdom (800 years under Islam and 200 years under the British), Hindus were made to forget their self-esteem, self-respect, and eminence and were made to undermine their greatest personalities like Shriram, Shrikrishna, Goutam, Mahavir, Shankaracharya, Chanakya, Patanjali etc., who were the products of the glorious Hindu cultural stock. Their situation of slavery also made them forget that they are the progeny of the cultural tradition of the great scriptures like Veda, Shastras, Puranas, Ramayana, Mahabharata, Gita etc. Therefore, VHP was formed to restore to Hindus their historical and cultural Hindu pride. It marks a new phase in the history of Hindutva as it operates as an indomitable force and strives to safeguard the core values, beliefs, and sacred traditions of Hinduism by resisting Christian conversions of Hindus, reclaiming converts through *ghar wapsi* programs, renovating Hindu temples and rendering social services to those in need.

The prominence of VHP became evident as early as 1966 with its vital involvement in the issue of Ram Janmabhoomi and by its launching of violent agitation activities against cow-slaughter in 1967. VHP also led movements on the issues of Shri Amarnath yatra, Shri Ramsetu, Shri Ganga Raksha, Go Raksha, the Hindu Mutt-mandir issue, the religious conversions of Hindus by the Christian Church, Islamic terrorism, Bangladeshi Muslim infiltration, etc. It was VHP that placed before the country the issue of the mosque in Ayodhya and which mobilized a massive movement to liberate the site.[160] It also sponsored several *dharma sansads* to discuss the ways and means to achieve this goal. On October 6, 1984, VHP campaigned for Hindu nationalist candidates who ran in the Lok Sabah elections, promising the public to champion Hindu demands, and particularly to replace the Babri Masjid which had stood since 1528 with the Sri Ram Temple.[161] With the political support of BJP, the activists of Sangh Parivar took the task into their own hands and proved their Hindu pride by destroying the Babri Masjid in December 1992. With this gruesome incident, VHP and the Sangh Parivar radicals gained immense momentum and the courage to violently attack religious minorities, particularly Christians and their institutions in the following years.

In both public and private, VHP has been on the forefront of communal and religious violence. On February 27, 2002, VHP and Bajrang Dal activists set the train returning from Ayodhya on fire. According to

159. Hasan, *Forging Identities*, 218.

160. Goel, *Hindu Temples*, vii.

161. Goel, *Hindu Temples*, vii.

human rights organizations, close to 2,000 Muslims were killed and as many as 100,000 Muslims were driven from their homes. Women were stripped and gang-raped, and parents were bludgeoned to death in front of their children.[162]

While speaking of the Gujarat carnage of 2002 at a press conference held in Jaipur on December 14, 2002, VHP general secretary Praveen Togadia commented that, "We will make a laboratory of the whole country. This is our promise and our resolve . . . . Rajasthan has already become the laboratory of Hindutva . . . The people of Gujarat have paid their tribute to the Ram Bhaktas of Godhra. Gujarat has become the graveyard of secular ideology and we will extend it to Delhi via Jaipur."[163] The Dangs district of Gujarat became the epicentre of the war against Christianity. VHP activists demonize Christianity as a dangerous foreign conspiracy to destabilize India and regularly threaten tribal Christians "to divide and communalise tribal communities and further distance them from justice."[164] Since 1998, quite a number of atrocities have been committed against Bhil and Warli Christian communities by VHP.[165]

VHP strives to constitute *Hindu Rashtra* ideals in sociocultural and religious spaces by means of various programs organised by its missionary wing called *Dharma Prasaar Vibhag* (Dharma Propagation Unit) and by violent activities by Bajrang Dal activists. Their slogan is *Ram Rajya* and their flag is the *bhagwa dhwaj* (the saffron flag of flame). While the RSS, the fountainhead of aggressive Hindu communalism, establishes differentiated cultural attitudes through stereotypes and symbols, VHP and BJP take advantage of technological opportunities like video films, audio cassettes, websites, stickers, and other means to popularize a Hindutva communal message.[166] The VHP rhetoric about the suppression of non-Hindus is often echoed in the language of their Hindu-right hate speeches and pamphlets,[167] igniting the anger of Hindu youth against religious others. VHP activists belligerently defend[168] their anti-Christian violence by engineering allegations against Christian activities and blanketing the nation with anti-Christian propaganda. Hate pamphlets are usually appeals made

162. See Roy, "Fascism's Firm Footprint in India."

163. *The Hindustan Times*, December 16, 2002. For more hate-speeches of VHP and other Hindu nationalists, see Gujarat Riots. "Gujarat Carnage 2002."

164. Mander, "Incursions of Hindutva."

165. Mander, "Incursions of Hindutva."

166. Basu, *Khaki Shorts,* ix.

167. Nussbaum, *Clash Within,* 27.

168. Tiwary, "VHP Defends Attack on Haryana Church."

to Hindus in the name of Ram and Lord Hanuman against Muslims[169] or Christians. Through a pamphlet written by A. Shankar titled, *Warning: India in Danger,* VHP advises Hindus to place large signposts in public spaces "highlighting Hindu principles," to fly saffron flags and to place *om* symbol stickers on doors and walls, and decals on private and public vehicles.[170] VHP also asks the readers of the book to photocopy and circulate the pamphlet among at least twenty more people.

BAJRANG DAL AND ANTI-CHRISTIAN MILITANCY

Bajrang Dal (BD) is a youth wing of VHP which looks after the training of young boys in the martial arts for the practical support of the vision of VHP. Bajrang Dal means "Troops of Hanuman"—the strong monkey deity worshipped as Ram's faithful servant, a traditional patron of wrestlers.[171] They are mostly active in times of communal conflicts with non-Hindu religious others.[172] BD recruits "untrained, volatile, semi-lumpen elements in contrast to the hand-picked and thoroughly-coached RSS cadres . . . "[173] It is known for its reckless, undisciplined acts of violence against Christians and Muslims.

BD was constituted by VHP in 1984 with a temporary, localized objective of awakening the youth of Uttar Pradesh to become involved in the Ram Janmabhoomi Movement.[174] Since BD received an abundant response from Hindu youths, in 1986, VHP decided to establish branches all over India. It has about 500,000 active workers who are devoted to the service of Mother India and Hindu Dharma.

BD plays a pivotal role in Hindu awakening and majoritarian aggression through anti-Christian propaganda, protests, and agitation activities. Its members vow to spring into action for the rescue of Hindus whenever there is a criticism or philosophical attack on their religion or Hindu society.[175] In 2006, Bajrang Dal activists were caught in the process of making bombs and other explosives in Malegaon, Maharashtra, to explode the mosque in that region.[176] In 2008, the National Commission for Minorities, the Indian National Congress, Lok Janashakti Party, and others

169. See Appendix F for an example of a hate-pamphlet of VHP against Muslims.

170. Basu, *Khaki Shorts,* 60.

171. Gold, "Organized Hinduisms," 581.

172. Basu, *Khaki Shorts,* 60, 68.

173. Basu, *Khaki Shorts,* 60, 68.

174. Vishva Hindu Parishad, "Bajrang Dal."

175. Vishva Hindu Parishad, "Bajrang Dal."

176. Swami, "Malegaon."

described BD as a communal, anti-secular, and anti-national organization and demanded its ban.[177]

Encyclopedia of Modern Worldwide Extremists and Extremist Groups includes BD as the most militant wing of the RSS, whose hostility was extended to Buddhists and Christians in the 1990s.[178] In addition to opposing by violent means Christian conversions and cow-slaughter, they file cases against Christians and Muslims, accusing them of involvement in forcible conversions. In most of the anti-Christian violent activities which have escalated since the 1990s, Bajrang Dal has been named as chief orchestrator or perpetrator. In December 2014, Dharm Jagran Samiti (DJS), an offshoot of the RSS, which works closely with the VHP in *ghar wapsi* programs, cooperated with BD and distributed propaganda pamphlets against Christians and Muslims in Aligarh, UP, saying "they are a problem" in India. Through those handbills, they also solicited funds for their reconversion programs. According to Dharm Jagaran Samiti, it costs Rs. 500,000 ($ 8,200) to reconvert a Muslim and Rs. 200,000 ($3,200) for a Christian.[179] During a *ghar wapsi* event in Agra on December 8, 2014, Rajeshwar Singh, the leader of BJS, publicly declared, "Our target is to make India a *Hindu Rashtra* by 2021. The Muslims and Christians don't have any right to stay here . . . So they would either be converted to Hinduism or forced to run away. I will ensure that India is freed of Muslims and Christians by December 31, 2021."[180] This sensational comment fetched him immediate suspension from the RSS in front of media and the public, and also a promotion in the RSS cadre in the following month.

INDEPENDENCE MOVEMENT AND CONFLICT OF INTERESTS

The leaders of the freedom movement like Dadabhai Naoroji, Gokhale, Lajpat Rai, Rajnarain Bose, Tilak, Aurobindo, and others made stirring appeals before their countrymen against the British and led the pre-Gandhian *Swadeshi Movements*. In the struggle for freedom, the participation of Indian Christian leaders and the support of foreign missionaries to the nationalist cause cannot be discounted. J. Kuruvachira notes that as early as 1887, there were 15 Indian Christians who participated in the Indian National Congress. H. C. Mukherjee, Madhu Sudhan Das, Kali Charan Banerjee, Brahmabandav Upadyay, Pandita Ramabai Saraswati, Triumbuck,

---

177. Ramaseshan, "Cabinet to Discuss Bajrang."

178. Atkins, *Encyclopedia of Modern Worldwide Extremists*, 264.

179. Nag, "RSS Body Dharam Jagran Samiti Sets Fixed Rates for Converting."

180. Srivastava, "We Will Free India of Muslims and Christians."

and Nikambe were among the earliest who called for "independence." In Tamil Nadu alone 103 Christians are believed to have participated in the freedom movement. Among the notable missionaries who gave full support to the nationalist cause were C. F. Andrews, J. C. Winslow, Varrier Elwin, Ralph Richard Keithahn, and Ernest Forrester-Paton.[181]

Due to frustration from the partition of Bengal in 1905, the Congress was split into two sections, the so-called extremists and the moderates. While the incensed extremists nurtured the spirit of militant nationalism,[182] the moderates continued with the ideological plans of Congress to represent the masses. The Indian National Congress (INC), which was the most prominent of all, was criticized by the extremists for its lack of aggressiveness in its struggle and approach for liberation. At times Lajpat Rai and Bankim Chandra Chatterji pointed out that the INC was deficient in advanced political ideas and would be proved unequal to the task. Until Mahatma Gandhi came to preside over its destiny, INC's leadership could not inspire India as a whole.[183]

Gandhi's Vision of Liberated India

Gandhi led the non-cooperation movement with two weapons—*Satyagraha* and *Ahimsa*, which proved powerful enough to affect the liberating of the nation. He denounced the militant aspect of nationalism and believed that freedom could be achieved by means of *Ahimsa* (non-violence), to which extremist leaders muttered, "Non-violence looks good only in the hands of those who have power, not in the hands of those who are without any."[184] Gandhi believed that unless Muslims joined Congress and worked together in the struggle for freedom, independence was not possible.[185] Undermining the conflicts between the Hindu extremists and Muslim Khilafats, Gandhi attempted to bring Muslims and Hindus together under the common cause of "freedom from the foreign dominion."

Gandhi dreamt of an independent India of *sarva dharma samabhava*, a Hindu concept of equality (equal respect) for all religions, as embraced and

181. Kuruvachira, "Indian Christians and the Independence Movement," 355–58. Contrarily, A. J. Appasamy, Eddy Asirvatham, and others argue that Indian Christian community as a whole did not participate in the freedom movement due to some political or spiritual reasons. See Appasamy, *Christian Task in Independent India*, 2; Asirvatham, *Christianity in the Indian Crucible*, 26.

182. Majumdar, *History of the Freedom Movement*, 145.

183. Majumdar, *History of the Freedom Movement*, 375.

184. Kelkar, *Lost Years of the RSS*, 5.

185. Kelkar, *Lost Years of the RSS*, 5.

advocated by Ramakrishna and Vivekananda. "*Sarva dharma samabhava*" is a dogma in Hinduism which means "all religions are equal" or "equal respect for all religions." However, in recent times this term has acquired many anomalies. It is now almost similar to the English idiom, "all roads lead to Rome," meaning, all religions are the same though they prescribe different paths to God. Alongside holding the concept of *sarva dharma samabhava*, Gandhi voiced strong opposition to Christian conversions.

Like Vivekananda, Gandhi was an inclusivist with a vengeance. Gandhi detested conversions to keep Hinduism intact. Even more, he criticized conversion to Christianity of the members of the depressed classes,[186] who for centuries had not enjoyed social equality in the traditional caste structure of Hindu society. B. R. Ambedkar's vision of constitutional reforms for the depressed classes and his ardent passion to purge untouchability and discrimination practiced by caste Hindus pushed Gandhi to consent to purifying Hinduism through voluntary reform by caste Hindus, including opening temples to the lower sections of Hindu society.[187] However, it was clear from the challenge of Ambedkar, who pledged that he would not die a Hindu, that there would be a religious exodus of the depressed classes from Hinduism sooner or later as Muslims, Sikhs, and Buddhists were making desperate efforts to capture those leaving.[188] Ambedkar, Bishop Pickett, and others viewed Gandhi's proposal of temple-entry and anti-untouchability reforms as being politically motivated.[189] Gandhi, who acknowledged that Ambedkar was a challenge to Hinduism, attempted various protectionist efforts, including the Poona Pact, to keep *harijans* within the Hindu fold. This proved impossible as shown in October 1956 in Nagpur when Ambedkar along with more than 200,000 people converted to Budhhism.

Although Gandhi detested Christian conversions practiced by missionaries and opposed them outrightly, he did not place converted Christians in the category of non-Hindu or "threatening other." He said, "I am not against conversion. But I am against the modern methods of it. Conversion nowadays has become a matter of business."[190]

At times, Gandhi suspected newly converted Christians' loyalty to the State as they were often persuaded by the Western way of life lived and introduced by foreign missionaries.[191] He also confronted missionaries'

186. Gandhi, *Hindu Dharma*, 352.

187. McPhee, *Road to Delhi*, 240.

188. McPhee, *Road to Delhi*, 241.

189. McPhee, *Road to Delhi*, 242.

190. Gandhi, *Truth is God*, 67.

191. Thomas, "Christian Missions in the Pluralistic Context of India," 192.

theological exclusiveness and proselytization efforts among the illiterate and the poor, but he did not mobilize Hindus against Christian converts or conversions. He rather cautioned Christian missionaries that their efforts would draw suspicion, if not hostility.[192] His resistance to conversions affirmed a Hindu past and created a sense of oneness among Hindus as did the common belief that conversions were the instrument of British colonialism and must be opposed.[193]

Hindu nationalists undoubtedly dislike Gandhi for making concessions to Muslims and for two oft-stressed things— first, that the "enmity against Englishmen or Europeans must be wholly forgotten"[194] and second, for the philosophy of *sarva dharma samabhava*[195] which binds the idea of religious tolerance to the upholding of equality of all religions. However, Gandhi's anti-conversion stance evidently produced a strange marriage between him and the Hindu nationalists.[196] They esteem Gandhi's ardent opposing to Christian conversions and herald him as voice of reason when opposed to Christian proselytization, making use of his anti-missionary rhetoric.

In 1935, when a missionary nurse asked Gandhi about the works of foreign missionaries, he replied, "If I had power and could legislate, I should certainly stop all proselytizing."[197] This political statement strengthens the idea of a legal prohibition to Christian conversions in India, an outcome which Hindu nationalists pursue. To bring about an anti-conversion spirit among ordinary Hindus, nationalists compile and distribute Gandhi's writings and speeches on how he reviled Christian conversions and opposed them to the core. For example, in 1950s, *The Hindu Outlook* of Hindu Mahasabha published a series of thought-provoking articles such as "Advent of Missionary Means Disruption of Hindu Households: How Gandhiji Developed Aversion to Conversions"[198] and "10,000 Hindus taken away from Hinduism Every Day: Call to Mahants to Save Country."[199]

Ram Swarup (1920–1998) is among the earliest who borrowed many of Gandhi's anti-conversion perceptions for his purposes and popularized those propositions in the 1980s. This lit a fire in the hearts of his fellow

192. Gandhi, *Truth is God,* 65–67.

193. Viswanathan, "Literacy and Conversion," 1, 3.

194. Nehru, *Discovery of India,* 112.

195. Gandhi, *Young India,* September 25, 1924.

196. Mills, *Conversion,* 273. See also Viswanathan, "Literacy and Conversion," 1, 3.

197. Gandhi, "Interview to a Missionary Nurse."

198. *The Hindu Outlook,* June 13, 1954.

199. *The Hindu Outlook,* March 28, 1954, 5.

Hindu nationalist scholars—Sita Ram Goel, Girilal Jain, Kanayalal Talreja, and later Arun Shourie and many others. In 1982, he constituted the Voice of India publishing house, which he used exclusively to promote a plethora of works aimed at Hindu apologetics and critiquing non-Hindu faiths, particularly Islam and Christianity. In 1981, H. V. Seshadri, a senior leader of RSS, compiled a booklet titled, *Christian Missions in the Eyes of Gandhiji*, in which Sheshadri carefully builds an anti-conversion argument by highlighting Gandhi's attitude toward Christian conversions and his anti-missional views.

Hindu Nationalist Construction of "Freedom"

The Hindu nationalist characterization of "freedom" is complex and beyond political parameters. The Hindu nationalists' perceived goal of liberation was not only to reclaim India from the long established Western socio-political and religious impositions, but also to get rid of the threatening others from within the country.[200] In order to clearly understand the Hindu nationalist perspective of freedom, Manjari Katju suggests that it "has to be read in the militant and majoritarian ideas of Hindu resurgence as articulated by the Sangh Parivar."[201] The advocates of Hindu nationalism fight tooth and nail against those religious others who try to assume freedom equal to Hindus in the areas of religion, social status, and legal provisions. They claim that the freedom which India achieved belongs only to the "Hindu race" and it cannot be expanded to non-Hindus. As Katju points out, they do not question the idea of freedom but engage in this ideological battle by re-defining the idea of freedom in a manner which would keep their privileges intact."[202]

India's Independence as Partial Freedom

The freedom which V. D. Savarkar and M. S. Golwalkar long envisioned was beyond territorial and political freedom, and was certainly not secularism. For Savarkar, it was *swarajya* with *swadharma*.[203] He emphasized that, "The command of God is, Obtain Swaraj, for that is the chief key to the protection of Dharma. He who does not attempt to acquire Swaraj, he who sits silent in slavery, he is an atheist and hater of Religion. Therefore,

---

200. Jaffrelot, *Hindu Nationalist Movement in India*, 2, 8.
201. Katju, "Understanding of Freedom in Hindutva," 19.
202. Katju, "Understanding of Freedom in Hindutva," 2.
203. Savarkar, *War of Independence*, 3–12.

rise for Swadharma and acquire Swaraj!"[204] Savarkar's watchword was "Hinduize politics and militarize Hinduism."[205]

Golwalkar had well represented the dream of Savarakar in his campaign speeches. Beginning in the 1940s he mobilized Hindus to look beyond India's political freedom. For him, the freedom which India achieved in 1947 was a partial one. He remarked that liberation was achieved on the idea of Hindu-Muslim unity, the result of which indicates that "Hindus were defeated at the hands of Muslims in 1947."[206] India's partition was not a freedom, but rather a shame. The bitter fruit of independence left Hindu nationalists in despair because they couldn't avenge Muslims adequately before the partition and they also lost a good portion of India to Muslims. For Golwalkar, the fight for independence had to continue until complete Hindu nationhood was achieved. Right-wing Hindutva advocates saw independence as incomplete because the British were gone but their place was taken by a secular, anti-Hindu leadership which challenged their ideology.[207]

HINDUS AS VICTIMS OF RELIGIOUS SLAVERY

On his 51st birthday, Golwalkar remarked, "Now that we are free from foreign rule and that steps are being taken to achieve economic freedom, let us endeavor to fight against our religious slavery."[208] In the minds of some people like Ram Swarup, "India became politically free in 1947," but "the old mental slavery continues and it (India) has yet to win its cultural and intellectual independence. India is entering into the second phase of its freedom struggle: the struggle for regaining its Hindu identity."[209] The literature of VHP, which largely reflects this imagery, portrays Hindus as if they were forced into a sort of non-Hindu cultural bondage, and VHP members as if they have sacrificially taken upon themselves the task of saving Hindus from those influences. For example, Swami Parmanand wrote in the bi-monthly of VHP, *Hindu Chetna,* that, "Today all that is happening in the country which did not even happen during the days of slavery (colonial rule). What we did not lose during the days of slavery we have lost in the era of freedom. We are increasingly coming under the grip

---

204. Savarkar, *War of Independence*, 10.

205. See SPPAI, January 1, 1944, 46, 3–5, quoted in Jalal, *Self and Sovereignty,* 426. See also Khare, "Militarising of Hindudom," 7.

206. Golwalkar, *Bunch of Thoughts*, 152.

207. Katju, "Understanding of Freedom in Hindutva," 9.

208. Devadas, *Ideologies of Political Parties*, 19. See also *Hitavada,* "RSS Rally," 3.

209. Swarup, *Hindu View of Christianity and Islam*, 114.

of Western culture. No political leader is thinking about this. . . ."[210] Such assertions indicate that India's current exercise of political independence is bestowed with cultural slavery due to which Hindus continue to lack freedom in their own independent country.

The Sangh Parivar, which feeds on this framework, relentlessly strives to bring India under the nationhood of Hindu culture and Hindu *dharma* mostly by marginalizing, suppressing and purging the non-Hindu others, especially Muslims and Christians. Since the last quarter of the twentieth century, especially when BJP gained a measurable acceptance in Indian politics, Hindu nationalists have boldly embarked on infringing upon Christian communities with concerted efforts to label them as alien, treacherous, anti-social, counter-cultural and anti-national.

MUSLIMS AND CHRISTIANS AS THREATENING OTHERS

Advocates of Hindutva philosophy portray Muslims and Christians as the common enemy of the land. As Jaffrelot indicated, "the development of a collective Hindu consciousness was inhibited not only by the extreme social and religious differentiation within Hinduism but also by a tendency to discount the importance of the Other and therefore to ignore the need for solidarity in the face of that Other."[211] By analyzing the doctrinal differences and missional commonalities between Islamic conquerors and western imperialists, Hindu nationalists tend to emphasize the affinity and mutual appreciation of Muslims and Christians in affecting or damaging Hindu religious traditions and culture in history. Ram Swarup stressed that Christians[212] contested and complemented Muslims for their own benefit. He adds that for Christians, "Islam was evil but its role in destroying idolatry with a strong hand was praiseworthy." However, "Islam . . . . as opposed to the Gospel . . . . is a 'curse,' but as the pre-appointed scourge of heresy and heathenism, as cleansing the world from the gross pollutions of idolatry, and preparing the way for the reception of a purer faith [Christianity], it may well be regarded as a blessing."[213]

Sita Ram Goel criticizes the attitude of Indian Muslims, stating that they "are not at all prepared to take pride in any period of pre-Islamic Indian history, or honour any hero who flourished in that period. They want the pre-Islamic period of Indian history to be disowned even by Hindus as an

210. Katju, "Understanding of Freedom in Hindutva," 16.

211. Jaffrelot, *Hindu Nationalist Movement in India*, 2.

212. Ram Swarup quotes Charles Forster, a clergyman of the Church of England, from *Mohammedanism Unveiled* (1829).

213. Swarup, *Hindu View of Christianity and Islam*, 14, 34.

'era of darkness'"[214] . . . and "show no appreciation for Hindu masterpieces of architecture, sculpture, and other plastic arts."[215]

To show Christians as a major threat over Muslims, Girilal Jain maintained that, "the British remained foreigners, while the Muslim invaders and immigrants made India their home, and that the British drained India of its wealth which Muslim rulers did not because the latter settled down here for good."[216] Contrarily, Ashis Nandy remarked that, between 1757 and 1830 "most Britons in India lived like Indians at home and in the office, wore Indian dress, and observed Indian customs and religious practices. A large number of them married Indian women, offered *puja* to Indian gods and goddesses, and lived in fear and awe of the magical powers of the Brahmans."[217]

Nehru's Secular Ideology and Religious Freedom

Along with the struggle for independence there came unending Hindu-Muslim conflicts and spiraling Hindu-non-Hindu disparities. After the assassination of Gandhi in January 1948, there was a cry for *Hindu Rashtra* during communal riots. It was the first Prime Minister of India, Jawaharlal Nehru, who led resistance to the communal onslaught. He gained an absolute majority in the 1951 elections, leaving the communal Hindu forces in despair. In contrast to the Hindu nationalist mantra that saw people of non-Hindu faiths as non-Indian, counter-cultural, and non-patriotic or anti-national, Nehru argued that Indian converts to the faiths of non-Indian origin "never ceased to be Indians in spite of a change of faith."[218] He favored and promoted the secular ideology which does not discriminate people based on religious differences or place one religion above the other. He did not agree with Hindu nationalists on the matter of monopolizing "Indian culture as Hindu culture" either. He refuted this idea saying, "It is misleading."[219]

Referring to the militant nationalist groups, Nehru said,

> New movements arose, narrow in outlook but representing a
> resurgent nationalism, and though they were not strong enough
> to build permanently, they were capable of destroying the

214. Goel, *Story of Islamic Imperialism in India*, 5.
215. Goel, *Story of Islamic Imperialism in India*, 5.
216. Jain, *Hindu Phenomenon*, 7.
217. Nandy, *Intimate Enemy*, 5.
218. Nehru, *Discovery of India*, 51.
219. Nehru, *Discovery of India*, 64.

empire of Moghuls. They were successful for a time, but they looked too much to the past and thought in terms of reviving it. They did not realize that much had happened which they could not ignore or pass by; that the past can never take the place of the present; that even that present in the India of their day was one of stagnation and decay. It had lost touch with the changing world and left India far behind. They did not appreciate that a new and vital world was arising in the West, based on a new outlook and on new techniques, and a new power, the British represented that new world of which they were so ignorant.[220]

In Nehru's opinion, conversion to Islam or Christianity aroused no particular opposition until the mid-twentieth century, except when force or some kind of compulsion was used by the Moors. He believed that conversions attracted widespread attention, indifferent attitudes and opposition largely due to political factors, especially to the introduction of separate religious electorates.[221] Apart from political topographies, he identified the growth of a tendency in Hinduism to proselytize and convert non-Hindus to Hinduism.[222]

The first president of India, Rajendra Prasad, was of the opinion that when people are identified as Hindu, Muslim, or Christian, it only indicates the differences in their religious beliefs, but all of them who reside in India belong to one and the same nation.[223] At the St. Thomas anniversary celebration on December 14, 1952, President Rajendra Prasad addressed the crowd, accentuating that "the freedom of religion granted by India's constitution is a 'genuine guarantee,'" while Prime Minister Nehru emphasized in his speech, "The various religions, creeds and faiths that exist [here] are equally of India; we all are partners in a great inheritance. . .To imagine that those who follow a slightly different path from ours are somehow foreign to India is wrong. The fact that a religion or a truth came from another country does not make it foreign. Truth is truth wherever it may originate."[224]

While the advocates of Hindu nationalism negatively pictured non-Hindu religious adherents as the plunderers of India's wealth, religious traditions and culture, Nehru viewed foreign conquest as the result of India's inadequacy and Britain's representation of a higher and advancing social

---

220. Nehru, *Discovery of India*, 133.

221. Nehru, *Discovery of India*, 264.

222. Nehru, *Discovery of India*, 264.

223. Prasad, *India Divided*, 79, 89.

224. *The Christian Century*, January 14, 1953, 58.

order,[225] not because of their religious superiority alone. While Hindutvavadis strive to reclaim India's ancient religious and cultural heritage and overcome embedded inferiority by showing the world its past greatness, Nehru
wanted to take India to compete at levels of social order equal to those of European countries. Nehru's theory was that India could not progress because
of its inherent limitations, particularly its "static society wedded to medieval
habits of thought."[226] Having said that, Nehru does not deny the economic
destruction, agricultural decay, and other calamities caused by the British
monopoly of economic policies, business, and administration.

THE RSS AND HINDUTVA REPRESENTATION
IN POLITICS

The founder of the RSS, Hedgewar refused to allow the movement to enter
into active politics. The RSS sometimes leaned on the political influence
of Hindu Mahasabha, but was not content with Mahasabha's representation in politics and looked for an adequate new platform.[227] But at the
juncture of independence, the leaders of the RSS, particularly Golwalkar
and Deoras, felt the need for political power in order to take advantage of
the achieved freedom for the Hindutva agenda and to tackle the secular
ideology espoused by the Congress Party. While Golwalkar wanted to keep
himself and the RSS away from active politics, Deoras, next in leadership
to Golwalkar, believed in and pushed Golwalkar on the idea of making the
RSS authoritative from the political perspective as a way to achieve Hindutva strategies. Some prominent Savarkarites (Savarkarites are anti-Gandhi,
anti-nonviolence, and anti-democratic) like Jayaprakash Narayan, Syama
Prasad Mukherjee, Deendayal Upadhyaya, K. M. Munshi, and others were
part of the Congress party even after independence, but their extremist
dogma was overshadowed by the secular, socialist, democratic ideals of
Congress headed by Nehru until they fell out with Nehru to create an opposition force against the Congress. Following the killing of Gandhi, the
RSS was banned with the arrest of Golwalkar along with 20,000 *Swayam-
sevaks* in January 1948[228]. After a 15-month trial, the government acquit-
ted Golwalkar and dropped charges against the RSS, lifting the ban, as
Nathuram Vinayak Godse, a former Hindu Mahasabha member, admitted

225. Nehru, *Discovery of India,* 280.

226. Nehru, *Discovery of India,* 290.

227. Sharma, "Bharatiya Jana Sangh," 16.

228. When RSS workers protested the arrest of Golwalkar, about 50,000 *swayamse-
vaks* were arrested. See Jhangiani, *Jana Sangh and Swatantra,* 14.

that he acted on his own.[229] The ban of RSS and the arrest of its leader led the RSS to feel the need to enter politics as some thought that if the RSS had political representation in parliament, it would not have been possible for the government to ban the RSS.

Bharatiya Jana Sangh (BJS)

Bharatiya Jana Sangh was an offshoot of the Hindu Mahasabha and a political arm of the RSS. The members of Arya Samaj, Ram Rajya Parishad, Hindu Mahasabha, and the RSS entered the political arena as Jana Sangh workers to engage in political combat with the Nehruvian secularism of the Congress espousing a narrow militant path.[230] In the late 1960s, the xenophobic dimensions of the BJS became more evident through the writings of its president, Balraj Madhok, who leaned on the views of Savarkar and Golwalkar to Indianize minorities.[231] Hence, BJS has been variedly labeled as "reactionary, communal, Hindu revivalist, ultra-rightist and militant Hindu nationalist in its ideological orientation and organizational behavior."[232] The Hindu Mahasabha has supported the Congress Nationalist Party in political spheres since 1937, providing its militant voice for the formation of *Hindu Rashtra* and opposed to the division of the nation along Hindu-Muslim population lines.[233] When the "calamity" (the Partition of India and separation of Hindus and Muslims) which the Mahasabha feared came to pass on August 15, 1947, alongside freedom, the movement eventually culminated as a political party in 1951.[234]

With Gandhi's murder, the influence of Hindu Mahasabha and the RSS reached their low ebb, though government was not able to prove the involvement of either of them in the crime. Syama Prasad Mukherjee, who was the vice-president of Mahasabha, could secure a position in Nehru's cabinet, but was not able to get along with the government led by the Congress Party for long due to ideological disparities. Neither was he able to cope with Hindu Mahasabha leaders on internal personality issues as he was an organized

229. However, the incident was and is still linked to RSS because the Hindu Mahasabha is the ideological arm of the RSS, and the RSS gave voluntary support to the Hindu Mahasabha, though these connections virtually ceased in 1940. For more information, see Anderson, "Rashtriya Swayamsevak Sangh," 673–68; Jeevan Lal Kapur Commission Report; Jhangiani, *Jana Sangh and Swatantra*, 14.

230. Frykenberg, "Hindu Fundamentalism," 243.

231. Jaffrelot, *Religion, Caste and Politics in India*, 47.

232. Puri, *Bharatiya Jana Sangh*, 5.

233. Baxter, *Jana Sangh*, 20.

234. Baxter, *Jana Sangh*, 20.

personality. Due to the lack of a dedicated cadre in the Hindu Mahasabha (HM), Savarkar often made independent decisions in the organization, which annoyed Mukherjee and strained his relationship with HM leaders, leading to his resignation from HM. Mookerji formed Bharatiya Jana Sangh in 1951 as a nationalist alternative to the Congress Party. While maintaining links with the right-wing *Swatantrata* party of C. Rajagopalachari, Jana Sangh shared an ideological platform with the Hindu Mahasabha and fed on the strategic plans of the RSS to infuse the ideals of Hindutva into political structures.[235] The RSS extended its cooperation and collaboration in the formation and progress of the party. According to Walter Andersen and Shridhar Damle, most of the leadership and the leading activists of the Jana Sangh underwent a period of training within RSS.[236]

In the 1952 elections, Jana Sangh marginally won three seats in Lok Sabha (LS) and thirty-four in Legislative Assembly (LA) while Hindu Mahasabha experienced similar or lesser outcomes. However, BJS rose to some prominence in the 1967 elections with thirty-five LS and two hundred sixty-four LA seats, leaving no luck for Hindu Mahasabha.[237] In 1957 Atal Bihari Vajpayee became a member of the parliament for the first time and moved to Delhi to assist BJS president Mukherjee. In 1969 Vajpayee and in 1973 L. K. Advani became presidents of the party. In 1977 BJS merged with several political movements that opposed the rule of the Indian National Congress and emerged as the Janata Party until it reemerged as the Bharatiya Janata Party (BJP) in 1980 under the leadership of Vajpayee.

BJS had its origins in a defense mechanism which had essentially religious moorings and was politicized since its inception.[238] Jana Sangh was the embodiment of an ideological view similar to that of Hindu Mahasabha, and it maintained the aspirations of the former Hindu revivalists who believed that political freedom was essential for religious and cultural freedom and hence supplied their fullest support to the development of Hindu pride over religious minorities, particularly in Rajasthan and Madhya Pradesh.[239] Although BJS did not include the minority or majority aspect in its 1951 election manifesto, its 1962 manifesto clearly spoke of nationalizing all non-Hindu Others by inculcating in them the Hindu culture and of freeing Indian Christians from the anti-national influences of foreign missionaries.

235. Sharma, *Bharatiya Jana Sangh*, 15.

236. Andersen, *Brotherhood of Saffron*, 5.

237. Sharma, *Bharatiya Jana Sangh*, 14.

238. Sharma, *Bharatiya Jana Sangh*, 3

239. Sharma, *Bharatiya Jana Sangh*, 11, 32, 39.

Bharatiya Janata Party and Communalism

The BJP is the child of the RSS, heir of Hindu Mahasabha and the successor party of the BJS. It embodies the ideology and political strategy of the RSS to subjugate minorities under the ideals of Hindutva.[240] Under the leadership of A. B. Vajpayee, in 1980, the BJP was founded as a separate Hindu nationalist party with a renewed vision and vigor. It is a member of Sangh Parivar, thoroughly nurtured by the ideology of the RSS.[241] The BJP considers Pandit Deendayal Upadhyaya, the former RSS member, general secretary, and president (1953–1968) of the BJS, as its ideologue. He advocated for integral humanism, an indigenous economic model that puts the human being at center stage, and held *Rashtra Dharma* as the party's philosophy of nationalism. However, the BJP is committed to the Hindutva dogma developed and articulated by V. D. Savarkar and expresses it in its governmental policies and implements it in various ways.

Beginning with only two seats in 1984, the BJP made political inroads and captured the attention of the masses by emerging as a powerful opposition party in 1991 with 120 seats in parliament. Drawing its strength from the Ram Janmabhoomi movement and politicizing controversial issues like Shah Bano Begam's case, the Uniform Hindu Civil Code, religious conversions, and Pakistan occupied Kashmir, it emerged as the largest party in the parliament in 1996 with 161 seats, though its power lasted for only two weeks. In 1998 the BJP reached its zenith with an unprecedented victory by winning 180 seats and held power until its defeat in the 2004 general elections.

Since its inception, the BJP has played its cards very carefully to have Hindutva idiom permeate into the secular aspects of Indian politics. For example, while in power, the NDA government was involved in revising the history textbooks in an attempt to "saffronize" Hindu history and introduced courses in Vedic Astrology in college curricula. Public places and projects were renamed after Hindu gods or Hindu heroes. The BJP's mobilization and political support in the destruction of Babri Masjid was another example of Hindutva extremism of the BJP.

Partha Ghosh mentions that it was the BJP which imparted political respectability to the concept of Hindu nationalism and then exploited it after acquiring political prominence.[242] Because the BJP employed religion and Hindu communalism to mobilize its support, the phenomenal rise of the BJP and the Hindu political resurgence have been variously branded as Hindu

---

240. Noorani, "BJP: Child of RSS."

241. See http://www.bjp.org/en/about-the-party/history?u=bjp-history.

242. Ghosh, *BJP and the Evolution of Hindu Nationalism*, 15.

fascism, Hindu revivalism, Hindu fundamentalism, Hindu nationalism, Hindu communalism, Hindutva force, and so on.[243]

The BJP maintains double standards in articulating its Hindutva stand. M. G. Chitkara says, "It is the misfortune of Hindutva Parivar Organizations, that BJP, a party with a difference, it speaks in one voice when in the Opposition; when in power, it goes astray, with dissidence, indiscipline rearing its ugly head."[244] In preparing ground for the upcoming elections, during his speech in the Lok Sabha on November 18, 2002, L. K. Advani did not mention anything like *Hindu Rashtra,* but tactfully said, "India accepted a Constitution which does not have the secular word in it but the secular concept is there—respect for all religions, equal rights, status for Hindus, Muslims, Christians and Parsis . . . This concept, which can be called secular, was accepted, unanimously at that, because Hindustan's ethos, Hindustan's culture never accepted the concept of a religious state."[245] He then summed up by saying, "Our concept of Hindutva, our concept of Hinduism, is the concept of Swami Vivekanandaji, the concept of Ramakrishna Paramahansa, the concept of Dayanandaji. These are the saints of the past."[246]

Since most of the office bearers of the BJP are from RSS backgrounds and the BJP website openly credits its ancestral roots to the ideology of the RSS, the attitudes of the BJP toward religious others in India is the same as that of the RSS and its leaders. One of the BJP's political agendas is to Hinduize India's secular concepts and bring every department of thought under the fold of the Hindutva framework, while maintaining inclusive language for the appeasement of religious minorities. As viewed by Savarkar, in the eyes of the BJP the loyalty of Indian Muslims and Indian Christians to India would remain suspect as long as Muslims and Christians do not give up their faith in favor of Hinduism.[247] In securing a strong bank of Hindu votes, through media and political campaigns the BJP repeats that Hindu communities are weak and fall under the threat of Muslims and Christians. By underscoring the idea that secularism has enabled Christian groups to attack the fabric of Indian society and hinder development, the BJP causes serious misgivings among middle class Hindu communities, causing them to turn against Christians. The religious intolerance which was spread undercover by Sangh Parivar until the 1990s has surfaced with open intensity since the BJP emerged as the main opposition party in the parliament and in power thereafter.

243. Ghosh, *BJP and the Evolution of Hindu Nationalism,* 16.

244. Chitkara, *Hindutva Parivar,* xvii.

245. Chitkara, *Hindutva Parivar,* 4.

246. Chitkara, *Hindutva Parivar,* 4.

247. Ghosh, *BJP and the Evolution of Hindu Nationalism,* 67.

4

The Christian Missionary Activities Enquiry Committee and its Report

DURING THE EARLY YEARS of independence, especially after the promulgation of the secular constitution, Madhya Pradesh witnessed an influx of foreign missionaries who initiated evangelistic activities in various backward regions of the state. There was general suspicion among the people that the missionaries, who came to India for the purpose of evangelistic, educational, medical, and social services, were also involved in extra-religious and political matters causing sociopolitical and religious tensions.[1] There were also allegations that "Christian Missionaries either forcibly or through fraud and temptations of monetary and other gain convert illiterate aboriginals and other backward people thereby offending the feelings of non-Christians."[2] The Christian missionaries denied these allegations and in turn, alleged that they were being harassed by non-Christian people and local officials.[3]

In the wake of complaints received from non-Christians and missionaries against each other, in April 1954, the state government of Madhya Pradesh appointed an enquiry commission called "Christian Missionary Activities Enquiry Committee" to probe these allegations and learn whether the activities of missionaries were objectionable to people and whether the missionaries were being harassed by the non-Christian communities and officials. After a two-year investigation, the committee submitted its report to the government of Madhya Pradesh in 1956. In the Report, the Committee showed

1. Report of the Christian Missionary Activities Enquiry Committee (Niyogi, *Report*, 1:3, 167.
2. Niyogi, *Report*, 1:169.
3. Niyogi, *Report*, 1:169.

the Christian grievances to be false and the non-Christian complaints to be valid. The Committee also made many recommendations to the government against the missionary methods of conversion activity.

This chapter discusses the various socio-political and religious contexts of the appointment of the Christian Missionary Activities Enquiry Committee in Madhya Pradesh[4] and the making of the report. It highlights the circumstances, purpose, and nature of the appointment of the Committee, the major thematic objections raised in the report against missionary enterprises, and its recommendations to the government against missionary activities.

THE HISTORICAL CONTEXT OF MISSIONARY PROBLEMS IN MADHYA PRADESH

Political and Religious Setting

Madhya Pradesh was the epicenter of political revolts in the 1800s. Ever since most of the central provinces came under British administration following the defeat of Nagpur and Sagar in 1818, British rulers and Western missionaries met with an increasing resistance from the princes, traditional landlords, Zamindars, and malguzars. The first round of resistance to Western domination took place between 1818 and 1826, followed by occurrences between 1842–43 and 1857–58.[5]

Under ancient Hindu law, a person converting from Hinduism to any other religion loses inheritance rights, which kept Hindus from converting. But with the Religious Disability Act of 1850, the government of EIC bestowed rights on converts to equally inherit property from their family members. Therefore, since the 1850s, the British administration was suspected of actively promoting the conversion activities by foreign missionaries. Dwarka Prasad Mishra notes that, "The Hindu Widows Remarriage Act of 1856, and the Religious Disability Removal Act of 1850 which gave protection of civil rights to Hindus who were converted to another religion, together with the aggressive proselytizing activities of Christian missionaries, created fear in the popular Hindu mind that the foreign government was out to destroy the social fabric and the traditions of the land and convert India to Christianity."[6] Thus, since the 1850s, "Hindu society in Madhya Pradesh . . . appears to have

---

4. Madhya Pradesh (M. P.), alluded to throughout this Report, refers to M. P. before the merger of Madhya Bharat, Vindhya Pradesh, and Bhopal State into M. P. on November 1, 1956.

5. Baker, "Colonial Beginnings," 511.

6. Mishra, *History of the Freedom Movement*, 59.

been sufficiently energetic to put up resistance against the encroachment of Christian missionary influence. . . and stoutly resisted the proselytizing activities of the missionaries"[7]

The revolt of 1857, known as the "Sepoy Mutiny," was largely due to the British government's interference with the religious and social customs of India.[8] The Mutiny indicated that "the new nationalism was prepared to use the Hindu religion in its attack on the British and incite violence in order to preserve Hindu beliefs."[9] Historians R. C Majumdar and Dwarka Prasad Mishra maintain that the dread of conversion to Christianity became a nightmare for the Indian soldiers who kept themselves aloof from the Christianizing efforts of the British in the army.[10] The cartridges given to the Hindu sepoys in the Jabalpur, Meerut, and Delhi cantonments were greased with the fat of cows, while Indian Muslim sepoys received cartridges smeared with pigs' fat. In order for a sepoy to use these cartridges, he had to bite the tip of the cartridge which, according to his religious customs, disqualified him being Hindu or Muslim.

Majumdar argued that those actions of the British convinced Hindu-Muslim sepoys that the government was determined to make them lose their social traditions and religious sentiments and eventually embrace Christianity.[11] George Smith reasoned that, "So far as a vague dread of Christianity was a cause of the Mutiny of 1857, the fear was based on ignorance of the fact that no loss of caste, no ceremonial defilement, no study of a mere book, can make a man a Christian."[12] Whatever the perceptions and misunderstandings may have been, the number of white Christians butchered by the mutineers was 1,500 of whom thirty-seven were missionaries, chaplains, and their families.[13]

The uprising did not result in the collapse of British administration because most of the native rulers or princes were either loyal to the British or remained neutral.[14] However, with the Mutiny, the British learned that, "it is not safer to interfere with the totems and taboos of the Hindu

---

7. Mishra, *History of the Freedom Movement*, 156–57.

8. Baker, "Colonial Beginnings," 17.

9. Baker, "Colonial Beginnings," 17.

10. Majumdar, *History of the Freedom Movement*, 1:226–33; Mishra, *History of the Freedom Movement*, 59.

11. Majumdar, *History of the Freedom Movement*, 1:226–33; Mishra, *History of the Freedom Movement*, 59.

12. Smith, *Conversion of India*, 57.

13. Smith, *Conversion of India*, 138.

14. Edwards, *Last Years of British India*, 19.

world."[15] Therefore, in 1858, the British pledged to "respect the rights, dignity and honor of the native Princes"[16] by letting them follow their own native interests. Fascinatingly, two years after the Mutiny, Prime Minister Lord Palmerstone, in a public meeting, said, "It is not only our duty but in our own interest to promote the diffusion of Christianity as far as possible throughout the length and breadth of India."[17] Furthermore, on another occasion, Lord Halifax, the Secretary of State, said that, "Every additional Christian is an additional bond of union with this country and an additional source of strength to British Empire."[18] Statements such as these from the higher officials of British government raised doubts about the British policies and practices in religious matters so that some Hindus began to accept the general allegation that "the growth of the Protestant Church during the period of British Raj in India was due mainly to the great patronage and support the church was getting from the government of India."[19] In supporting such a view, RSS Chief M. S. Golwalkar alleged that "During the War of Independence in 1857, some bishops had raised platoons to help the British government in suppressing the uprising . . . The British too were helping the Christian missionary activities in various ways."[20]

After the 1857 revolt, Britain sought to strengthen its rule through winning over the Indian princes, chiefs, and landlords. There were 562 princely states (also called native states) in India that were not part of nor annexed by British India but were subject to subsidiary alliances. These princely states, which were allied with the British, were "subject to fixed laws, controlled by Brahmanical influence, military independence and popular opinion."[21] The British controlled only their external affairs and did not interfere in their local religious affairs. Since the British showed neutrality on missionary matters, Hindu Rajas in some of the princely states of Madhya Pradesh upheld local religious practices and restricted the entry of missionaries and conversion activities in the areas of their jurisdiction. Under the Political Department, some states had passed anti-conversion acts as early as the 1930s.[22] For example, there was the Raigarh State Conversion Act in 1936, the Patna Freedom of Religion Act of 1942, the Surguja State Apostasy Act in 1945, and

15. Edwards, *Last Years of British India*, 17.

16. Edwards, *Last Years of British India*, 182.

17. Niyogi, *Report*, 1:40.

18. Niyogi, *Report*, 1:40.

19. Niyogi, *Report*, 1:41.

20. Golwalkar, *Bunch of Thoughts*, 141.

21. Mill, *History of British India*, 320.

22. Niyogi, *Report*, 1:9.

the Udaipur State Anti-Conversion Act in 1946. Similar laws were enacted against Christianity in Jodhpur, Bikaner, Kota and Kalahandi and many other princely states.[23] Under the operation of these laws, "no churches were allowed to be built, no Christian schools permitted and no priest allowed to reside within the limits of the States."[24] In spite of these Acts, some missionaries surreptitiously entered Surguja, Raigarh, and other states to carry on the propagation of the Christian faith and to encourage nationalism.[25] Through the Government of India Act of 1935, the British established a federal form of administration, hoping in vain to bring the princely states politically into the government of the whole of India and to apply common policies for all of these states. However, as long as Britain remained in power, princely self-interest drew these states together.

As the freedom movement intensified under the leadership of Gandhi in the second quarter of the twentieth century, and the transfer of power was nearer, the Indian National Congress (INC) suspected that the friendly alliance of the princely states with the British would be a challenge. In 1938, Gandhi warned the princes that it would be wise for them to cultivate a friendly relationship with INC rather than with the British in order for a fair future in India.[26] In 1939, by hinting to the princes about the upcoming secular democratic governance of India, Nehru said, "We recognize no such treaties [between the states and the Crown] and we shall in no event accept them . . . The only paramount power that we recognize is the will of the people."[27] In 1942, through the "Quit India Movement," Gandhi led a mass civil disobedience campaign and gave a clarion call to the nation to force the British to leave India. After India achieved freedom in 1947, the foremost challenge for the democratic self-governing India was the merger of the princely states into the Indian dominion. Sardar Vallabhbhai Patel, the first Home Minister and Deputy Prime Minister of India, invited the princes to form a democratic constitution in the national interest and persuaded them to surrender their defense, foreign affairs, and communication to the government of India. To that effect, in 1948, many princely states were integrated into Madhya Pradesh.

23. Anant, "Anti-Conversion Laws."

24. *The Hindustan Times*, Tuesday, May 4, 1954, 8.

25. Niyogi, *Report*, 1:9.

26. Edwards, *Last Years of British India*, 181.

27. Edwards, *Last Years of British India*, 181.

The Liberal Constitution and Religious Foment in the 1950s

With the support of the colonial government in pre-independent India, the erstwhile rulers of the feudal states of Raigarh, Udaipur, Jashpur, and Surguja had practiced the prohibition of religious conversions and had restricted the entry of missionaries into the pre-merged princely states of Madhya Pradesh.[28] Freedom of Religion Acts, also known as Anti-Conversion Laws, have been in effect in the princely states since 1930s. These laws [i.e., the Raigarh State Conversion Act of 1936, the Patna Freedom of Religion Act of 1942, the Surguja State Apostasy Act of 1945, and the Udaipur State Anti-Conversion Act of 1946] were enacted to preserve Hindu religious identity, and to protect Hindus and tribal people from conversions by missionaries. Similar laws were also in effect in Bikaner, Jodhpur, Kalahandi, Kota, etc. until independence.[29]

At the juncture of independence, India was at a crossroad of political uncertainty with the country's partition on one side and protracted Hindu-Muslim conflicts on the other. For Nehru's government, it took a little over two years after independence to define and assure the citizens of free India of their constitutional rights. On November 26, 1949, the Constituent Assembly solemnly resolved to constitute India into a Sovereign Democratic Republic and to secure for all its citizens: socioeconomic and political justice; liberty of thought, expression, belief, faith, and worship; equality of status and opportunity, and fraternity of individual dignity and unity of the nation. The constitution officially came into effect on January 26, 1950. The Preamble of the Constitution was amended in 1976 to read that India is a "Sovereign Socialist Secular Democratic Republic."

The principal rights of religious communities are incorporated in Articles 25 to 30 of the Indian Constitution. Article 25, "Right to Freedom of Religion," states that, "all persons are equally entitled to freedom of conscience and the right freely to profess, practice, and propagate religion."[30]

This secular democratic constitution marked a great turning point for both Hindu nationalists and Christian missionaries. As individual freedoms began to emerge from the liberal principles of the constitution, the idea of freedom itself acquired varied meanings, inflections, and implications.[31] Hindu nationalists and missionaries viewed freedom quite differently. Christian mission agencies, especially foreign missionaries,

28. Niyogi, *Report*, 1:6, 9. It is contended that these laws have been foundational to the anti-conversion laws in independent India.

29. Menon, "Old Debate."

30. *Constitution of India*, 13.

31. Katju, "Understanding of Freedom in Hindutva," 3.

celebrated the aspect of religious freedom guaranteed by the constitution. They began to express a great deal of optimism for the expansion of Christianity[32] as the constitution had made things smoother for them to surge forward with renewed fervor. For example, *Gharbandhu*, a magazine of Gossner Evangelical Lutheran Church, said in 1952 that, "With the advent of *swaraj* the gates for the preaching of the gospel have been thrown open."[33] In contrast, Hindu nationalists perceived such optimism as threatening to their vision, cultural unity, identity, and religion.

With the merger of the minor states into Madhya Pradesh in 1948 and by the promulgation of the Secular Democratic Constitution in 1950, Christian missionaries liberally assumed the lifting of Anti-Conversion Acts and freely toured in the backward regions of the state where missionary entry was previously restricted. They began to boldly initiate various charitable and evangelistic works.[34] The assumption that the princely states' pre-existing anti-conversion laws would be revoked was due to the assurance given by Article 25 of the Constitution, which said, " . . . all persons are equally entitled to freedom of conscience and the right freely to profess, practice and propagate religion."[35] Since the constitutional freedom of religion was not instigated on the local level due to either ignorance or respect for the former conversion bans, some Hindu groups openly opposed missionary infiltration, while others politicized the issues to attack the secularism of the government.

With the increase of foreign missionary activities, Hindu nationalists became apprehensive that under the shadow of constitutional freedom, Westerners could perhaps attempt to take India back to some sort of colonial bondage through the foreign missionary enterprise. For example, in the early 1950s, while encouraging people to fight foreign influence in India, RSS leader Golwalkar said, "A few years ago, there was an All-India Conference of Christians wherein they called up on to pledge themselves to establish Christian Empire in Bharat. And one of our central ministers was present there to bless the proceedings. Such is the role of Christian gentlemen residing in our land today, out to demolish not only the religious and social fabric of our life but also to establish political domination in various pockets and if possible all over the land."[36] Analyzing the

32. Niyogi, *Report*, 1:108.

33. Goel, *Pseudo-Secularism*, 10.

34. Missionaries from Belgium and Germany had established themselves in various Adivasi areas of Orissa, Bihar, and Madhya Pradesh since 1834 and had converted a large number of aboriginal people to Christianity. Niyogi, *Report*, 1:9.

35. Constitution of India, 1949, Article 25 (1).

36. Golwalkar, *Bunch of Thoughts*, 193.

situation between Hindus and missionaries, John T. Seamands,[37] a long-time missionary in India, noted that with the coming of independence, the attitude of Hindus toward Christianity quickly changed from that of defense to that of confident attack.[38]

The Influx of Foreign Missions and its Repercussions

In the first decade of independence, there was frequent communal strife between Muslims and Hindus, which caused the exodus of millions of Hindus to India from West Pakistan and East Pakistan. Partha Ghosh estimates that between 1950 and 1960 India received about 5.5 million Hindu refugees from the two regions of Pakistan. Due to strife, altogether about 14 million Hindus migrated to India from Pakistan in the first two decades of Independence.[39]

While the wounds from India's partition were still fresh and the communal conflicts between Muslims and Hindus were not fully forgotten, the constitutional provision of religious freedom came as an acid-test for Hindu nationalists as it directly contributed to an influx of foreign missionaries, whose number grew from 2,400 to 4,800 in the first few years of independence.[40] After the promulgation of the constitution, it was reported that there were about 4000 converts from the Uraon tribes in the Surguja district of Madhya Pradesh (now in Chhattisgarh) alone, where conversion had been prohibited in the pre-independent era.[41] When missionaries experienced opposition from non-Christians, they often quoted the rights of religious freedom guaranteed in Article 25 of the Indian constitution. For example, E. Stanley Jones, a well-known missionary in India, wrote several articles in Indian newspapers indicating that missionaries held to the constitutional right to boldly "profess, practice and propagate" their faith. He said, "Whatever individual Hindus may say for or against Christian missions, we feel we have friendliness at the center—friendliness in two ways: the constitution is friendly to Christian missions and the persons who are at the center are friendly."[42]

---

37. John Seamands served as a Methodist missionary in India for twenty years prior to joining the faculty of Missions at Asbury Theological Seminary.

38. Seamands, "Present-Day Environment of Christian Missions," 13.

39. Ghosh, *BJP*, 80.

40. Fey, "Report Urges Ban on Missionaries," 892.

41. Niyogi, *Report*, 1:123.

42. Jones, *Evangelism in India*, 3.

HINDU NATIONALISM AND INTOLERANCE

Among the central states, Madhya Pradesh and Madhya Bharat were the two states where Hindu nationalism maintained its powerful presence through the RSS network and the BJS' political influence in the 1950s. Since 1952, by the influence and strength of the RSS, the BJS has evolved as a nationalist, alternate party to the Congress Party.[43] It has gained a strong foothold and become the largest opposition party in M.P., posing a serious challenge to the Congress Party in the state and Nehru's secularism in the country.[44] The BJS, which did not believe in doctrinaire socialism, derived its inspiration from the values of Bharatiya culture and life following the reformist tradition of Swami Dayananda and Gangadhar Tilak.[45] According to Motilal A. Jhangiani, "it was an expression of nascent nationalism."[46] Ram Rajya Parishad, Hindu Mahasabha, and Jana Sangh, who supported each other politically in M.P., in their urge to promote Hindutva ideology in secular India, became cautious of religious development of non-Hindu faiths, particularly Christian missionary enterprises in India.

In narrating the causes of conflicts between missionaries and non-Christians in M.P., O. M. Thomas, a Christian scholar and a lawyer at Allahabad High Court, said, "Since the coming into operation of the Constitution of India Christian missionaries moved into the prohibited areas and converts openly professed the Christian religion therein. This alarmed the communalists of the Hindu Mahasabha, the Rashtriya Swayamsevak Sangh, the Ram Rajya Parishad, and the Arya Samaj, whose subtle machinations turned the authorities of Madhya Pradesh against Christian missionaries and Christian converts."[47] Opposition to missionary work was also experienced in the princely state of Surguja as a natural reaction to the entry of missionaries into the state which had been closed to the gospel in pre-independent India. According to NCCI, at the juncture of the integration of Surguja with Madhya Pradesh, especially from 1950 onwards, opposition intensified and appeared in an organized form because the gospel had positively resulted in conversions.[48] On various occasions, Hindu nationalists printed and distributed handbills with the signatures of the Maharaja of Surguja and of local MLA, condemning the activities

---

43. Jhangiani, *Jana Sangh and Swatantra*, 13.

44. Jhangiani, *Jana Sangh and Swatantra*, 201.

45. Jhangiani, *Jana Sangh and Swatantra*, viii.

46. Jhangiani, *Jana Sangh and Swatantra*, 10.

47. Thomas, "Christian-Baiting in Madhya Pradesh," 25–26.

48. NCCI, *Minutes*, 11.

of the missionaries.[49] In the process, they politicized the influx of foreign missionaries, intensified propaganda against missionary activities, and mobilized non-Christian organizations to present a united front against Christians and the Jharkhand movement.[50]

The situation created such an uproar that the government of India has significantly refused missionary visas since April 1, 1952, in order to limit the entry of missionaries into India.[51] Through *The Hindu Outlook,* N. C. Chatterjee, President of ABHM, exhorted Hindus that they "ought to face boldly the activities of the Christian missionaries" and challenged that "Hindu Mahasabha, Jana Sangh, Arya Samaj and other Hindu nationalist organizations must form a Front against Christian missionaries in the coming five years."[52] He proposed various programs to combat the proselytizing activities of the Christian missionaries.[53] He advocated for the integration of tribal people and *harijans* (downtrodden and marginalized people of Hindu society) into the Hindu social organism, and he also pressed Hindus to realize that "change of religion under foreign auspices connotes change of nationality."[54]

THE EFFORTS TO HINDUIZE ADIVASIS

Madhya Pradesh was one of the most backward states in India. The British officers of the Census of India before 1931 called aboriginal people (forest-dwellers) a "primitive" tribe and designated them as "animists" to maintain their religious distinction.[55] Since tribal people were illiterate and socioeconomically backward, foreign missionaries focused on the tribal regions of the state, to improve the conditions of the people alongside propagating the gospel.[56] Bhagatism (meaning religious devotion), a religious movement which sprang up around 1914 in the Oraon region of Chota Nagpur,[57] used similar developmental strategies, and, in so doing, counteracted the missionary enterprise, especially its evangelistic activities, to impede tribals from coming under the influence of missionaries. Missionaries and Bhagatists brought great change to the lives of tribals, which eventually led to their

49. NCCI, *Minutes*, 11.

50. Niyogi, *Report*, 1:18.

51. NCCI, *Minutes*, 4.

52. *The Hindu Outlook*, July 18, 1955, 8.

53. *The Hindu Outlook*, July 18, 1955, 1, 8.

54. *The Hindu Outlook*, July 18, 1955, 1.

55. Mehta, *Constitutional Protection*, 26.

56. Thomas, *Christian Missions*, 39.

57. Srivastava, *Essentials of Cultural Anthropology*, 229.

religious stratification within the classification of their ethnic identity such as Bhagats, Isaai, animist and so on.[58] Bhagatism was a reform movement which worked among Bhil tribals in central India for the eradication of the evils of bride price, polygamy and habits of drunkenness. Educationist P. C. Jain contends that the Bhagat movement was not a movement of Hinduization, but a movement of progress and development.[59]

According to Amita Baviskar, a sociologist, several Bhagat sects were integrated into Hinduism by Sangh Parivar which renders them its philanthropic and educational services and assists them in performing pilgrimages to Hindu temples.[60] After independence, Indian anthropologists began to claim adivasis as "Backward Hindus," to prevent them from converting to Christianity and to Hinduize them. Anita Srivastava Majhi, an Indian anthropologist, argues that the tribals consider the Hindu social structure as their model for imitation, and thus they are close to Hindus in their habits and behavior.[61] Sangh affiliated organizations like Sewa Bharti, Vanvasi Kalyan Ashram, and Friends of Tribal Society were often involved in mobilizing tribals for the support of Hindu gods, culture, and traditions. The tribals were supplied with calendars with Hindu deities and were encouraged to celebrate Hindu festivals. Their regional meetings were supplemented by rituals of purification, *deeksha* (religious initiation), and lectures of an anti-Christian and anti-Muslim nature.[62] As they were being Hinduized, they were exhorted to defend their Hinduness when threatened or induced by missionaries for conversion into Christianity.

In 1952, with the support of state government and the RSS, Ramakanth Keshav Deshpande founded Vanvasi Kalyan Ashram (VKA, Center for Tribal Welfare), also called Vanvasi Kalyan Manch (VKM), in Jashpur, Madhya Pradesh. The aim of this society was to provide education to tribals, especially to counter the appeal of Christian mission schools.[63] Under the influence of the RSS and VKA, Bharatiya Jana Sangh took advantage of local socio-religious conflicts, particularly those of tribal interest, and politicized them for their own purposes. Deshpande, who also served as an officer in the State Tribal Welfare Department during 1948 and 1957, followed Golwalkar's ideology and strategy, hinting to the public and

58. Jain, *Christianity, Ideology and Social Change*, 34.
59. Jain, *Christianity, Ideology and Social Change*, 36.
60. Baviskar, "Adivasis Encounter," 5108.
61. Majhi, *Tribal Culture*, 183.
62. Majhi, *Tribal Culture*, 183.
63. Jaffrelot, *Hindu Nationalist Movement*, 322.

alerting the government that missionary work would encourage separatism among the tribes.[64]

THE HARASSMENT OF MISSIONARIES

After the merger of princely states into Madhya Pradesh, especially after the promulgation of the secular constitution which guaranteed freedom of religion, some local authorities continued to place restrictions on the entry of missionaries in the regions of Raigarh, Jashpur, Surguja, and Udaipur, based on former State anti-conversion acts and caused tensions between missionaries and authorities. Missionaries were not allowed to visit their Christian members more than four times a year, for 48 hours each visit. In April 1948, Father Stanislaus Tigga entered the Udaipur region without the permission of the authorities and was imprisoned because he stayed more than 48 hours.[65] After serving a portion of his sentence, Tigga appealed to the court against the sentence, but was denied by the session's judge of Raigarh who upheld the former missionary restrictions as valid. The following year, Christian leaders approached Chief Minister Pandit Ravi Shankar Shukla who made it clear to them that there were no restrictions or bans on missionary entry into those regions.[66] He also promised that he would permit the entry and residence of priests if they give him assurances in writing that they would not meddle in politics. The Bishop of Ranch, O. Servin, hastily went to Nagpur and submitted a written statement to that effect.[67] As per the account of O. M. Thomas, a lawyer at Allahabad High Court, "For five years from the time of the merge of the Raja-ruled enclaves in Madhya Pradesh Christian organizations and leaders had petitioned the Government of the State for protection against harassment and unfair discrimination by officials. The State authorities took no notice of these representations."[68]

Meanwhile, in many places of Madhya Pradesh, Hindu nationalists moved swiftly to limit the work of Christian missions by means of agitation and the politicization of religious issues. When it became such a problem by early 1952, the National Christian Council of India (NCCI), Nagpur, sent a letter to Prime Minister Jawaharlal Nehru elucidating the harassment faced by missionaries in Madhya Pradesh.[69] Referring to the complaints received from both foreign missionaries and Indian Christians, in a private circular

64. Jaffrelot, *Hindu Nationalist Movement*, 322.
65. See Francis, "Background of the Niyogi Report," 109–10.
66. See Francis, "Background of the Niyogi Report," 112.
67. See Francis, "Background of the Niyogi Report," 112.
68. Thomas, "Christian-Baiting in Madhya Pradesh," 26.
69. Menon, "Old Debate."

dated 17 October 1952, Nehru advised the chief ministers to maintain religious harmony within their states, requesting them to be mindful of India's constitutional values and to be tolerant toward Christians and their mission. The gist of the circular reads:

> I have sometimes received complaints from Christian Missions and missionaries both from foreign and Indian, about the differential treatment accorded to them in certain states . . . . . I know that there is a hangover still of the old prejudice against Christian missions and missionaries . . . . .But remember that Christianity is a religion of large numbers of people in India and that it came to south India nearly 2000 years ago. Our policy of religious neutrality and protection of minorities must not be affected or sullied by discriminatory treatment or harassment . . . We permit, by our constitution, not only freedom of conscience and belief but also proselytism[70]

Perhaps this circular further ignited Hindu nationalists to oppose and resist the Christian missionary enterprise in Madhya Pradesh, as it generally appeared that Nehru favored Christians in his secularism. The issue gained political attention as the RSS, Hindu Mahasabha, Arya Samaj, and the Bharatiya Jana Sangh mobilized protests against missionary work in various regions of India, particularly in Madhya Pradesh,[71] while Hindu revivalists such as VKA took measures to Hinduize those who were typically outside pure Hinduism.[72]

Whenever missionaries faced objections, they complained to the local authorities, but this only led to more harassment from the officials. Counter-charges were filed against missionaries as if they were involved in conversion through force, fraud, and inducement.[73] With this background, anti-conversion sentiments brewed in various parts of Madhya Pradesh and Madhya Bharat, giving rise to the appointment of enquiry commissions by the state governments.

---

70. Gopal, *Selected Works of Jawaharlal Nehru*, 733–34, also quoted in Goel, *Pseudo-Secularism*, 8.

71. Niyogi, *Report*, 1:18.

72. *The Hindu Outlook*, July 18, 1955, 8.

73. *Hitavada*, January 23, 1954, 5; *The Hindustan Times*, May 4, 1954, 8; Niyogi, *Report*, 1:1.

THE APPOINTMENT OF THE NIYOGI COMMITTEE

On April 14, 1954, the state government[74] of Madhya Pradesh officially passed notification under Resolution No. 318–716–V–Con. of the appointment of a six-member committee under the chairmanship of M. Bhavani Shankar Niyogi, former chief justice of the Nagpur High Court, to conduct an inquiry into the growing religious agitations held by both Hindus and Christian missionaries in various parts of the state. On April 14 and 16, 1954, in press notices released to the public, the government briefly explained the circumstances and the purpose of the appointment of the committee as follows.

> Representations have been made to Government from time to time that Christian Missionaries either forcibly or through fraud and temptations of monetary and other gain convert illiterate aboriginals and other backward people thereby offending the feelings of non-Christians. It has further been represented that Missions are utilised directly or indirectly for purposes of political or extra-religious objectives. The Christian Missionaries have repudiated these allegations and have asserted on the other hand that their activities are confined solely to religious propaganda and towards social, medical and educational work. The Missionaries have further alleged that they are being harassed by non-Christian people and local officials, as agitation has been growing on either side, the State Government consider it desirable in the public interest to have a thorough inquiry made into the whole question through an impartial Committee.[75]

The press release also listed the six names and the qualifications of the members of the committee with M. Bhavani Shankar Niyogi as the chairman. It further said, "On a thorough review of the question from historical and other points of view, the Committee may also make recommendations to Government as to the action that Government should take to deal with the situation as disclosed by the inquiry. The Committee has been authorized to frame its own procedure for conducting the enquiry and requested to submit its report to Government with all possible expedition."[76]

There were also press notices by the state government on April 30 and November 12, 1954, inviting the cooperation of the public in the investigation of the Committee.

74. Madhya Pradesh was ruled by the Congress Party.
75. Niyogi, *Report,* 1:169.
76. Niyogi, *Report,* 1:167.

Public are aware that the Committee appointed by the Government of Madhya Pradesh, to enquire into the activities of Christian Missionaries in this State undertook a tour of some districts in the State with a view to secure preliminary information regarding the nature of the problem. In the course of these tours, various sections of the people were contacted and they gave information, oral as well as in writing, to the Committee. The Committee received correspondence from the Christians as well as the non-Christians and have also gone through some records of the State Government. They have prepared a questionnaire which is being released separately to the general public. Members of the public and representatives of the various Christian and non-Christian organizations and institutions are requested to furnish such information on the subjects referred to in the questionnaire, as may be in their possession, supported by documents, if any. Copies of the questionnaire will be supplied to anyone asking for it by the Assistant Secretary, Christian Missionary Activities Enquiry Committee, Secretariat Building, Nagpur-1.[77]

The Circumstantial Backdrop of the Committee's Appointment

Sociopolitical Unrest

In January 1948, the government announced the integration of the princely states of central India, Raigarh, Udaipuar, Jashpur, and Surguja, into Madhya Pradesh. The government faced many challenges in integrating the minor states into linguistically planned states while cautiously distributing aboriginals between the merged states. There was political tension between Madhya Pradesh and Bihar regarding certain border districts of the Chhattisgarh region (now a separate state), where aboriginals of the Jharkhand movement relentlessly fought for a separate state. Missionaries, who had worked in these tribal regions since the mid-nineteenth century for the spiritual, educational, and economic emancipation of aboriginals, were perceived as surreptitious conspirators of various adivasi agitations.[78] According to B. N. Banerjee, the Jharkhand movement was the real trouble which led to the appointment of the Niyogi Commission, as politicians often linked this movement with Christian conversion and missionary activities, although the movement was headed by many Marxist and Naxalite leaders.[79]

77. Niyogi, *Report*, 1:171–72.
78. Niyogi, *Report*, 1:9.
79. Banerjee, *Religious Conversions*, 226. See also Niyogi, *Report*, 1:6–23.

According to the Niyogi Report, the chief unrest could be located against the following historical setting:

a. Oppression and misgovernment which existed prior to Integration [of princely states] . . .

b. The expectations of the people of the Integrated States of immediate improvement in their moral and material conditions as a result of Integration were pitched so high that almost inevitably they were bound to be disappointed to some extent.

c. Almost from the very beginning interested parties, including Christian Missionaries, began to intermeddle and create dissatisfaction by exploiting the situation. An end was put to the activities of such persons by the decision of the Union Ministry of States in May 1948, but according to Government reports the activities of Missionaries continued further though surreptitiously.

d. The reports which the Government of Madhya Pradesh had obtained from the former States in respect of the activities of Missionaries show that their role in the past had not been healthy, their methods not savoury. Two or three times there were rebellions in the States and even the Political Department, which was in the hands of the European Christians, was compelled to put restrictions on the entry of Missionaries and their movement in the former States.[80]

Parliamentary Discussions on Missionary Issues

In 1952, *The Hitavada,* a popular newspaper in central India that leans toward right-wing Hindu ideals, repeatedly published anti-missionary complaints and replies sent by various people to the editor. In the same year, Roman Catholics and the National Council of Churches in India (NCCI) officially complained to Prime Minister Jawaharlal Nehru about the troubles Christians were facing from Hindu activists in various parts of India, especially in the Madhya Pradesh region. The missionaries' complaints to Nehru regarding harassment by government officials in Madhya Pradesh not only compelled Nehru to write to all chief ministers exhorting them to render respect and tolerance toward Christians, but also brought the issue to the floor of parliament as early as 1952. E. Stanley Jones, a prominent missionary friend of Gandhi, had also personally written an Open Letter

80. Niyogi, *Report,* 1:6–7.

to every governor and chief minister of state in early 1953 expressing his concern and fear over parliamentary debate on the missionary situation in India.[81] G. X. Francis, the president of the Catholic Regional Council of M.P., Bihar and Orissa had filed a case in the Nagpur High Court against the harassment of missionaries by local authorities and non-Christians. The government officials who troubled missionaries initially were R. K. Deshpande and his associates. They were part of the state welfare department as well as the leaders of the RSS managed VKA.[82]

When Nehru called for a report from the Madhya Pradesh government, the State sent him a report in which "no effort was spared to malign the tribal Christians and missionaries as anti-nationalist, as fostering plans for Jharkhand, as engaged in immoral traffic, as joining hand with Muslims to abduct Hindu girls, etc."[83] With the knowledge of this report, Home Minister Kailash Nath Katju made a statement in the Parliament in 1953 that "the activities of Christian Missionaries were offensive to the feelings of the non-Christian population in the State of Madhya Pradesh."[84] In response, Prime Minister Nehru ordered Home Minister Kailash Nath Katju to suggest to the state government to thoroughly investigate the matters concerned. The parliamentary debates on anti-missionary allegations affected the granting of missionary visas to foreign Christians so that in 1953, the government denied 53 missionary visa applications.[85]

In pursuance of the instructions from the government of India, in May 1953, the state government decided to appoint a three-man committee under M. Bhavani Shankar Niyogi to make an inquiry into the missionaries' complaints.[86] The three-man committee included M. B. Niyogi, former Chief Justice of Nagpur High Court, G. S. Gupta, former speaker and Member of Parliament, and Seth Govind Das, Member of Parliament. It was at this time that Christians demanded Christian representation on the committee. The fact-finding committee did not begin its work until the state government of Madhya Pradesh officially appointed a six-member enquiry

81. For Jones' letter and the replies of Nehru, state governors, chief minsters, see Jones, "Missionaries in India."

82. Niyogi, *Report,* Part A, 2:18, 19, 22, 52, 128; 1:3.

83. Quoted by Thomas in "Christian-Baiting," 27. See also Hermanns, *Hinduism and Tribal Culture,* 47; Soares *Truth Shall Prevail,* 116–22.

84. Quoted by Thomas in "Christian-Baiting," 27.

85. Plattner, *Catholic Church in India,* 12.

86. *The Hitavada,* "Inquiry into Missionaries' Complaints," 5. See also *The Hitavada,* "Activities of Missionaries," 5.

committee a year later.[87] During this time, the anti-missionary allegations by the Hindu nationalist groups intensified.[88]

ANTI-MISSIONARY PROPAGANDA

After Catholic leaders lodged a formal complaint in 1952 in the Nagpur High Court against the harassment of missionaries, various newspapers and fortnightlies such as *Yugdharm,* the *Hitavada, Sanmarg, Swatantra Bharat, The Organiser,* and *The Hindu,* published anti-missionary opinions and complaints that missionaries in Madhya Pradesh were conspiring against India's independence.[89] Those accusations were substantiated by taking the examples of Nagas' demand for a separate Christian state in the north-east and of the alleged missionary support to the Jharkhand movement.[90] Missionaries were portrayed as disloyal to the country in which they worked. On March 25, 1954, *Yugdharm,* a Hindu nationalist newspaper, published an article under the title, "'Sisters' being employed to create hatred against Hinduism," in which the author claimed that missionaries were engaged in secret works in the border districts of Orissa and M. P., enticing illiterate and backward people into Christianity by charitable activities.[91] In *Sanmarg,* Sant Tukdoji, an influential Hindu activist from Nagpur who was honored by President Rajendra Prasad as a Rashtriya Sant (national saint) in 1949, wrote an article under the title, "Christian Missionaries' Heinous Activities in Jashpur."[92] He claimed that the missionaries had received two million dollars for conversion activities and had converted 150,000 out of a population of 250,000 in Jaspur.[93] *Yugdharm* also published an article, "Missionaries Active in Surguja," which claimed that about nine missionaries, both Indian and foreign, assisted by 500 propagandists, were busy day and night in forcible conversions.[94] The Hindu Mahasabha's mouthpiece, *The Hindu Outlook,* regularly published lengthy articles on the negative aspects of Christianity and conversions.[95]

87. See Jones, "Missionaries in India," 2.

88. Niyogi, *Report,* 1:18.

89. Jones, "Missionaries in India," 7.

90. *Hindustan Samachar,* "Christian Missionaries May 7, 1954." See also *The Hitavada,* "Inquiry into Missionaries' Complaints," 5.

91. Jones, "Missionaries in India," 8.

92. Jones, "Missionaries in India," 9.

93. *Sanmarg,* March 24, 1953.

94. *Yugdharm,* Nagpur, dated March 21, 1953.

95. See *The Hindu Outlook,* November 29, 1953; December 27, 1953; March 28, 1954; July 11, 1954; June 13, 1954; July 14, 1954; July 18, 1954, July 24, 1956; September

ANTI-MISSIONARY AGITATIONS

In the early 1950s, anti-missionary agitations flared up in various parts of India because Hindu nationalists built up a view that the motive of conversions was "to strengthen the British Empire in India and to disintegrate the unity of the Indian nation and people."[96] In Nasik, an important Hindu religious center, the Hindu Mahasabha led a public procession under the leadership of the former mayor of Poona to protest the presence of Christian missions.[97] Taking political advantage of the local unrest, the newly formed Hindu nationalist party the Bharatiya Jana Sangh (BJS) launched a protest, "Anti-foreign Missionary Week" in Nagpur in early 1954 to curtail the work of Christian missions in Madhya Pradesh. By this time, BJS had officially become an opposition party in the state, closely allied with the RSS on the ideological platform of Hindu Mahasabha.

In the wake of the unrest between non-Christian adivasis and missionaries, the Arya Samaj invited Rajendra Prasad, the Premier of the Union, to inspect the districts of Raigarh and Surguja to understand the magnitude of the problem. During his visit, the Arya Samajists organized various processions to pass before him shouting anti-missionary slogans.[98] Sant Tukdoji Maharaj[99] (1909–1968), a well-known Hindu guru and anti-British revolutionist, who later served as the vice-president of the VHP, also visited those places of uproar and demanded immediate action from the governments (Central and State) to stop the activities of foreign missions which he believed were causing trouble among Indians. While appealing to both the public and the government through a press conference, he alleged that,

> The Missions were in the habit of advancing debts to *Adivasis* and then seeking conversion for non-payment. Free education to children in Mission Schools, money grants, clothes, food and medical aid were the usual methods through which conversion was being sought. The missionaries wielded such great influence on the 75 percent *Adivasi* population of this area, that they prevented many from attending his bhajan meetings. Controlled as they did such huge funds the missionaries had even corrupted

---

18, 1956.

96. Pachpore, "Peep into the History of Anti-Conversion Laws."

97. Smith, *India as a Secular State*, 201.

98. Jones, "Missionaries in India," 1.

99. Tukdoji Maharaj was involved in social reforms and contributed to nation-building through his writings and Hindu revitalization movements. The President of India bestowed on him the title of "Rashtra Sant" for his wisdom and involvement in rural development and national reconstruction.

the local officials and police . . . . What looked like movement for
Jharkhand was a movement for 'Christian-Khand' in reality.[100]

The Hitavada regularly published Hindu-Christian complaints against
and replies to each other, particularly of the allegations[101] that Christian
missionaries "either forcibly or through fraud and temptations of monetary
and other gain convert illiterate aboriginals and other backward people
thereby offending the feelings of non-Christians," while missionaries alleged that, "they are being harassed by the non-Christian people and local officials."[102] Responding to religious disputes, the Law Minister Kailash
Nath Katju said that, "if anybody starts a comparative race and says, 'your
faith is utter idolatry' it is not a question of religion, it will be a question of
law and order: people will not tolerate it now."[103]

> In 1952, leading citizens of the district, including the Maharaja
> of Surguja distributed pamphlets and addressed gatherings
> advising the Adivasis not to give up their religion for the sake
> of monetary benefits or temptations. Members of the Rash-
> triya Swayamsevak Sangh and the Arya Samaj joined hands
> and intensified propaganda against Missionary activities. The
> services of a large number of enthusiastic workers could be
> secured by them and reconversions took place in some num-
> bers. A conference of Virat Hindu Rashtriya Sammelan was
> convened at Ambikapur where all non-Christian organizations
> were asked to present a united front against the Christians and
> the Jharkhand movement. Thus, acute tension prevailed in the
> area and the authorities thought that the situation may result
> in serious trouble unless handled properly.[104]

Although no formal complaint was filed with the government against
Christian missionaries in Madhya Pradesh, considering the magnitude of the
problem, the government of Madhya Pradesh appointed a six-member fact-
finding committee on April 14, 1954, to investigate whether the Christian missionary activities in Madhya Pradesh had been offensive to non-Christians.

100. Jones, "Missionaries in India," 1.

101. *The Hitavada*: April 23, 1953, 4; April 24, 1953, 4; April 30, 1953, 4; May 2,
1953, 4; May 3, 1953, 4; May 12, 1953, 4; May 19, 1953, 5; September 1, 1953, 6; October
22, 1953, 4; October 26, 1953, 4; October 31, 1953, 4; November 9, 1953, 4; January 23,
1954, 5; March 1, 1954, 5; April 17, 1954, 1; April 20, 1954, 2; April 23, 1954, 5; April
25, 1954, 5; May 1, 1954, 5, etc. . . .

102. *The Hitavada*, January 23, 1954, 5; *The Hindustan Times*, May 4, 1954, 8; Niyogi, *Report*, 1:1, 16.

103. Jones, "Missionaries in India," 1.

104. Niyogi, *Report*, 1:18.

However, "From 1948 onwards Christians in Madhya Pradesh have made definite charges of being harassed by the civil authorities in the State. But not a single complaint or allegation against Christian Missionaries or tribal Christians has been registered before April 14, 1956, the date of the Resolution appointing the Niyogi Committee." If so, it seems like missionaries invited disaster upon themselves by lodging complaints against Hindu authorities in the state where they experienced harassment.[105]

The Purpose and Nature of the Committee

> It was represented to Government from time to time that the conversion of illiterate aboriginals and other backward people was effected by the Christian Missionaries either forcibly or through fraud or temptations of monetary gain, and the Government were informed that the feelings of non-Christians were being offended by conversions brought about by such methods. The Christian Missionaries repudiated before Government these allegations and charged local officials and non-Christians of harassment and as the State Government found that an agitation was growing on either side, it considered it desirable in the public interest to have a thorough enquiry made into the whole question.[106]

The purpose of the committee, therefore, was to make a "thorough enquiry into the whole question and to make recommendations on a review thereof from historical and other points of view."[107] In its press note, the government said, "The purpose of the committee is to conduct an impartial enquiry into certain complaints and counter-complaints regarding the missionary activities in the State."[108]

Since the committee was appointed under the inherent powers of the state and not under the guidelines of the Commission of Enquiry Act IX of 1952, the committee functioned purely on a voluntary basis.

> It had neither the power to compel any one to attend before it, nor to make any statement, oral or written, nor to administer an oath. The Committee thus had no coercive power in any shape or form. No one was bound to answer all or any question contained in the Questionnaire or to answer it in a prescribed manner. The enquiry was riot judicial, in the sense that it was calculated to have an operative effect. As the Committee

---

105. See Thomas, "Christian-Baiting," 28.

106. Niyogi, *Report*, 1:1; See also *The Hindustan Times*, Tuesday, May 4, 1954, 8.

107. Niyogi, *Report*, 1:1, 2.

108. Niyogi, *Report*, 1:171.

interpreted the Terms of Reference, it appeared to it that the object of the enquiry was to ascertain the facts from the people directly at first-hand, unlike a judicial enquiry which proceeds on the material brought before it by an investigating authority. The attitude of the Government, as well as that of the party in power, was perfectly neutral.[109]

Members of the Committee

The following made up the six-member fact-finding committee.

A. M. Bhavani Shankar Niyogi was appointed as the chairman of the committee. He was a Brahmin, who had previously served in various important government positions including as Chairman of the Public Service Commission and Chief Justice of the High Court of Madhya Pradesh in Nagpur. He participated in the freedom movement and was believed to have been influenced by Gandhi's philosophy[110] of anti-religious conversions.

B. Ghanshyam Singh Gupta, leading member of the committee, who hailed from Durg, was ex-speaker of the Madhya Pradesh Legislative Assembly and member of the Constituent Assembly of Central Provinces and Berar. He was an Arya Samajist,[111] who followed the principles of Dayananda Saraswati. He was the author of "The Case of Arya Samaj and Regional Language Formula in Punjab" in which he promoted Hindu unity at the local level along linguistic lines.

C. S. K. George was a professor at Commerce College, Wardha. He was appointed as the Christian representation on the committee. George was a Dalit theologian with a membership from the Syrian Church in Kerala and a pioneer of pluralism in theology.[112] He obtained a Bachelor of Divinity degree from Bishop's College in 1927 and served as a tutor there until 1932. He also taught in other colleges before joining Commerce College in Wardha.

D. Ratanlal Malaviya was a Member of Parliament from Manendragarh. He was appointed in the place of Seth Govind Das, who resigned from the committee due to being preoccupied with other responsibilities (vide Resolution No. 419–860–V–Con., dated May 8, 1954).

109. Niyogi, *Report*, 1:4.
110. Moon, *Growing Up Untouchable in India*, 125.
111. Soares, *Truth Shall Prevail*, vii.
112. Aleaz, "S. K. George," 315–40.

E. Bhanupratapsingh Giri Raj Singh Deo, Member of Parliament, was appointed in the place of Kirtimant Rao who resigned from the committee (vide Resolution No. 18–279–XXX–MR, dated January 4, 1955).

F. B. P. Pathak, Secretary to the Government of Madhya Pradesh, Secretary to the Committee.

CHRISTIAN RESPONSE TO THE SELECTION OF MEMBERS

Christian leaders in general and Catholics in particular were displeased with the State's selection of committee members and approached the Prime Minister of India, strongly protesting against the composition of the committee and expressing their unwillingness to cooperate with the investigation.[113] Letters of a similar nature were sent to the Madhya Pradesh government by various leaders of Christian organizations and churches. While some questioned the choice of S. K. George as the Christian representation on the Committee, others raised doubts about the propriety of the appointment of M. B. Niyogi as the chairman as he had exhibited his anti-missionary attitude in a meeting held in Jabalpur earlier that year.[114]

Christian leaders in Madhya Pradesh disliked George's Christian representation as he was ignorant of the language in which most of the investigation was carried out. No church, including the Syrian Church in Kerala, endorsed his continued Christian membership or subscribed to his theology.[115] George was the first Indian Christian theologian to affirm a pluralistic theology of religions.[116] In the words of P. N. Benjamin, "George was a social leper in theological circles" and "was regarded as disloyal to the church . . . His [George's] conviction to follow the Gandhian way also gave him enough audacity to express theological doubts pertaining to the exclusive Divinity of Christ. Theologians, who were taken by surprise at George's affirmations, postponed his ordination as a priest of the Church, hoping that he would come back to the real faith of the Church."[117] S. K. George's appointment to the committee was like adding "insult to injury" as he did not believe in the divinity of Christ and showed deep animus against Christian churches and missionary endeavors.[118] B. N. Banerjee

---

113. Jones, "Missionaries in India," 2.

114. Jones, "Missionaries in India," 2.

115. Thaliath, "Improper Choice," 34.

116. See Aleaz, "S. K. George," 315–40.

117. Benjamin, "Prof. S. K. George."

118. See Soares, *Truth Shall Prevail,* vii; NCCI, "Proceedings of the Thirteenth Meeting," 57; Pothacamury, *Church in Independent India,* 18.

was of the opinion that George was chosen for the committee because he was opposed to the idea of conversion and missions.[119]

On April 29, 1954, Christian members of Parliament together with other prominent Christian leaders convened a meeting at the residence of Health Minister Rajkumari Amrit Kaur and asked her to influence Prime Minister Nehru to intervene in the matter and to suggest to the state that at least one more Indian Christian be put on the committee from the following names instead of, or in addition to, S. K. George.[120]

1. Kanwar Sir Dalip Singh, ex-judge of the undivided Punjab High Court

2. Professor C. P. Mathew, Member of Parliament

3. Mrs. John Mathai

4. Shri M. J. Mukerji, M. L. C.

At one stage, the names of Horace Alexander and David Groom were suggested to represent Christian communities in the place of S. K. George. Though Rajkumari herself attempted to suggest to the state government some names of her choosing, her request was turned down on the grounds that the names of committee personnel had already been announced.[121] Government had supported the Christian representation of S. K. George by affirming that he was "a devout Christian belonging to the oldest Church in India–the Syrian Christian Church, and he has been an educationist and public worker for more than twenty years standing. He has pursued theological studies both in India and at Oxford and was also working in Shantiniketan."[122] Furthermore, about the composition of the committee, the government clarified its stand by saying, "The persons nominated have been chosen for their unbiased and impartial outlook"[123] and requested the cooperation of the people with the committee's investigation.

The Committee's Investigation Procedures

The Committee was authorized to frame its own procedure for conducting the enquiry.[124] While going through all the relevant material from certain government files, "the Committee thought it necessary and desirable to meet representative members of the contestant parties at various important

119. Banerjee, *Religious Conversions in India*, 237.

120. Jones, "Missionaries in India," 2.

121. Jones, "Missionaries in India," 2.

122. Niyogi, *Report*, 1:171.

123. *The Hindustan Times*, "Missionary Activities," 5.

124. Niyogi, *Report*, 1:1–2, 170.

centers in the State and to ascertain the specific points in the controversy."[125] It undertook a tour of several adivasi regions and visited many Christian centers for investigation.

The Committee used mixed methods of enquiry—participant observation, interviews, and mission-history to probe into the problem. It received 385 replies to its questionnaires[126] out of which the committee published only 13 replies from Christians which were either in defense of missionaries or neutral and 5 from non-Christians which were against missionaries.[127] In a span of two years, the committee contacted 11,360 people in person and by letter. In order to gain firsthand knowledge of the workings of the various mission institutions, "the Committee visited institutions like hospitals, schools, churches, leper homes, hostels, etc., maintained by the various Missions operating in Madhya Pradesh and also had an opportunity of contacting local people amongst whom activities of the Missions were carried on and also the areas in which the various Missions were functioning."[128] The persons whom the committee interviewed came from about 700 villages and the statements of a large number of spokesmen from amongst them were also recorded.[129]

THE QUESTIONNAIRE

The committee prepared a questionnaire in Hindi, Marathi, and English with 99 questions under the subject of enquiry heads—Conversion, Social Relations, Missions, Hospitals and Schools, and Remedies.[130] The largest portion of the questionnaire was on "missions" with 26 questions; 21 questions were on "Christian methods of conversion," 15 were on schools, 9 were on hospitals and the rest were on social relations and remedies. Some questions on conversion were multiple choice, while others were yes/no questions. The most significant questions include:

> What, to your knowledge, are the methods used for conversion?
> Are any of the following methods used?
>
> a. Advancing loans. If so, what are the terms on which loans are advanced?

125. Niyogi, *Report*, 1:1–2.

126. Niyogi, *Report*, Part A, 2:189. According to Volume I of the report, the number of written statements received by the committee was 375. See Niyogi, *Report*, 1:2.

127. Niyogi, *Report*, Part A, 2:189.

128. Niyogi, *Report*, 1:2, 171.

129. Niyogi, *Report*, 1:2, 171.

130. *The Hindustan Times*, Tuesday, May 4, 1954, 4.

b. Promising or providing free medical facilities.

c. Giving free education to children.

d. Promising help in litigation.

e. Promising relief from social disabilities suffered in ancestral religion and class, and a better social status as Christians.

f. Offering employment.

g. Holding out hopes of better marriages and greater social freedom.

h. Extolling Christianity and foreign culture.

i. Extolling Jesus Christ and decrying non-Christian deities.

j. Threatening danger of eternal damnation to unconverted souls.

k. Holding out hopes of political advantages.

l. Threatening social boycott and harassment.

m. Other fraudulent and unfair means.

Where does Christian preaching, with a view to conversion, usually take place? Do you know of this being done in any of the following?

a. Houses of individuals and Mukhias in villages,

b. Schools,

c. Hospitals,

d. Orphanages and other charitable institutions,

e. Bazars,

f. Fairs,

g. Churches, and

h. Any other place?

Are patients obliged to take part in Christian prayers and other religious exercises? Are favours shown to those who attend prayers? Are there Christian Pracharaks employed in the hospital?

What is the procedure of recording names of students in school registers? Do you know of cases of students being shown as following a religion other than the one to which they or their parents belonged at the time of admission? Cite specific instances.

What fees are charged in the school? What scholarships and freeships are offered? Is the offer of a freeship used as an inducement to students or their parents to change their religion? Give specific instances, if any.

How many literate people (persons of the Matriculation standard and above) and how many well-to-do people (persons with an annual income of Rs. 1,000 and above) have been converted, in your district, since 1947?

Do you know of cases where conversion has been the result of religious conviction? If so, what were the educational, social and financial status of such people?

Do you think that conversion to Christianity adversely affects the national loyalty and outlook of converts? Give instances and state reasons.

Does change of religion necessarily imply change of culture?

The State being secular, has it any right to interfere with the methods of propagation of any particular faith? Do you think that if other religions showed the same zeal and enthusiasm as Christian Missions, there would be unpleasant consequences?

The Catholic Association approached the Supreme Court with a petition against the Committee's mode of the enquiry, arguing that the questionnaire was purely based on biased assumptions and therefore, it would widen the scope of an impartial enquiry. Although the court rejected their petition, the Chief Justice made certain valuable observations that "the questionnaire was in the nature of an inquisition and in others contained unfortunate innuendoes."[131] Justice suggested that the matter could be rectified because the report had not yet been submitted. According to NCCI, he also expressed that "the impropriety of some members of the committee having indulged in the expression of partisan opinions even before the committee began its work."[132] NCCI said the committee was aware of these comments but they continued the investigation in their own way.

Field Visits and Interviews

The committee toured different parts of the state where missionary work was carried out, including the most interior and almost inaccessible rural areas inhabited mostly by tribals. They visited seventy-seven centers in the

131. *NCCR* 76 (1956) 319.
132. *NCCR* 76 (1956) 319.

districts of Raigarh, Surguja, Raipur, Bilaspur, Amaravati, Nimar, Yeotmal, Akola, Buldana, Mandla, Jabalpur, Betul, Chindwara, and Balaghat, and took notes at every center.[133] The people they interviewed came from 700 villages and the committee recorded every complaint. Out of the 14 districts they visited, the report included the tour reports of 12 districts.

HISTORICAL RESEARCH

To study missionary efforts from the historical point of view, the committee extensively consulted historical documents on the world missionary enterprise, especially the conversion schemes employed by Western missionaries in various parts of Asia, Europe, and other developing nations. Although the committee embarked on an empirical study of the problem, for drawing inferences in the Report on missions, conversions, and proselytism, it depended very much on self-critiqued Christian literature, government records, and various publications of missions operated in India and by mission boards abroad.

Among eighty-three writings that the Committee consulted, the most frequently quoted were the writings of K. M. Panikkar, M. K. Gandhi, Eddy Asirvatham, J. W. Picket, Roland Allen, Arnold Toynbee, and M. C. Parekh. For example, the Committee depended on Panikkar's *Asia and Western Dominance* to contend that since the arrival of Portuguese colonizers, Christianization was a state enterprise and that without the State it was not possible to spread the Christian religion in India.[134] Quoting from Gandhi's work, *Christian Missions,* it tried to emphasize that Christianity is synonymous with denationalization and Europeanisation,[135] and that it was advanced by foreign money.[136]

The Committee used the self-critiqued Christian works of Roland Allen (*The Spontaneous Expansion of the Church* and *Missionary Methods: St. Paul's or Ours?*) and Eddy Asirvatham (*Christianity in the Indian Crucible*) to argue that "one chief reason why India Christians in general still welcome foreign missionaries is economy."[137] The Committee illustrated this opinion by showing that ninety-four percent of the funding of NCCI was from mission boards abroad.[138] From Pickett's *Christian Mass Movements in India,*

133. Niyogi, *Report,* 1:2. See also Appendix B for the tour map of the Committee.

134. Niyogi, *Report,* 1:65.

135. Niyogi, *Report,* 1:124.

136. Niyogi, *Report,* 1:96–104.

137. Niyogi, *Report,* 1:102–4.

138. Out of a total income of Rs.1,12,500, NCCI's received only Rs.6000 from Indian sources. The rest was from abroad during the year of investigation. See Niyogi,

the Committee quoted, "Roman Catholic Missions are aggressively seeking to win converts from Protestant Christian groups and are accused of offering financial inducements through Co-operative Societies loans, employments, free or reduced tuition in schools, financing of court cases, etc."[139] "The economic benefits have come to many participants in Christian mass movement."[140] "The adoption of European names, European modes of life, and European dress has sometimes been followed by the development of a contemptuous attitude towards those of their fellow countrymen who have continued to honour Indian traditions."[141] In *Christian Proselytism in India*, M. C. Parekh heavily criticizes the proselytizing activities of missionaries by contending that they were carried out under the shadow of the British administration and by means of various philanthropic and educational institutions.[142] The Committee used those theses to substantiate that social activities were used as means for conversions. In his Reith lectures, Arnold J. Toynbee stated that the "West had invaded the world, particularly Asia which adopted technology and nationalism but not Christianity, and he suggested that nationalism would be dangerous unless it was balanced by Christianity."[143] Based on this argument, the Committee contended that "To overcome this tide of nationalism the conversion of the people to Christianity apparently offered itself as an effective instrument."[144]

Hindu Nationalist Participation in the Investigation

ABHM deputed L. B. Chelpe, secretary of Nagpur City Hindu Mahasabha, and Dyaneshwar Gajbhiye, advocate, to observe the field proceedings of the Niyogi Committee wherever they went.[145] Along with another Hindu Mahasabha worker, Baburao Miralal, they accompanied the investigation team to Raipur. V. G. Deshpande, M. P., and the General Secretary of ABHM, met with the chairman of the Committee M. B. Niyogi and with his permission, decided to send along two of ABHM's representatives to direct and supervise the investigation in the Rajgarh-Surguja regions.[146] According to

Report, 1:102.

139. Niyogi, *Report*, 1:114.

140. Niyogi, *Report*, 1:101.

141. Niyogi, *Report*, 1:126.

142. Parekh, *Christian Proselytism in India*, 87–88, 234, 252–54, 256. See Niyogi, *Report*, 1:101.

143. Niyogi, *Report*, 1:58.

144. Niyogi, *Report*, 1:58.

145. *Hitavada*, "Niyogi Committee Proceedings."

146. *Hitavada*, "Niyogi Committee Proceedings."

Hitavada, Deshpande himself accompanied the Committee to some areas and accused missionaries of forced conversions alongside anti-missionary complainants.[147] During the investigation, in order to influence the witnesses against missionaries, the Hindu nationalist leaders organized various rallies and campaigns against the missionary enterprise. For example, N. B. Khare, Member of Parliament and the Vice-President of ABHM, planned and executed a rally in Nagpur on July 25, 1954.[148] Such rallies by politicians not only created fear among adivasis, but also strengthened local challengers to threaten the backward Christians to sign or give thumb-impressions on anti-missionary documents during the investigation.[149]

H. V. Seshadri, a prominent leader in the RSS, admits that,

> A senior Sangh Pracharak working in Madhya Pradesh took upon himself the task of mobilizing the necessary witness. It was mainly because of his efforts that about 5,000 vanavasis and others adduce evidence in person before the commission. That help proved crucial for the commission in preparing a well-documented and authentic report which laid bare the underlying motive of the Christian missionary activities. For the first time, because of that historic report, the nefarious activities indulged by the Christian missionaries came to light.[150]

The Hindu responses to the questionnaire received by the Committee were mostly from influential Hindu nationalists. For example, P. S. Shekar filled out the questionnaire on behalf of Hindu Sabha and Arya Samaj.[151] One questionnaire was submitted by Sohanlal Aggarwal, the secretary of Vedic Sanskriti Raksha Samiti. The other was by M. N. Ghatate, the RSS Sanghchalak of the Nagpur Chapter. Another reply came from R. K. Deshpande, pleader, a staunch follower of Hindutva ideology and supporter of the RSS, which, at sixty-three pages, superseded all other questionnaires.

THE MAKING OF THE NIYOGI REPORT

The Committee produced a 939-page report in two volumes. Volume 1 (182 pages), which was initially published by the government of Madhya Pradesh, dealt with the circumstances leading to the appointment of the committee, castes and tribes in M. P., a history of missions, religious liberty in other

147. *Hitavada,* "Probe into Missionary Activities," 3.
148. *Hitavada,* "Foreign Missionaries," 6.
149. *Hitavada,* "Christian Tribals Forced to Sign," 5.
150. Seshadri, *RSS,* 74.
151. Niyogi, *Report,* Part A, 2:279.

countries, missionary activities in M.P. and conclusions and recommendations. It also has appendices and a bibliography. Volume II was published in
two parts; Part A (383 pages) and Part B (374 pages). Part A contains maps of
the Committee's tours, exploratory tour notes, the questionnaire, and replies
to the questionnaire. Part B has details of the Committee's correspondence
with Roman Catholics and state and central governments, as well as Catholic literature on methods of Christian propaganda, missionary activities and
proselytization, and oral statements from the field investigation.

At the very outset, it was mentioned that, "In all the places visited by
the committee, there was unanimity as regards the excellent service ren-
dered by the missionaries in the fields of education and medical relief . . .
" and that "there was no disparagement of Christianity or of Jesus Christ,
and no objection to the preaching of Christianity and even to conversion to
Christianity."[152] However, the committee, which embarked on investigating
the two-fold problem of "complaints and counter-complaints regarding the
missionary activities in the state,"[153] appears to have conducted a thorough
enquiry only on the non-Christian complaints against missionaries, not on
the complaints of missionaries against the non-Christian harassments. The
ninety-nine-point questionnaire is self-evident of such one-sided enquiry
because it was set to study only the missionary activities in the light of
non-Christian complaints. The field notes taken down by the Committee
were mostly from non-Christians. Out of a total of 279 written statements
recorded and summarized in Volume II–A of the Report, only 66 statements were from Christians and the rest were from non-Christians.[154]
Throughout the report, the Committee's historical survey of missions was
also inclined to show only the negative or objectionable aspects of Christian activities and missionary methods.

The Niyogi Committee, nevertheless, gave some clarification on its
investigation of missionary grievances against non-Christians. Referring
to some older governmental enquiry files on missionaries, the Committee
attempted to establish that the state officials, at times, had to deal severely
with the missionaries because of their unlawful activities. As an example,
the Committee showed the case of J. C. Christy, head of a mission, and
two other villagers, who were prosecuted on charges of smuggling rice
to Bihar in contravention of Food Control Regulation.[155] The report also
briefly narrated a few cases filed by missionaries against the authorities

152. Niyogi, *Report*, 1:3.
153. Niyogi, *Report*, 1:171.
154. See Servin, *Annotations on the Niyogi Report*, 154.
155. Niyogi, *Report*, 1:18, 22.

and ascertained that "missionaries deliberately put up false and frivolous complaints against Government servants, so that the activities of the Missionaries could be carried on without being brought to the notice of the higher authorities."[156] The Committee further contended that,

> After careful enquiry Government found that the complaints made by Rev. Christy . . . and the National Christian Council had no basis whatsoever, in fact. All the allegations of discrimination and harassment were totally false. They found that the allegations had been clearly magnified and what was being done in the ordinary process of law was given the shape of deliberate harassment so as to conceal the objectionable activities of Rev. Christy and other Missionaries in the areas concerned. Government noticed that a considerable amount of discontent and resentment prevailed amongst the local population of the Surguja district over the antireligious and anti-national activities of Christian Missionaries engaged in efforts to gain a foothold in the Surguja district which was hitherto a closed ground for them.[157]

After this conclusion on the complaints of missionaries, the Committee moved on to conduct a thorough enquiry against missionary activities from various historical sources, questionnaires, and field notes to ascertain that the anti-missionary allegations were truer than the missionaries' grievances. The report said,

> The [non-Christian] objection was "to the illegitimate methods alleged to be adopted by the Missionaries . . . such as offering allurements of free education and other facilities to children attending their schools, adding some Christian names to their original Indian names, marriages with Christian girls, money-lending, Distributing Christian literature in hospitals and offering prayers in the wards of in-door patients. Reference was also made to the practice of the Roman Catholic priests or preachers visiting new-born babies to give ashish (blessings) in the name of Jesus, taking sides in litigation or domestic quarrels, kidnapping of minor children and abduction of women and recruitment of labour for plantations in Assam or Andaman as a means of propagating the Christian faith among the ignorant and illiterate people. There was a general tendency to suspect some ulterior political or extra-religious motive, in the influx of foreign money for evangelistic work in its varied forms. The concentration of Missionary enterprise on the hill tribes in remote and

156. Niyogi, *Report,* 1:19.
157. Niyogi, *Report,* 1:22.

inaccessible parts of the forest areas and their mass conversion with the aid of foreign money were interpreted as intended to prepare the ground for a separate independent State on the lines of Pakistan. In the Raigarh and Surguja districts, the Christians complained against the petty Government officials, but there were practically none in other districts including Berar.[158]

According to John Dayal, member of the National Integration Council, former president of the All-India Catholic Union, and one of India's foremost voices on human rights and religious minorities, "Ravi Shankar [chief minister of Madhya Pradesh at the time of the *Report*] and Niyogi [were] both pathologically hostile to Christianity" so that "the Report was a forgone conclusion."[159]

The Report's Narrative of the History of Missions in India

For a significant portion of western missionary history in India, the Committee selectively relied on Julius Richter's work, *A History of Missions in India*, K. M. Panikkar's work, *Asia and Western Dominance* and Arthur Mayhew's work, *Christianity and Government of India*. The historical narration of these works clearly brought out two major historical developments, namely missionary aggression in history and the British colonial government's favor and support of the missionary work.

In order to provide background to the expansion of Christianity in India, particularly regarding opposition to missionary activity in Madhya Pradesh, the Report presented a brief description of the origin of the Christian faith in India beginning from the Syrian period, but emphasizing the advent of European Christianity with the arrival of Latin Christian Missionary John de Monte Corvino. The Report consistently highlighted how Christian missionaries were met with opposition from locals in their expansion efforts and how they used their political and economic powers to achieve their Western Christian intentions in India.

AGGRESSIVE MISSIONARY ERA

The Niyogi Committee marked the missionary work commenced at the entry of the Portuguese in 1498 as the start of an aggressive missionary era by the Catholic Church.[160] However, the birthday of Roman Catholic Missions

---

158. Niyogi, *Report*, 1:3.

159. Speech by John Dayal delivered in the Catholic Council of India on December 2, 2007, quoted in Bauman, "Postcolonial Anxiety," 19.

160. Niyogi, *Report*, 1:35.

in India is marked by the arrival of Francis Xavier in 1541, who is said to have baptized 60,000 people on the fisher coast in south India in about four and a half years' time. At Xavier's request, the King of Portugal issued orders that in all Portuguese settlements, "all idols shall be sought out and destroyed, and severe penalties shall be laid upon all such as shall dare to make an idol or shall shelter or hide a Brahmin."[161] The King also extended special privileges to converts who submitted to the yoke of Christianity.[162] By 1600, Jesuit and Augustinian Catholics had entered Agra, Delhi, Lahore, Bengal, and other parts of India, winning about 270,000 converts.

Robert de Nobile saw that "the policy of Xavier and other Catholic Fathers who were making mass conversions of lower castes by using the secular power of the State was disastrous"[163] and attempted to accommodate Hindu thoughts and practices in the presentation of the gospel in order to attract higher caste men into the Christian faith. The Report pointed out that Nobile's method "passed for a genuine work until the Protestant Missionaries exposed the fraud about the year 1840."[164] According to the Niyogi Report, Nobile had converted about 100,000 persons.[165] The Report also states that, "By 1700, India had 600,000 of Catholics."[166] Again, by quoting from the Catholic Directory of 1950, the Report claimed, "Within two hundred years after the Portuguese landed in India, . . . the Catholic Church had 958,000 adherents in India."[167]

According to the Report, Protestant work in India began in 1706 with the arrival of the Dutch, Danes, German Lutherans, Calvinists, and British Baptists. William Carey landed in Calcutta in 1793 and greatly contributed to the expansion of the Christian mission in India. The Serampore trio, viz., Carey, Marshman, and Ward, carried on "a vigorous crusade, pouring coarse and scurrilous invectives against both Hinduism and Islam."[168] In 1813, Mr. Charles Marsh, a retired barrister from Madras, opposed missions in a vehement speech delivered in the Parliament on the subject of sending out missionaries to India. He said, "What will have been gained to ourselves by giving them Calvinism and fermented liquors; and whether

---

161. Niyogi, *Report*, 1:36, quoted from Richter, *History of Christian Missions in India*, 53–54.

162. Niyogi, *Report*, 1:36.

163. Niyogi, *Report*, 1:36.

164. Niyogi, *Report*, 1:36.

165. Niyogi, *Report*, 1:38.

166. Niyogi, *Report*, 1:36.

167. Niyogi, *Report*, 1:36.

168. Niyogi, *Report*, 1:39, quoted from Parekh, *Christian Proselytism in India*, 39.

predestination and gin would be compensation to the natives of India for the changes which will overwhelm their habits, morals and religion?"[169] The Scottish missionary, Alexander Duff, who arrived in India in 1830, proposed the idea of educating Brahmins in English in order to provide them with Christian instruction and eventually Christianize them by employing them in the government sector.[170]

The Government's Assistance in Missionary Efforts

Quoting from Arthur Mayhew's work, *Christianity and Government of India*, the Committee asserted that as early as 1853, several witnesses before the Parliamentary Committee affirmed that "government schools were doing pioneer work for Christianity."[171] The underlying educational policy of the British government was to let missionary institutions impart the knowledge of the Christian religion directly, while government run schools did the same indirectly.[172] With the support of British residents, Protestant missionaries established churches and mission centers all over India.[173] The Niyogi Report underlined that,

> The growth of the Protestant Church during the period of British Raj in India was due mainly to the great patronage and support the Church was getting from the Government of India. Instances of Land grants and financial aid to build Churches, missionary centres, hospitals, educational institutions etc., are numerous. All Cathedrals entrusted to the Bishoprics under the Ecclesiastical establishments were built from State funds. Not only in cities and towns and in military stations in British India, but in almost every Indian State we can find big Churches and Missionary buildings erected almost entirely with Government aid. To protect the Christian converts and their inheritance in British India, Act XXI of 1850 was passed, as the then prevailing customary law stood as an impediment to conversion of Hindus to other religions. All the concessions given to missions in about 350 major Anglican centres need not be mentioned in detail in our Report.[174]

169. Niyogi, *Report*, 1:39, quoted from Marshman, *Life and Times*, 36.

170. Niyogi, *Report*, 1:40.

171. Niyogi, *Report*, 1:40, quoted from Mayhew, *Christianity and the Government of India*, 177.

172. Niyogi, *Report*, 1:40.

173. Niyogi, *Report*, 1:40.

174. Niyogi, *Report*, 1:41.

Missionary Conversion Attempts of the Aboriginal Peoples

According to the Report, until the Permanent Settlement Policy (PSP) initiated by Lord Cornwallis in 1793, "the custom was to regard the aboriginal as owner of the land in the forest, which he reclaimed it and the Zamindars were only farmers of revenue. The cultivators had to render certain feudal services in return for the lands which they held."[175] The Zamindars and Rajas were tax collectors, never owners of the land. But the British PSP affected the tribal economy and gradually allowed the Rajas and Zamindars to become the landlords and the tribals to become mere caretakers of their own lands. By pointing to these historical developments, the Report ascertained that the British created a pathetic situation for aboriginals, opening opportunities for Christian missions to provide the aboriginals with schools, colleges, hostels, hospitals, and co-operatives of various sorts.[176]

In the process, according to the Report, missionaries had not only helped aboriginal people to realize their land rights, but also assisted them to fight against their landlords. "The disputes between them and the Zamindars arose when a number of the aborigines embraced Christianity."[177] Referring to some governmental records of Lord Northbrook, the Report noted that Catholic Jesuit missionaries entered the tribal regions of Chhota Nagpur in 1885 and "tried to exploit the agrarian grievances of the aboriginals"[178] in order to gain a larger following for the Christian faith.

THE ENTRY OF MISSIONARIES AND LOCAL RESTRICTIONS

According to the Report, Deputy Commissioner Hanington invited four German missionaries from Calcutta to Chhota Nagpur in 1845. They began their work under the banner of the Gossner Evangelical Lutheran Mission (GELM) with some orphan children who were handed over to them during a famine. They extended their mission to Ranchi and also operated in the princely states of Madhya Pradesh—Jashpur, Surguja, Udaipur, and Raigarh. In 1885, Catholic missions also entered these areas.[179] Under the benevolence of Sir Andrew Fraser, the Commissioner of Chhattisgarh, Catholic missionaries were able to acquire some land for mission purposes in Bastar State.

175. Niyogi, *Report,* 1:43.
176. Niyogi, *Report,* 1:43.
177. Niyogi, *Report,* 1:43.
178. Niyogi, *Report,* 1:44.
179. Niyogi, *Report,* 1:42.

As missionaries were able to initiate various social and developmental activities among the adivasi people, there were movements of conversion in Jashpur and Udaipur in 1907 and in 1935 respectively.[180] These conversions also had impact on Udaipur and Raigarh regions. As a result, local Rajas in all these areas began to place restrictions on missionary activities to control conversions. In 1936, the princely state of Raigarh officially came up with an anti-conversion law, which, for about nine years, did not allow missionaries to establish or erect mission centers in the state. Similarly, until 1941, by law no priest or catechist was allowed to enter Udaipur, although missionaries ignored this many times with the moral support of local tribal people. From 1941 to 1949, Christian priests were conditionally allowed to enter those states four times a year to visit dangerously ill persons or conduct mass. However, the law did not permit a priest to stay in those feudal states for more than 48 hours.

Conversion Activities in Restricted Areas

As hinted above, since the mid-nineteenth century a number of missionary societies focused on Christianizing the backward sections of society by adopting various methods effective to that goal. When Christian missionaries entered the backward areas in M. P., they "could provide the aboriginals with schools, colleges, hospitals, hostels and cooperatives of various sorts. . ."[181]

In order to explain that missionaries made successful inroads into backward community areas, the Niyogi Report underlined Sir Bamfylde Fuller's account that, "Christianity has been offered to classes that have remained outside the pale of Hinduism, hill tribes and the lower strata of the cooly population . . . Among the higher and better educated classes evangelism has been less successful . . . For a century it has not only been preached in the streets but has been taught in numerous schools and colleges; it has behind it the presage of the ruling race. . ."[182] From other records, the Niyogi committee also claimed to have found that during 1936–37 Jesuit missionaries entered Udaipur State, where proselytization was forbidden, and offered loans to people to attract converts. They opened mission schools without permission from the local authorities which caused clashes between officials and the missionaries. The missionaries were warned by the government to avoid further mission development in those areas and were "told to maintain a register showing in the case of each new convert, his name, his father's

180. Niyogi, *Report*, 1:43.
181. Niyogi, *Report*, 1:43.
182. Niyogi, *Report*, 1:42, quoted from Fuller, *Empire of India*, 364.

name and other particulars including any kind of material benefit given to the converts at the time of their conversion."[183]

Christian Activities as Disloyal, Treasonous, and Anti-national

The Niyogi Report states that the more adivasis embraced Christianity, the more they entered into disputes with the Zamindars and successfully attempted to reclaim their lands in court, because they "were backed by moral support and sometimes by the financial support of the European missionaries."[184] In order to emphasize the separatist tendency in converts, the Report made a reference to the words of M. H. Dampier who said in the Bengal Council in 1868 that, " . . . the Kols who embraced Christianity imbibed more independent notions, and in several instances successfully asserted their rights. . . . .When the Kols go to the Court as Christians they are more uniformly successful than those who have not changed their religion."[185]

From several historical sources, the Niyogi Committee traced the involvement of missionaries and Indian Christians in the tribal rebellions to ascertain that "conversions" not only create social tensions, but also promote an anti-national spirit. For example, it pointed out that the uprising of aboriginals in 1895 was led by a German Mission convert named Birsa, whose revolt was suppressed with the help of the military. From the official records of Bastar state, the Niyogi Committee claimed to have found that an American missionary by the name of Ward led a rebellion in 1910 against the state where he was charged by the state officials many times. An officer called Ward "the most dangerous man in Bastar state."[186] According to the Committee's account, J. May, an official of the state, wrote to the mission authorities at Raipur to say that on enquiry, "he [Ward] was satisfied that he and the Christians were instrumental in causing a great deal of disloyalty and discontent."[187]

The Niyogi Committee also claimed to have discovered from the oral reports that in 1948, Joel Lakra, the head of the German Lutheran Mission "carried on propaganda for a separate Jharkhand Province, which would be administered by Christians, who predominated in the area concerned. Three meetings of Christians were held in the Jashpur State for the purpose of carrying on this propaganda." Lakra was also suspected of "dissuading

183. Niyogi, *Report*, 1:45, quoted from Col. Meek's Report.

184. Niyogi, *Report*, 1:42, quoted from S. Haldar, *Legends of the Kols*, 16.

185. Niyogi, *Report*, 1:43.

186. Niyogi, *Report*, 1:44.

187. Niyogi, *Report*, 1:44.

Christians from participating in Mahatma Gandhi's Ashes Immersion Ceremony observed at Jashpur on 12th February [1948]."[188] According to the Report, Julias Tigga, secretary of Adivasi Sabha, Ranchi, and Jaipal Singh, the father of the Jharkhand movement were also found to have indulged in objectionable activities in Jashpur and Ambikapur. By presenting these examples, the Niyogi Reports attempts to establish that missionaries and converts were involved in extra-religious purposes.

In substantiating the allegation that Christians were involved in anti-national or denationalizing activities, the Report also quoted extensively from Gandhi's work, *Christian Missions,* and suggested reading an anonymous Indian author's work, *The Heritage of the Indian Christian,* published in 1942 by S. P. C. K. Madras. Inclining to Gandhi's self-opinionated remarks on Western Christianity, the Report emphasizes that, "It is not unusual to find Christianity synonymous with denationalization and Europeanisation."[189] When the Committee visited Jashpur, an oral testimonial brought to its notice said that "the preachers told the villagers that Jawahar Raj had come and there was no happiness, and they assured them that Jawahar's Raj would go and that the Christian Raj would come."[190] In Jashpur, some people gave witness that missionaries wished to substitute "Jai Hindu" with "Jai Yesu," and that they hoisted the Christian flag over the national flag in a drama staged in one of their schools.[191] The Backward Classes Commission Report of the government of Madhya Pradesh stated that, "it is true that foreign or proselytizing agencies sometimes consciously or unconsciously foster anti-national and separatist tendencies among the backward classes."[192]

Illegitimate Means of Evangelism and Conversions

The Niyogi Committee showed from its field investigation and from the historical records that conversions had been brought about by various non-spiritual methods, which were labeled as conversions by "allurement," "inducement" or "force."

188. Niyogi, *Report,* 1:11.
189. Gandhi, *Christian Missions,* 160 quoted in Niyogi, *Report,* 1:125.
190. Gandhi, *Christian Missions,* 160 quoted in Niyogi, *Report,* 1:125.
191. Niyogi, *Report,* 1:125.
192. *Hitavada,* "Anti-National Tendencies," 3.

Foreign Funds as a Western Strategy of Mission

There is a section in the Report entitled "Foreign Money" which deals with the details of mission funds received from donor nations. According to the assessment of the Committee, mass conversions, extra religious activities, and separatist tendencies were the result of the foreign aid which was given for social services.[193] During the Committee's investigation visits, some informants alleged that the American government financially aided the missionary enterprise in India and also supplied missionary literature, films, books, pamphlets etc. for propaganda.[194]

While going through the mission magazine *Grahabandhu*, the Niyogi Committee discovered that there was keen competition between various missions in the 1950s regarding the advancement of conversions. The Report contends that, in 1948, J. Lakhra, the head of the Lutheran mission and principal of the Theological College at Ranchi, attended the First Assembly of the World Council of Churches held in Amsterdam. His adivasi representation at the conference fetched mission grants from the United Lutheran Mission in America of $8,000 and $20,000 in 1952 and 1953 respectively in order to advance conversions on a mass scale in Surguja district. With some of these funds, in 1953, "12 Uraon congregations had been established with a baptised membership of 1,010. Three Gossner Pastors, eighteen paid evangelists, four Bible women were put on this work."[195] The Committee also found out from various reports that, in order to progress in the number of conversions, missionaries of different agencies competed with each other and offered some converts Rs.30 each as an inducement to change their religion.[196]

In 1954, Lutheran National Missionary Society (India) requested a financial grant from abroad for engaging the services of Uraon personnel for mass conversion work in Surguja. They secured a grant of 1,500 dollars.[197] The Report states that, "There was practically an invasion in the Surguja State of Missionary enterprise backed by substantial finance and personnel with the result that there were more than 5,000 conversions."[198]

---

193. Niyogi, *Report,* 1:96–105.

194. *Hitavada,* "American Aid," 3.

195. Niyogi, *Report,* 1:45, 98–100.

196. Niyogi, *Report,* 1:45.

197. Niyogi, *Report,* 1:45. Niyogi Committee collected information from *The National Missionary Intelligencer,* April 1954, 5.

198. Niyogi, *Report,* 1:45.

The Report also inferred that, "without the lure of money none would have sought to become Christian."[199]

WAYS OF EVANGELISM: SCHOOLS, HOSPITALS, AND ORPHANAGES

By assessing the information collected from the various historical sources and field interviews, the Niyogi Committee deduced that missionaries used hospitals, schools, philanthropic works, and material gifts for the purpose of evangelizing India. In substantiation of this deduction the Committee quoted Richter's words, "Missions have neither a call nor a mandate to teach English literature, history, mathematics or natural science, the preaching of the Gospel to the heathen and the exercise of pastoral care over the relative churches is the head and front of all Missionary labour, and everything must be considered as pure waste which does not directly further this end."[200] It also referred to Arthur Mayhew's work, *Christianity and the Government of India,* to maintain that missionaries' primary object of education was religious conversion rather than intellectual improvement.[201] It highlighted a portion of the report of the World Conference of the International Missionary Council (IMC), held at Thambaram in 1938, which stated that, "Care should be taken to secure that evangelism has a central place in all medical and educational institutions."[202] The Niyogi Committee gathered a few of these kinds of statements from various sources including Catholic mission bulletins, government records, and other missionary reports to maintain that evangelism is the major thrust of all mission activities including the schools, hospitals, and orphanages.

Regarding schools, the Committee considered the allegations made by some individuals that the Roman Catholic Church offered free room and board to school children with the aim of attracting their parents to attend church services, while making it a rule for the children to follow Christian religious regulations in its facilities. The Committee claimed to have found that in the school records the names of some children were changed from Hindu names to Christian names with Western last names such as "Walter."[203]

The Committee gave accounts of the various Christian hospitals it had visited, where it had learned that lady preachers and Bible women were

199. Niyogi, *Report,* 1:115.

200. Niyogi, *Report,* 1:106, quoted from Richter, *History of Christian Missions in India,* 314.

201. Niyogi, *Report,* 1:106.

202. Niyogi, *Report,* 1:107.

203. Niyogi, *Report,* 1:108.

employed to offer prayers to patients as a divine aid for healing. It was mentioned in the Report that a lady named Sarjabai Yengad in Washim was reported to have been giving her Christian witness from room to room, while a man, Sampad Shinde, of the Church of the Nazarene, visited the hospital daily to talk about Christ with the patients.[204] In Washim, Hanumant Bhatkhande complained that when his wife was in the mission hospital for treatment, a nurse named Sathe tried to influence her to become Christian. When the investigation team visited Raipur, similar complaints were heard. The committee also posited that the leper asylum made a lot of patients Christian as long as it was under mission management. When the management was taken over by the government and when a Hindu doctor was placed, as many as 100 Christian patients openly gave up their Christian faith and reverted to Hinduism.[205] The Committee uncovered various hospital records about the conversion of patients from 1898 until the 1950s to prove the allegation that mission hospitals indulged in proselytization work.

According to the Niyogi Report, Christian orphanages were another precinct where the Christian population undoubtedly multiplied. In order to explain why there were more Christians from the backward communities than from well-to-do society, the Committee states that it was due to missionaries' focus on people who are economically, socially, and physically disadvantaged. "A large number of such orphans were gathered into the Christian fold during famine, natural calamities like the floods and the earthquakes" and "most conversions have been doubtless insincere admittedly brought about in expectation of social service benefits and other material considerations."[206]

The Committee maintains further that "conversions were induced on the promise of gifts of salt, plough, bullocks and even milk powder received from abroad."[207] In an interview on June 12, 1954, John Lakra of Pithora at Dhorpur admitted that he saw in people "some sort of willingness to become Christians to improve their lot. We have got a Mutual Aid Society to advance money. In all the centres at Jashpur there is Mutual Aid Society. . .We have got several committees in foreign countries from which amount is collected. This is received here and spent by the Bishop . . . if parents embrace Christianity their minor children are also baptized."[208] The Committee claimed that from oral testimonials it had found that the

204. Niyogi, *Report*, 1:110.
205. Niyogi, *Report*, 1:110.
206. Niyogi, *Report*, 1:113.
207. Niyogi, *Report*, 1:116.
208. Niyogi, *Report*, 1:116.

Roman Catholic Church used the influence of village officers and sometimes employed the village heads to distribute Christian tracts and invite
people into the church. They found contextual methods of evangelism such
as Hindu-styled Christian ashrams, jatra, bhajans, dramas and story-telling
as unnecessary counterfeits of Hindu traditions to affect Hinduism and to
attract converts into Christian faith.[209]

FRAUDULENT AND FORCED CONVERSIONS

From government records, mission statements, and oral evidences, the Report claimed to have ascertained that Jesuit missionaries made unauthor-
ized attempts to enter Udaipur state during 1936–37, offered loans to people
"to attract converts," and opened schools without permission from the local
authorities.[210] Roman Catholic missions employed various devices for proselytization, creating situations that forced people to walk into Christianity.
Money-lending was one of the schemes.

When the Committee visited the districts of Surguja, Raigarh, and
Mandla, they learned that missionaries advanced loans to economically poor
adivasis and *harijans* on various conditions, failing which would require the
borrower to repay the loans with interest.[211] One of the conditions was that
if one chose to become a Christian, it would be easy for him to obtain loans
with no interest or no repayment at all.[212] Similar conditions made the bor-
rowers obliged either to convert or to burden themselves with financial debts.
In many cases "when one member of a family had taken a loan, all the other
members of that family were entered in the book as potential converts."[213]
The Committee also found Col. A. S. Meek's letter No. 751, dated April 20,
1935, which indicated that these sorts of missionary practices had been in
place for many decades and that Meek himself enforced restrictions on the
conversion activities of missionaries.[214] The Report argues that since Meek
had imposed several restraints on the activities of missionaries, the missionaries found other ways such as hospitals and educational institutions to carry
out the business of making converts.

209. Niyogi, *Report*, 1:118–24.
210. Niyogi, *Report*, 1:45.
211. Niyogi, *Report*, 1:113.
212. Niyogi, *Report*, 1:114.
213. Niyogi, *Report*, 1:115.
214. Niyogi, *Report*, 1:114.

Religious Liberty: The Indian Constitution vs Other Constitutions

The Report dedicated two chapters to comparing the religious freedom of various nations with India's constitutional provision of freedom of religion, contending that India went too far in generously granting religious freedom to Christian missionaries. In 1944, the Joint Committee appointed by the Federal Council of Churches of Christ in America and the Foreign Missions Conference of North America made a statement on Religious Liberty stating that, "Religious Liberty shall be interpreted to include freedom to worship according to conscience and to bring up children in the faith of their parents; freedom for the individual to change his religion; freedom to preach, educate, publish and carry on missionary activities; and freedom to organise with others, and to acquire and hold property, for these purposes."[215] The Niyogi Committee agreed with this definition and claimed that India had practiced such religious liberty from time immemorial.

However, the Report stated that, "Hindu India has maintained this spirit of religious toleration," but that "intolerance in religion came in the wake of the advent of Christianity,"[216] that the Christian dogma of exclusive salvation in the only God makes them intolerant toward other faiths. In substantiating this contention, it quotes from Searle Bates' work, *Religious Liberty: An Inquiry,* which says that, "The antagonist in the major struggle of mankind for religious freedom has been Christianity, which accentuated the elements of intolerance included in its Hebraic heritage and supplemented them by the introduction of two new and potent incentives—the idea of a universal mission, a rigid dogma, the conception of the Church as an indispensable mediator between God and man."[217] It further quoted from Bates that,

> When the idea of a single and universal God was set, first by the Hebrews and then by the Christians, against the ancient polytheism, there arose a new form of religious exclusivism, contrary to the old not less in its basis than in its effects. The Gods of the other peoples were said to be false and fallen and religion lost its national and public character and became on the one side cosmopolitan and on the other proper to each single individual. From this followed not only *an inextinguishable spirit of proselytism but also the principle that he only could be saved who*

---

215. Niyogi, *Report,* 1:61, quoted from Bates, *Religious Liberty,* 309.

216. Niyogi, *Report,* 1:62.

217. Niyogi, *Report,* 1:61, quoted from Bates, *Religious Liberty,* 132.

worshipped the true God, that is to say, the principle of absolute intolerance.[218] [italics added by the Committee]

The Committee cited Bates forty times in the report to show that Christianity has been a religion of intolerance from the beginning. By pointing to Catholic intolerance toward Protestants in Spain, the Report questioned the majoritarian attitude of the Catholic Church over other religious minorities or minority Christian sects. On the other hand, while showing how countries such as Denmark, Greece, Germany and Japan moved from general religious freedom to self-centered religious freedoms in the wake of aggressive Christian proselytization, the Report questioned India's constitutional religious freedom which granted more religious liberty to the minority than others.

Ironically, the Report bragged about its secular values, contending that Christians, unlike Hindus, were intolerant of religious others. "Notwithstanding the unpleasant memories associated with the advent of the Western Christian Missionary activities in India and the methods used by foreigners under a foreign Government, notwithstanding that in the fight for Independence Christians as a whole had little or no share . . . a secular and democratic State was set up"[219] to treat the minorities equally with no special consideration for majority Hindus. But, "the attitude of the minorities may not have been very helpful in the past, backdoor methods to sabotage the national movement may have been used."[220] The Report underlined Japan's definition of religious freedom according to which, "Freedom is limited to belief. It is to be exercised within the limits of the law of the land and consistent with the duties of the individual to the State as its Subjects."[221] The bottom line, according to the Niyogi Report, was that the religious freedom guaranteed in India's constitution was subject to limitations and could not be interpreted and exploited by missionaries in their own way.

Major Findings and Interpretations

From their overall evaluation of the activities of Christian missionaries in Madhya Pradesh, the Committee made the following inferences in the Report: [222]

218. Niyogi, *Report*, 1:61, quoted from Bates, *Religious Liberty*, 132.

219. Niyogi, *Report*, 1:95.

220. Niyogi, *Report*, 1:95.

221. Article XXVIII of the Constitution of Japanese Empire. See Niyogi, *Report*, 1:82, quoted from Bates, *Religious Freedom*, 49.

222. Niyogi, *Report*, 1:133–62.

1. *Problem of the Secular Constitution:* Since the Indian secular constitution, which guaranteed religious freedom, came into effect, not only had the American personnel of missionary organizations increased, but also mass conversions in the adivasi regions had been advanced by educational, medical and evangelistic activities.

2. *The Power of Foreign Funds:* Enormous sums of foreign money were used for proselytization work. Therefore, evangelization was a foreign strategy that affected the faith of other religions by the power of money.

3. *Illegitimate Methods of Conversion:* Conversions were not brought about by spiritual convictions, but by undue influence, misrepresentation and various forms of material inducements.

4. *Denationalization of Converts:* Missions in some places served extra-religious ends, causing converts to be disloyal to their own country or to show separatist tendencies.

5. *Christian Attacks on Hinduism:* A vile propaganda campaign against the religion of the majority community was being systematically carried out so as to create a breach in the public peace.

6. *Evangelism as Western Supremacy:* Evangelization in India appeared to be part of a uniform world policy to revive Christendom in order to reestablish Western supremacy and was not prompted by spiritual motives.

7. *Proselytization:* Schools, hospitals and orphanages have been used as means to facilitate proselytization.

8. *Tribals and Harijans:* These groups were targets of aggressive evangelism because they were mostly non-literate.

The Committee's Recommendations

"The committee had to consult a number of published books, pamphlets and periodicals for determining the nature and form of their recommendation."[223]

The following is a summary of recommendations provided by the Niyogi Committee in the report.

223. Niyogi, *Report,* 1:4.

1. Those Missionaries whose primary object is proselytization should be asked to withdraw. The large influx of foreign Missionaries is undesirable and should be checked.

2. The best course for the Indian Churches to follow is to establish a United Independent Christian Church in India without being dependent on foreign support.

3. The use of medical or other professional services as a direct means of making conversions should be prohibited by law.

4. To implement the provision in the Constitution of India prohibiting the imparting of religious education to children without the explicit consent of parents and guardians, the Department of Education should see that proper forms are prescribed and made available to all schools.

5. Any attempt by force or fraud, or threats of illicit means or grants of financial or other aid, or by fraudulent means or promises, or by moral and material assistance, or by taking advantage of any person's inexperience or confidence, or by exploiting any person's necessity, spiritual (mental) weakness or thoughtlessness, or, in general, any attempt or effort (whether successful or not), directly or indirectly to penetrate into the religious conscience of persons (whether of age or underage) of another faith, for the purpose of consciously altering their religious conscience or faith, so as to agree with the ideas or convictions of the proselytizing party should be absolutely prohibited.

6. Religious institutions should not be permitted to engage in occupations like recruitment of labour for tea gardens.

7. It is the primary duty of Government to conduct orphanages, as the State is the legal guardian of all minors who have no parents or natural guardians.

8. Government should issue an appeal to authoritative and representative Christian Missionary Organizations and to Christians in general to come together and to form an authoritative organization which should lay down and inform Government in clear terms the policy which the Missions and Christians in general will follow in respect of propagating their religion, the methods to be followed in conversions, the type of propaganda which will be promoted and the attempts which will be made to confine their evangelistic activities within the limits of public order, morality, and health.

9. An amendment of the Constitution of India may be sought, firstly to clarify that the right of propagation has been given only to the citizens of India, and secondly that it does not include conversion brought about by force, fraud or other illicit means.

10. Suitable control on conversions brought about through illegal means should be imposed. If necessary, legislative measures should be enacted.

11. Advisory Boards at State level, regional level, and district level should be constituted of non-officials, minority communities like Tribals and Harijans being in a majority on these boards.

12. Rules relating to the registration of Doctors, Nurses and other personnel employed in hospitals should be suitably amended to provide a condition against evangelistic activities during professional services.

13. Circulation of literature meant for religious propaganda approval of the State Government should be prohibited.

14. Institutions in receipt of grants-in-aid or recognition from Government should be compulsorily inspected every quarter by officers of Government.

15. Government should lay down a policy that the responsibility of providing social services like education, health, medicine, etc., to members of scheduled tribes, castes, and other backward classes will be solely of the State Government, and adequate services should be provided as early as possible, non-official organizations being permitted to run institutions only for members of their own religious faith.

16. A separate department of Cultural and Religious affairs should be constituted at the State level to deal with these matters which should be in charge of a Minister belonging to a scheduled caste, tribe or other backward classes and should have specially trained personnel at the various levels.

17. No non-official agency should be permitted to secure foreign assistance except through Government channels.

18. No foreigner should be allowed to function in a scheduled or a specified area either independently or as a member of a religious institution unless he has given a declaration in writing that he will not take part in politics.

19. Programmes of social and economic uplift by non-official or religious bodies should receive prior approval of the State.[224]

CHRISTIAN CRITIQUE OF THE REPORT

The Catholics, the NCCI,[225] mission agencies, and various prominent foreign missionaries expressed their concern at the outcome of the investigation of the Niyogi Committee. Christians throughout India condemned the Report and the way it was framed. In order to prepare a counter report against the Niyogi Report's findings, the management of the *Saptahik Madhya Pradesh (SMP)*, a Hindi weekly newspaper, proposed to conduct an independent enquiry into the Niyogi Report's allegations against missionaries and invited various Christian representatives to take part in the enquiry.[226] The NCCI declined to participate in the reinvestigation process as it would not affect the Niyogi Report's inferences and recommendations in anyway.[227] Further information is not available to show whether SMP moved forward with such a proposal. However, the Catholic Church took drastic steps to critique the Report by revisiting the fields of investigation to cross-examine the facts. It also conducted various symposiums and discussion forums and published counter answers to the major claims of the report.

The Response of Catholics

Catholic leaders were greatly disappointed and angry at the Report and asserted that it was a "distortion of historical perspective; irrelevant fact, false allegation, gratuitous inference, blatant lie, malicious suspicion, etc., and a one-sided Report with void of sense and truth.[228]" They attempted to scrutinize every detail of the Niyogi Report and to refute the unwarranted claims and assertions by pointing to how the enquiry committee misquoted Christian mission history from a selective list of Christian publications, how it had prepared a ponderous questionnaire, and how

---

224. Niyogi, *Report*, 1:163–65.

225. The National Christian Council of India (NCCI) was formed in 1921 as the successor of National Missionary Council of India founded in 1912. Since 1979, it has been known as the National Council of Churches in India.

226. *Minutes of the Meeting of the Executive Committee of the NCCI, Nagpur,* February 25–27, 1959, 39, 40.

227. *Minutes of the Meeting of the Executive Committee of the NCCI, Nagpur,* February 25–27, 1959, 39, 40.

228. Servin, *Annotations on the Niyogi Report Relating to Raigarh and Surguja,* 1.

it had blacked-out relevant Christian-favored statements and facts in the process of making the Report.

ANNOTATIONS ON THE NIYOGI REPORT RELATING TO RAIGARH AND SURGUJA

In a 247-page detailed work, Oscar Servin, the Bishop of Raigarh-Ambikapur, dealt with the Niyogi Report chapter by chapter and subject by subject and pointed to each error related to the Raigarh and Surguja regions. He contended that in order to explain a tense situation between missionaries and non-Christians, in 1954 the Committee gave blind credence to various unwarranted reports published by the press against missionaries and grossly misinterpreted them to strengthen those allegations. He condemned the Report's broad attack on missionaries which said that they meddled in the politics of pro-Bihar agitation, Jharkhand and Christianistan (land of Christians), and challenged anyone to prove that any missionary played on the religious feelings of the primitive Christian converts in Madhya Pradesh. By wondering "what on earth is Christianistan?" he contended that "Catholic missionaries have absolutely nothing to do with politics, either directly or indirectly."[229] To substantiate this point, he included in the appendices of this book the various official Catholic statements regarding missionary political involvement. He argued that it was the work of a certain Sadhu named Swami Jagat Guru Ramanuj Saraswati, who went as far as publishing in the press a statement accusing the missionaries of possibly establishing Christianistan![230]

Servin showed that the committee had utilized the statements of lapsed Catholics such as Col. Meek and anti-missionary Zamindars in Madhya Pradesh to insist that mass conversions of Oraons, Kharias, and other backward communities were due to the proselytization efforts of missionaries.[231] M. B. Niyogi, the chairman of the enquiry committee, maintained that the aboriginals were not capable of true conversion due to lack of intelligence, and therefore, by force, fraud, or inducement they had been brought into Christian faith.[232] Servin countered the validity of the Report's "objection to conversion" by pointing to the conversion of M. B. Niyogi himself to Buddhism in Nagpur in October 1956 along with B. R. Ambedkar and some 200,000 untouchables.[233] According to Smith's account, 300,000 Hindus were

229. Niyogi, *Report*, 1:7, 16.
230. Niyogi, *Report*, 1:16–17.
231. Niyogi, *Report*, B, 2:325–75.
232. Niyogi, *Report*, B, 2:325–75.
233. Servin, *Annotations on the Niyogi Report*, 27.

converted to Buddhism including M. B. Niyogi.[234] After his conversion, every Sunday evening M. B. Niyogi used to deliver lectures on Buddhism to the educated people in Nagpur and to conduct conversion ceremonies (puja) for Buddhism.[235] N. C. Mukerji, a lecturer at Allahabad University, had also made a similar criticism. If "the Chairman of the Committee, Dr. Niyogi, has himself walked on the road to conversion," "what will be the repercussion of his act on the value of the Report . . . " and "how much of it will have to be rewritten," and how much of it has to be rejected?[236]

REPLY TO NIYOGI COMMITTEE

In 1957 the Catholic Association of Bombay (CAB) published a collection of articles under the title, *Truth Shall Prevail: Reply to Niyogi Committee*, edited by Aloysius Soares, vice-president of CAB. Eight Catholic writers of scholarly repute and ecclesial leadership contributed articles to critique the issues raised by the Committee in the Report.

Reacting to the Niyogi Committee's orientation on Christian conversions, Soares wrote a lengthy leading article, "Conversion—Means and Ends," in which he argued that it was wrong to assume that "the aim and purpose of Christian Missionary activity all over the world is said to be conversion."[237] He puts it in perspective by emphasizing that the purpose of Christian missions is evangelization—"the presentation of the life and teaching of Jesus Christ," which may or may not result in conversion. Conversion of an individual is the response of that individual to the Gospel, which is borne out of his own will and thus it is not something imposed from outside.[238] The act of conversion is a process and not an instant work because when a would-be convert expresses his wish to be baptized, his belief is tested through catechetical instruction that lasts for months or even years. Therefore, "forced conversion," according to Soares, is not possible and is a contradiction in itself.[239]

He also strongly condemned the Niyogi Committee's contention that the schools, hospitals, and other charitable works which proceed from religious orders and congregations were used as baits to entrap non-Christians into the Church. While strongly defending the theological and social aspects of evangelism, he argued that, given the Indian context of

234. Smith, *India as a Secular State*, 167–68.
235. Moon, *Growing Up Untouchable in India*, 146, 151.
236. Mukerji, "Communalism of the Niyogi Report," 38.
237. Soares, "Conversion—Means and Ends," 1.
238. Soares, "Conversion—Means and Ends," 1.
239. Soares, "Conversion—Means and Ends," 2.

the time, the Niyogi committee sided with religious intolerance bred from dogmatism at both the civil and political levels, which hatched a purposeful misinterpretation of the Christian concept of conversion because of the positive impact of conversion on the people.[240]

In his article, "The Niyogi Report and Its Sources," William Coelho attempted to show how the pre-conceived notions of the committee were applied through various stages of the investigation in order to build upon the allegations rather than to cross-examine the witnesses.[241] For example, he pointed out that the questionnaire, which was framed to fish for opinions rather than only find facts, "provided opportunities to anti-Christian leaders to make inflammatory speeches or to coach and prompt villagers to complaint against missionaries."[242] Coelho also charged the Committee with tampering with the materials. He dedicated several pages to clearly showing how the Niyogi Committee selectively chose Christians sources to show that anti-foreign missionary feelings were expressed not by Hindus alone, but also by Christians.[243] He also spotted several misquotes and misrepresentations of Christian literature and testimonials in the Report. He discovered that out of 250 quotations cited in the Report, there were 85 errors, 23 misquotations, and 29 quotes out of context. In addition, he found that there were 33 mutilations in the gathered testimonials.

An Anthropological Verdict on the Niyogi Report

Allen Mathias Hermanns, Indian anthropologist, was of the opinion that the Niyogi Report gave a false impression that its investigation was thoroughly substantiated by scientific evidence. Chapter III of the Niyogi Report, Volume I, dealt with the "Castes and Tribes of Madhya Pradesh" in which the Committee contended that Hinduism had its roots in the very hearts of the aboriginal tribes and that they belonged to a pre-developed stage of Hinduism. Therefore, they shared in Hindu heritage whereas Christian missionaries promoted separatist tendencies among them.[244]

In his well-researched work, *Hinduism and Tribal Culture: An Anthropological Verdict on the Niyogi Report,* Hermanns countered the Report's portrayal of tribal people as Hindus. He went back to the Niyogi's sources, particularly the works of G. S. Ghurye, M. M. Kunte, and other orientalists'. To question the Report's scholarly sources, Hermanns showed that Kunte's

240. Soares, "Conversion—Means and Ends," 3–106.

241. Coelho, "Niyogi Report and its Sources," 140–73.

242. Coelho, "Niyogi Report and its Sources," 142.

243. Coelho, "Niyogi Report and its Sources," 148–73.

244. Niyogi, *Report*, 1:29.

actual source for *The Vicissitudes of Indian Civilization* was "Mahabharata," which is not generally accepted by scholars as a real historical document, but rather as a beautiful myth or saga.[245] In discussing Ghurye's understanding, classification, and construction of tribal identity, Hermanns argued that the committee misquoted or misrepresented his ideas to establish that since Vedic times, Aryans and non-Aryans intermingled by intermarriage and thus aboriginals are Hinduized by acculturation. By presenting the scholarly facts regarding tribals, he pointed out that "the Committee members were not objective searchers of the truth but were extremely prejudiced against Christian missionaries and Christians."

A Symposium on the Niyogi Report

In 1957, O. M. Thomas, a Jacobite Syrian Christian of Travancore, organized a topical symposium and invited a few Christian men of repute from different churches to deliberate on the Niyogi Report's attacks on missionaries and Christians. The symposium was attended by Joseph Thaliath, a Catholic and retired Justice of the High Court of Travancore; N. C. Mukerji, a Presbyterian and professor at Allahabad University; and M. Ruthnaswamy, a distinguished scholar, retired vice chancellor of Annamalai University, and the president of the Catholic Union of India. Their papers were published under the title, *Voice of Truth: A Topical Symposium, Replies to the Niyogi Report and Sardar K. M. Panikkar's Attacks on Missionaries and Christians.*

In his paper, "Christian-baiting in Madhya Pradesh," O. M. Thomas gave a detailed account of how trouble was created for Christians in Madhya Pradesh by Hindu nationalist groups—the Hindu Mahasabha, the RSS, the Ram Rajya Parishad, and the Arya Samaj. By critically analyzing the enquiry procedures of the Niyogi committee and the claims therein, he established that these groups harrowed the ground for oppression of Christianity through a report like the Niyogi.[246] In "Communalism of the Niyogi Report," while questioning whether Christian missionary work should be permitted at all in India, N. C. Mukerji argued that "the real standpoint of the Report is that of the Hindu Mahasabha which openly stands for the establishment of a *Hindu Rashtra*, with Hinduism as the state religion and the domination of all minorities by the Hindu majority."[247]

M. Ruthnaswamy, in his article, "Obsession of the Niyogi Committee," expounded on how the Report was pregnant with baseless suspicion of Christian loyalty to the state. In his paper, "A Critique of the Niyogi Report,"

245. Hermanns, *Hinduism and Tribal Culture*, 2.
246. Thomas, "Christian-Baiting in Madhya Pradesh," 24–33.
247. Mukerji, "Communalism of the Niyogi Report," 38–39.

O. M. Thomas criticized at length the micro details of the major accusations of the Report. He pointed out that the positive Christian responses obtained from the mission field and from Christian organizations during the investigation were purposefully not considered or included in the Report. He also pointed out how the media and government officials were controlled by the majority mentality and the shifty tactics of Hindu nationalists to represent only the voice of Niyogi Committee's investigation, rather than its opponents as well. He stressed that the Report misrepresented the Christian history of missions and lapsed from accuracy. He asserted that the primary reasons for the Niyogi Report's attacks on Christian missions and methods of conversion were the committee's dislike of conversions and their desire to keep up the supremacy of caste and Hindu law.[248]

National Christian Council of India (NCCI)

The National Christian Council of India, now known as the National Council of Churches in India, which has broadly represented Protestant Churches in India since 1921, expressed its apprehensions about the outcome of the report as it was clear that the Committee was not following any accepted judicial procedure in the conduct of its enquiry. When the report came out, NCCI remarked that,

> The Report of the Committee has deeply injured the Christian Community in India. The spirit of the Report is not in keeping with the best traditions of our country. Not only has it tarred with one brush all Christian Missionaries in India, ignoring the devoted work done by them in uplifting the down-trodden and serving the sick and the lost, but it has slandered Christian Indians by dubbing them as alien agents. The Report is an incitement to communal hatred and shows poor understanding of the spirit of secularity and unity in diversity which India has accepted as her ideal.
>
> Already, much harm has been done by the publication of this Report. We can now only hope that everyone concerned will ignore it and consign it to oblivion. We hope no further bitterness will be engendered by it . . . .[249]

NCCI's plans of publishing "a book dealing with issues raised by the Niyogi Report" were never followed up by the council.[250]

---

248. Thomas, "Critique of the Niyogi Report," 52–160.

249. NCCI, *Proceedings of the Thirteenth Meeting*, 62–63.

250. NCCI, *Proceedings of the Thirteenth Meeting*, Appendix, VI, 12.

THE STATE GOVERNMENT'S RESPONSE
TO THE REPORT

The government of Madhya Pradesh did not legally act upon the recommendations of the Report against Christian missionary enterprise. However, it published the Report as a public document of investigation on missionary activities in the state. Since the Report was result of the investigation committee headed by M. B. Niyogi, a reputable, educated, retired high government official, and since it was a governmental investigation report, it was generally considered credible. According to NCCI, after the publication of the report, the government of India was "watchful of the plans, utterances, and the writings of Indian Christians and missionary publicists."[251] Donald E. Smith states that, "this official document is significant as an expression of the extremist Hindu sentiment which is sometimes found where it would not be expected."[252] It has provided ideological impetus to Hindu nationalist politicians in the parliament to embark on their political agendas against Christian missionary activities and has particularly influenced the advocates and followers of Hindutva thought, which is discussed in the next chapter.

251. NCCI, *Proceedings of the Thirteenth Meeting*, Appendix, VI, 13.
252. Smith, *India as a Secular State*, 201.

5

The Significance of the Niyogi Report on Hindu Nationalism

THIS CHAPTER TRACES THE impact of the report on sociopolitical and religious events in independent India, particularly how it has shaped the perspectives and attitudes of the RSS, the VHP, and the BJP against Christianity and its missionary work. It also presents how Hindutvavadis circulate the redactions and recensions of the Report in print, electronic, and social media to stereotype the history of the spread of Christian missions in India and attempt to raise resistance to Christian conversion activities.

Sebastian Kim, who has scrutinized the Hindu-Christian debates on conversion in independent India, observed that, "The report was significant because it gave historical and social justification for Hindu objections to Christian conversion by providing factual evidence for the problems surrounding the Christian campaign of conversion, adding to the theological groundwork against conversion laid in the previous century by Roy and the moral, religious and philosophical basis on which, at a later date, Gandhi had challenged Christian conversions. Even more significantly, the report also implicitly promoted the idea that the people of India should conform to Hindu ideology."[1] Leaning to Christophe Jaffrelot's analysis, he argued that the Niyogi enquiry process was the political strategy of the Hindu nationalist party of the day in Madhya Pradesh to intimidate religious minorities and to paint the issue of conversions as entirely political, not religious or spiritual.[2]

---

1. Kim, *In Search of Identity*, 72.
2. Kim, *In Search of Identity*, 72.

Chad Bauman argued that the Niyogi enquiry in the 1950s was the result of the post-colonial anxiety of nationalist Hindus about the survival of the fledging Indian nation. He noted that, "the Report remains an influential document today"[3] because "it is often invoked by contemporary Hindu nationalists as an indication of the methods and goals of Christian missionaries, even contemporary missionaries."[4]

According to Goldie Osuri, who examined various scholarly discussions on Indian secularism, Hindu nationalism, and conversion, "In a post-independent era, the Niyogi report was responsible for framing Christian missionary activities as a threat to the public order of nation-state sovereignty."[5] Citing the arguments of Ronald Neufeldt, Gauri Vishwanathan, Parvati Menon, Chad Bauman, and others, Osuri indicates that the Report, which affirmed the idea that "conversion means a change in nationality at the feet of missionaries"[6] and which appeared to be concerned about nation-state sovereignty and public order, formed the basis for contemporary anti-conversion publications, campaigns, and Hindu nationalists' demands for the passing of Freedom of Religion laws in various states.[7]

THE INFLUENCE OF THE REPORT ON THE SOCIOPOLITICAL DEVELOPMENTS

In 1956, the state government of Madhya Pradesh published the Niyogi Report and made it available to the public, but it did not implement the Report's recommendations against the conversion activities of missionaries or the church. There were at least two possible reasons why the government maintained neutrality on the report. First, Madhya Pradesh was ruled by a government which belonged to the Congress Party. The Congress Party believed in the ideology of democracy and secularism. Though Chief Minister of Madhya Pradesh Ravi Shankar Shukla, under whose government the Enquiry Committee was appointed, was hostile to Christians,[8] as a member of the Congress Party, Shukla and his government theoretically shared in the ideology of the party and were obliged to show due respect to party principles. Shukla was

---

3. Bauman, "Postcolonial Anxiety," 4.

4. Bauman, "Postcolonial Anxiety," 4.

5. Osuri, *Religious Freedom in India*, 33.

6. Osuri, *Religious Freedom in India*, 36.

7. Osuri, *Religious Freedom in India*, 29–36.

8. Thomas, "Christian-Baiting," 26; Bauman, "Postcolonial Anxiety," 19. According to Richard Fox Young, the state government under Shukla's leadership approved anti-Christian activities in the state while theoretically maintaining secular goals of the Congress Party. See Brown, "Indian Christians," 226.

also aware of a previous letter from Prime Minister Jawaharlal Nehru, which instructed him to render respect and protection to all Christians in the state in light of India's constitutional freedom.[9] Passing restrictions on the religious activity of Christian missionaries as recommended by the Report would be against Shukla's own party's secular ideals and becomes questionable in the context of India's secularism.

Second, there was political instability within the state in the years following the publication of the Report. Chief Minister Shukla died in December 1956, a few months after the report was submitted to the government. Bhagwantrao Mandloi became Chief Minister for 30 days before Kailash Nath Katju took over the office of Chief Minister in January 1957. Prior to becoming Chief Minister, Katju served as the Home Minister of India between 1951 and 1955 under Nehru's leadership. After his term was over, Bhagwantrao Mandloi became Chief Minister again in March 1962 for one and a half years until replaced by Dwarka Prasad Mishra in 1963. During these years, there were political debates in the state assembly on the issue of "conversions by force, fraud or inducement," but no legal decision was made until after the death of Nehru when the state was ruled by the non-Congress government.

Report as an Anti-missionary Propaganda Document

After the official publication of the Report by the state government, the Hindu Mahasabha and the RSS voluntarily reprinted tens of thousands abridged versions of Volume I of Report,[10] which they freely distributed in offices, schools, colleges, and other places to "exploit the situation created by the odious document against Missionaries and Christians." This version had only 77 pages of summarized information from the original report of 182 pages. The abridged version was perhaps Part IV of the Report which contained the key findings, conclusions, and recommendations about missionaries and their activities.[11] It was priced 4 Annas (1 anna is 1/16 of a rupee).

Pro-Hindu newspapers and magazines such as *Hitavada, Yugdharm,* and *The Hindu Outlook* printed the committee's key findings against missionary activity.[12] All India Arya (Hindu) Dharma Seva Sangh, the highest propaganda body of the Arya Samaj, also published an abridgement of the

9. Gopal, *Selected Works of Jawaharlal Nehru,* 733–34.

10. Thomas, "Preface," 5. To know how RSS was involved in the Niyogi's investigation, see Seshadri, RSS, 74. See also Appendix C on the republications of the summaries and redactions of the Report.

11. Thomas, "Preface," 5.

12. *Hitavada,* July 18, 19, 1956; *The Hindu Outlook,* July 24, 1956.

Report for inexpensive circulation.[13] Through republicizing the Report, "Extremist Hindu organizations tried to raise anti-missionary and anti-Christian feelings in several parts of India."[14]

Sita Ram Goel mentions a *sanyasi* named Baba Madhavdas from Andhra Pradesh whom he met in the early 1980s. Goel reports that Madhavdas got involved in Hindu resistance to Christian missions and "got several thousand copies of a summary of the report printed in English and Hindi and distributed them widely as he moved along"[15] in the tribal regions of various states of India. He also presented copies to "the leaders of Arya Samaj, Jana Sangh, Hindu Mahasabha and Vishva Hindu Parishad . . . and various rich men known for their sympathy toward Hindu causes."[16] All that he wanted from them, according to Goel, was "to read the Report and mobilize public opinion for persuading the Indian state to stop the flow of massive foreign funds which Christian missionaries were using for conversions by means of force, fraud and inducements."[17]

Bharatiya Jana Sangh and the Report

After the publication of the Niyogi Report, "the working committee of the Jana Sangh . . . endorsed the report in its entirety, accepted the conclusions and called for the implementation of the recommendations."[18] Sita Ram Goel, who was the political candidate of the BJS in Madhya Pradesh at that time, writes that some BJS party-men requested that Pandit Prem Nath Dogra, the president of BJS, make the Niyogi Report known to the country at large through its political avenues.[19] The party's working committee agreed to their appeal at a later time and included the Report as one of the agendas of their upcoming election manifesto.[20] This was one of the major steps taken by the party before the 1957 elections. The BJS revised its election manifesto in 1957 with two key elements which included:[21]

1. "Creating a feeling of equality and oneness in the Hindu society by liquidating untouchability and caste-ism.

13. Baxter, *Jana Sangh*, 143.

14. Thomas, *Christians in Secular India*, 133.

15. Goel, *Pseudo-Secularism*, x.

16. Goel, *Pseudo-Secularism*, x.

17. Goel, *Pseudo-Secularism*, x.

18. Baxter, *Jana Sangh*, 145.

19. Goel, *Pseudo-Secularism*, viii.

20. Baxter, *Jana Sangh*, 158.

21. The text of the manifesto was published in *The Organiser* 10 (February 25, 1957).

2. Nationalizing all non-Hindus by inculcating them in the idea of Bharatiya Culture.

The recommendations of the Niyogi Committee and the Rege Committee[22] will be implemented to free Bharatiya Christians from the anti-national influence of foreign missionaries."[23]

The Influence of the Report on Hindu Activism

Brojendra Nath Banerjee, who analyzed "the issue of religious conversions in secular India," states that, "The Report has done incalculable harm in embittering relations between communities."[24] According to historian Felix Alfred Plattner, as a result of the Report "foreign missionaries have become suspect in the eyes of many Indians."[25] A year after the publication of the Report, Goss Memorial Centre, maintained by American Evangelical Mission in Raipur (now the capital city of Chhattisgarh), was looted and burned to the ground by a Hindu mob.[26] Since the Report made ample references to the involvement of the Lutheran Mission in proselytizing and political activities,[27] there was a possibility that the report had triggered the anger of Hindu activists against Goss Memorial Center. The NCCI reported that, "the animosity created by it [Niyogi Report] had not died down and the events that happened at Raipur in August 1957 leading to the total destruction of the Goss Memorial Center was a direct outcome of the ill will engendered by the Report."[28]

The Report gained further momentum after the Union government granted the demands of Christian Nagas in the northeast of India for an autonomous state, which resulted in the formation of Nagaland in 1963. As sociologist Sarbeswar Sahoo observed, the creation of Nagaland as a separate state because of the demands of majority Christians "provided increasing legitimacy to the Niyogi Report"[29] since it had already cautioned about the influence of foreign missionaries on Christian Naga tribes and

22. The Rege Committee was the counterpart of the Niyogi Committee appointed by the state government to study missionary activities in Madhya Bharat.

23. Bharatiya Jana Sangh: Party Documents, 82; Baxter, *Jana Sangh,* 158; Elst, *Decolonizing the Hindu Mind,* 287.

24. Banerjee, *Religious Conversions in India,* 236.

25. Plattner, *Catholic Church in India,* 11.

26. Smith, *India as a Secular State,* 437; Plattner, *Catholic Church in India,* 11; Bauman, "Postcolonial Anxiety," 17.

27. Niyogi, *Report,* 1:42, 49, 55, 98, 100.

28. NCCI, *Minutes of the Meeting of the Executive Committee,* 26.

29. Sahoo, "Religious Violence," 186.

their secessionist attitudes.[30] The RSS, which held the Christian missionary influence responsible for the separation of Nagaland,[31] propagated Christians as "hostile elements" and "internal threats."[32] The chief of RSS, M. S. Golwalkar, commented that the role of Christian missionaries in India was "to demolish not only the religious and social fabric of our life, but also to establish political domination in various pockets and if possible all over the land."[33] As maintained in the Niyogi Report, Hindu nationalist organizations began to view "separation" as "denationalization" and the missionaries who caused it as the main adversaries.[34]

A year after Nagaland was granted statehood, at the instigation of RSS chief Golwalkar and by the impetus provided by the Niyogi Report, Hindu nationalist advocates, Shivram Shankar Apte, K. M. Munshi, C. P. Ramaswamy Iyer, and others gathered to form Vishva Hindu Parishad to ensure the religious unity of Hindus and to prevent ongoing conversion activities in India.[35] Three years after the formation of VHP, Freedom of Religion bills against forced or fraudulent conversions were passed by the state governments in Orissa (1967) and Madhya Pradesh (1968) under the influence of the recommendations of the Niyogi Report.

The Impetus of the Report on Conversion Laws

Gauri Viswanathan mentions that, "In the Constituent Assembly discussions that were held between 1946 and 1950, there was a strong move by powerful Hindu lobbies to ban conversions altogether."[36] Although it is difficult to ascertain whether the deliberations in the Legislative Assembly were to "ban conversions altogether" or not, during the time when the Indian constitution was being drafted, some political leaders, who subscribed to the philosophy of Hindu nationalism, recommended the inclusion of "clause 17" to control "conversions brought about by coercion or undue influence." Clause 17, which was proposed by the Fundamental Rights Committee headed by Sardar Vallabhbhai Patel, states that "Conversion from one religion to another brought about by coercion or undue influence shall not be recognized by law." K. M. Munshi proposed an amendment to the clause

30. Niyogi, *Report,* 1:50, 145.

31. Golwalkar, *Bunch of Thoughts,* 191; Seshadri, *RSS,* 61; Pachuau, *Ethnic Identity and Christianity,* 20.

32. Golwalkar, *Bunch of Thoughts,* 188–94.

33. Golwalkar, *Bunch of Thoughts,* 193.

34. Jaffrelot, *Religion, Caste and Politics,* 160.

35. Parishad, "Inception of VHP." See also Rai, "VHP at a Glance."

36. Viswanathan, "Literacy in the Eye," 272.

to read, "Any conversion from one religion to another of any person brought about by fraud, coercion or undue influence or of a minor under the age of 18 shall not be recognized by law." M. Ananthasayanam Ayyangar, R. V. Dhulekar, and R. P Thakur are among those who supported the clause. After a long discussion on whether it should be included in the fundamental rights, the assembly moved not to include it in the fundamental rights and thus the proposal was not adopted.[37] "Clause 17" was dropped by the Assembly because Sardar Vallabhbhai Patel suggested that such a clause was unnecessary as no one ever recognized conversion by coercion or undue influence.[38] The Indian Constitution which was adopted in November 1949 declared India to be a sovereign democratic republic with the conceptual provision of religious freedom to all its citizens. Article 25 and 26 under the title "Right to Freedom of Religion" read,

> 25. (1) Subject to public order, morality and health and to the other provisions of this Part, all persons are equally entitled to freedom of conscience and the right freely to profess, practice and propagate religion. (2) Nothing in this article shall affect the operation of any existing law or prevent the State from making any law— (*a*) regulating or restricting any economic, financial, political or other secular activity which may be associated with religious practice; (*b*) providing for social welfare and reform or the throwing open of Hindu religious institutions of a public character to all classes and sections of Hindus.

> 26. Subject to public order, morality and health, every religious denomination or any section thereof shall have the right— (*a*) to establish and maintain institutions for religious and charitable purposes; (*b*) to manage its own affairs in matters of religion; (*c*) to own and acquire movable and immovable property; and (*d*) to administer such property in accordance with law.

While the constitutional right of religious freedom provided courage to Christian missionaries to boldly carry out their religious activities in various parts of India, Article 25 became "the bone of contention"[39] to some members of the Constituent Assembly, who, according to Felix Plattner, argued that, "in the past as well as in the recent times religion has been the cause of disruption in the country. The Christian Religion,

37. Constituent Assembly of India Debates, 5, May 1–August 30, 1947. See also Choudhary, *Dr. Rajendra Prasad*, 43.

38. Constituent Assembly Debates, 1947, 3:427–28. See also Thomas, *RSS-Christian Perspective*, 11; Smith, *India as a Secular State*, 182.

39. Plattner, *Catholic Church in India*, 5.

essentially and consciously a missionary religion, could perhaps increase the number of its adherents to such as extent that they would become the majority in certain parts of India. The Christians could then create political problems by demanding a State of their own."[40] Though these objections were strongly refuted by several other leaders within the Congress Party, as Plattner points out, "the narrow minded Hindus and fanatical communists . . . tried to interpret the rights" and called the article into question both in the parliament and in individual states.[41] There was also a question raised in parliament about whether the right to propagate one's religion was applicable only to Indian citizens or also to foreigners residing in India. In March 1954, the Supreme Court gave its response that the right of freedom of propagation was applied to citizens and non-citizens alike.[42] With such a ruling, as Plattner notes, "the enemies of the Church tried to restrict her right to propagate the faith in other ways."[43]

In 1954, Jethalal Joshi, a member of the Congress Party, introduced in Lok Sabha, the lower house of parliament, a bill on conversion which, "if passed, would have handicapped the work of missionaries."[44] This bill was called Indian Converts (Regulation and Registration) Bill, 1954, and required compulsory licensing of missionaries and the registration of converts all over India. The basic provisions of the bill were: "Persons or institutions engaged in converting people would have to secure a license from the district magistrate; a prospective convert would have to make a declaration of his intensions to the district magistrate one month prior to the actual date of conversion; the license-holder and the convert would be required to give particulars regarding the conversion within three months after it took place."[45] The bill was opposed by Pocker Sahib, a Muslim member, who argued that, "When such conditions are put, then it means that the conversion of a man from one religion to another is dependent upon the discretion of the district magistrate, which, I submit, is a virtual denial of the right."[46] Meanwhile, the National Christian Council also sent a memorandum to the Prime Minister Nehru against the bill.[47]

40. Plattner, *Catholic Church in India*, 5.

41. Plattner, *Catholic Church in India*, 6.

42. Plattner, *Catholic Church in India*, 7.

43. Plattner, *Catholic Church in India*, 7.

44. Plattner, *Catholic Church in India*, 7.

45. Smith, *India as a Secular State*, 184.

46. *Lok Sabha Debates*, 4078–79.

47. NCCI, *Minutes of the Meeting of the Executive Committee*, February 14–16, 1956, 2.

Debate on the bill resumed in September 1955. It was supported by G. H. Deshpande, another Congress member who accused missionaries, saying, "There is a political motive behind this conversion . . . What we suspect is that there are some imperialist powers who are not free even today from their dreams of imperialism. They probably think there was a Pakistan, why should there not be in India a Christianstan even?"[48] In a response, Prime Minister Jawaharlal Nehru remarked, "Personally, I would not pass such a measure unless it has the fullest support from the principal parties who are likely to be affected by it. If this measure apparently is meant to apply to Christian missionaries carrying on this conversion, I would like the real decision to lie with the Christian members of this house. Let them decide."[49] "I fear that this bill will not help very much in suppressing evil methods, but might very well be the cause of great harassment to a large number of people . . . Christianity is one of the important religions of India, established here for nearly two thousand years. We must not do anything which gives rise to any feeling of oppression or suppression in the minds of our Christian friends and fellow-country men."[50] At the conclusion of his speech, the bill was rejected by an overwhelming majority.

In September 1956, two months after the publication of the Niyogi Report in Madhya Pradesh, as Plattner reports, "a question was raised in the Parliament about an alleged increase in the anti-Indian activities on the part of foreign Christian missionaries."[51] B. N. Datar, the Minister of State for Home Affairs, strongly opposed the argument stating, "There is no factual basis for the assumption made in the question, according to the information available with the Government of India . . . and no steps would be taken to check the work of foreign missionaries."[52]

Scholars argue that the summary of the findings and recommendations of the Niyogi Report provided the rationale and ideological impetus for Madhya Pradesh, Orissa, and other states to enact state-wide Freedom of Religion laws to control conversions brought about by means of force, fraud, or allurement. In view of prohibiting fraudulent conversions, a Hindu Mahasabha MLA from Madhya Pradesh Assembly introduced a conversion bill in the state assembly in 1958 which took up the terms of the Niyogi Report.[53] Discussion on the bill continued in the assembly in Madhya Pradesh

---

48. Speech reproduced in *NCCR* 76 (1956) 19–21.

49. *NCCR* 76 (1956) 19–21; Smith, *India as a Secular State*, 185.

50. Plattner, *Catholic Church in India*, 7; Smith, *India as a Secular State*, 185.

51. Plattner, *Catholic Church in India*, 7; Goel, *Pseudo-Secularism*, 64.

52. Plattner, *Catholic Church in India*, 7.

53. Jaffrelot, *Religion, Caste and Politics in India*, 157.

until it was rejected by the Congress majority in 1961 under the constitutional provisions of religious freedom.[54]

In 1967, Jana Sangh MLA, Virendra Kumar Sakhlecha, re-proposed the conversion bill in the Vidhan Sabha (state assembly) of Madhya Pradesh "to provide for the prohibition of conversion from one religion to another by use of force or allurement or by fraudulent means."[55] During this time, the state was under the leadership of Chief Minister Govind Narayan Singh of Lok Sewak Dal (LSD). LSD was founded by Govind Narayan Singh in 1967 after he resigned from Indian National Congress. He became the chief minister of Madhya Pradesh on July 30, 1967, and remained in office until March 12, 1969. LSD was supported by Samyukta Vidhayak Dal (SVD), a coalition made up of Bharatiya Kranti Dal, Samyukta Socialist Party, Praja Socialist Party, and Bharatiya Jana Sangh. SVD, which consisted of "Congress defectors, Jana Sangh and Socialist members,"[56] stood in opposition to the Congress Party. The SVD government had also generously supported the activities of VKA in Madhya Pradesh during 1967 and 1968.[57]

L. S. Herdenia observes that, "When the SVD government assumed power, the Jana Sangh strongman, late Virendra Kumar Sakhlecha, who was deputy chief minister holding the crucial home portfolio, moved the bill, which was passed in the absence of the Congress members."[58] The bill became law at the ascent of the Governor on October 19, 1968, and was known as The Madhya Pradesh Dharma Swatantrya Adhiniyam (MPDS), 1968. The passing of this Religious Freedom Act became possible "after the death of Nehru and before the rise of Indira Gandhi to supreme power" because Jawaharlal Nehru neither supported such bills in the parliament, nor would have encouraged states controlled by Congress Party leaders to vote for such laws. The key text of the MPDS Act reads,

> No person shall convert or attempt to convert, either directly or otherwise, any person from one religious faith to another by the use of force or by allurement or by any fraudulent means nor shall any person abet any such conversion . . . Whoever converts any person from one religious faith to another either by performing himself the ceremony necessary for such conversion as a religious priest or by taking part directly or indirectly in such

54. *Hitavada*, April 13, 1961, 6. See also Jaffrelot, *Religion, Caste and Politics*, 157.

55. Madhya Pradesh Act, No. 27 of 1968, *The Madhya Pradesh Dharma Swatantrya Adhiniyam, 1968*.

56. Herdenia, "Debating Religious Conversions."

57. Jaffrelot, "India: The Politics of (Re)conversion," 206.

58. Jaffrelot, "India: The Politics of (Re)conversion," 206. Also see Agrawal, "Church Goes Political in India," 249.

ceremony shall, within such period after the ceremony as may be prescribed, send an intimation to the District Magistrate of the district in which the ceremony has taken place of the fact of such conversion in such form as may be prescribed.[59]

The Act has provided the definition of what allurement, force, or fraud means.

a. 'allurement' means offer of any temptation in the form of

    i. any gift or gratification either in cash or kind;

    ii. grant of any material benefit, either monetary or otherwise.

b. 'conversion' means renouncing one religion and adopting another;

c. force shall include a show of force or threat of injury of any kind including threat of divine displeasure or social excommunication;

d. 'fraud' shall include misrepresentation or any other fraudulent contrivance;

e. 'minor' means a person under eighteen years of age.[60]

The definitions of conversion, force, inducement, and fraud in the Act are comparable to the text in the recommendations of the Niyogi Report which indicate that the bill was influenced by the Niyogi Report. For example, one of the recommendations of the Report reads, "Any attempt by force or fraud, or threats of illicit means or grants of financial or other aid, or by fraudulent means or promises, or by moral and material assistance, or by taking advantage of any person's inexperience or confidence, or by exploiting any person's necessity, spiritual (mental) weakness or thoughtlessness, or, in general, any attempt or effort (whether successful or not), directly or indirectly to penetrate into the religious conscience of persons (whether of age or underage) of another faith, for the purpose of consciously altering their religious conscience or faith, so as to agree with the ideas or convictions of the proselytizing party should be absolutely prohibited."[61]

59. *Madhya Pradesh Gazette*, "Madhya Pradesh Dharma Swatantrya Adhiniyam, 1968."

60. *Madhya Pradesh Gazette*, "Madhya Pradesh Dharma Swatantrya Adhiniyam, 1968."

61. Niyogi, *Report*, 1:63.

This recommendation was broadly and redundantly clarified with reasons in Part IV of the Niyogi Report, Volume I.[62]

It is not accidental that the text of the MPDS Act parallels the language of the Report. It is evident from Hindu nationalist writings that the Niyogi report had provided ideological impetus and terminology to Madhya Pradesh's conversion law. Virag Shrikrushna Pachpore, a journalist and a full-time worker of Vivekananda Kendra, is of the opinion that Madhya Pradesh Deputy Chief Minister Virendra Kumar Sakhlecha, who proposed the bill in the assembly, used the Niyogi Report "as the basis for drafting the Freedom of Religion's Bill in 1967."[63] Swaminathan Gurumurthy, a journalist and political analyst, writes, "The Madhya Pradesh government did not wake up one fine morning and pass this law. In the 1950s it had appointed a committee headed by Justice Neogi [sic] . . . to study allegations of forcible and fraudulent conversions of tribal and illiterate people by foreign missionaries. The Committee submitted a voluminous, unanimous report detailing fraudulent conversions by the Church. The MP Government . . . merely enacted the recommendations of the Neogi [sic] committee."[64] H. V. Seshadri, a prominent leader of RSS, records, "The first to take steps at the governmental level in uncovering the ulterior motive behind Christian Missionary activities was the Government of Madhya Pradesh"[65] and it "followed up the Commission's Report with legislation prohibiting illegal and forcible conversions in the State."[66]

Orissa passed a Freedom of Religion law nine months before Madhya Pradesh enacted its conversion law, "to provide for the prohibition of conversion from one religion to another by use of force or allurement or by fraudulent means."[67] E. D. Devadason reports that Rajendra Narayan Singh Deo, who had been the feudal Raja in the former Bolangir-Patna state before becoming the Chief Minister of Orissa, proposed the Freedom of Religion bill in the State Assembly in 1967.[68] Devadason mentions that this was the same person who, during the British regime, passed the Freedom of Religion Act in 1942.[69] According to Devadason, Rajendra Narayan Singh

---

62. Niyogi, *Report*, 1:131–65.

63. Pachpore, *Indian Church?*, xxii.

64. Gurumurthy, "Conversion and Anti-Conversion," 8.

65. Seshadri, *RSS*, 74.

66. Seshadri, *RSS*, 75.

67. *Orissa Gazette*, "Orissa Freedom of Religion Act," 363.

68. Devadason, *Study on Conversion and its Aftermath*, 23.

69. Devadason, *Study on Conversion and its Aftermath*, 23.

Deo "got the Orissa Freedom of Religion Act, 1967 passed by the Legislative Assembly without debate or discussion."[70]

The Orissa Freedom of Religion Act, 1967, which came into effect in January 1968, also reflects the language of the Niyogi Report as does the MPDS Act, except with the arrangement of text and slight variance in punishments and the legal requirements for conversion-aspirants. In the definition of terms, the MPDS Act uses "allurement," whereas the Orissa Act uses "inducement." Both of these words were used interchangeably in the Niyogi Report.[71] The Arunachal Pradesh Freedom of Indigenous Faith Act which was passed in 1978[72] is not much different from the conversion laws of Madhya Pradesh and Orissa, except that it included definitions of "indigenous faith" and tribes.[73] The anatomies of the Gujarat Freedom of Religion Act 2003, the Himachal Pradesh Freedom of Religion Act 2006, the Rajasthan Freedom of Religion Act 2008 and the Maharashtra Freedom of Religion Bill 2008 are analogous to the freedom of religion laws of Madhya Pradesh, Orissa and Arunachal Pradesh. The sole intent of all these laws is to prohibit "forcible conversion" by using the following body of text: "No person shall convert or attempt to convert, either directly or otherwise, any person from one religion to another by use of force or by inducement or by any fraudulent means, nor shall any person abet any such conversion."[74]

On December 2, 1978, Om Prakash Tyagi, the Lok Sabha Member of the Janata Party from Uttar Pradesh, proposed a bill on the "Freedom of Religion" in the parliament "to provide for prohibition on conversion from one religion to another by use of force, or inducement or by fraudulent means." This proposal is similar to the Religious Freedom Acts passed by Madhya Pradesh, Orissa, and Arunachal Pradesh. It was word-to-word identical to the one passed by Madhya Pradesh.[75] Sita Ram Goel notes that, "The Bill followed the pattern of the Bills passed by the congress governments [sic] of Orissa (1967), Madhya Pradesh (1968), and Arunachal Pradesh (1977) following the recommendations of. . .the Niyogi Committee."[76] Due to lack of support, the Bill could not be voted for in the house.

70. Devadason, *Study on Conversion and its Aftermath*, 24. See also Agrawal, "Church Goes Political in India," 249.

71. Niyogi, *Report*, 1:131–65.

72. Arunachal Pradesh Act No. 4 of 1978 has not been implemented due to a lack of enabling legislation. See India 2014 International Religious Freedom Report, 3, http://www.state.gov/j/drl/rls/irf/religiousfreedom/index.htm#wrapper.

73. Compare wordings in the Freedom of Religion Laws in Appendix G.

74. Compare wordings in the Freedom of Religion Laws in Appendix G.

75. Compare wordings in the Freedom of Religion Laws in Appendix G.

76. Goel, *Pseudo-Secularism*, 68.

Om Prakash Tyagi held press conferences in Delhi and other places in 1979 and issued various statements to the media in order to draw positive public response for the proposal so that he could push forward the bill again in the Parliament. When reporters asked Tyagi for evidences of false conversions in support of the bill, he promptly cited the Rege and Niyogi Committee Reports.[77] He attempted to influence political leaders of the Congress, in addition to obtaining favorable statements on the proposed bill from reputed former judges of the High Court. He and Janata Party members had the leading newspapers publish various articles and special editorials in support of the bill.[78] The then Prime Minister, Morarji Desai, was also in favor of having the bill proposed again in the parliament. But within a few months, the Janata Party split and Morarji Desai had to resign from his post. Therefore, Tyagi's proposal did not reach the corridors of the Parliament again.

Foreign Contribution Regulation Act (FCRA)

Alongside the issue of conversions, as early as the 1950s, there were deliberations on the need to scrutinize the inflow of foreign funds to India. The Niyogi report, which dealt with foreign funds and their impact on conversions, claimed that "foreign money has played a great part, from the very beginning of the missionary enterprise in India, in securing proselytes from the poor classes."[79] The Report went on to say, "the churches have become more closely associated with political parties and policies than is good for spiritual independence."[80] In its summary of recommendations, the Report said, "No non-official agency should be permitted to secure foreign assistance except through government channels."[81]

The ideas highlighted in the Report's recommendations, which stirred debates in the late 1960s causing the passing of anti-conversion laws in Madhya Pradesh and Orissa, have also intensified discussions regarding the receipt of foreign funds in India.[82] According to *AccountAid India,* a financial accounting agency based in New Delhi, the Niyogi Report's language of financial suspicion has played a role in the murmurings about the use

---

77. Goel, *Pseudo-Secularism,* 69.

78. *The Hindu* (Madras Edition), April 29, 1979.

79. Ram Mohan Roy contended that "a body of English gentlemen who were called Missionaries of the poor classes who are prompted by the desires of gain or any other motive." Niyogi, *Report,* 1:101.

80. Niyogi, *Report,* 1:100.

81. Niyogi, *Report,* 1:162, 165.

82. For a brief overview of the history of FCRA, see Account Aid, "History of FCRA."

and misuse of foreign funds, leading to constitutional discourses on how to regulate the inflow of foreign contributions to India.[83]

On March 20 and 23, 1967, questions were raised in the parliament regarding the contributions received by various organizations from the USA, some of which were allegedly sent with the aim of defeating forty-four progressive candidates in the 1967 elections.[84] Based on investigative reports by the Intelligence Bureau, on May 14, 1969, Home Minister Y. B. Chavan stated in the parliament that "government will bring a comprehensive legislation to impose suitable restrictions on the receipt of funds from foreign sources, except those in the ordinary course of business."[85] The discussions continued until the FCRA bill was introduced in Rajya Sabha in December 1973. It was referred to the Joint Parliamentary Committee of sixty MPs under the chairmanship of Manubhai Shah for final shaping. In January 1976, JPC submitted its report to the Parliament with notification of the rules and regulations that the FCRA would demand. On August 5, 1976, President Fakhruddin Ali Ahmed signed the bill, making it a law.

Through FCRA, the government can track how non-governmental organizations (NGOs) spend their foreign funds. No NGO registered under FCRA is permitted to get involved in electoral politics or receive funds on behalf of political parties.[86] Under FCRA rules, the applying NGO or the person applying has to ensure that he "has not been prosecuted or convicted for indulging in activities aimed at conversion through inducement or force, either directly or indirectly, from one religious faith to another."[87] This clause is proportional to the Niyogi's recommendations on conversions and the use of foreign funds. Since the BJP came to power in 2014, there have been apprehensions about the restrictions of foreign funds for missionary purposes as the government has been closely studying the level of compliance with the norms stipulated under FCRA. In April 2015, the Ministry of Home Affairs cancelled the licenses of over 8000 charitable organizations, both religious and non-religious, due to non-compliance with the reporting requirements stipulated under the Act.[88]

83. Account Aid, "History of FCRA."

84. Account Aid, "History of FCRA," 2.

85. Account Aid, "History of FCRA."

86. Account Aid, "History of FCRA," 4. Also, see *The Gazette of India,* Part II, Section I, 2010, 5.

87. *The Gazette of India,* Part II, Section I, 2010, 9.

88. Lexology, "Overview of the Foreign Contribution Regulation Act."

The Re-publicizing of the Report

In 1986, the Deendayal Research Institute published *Politics of Conversion,* edited by Devendra Swarup, which refloated the views and interpretations of the Niyogi Report against current missionary activity. This volume, which was a study on the issues of mass conversion of *harijans* (Hindus and Christians) to Islam in Meenakshipuram, Tamil Nadu, in 1981, included various articles from Hindutva thinkers who dealt with the politics of conversions from the Niyogi Report's point of view. In his chapter, "Church as a Tool of Imperialism in the World," T. R. Vedantham relied on the views of the Report to contend that force, guile and incentives were used in gaining converts.[89] S. Saraswati, in his article, "British Policy Towards Religion in India," quotes from the Report that "growth of the Protestant church during the period of British Raj in India was due mainly to the great patronage and support church was getting from the Government of India . . . ."[90] The other authors who utilize the framework and the views of the Niyogi Report in their articles include Sita Ram Goel, S. K. Agrawal, and Ravidra V. Ramdas. Some of their chapters were also published independently and are freely available online.

In 1998, Sita Ram Goel published "Pseudo-Secularism, Christian Missions and Hindu Resistance," which included a redacted summary of the Niyogi Report, especially the findings and recommendations of the committee against Christian missionaries and their conversion activities. In this work, Goel described the communal circumstances that paved the way for the appointment of the Niyogi Enquiry Committee in the 1950s. Drawing upon the inferences of the Report, he elucidated how Christian missionaries have exploited the situation in India and around the world over the centuries through their illicit conversion activities. He contended that the anti-conversion laws were the result of the Niyogi Report's impartial investigation and recommendations.[91]

In 1998, the Voice of India publishing house republished the two-volume Niyogi Report in one volume under the title, *Vindicated By Time: The Niyogi Committee Report on Christian Missionary Activities.* Goel wrote the preface to the book, arousing the interest of readers by emphasizing how praiseworthy and credible was the work of the Niyogi Commission, which unveiled the evil side of Christian missionary activities. He adds his personal story of how he was drawn into the discussion and promotion of the Niyogi Committee Report which exposed the true color

89. Vedantham, "Church as a Tool of Imperialism," 72–73.
90. Saraswati, "British Policy," 105.
91. Goel, *Pseudo-Secularism,* x.

of Christianity. Additionally, his book, *Pseudo-Secularism, Christian Missions and Hindu Resistance* was added as an introductory chapter to the 939-page Niyogi report.

The Report in the Electronic Campaigns for Hindutva

Apart from the websites of the RSS, the VHP, and the BJP, there are dozens of full-fledged Hindutva websites which seek worldwide Hindu consolidation through publication of various socio-political articles, stories of the Mahabharata, and Hindu cultural programs. Many of these websites show their allegiance to the Hindutva ideology defined by Hindu Mahasabha and the Sangh Parivar. They play a critical role in shaping the Hindutva narrative and command a decent online following. To exemplify how electronic campaigns are being conducted, I will briefly analyze the content of the websites of a few selected organizations and highlight the influence of the Report.

The Hindu Janajagruti Samiti (HJS) is a Hindu organization which has an active website with the tagline "for the establishment of the *Hindu Rashtra*." It aims to awaken Hindu masses to unite against the sociocultural and religious threats Hinduism faces. On its website, www.hindujagruti. org, it publishes various kinds of news, articles, stories, and provocative information against religious others, particularly Christians and Muslims. It also mobilizes activism through its Facebook page which has 867,673 likes and several thousand regular followers as of March 1, 2016. By showing how the worldwide missionary enterprise is operated based on the Western ideological hegemony and flow of funds, the HJS invented an eleventh commandment, "Thou shall not convert."[92]

Drawing upon the Report's views, the HJS attempts to propagate that Christianity has a separatist tendency and contributes to disharmony among the aboriginals. The site uses extracts of the Niyogi Report to portray Christianity as treacherous and threatening to Indian society. It alleges that missionary conversion efforts are "a fraud on humanity."[93] While criticizing the Western character of Indian churches, the HJS equally finds fault with culturally Indianized churches by contending that Christians in India use the process of inculturation or the adaption of Hindu cultural methods "to confuse, corrupt and change the minds of gullible masses."[94]

Differing from the historical narration, the HJS gives its own redacted account of the circumstances of the appointment of the Niyogi Committee in Madhya Pradesh. The HJS alleges that during the 1950s, there was

92. Hindu Janajagruti Samiti, "Eleventh Commandment."
93. Hindu Janajagruti Samiti, "Eleventh Commandment."
94. Hindu Janajagruti Samiti, "Eleventh Commandment."

uproar among Hindus against missionaries because the "USA (A Christian Country) put certain conditions on Bharat before agreeing to supply wheat. One condition was to permit Christian missionaries to spread Christianity in Bharat. Since there was tremendous opposition to this condition, Nehru appointed a committee under the Chairmanship of Justice Bhawani Shankar Niyogi."[95] Nowhere in the Niyogi report was it mentioned that the United States demanded permission for the spread of Christianity in return for the wheat it supplied nor did such a thing cause the uproar against missionaries. It also emphasizes that, "In its report the committee had clearly put forth, with many examples and evidence, how the Christian church and missionaries had political motives in the propagation of their religion. The committee had also suggested putting a stop to the foreign aid they were receiving. The Nehru Government, however, chose to completely ignore this report."[96] The HJS blames Prime Minister Jawaharlal Nehru for not implementing the recommendations of the Report and holds him responsible for the continuation of missionary activities in India. It has published the recommendations of the Niyogi Report and seeks the solidarity of Hindus to stop ongoing Christian conversions in the country.[97] The HJS has a "Jago SMS" (cellphone texting service) scheme through which they continue to encourage young people to remain Hindu and provide them with guidance in emergencies, particularly during times of religious infiltrations.

Hindu Vivek Kendra (HVK) is another scholarly branch of the Hindutva movement, managed by the Sangh Parivar, which seeks to promote its ideology by publishing various resources that provide intellectual arguments against conversions. Examples of its publications on conversions, available on its website (www.hvk.org), include, *Christianity in India: A Critical Study (1979)*, *Religious Conversions: Frequently Asked Questions*, *Christianity in India: The Hindu Perspective*, and *A Perception of Christian Missionary Activities*, in which the recommendations of the Niyogi Report are summarized.[98] All these works reflect the rationale of the Niyogi Report in one way or another. For example, in *Religious Conversions: Frequently Asked Questions*, HVK explains that conversions are the exploitation of one's free will by means of force, inducements, or fraud. Every conversion is portrayed as illegitimate if the process of conversion has any elements

---

95. Hindu Janajagruti Samiti, "What was the Main Cause."

96. Hindu Janajagruti Samiti, "What was the Main Cause."

97. Hindu Janajagruti Samiti, "Eleventh Commandment."

98. Hindu Vivek Kendra. "Summary of the Recommendations of the Niyogi Committee."

of social services or faith healing.[99] By referencing the Niyogi Report, HVK states that foreign funds have been utilized with an ulterior motive to aggressively proselytize Hindus.[100] Drawing upon current examples of missionary enterprise, HVK tries to make the case for the relevance of the report in a present-day context.[101] According to HVK, conversion is an issue not just for the *Hindutvavadis* alone, but for the whole Hindu *Samaj*.[102] While condemning the violent activities that have been taking place against Christians in various states, it concludes that, "the prime cause of the violence is the action of conversions."[103]

Voice of Dharma (www.voiceofdharma.org), the online publishing house of Voice of India publications, Delhi, is a free storehouse of Hindutva literature, which reaches Hindus through the publication of various academic writings and featured articles. The main purpose of this website is to revitalize the history of Hindu culture, as well as the dignity and pride of dharma by emphasizing that Indian history has been twisted by the victors of the colonial past and that there is a richness to the Hindu past of which every Indian should be proud and embrace. In 1998, it published the Niyogi Report in its entirety under the title *Vindicated by Time,* as well as various other books which criticize Christian mission history and conversion activities. Its Facebook page[104] serves as a public platform where Hindus from all over the world are able to post about the current affairs of Hindu programs or new findings against Muslims and Christians.

Bajrang Dal's website is Hindutva Brotherhood (www.hindurashtra. org), which states that,

> "Hinduism is on the attack from three main groups and each is as dangerous as the other. Firstly, the Christians have an upper hand on us with the economies under their control . . . , secondly . . . Muslims and thirdly, from within us, the Hindus who either falsely or for some ulterior motives believe that Hinduism can survive the onslaught in modern times as it has in the past.

---

99. Hindu Vivek Kendra, "Summary of the Recommendations of the Niyogi Committee."

100. Hindu Vivek Kendra, "Summary of the Recommendations of the Niyogi Committee," Question 14.

101. Hindu Vivek Kendra, "Summary of the Recommendations of the Niyogi Committee," Question 17, 18.

102. Hindu Vivek Kendra, "Summary of the Recommendations of the Niyogi Committee," Question 33. See also Chowgule, *Christianity in India*, 27.

103. Hindu Vivek Kendra, "Summary of the Recommendations of the Niyogi Committee," Question 25.

104. https://www.facebook.com/VoiceOfDharma.

> In times when the Christians have openly taken on the task of harvesting us to Christianity . . . , who will stop at nothing, the gravity of the situation will have to be realized now or the very survival of Hinduism is at risk. Join us for free, together we can make the difference and fight as one."

In its lengthy list of the Hindu agenda, the language of the Niyogi report is clearly reflected. For example, "Change of religion means change of nation."[105] "The anti-national activity of religious conversion of Hindus by force, fraud or false propaganda by exploiting the innocence of the poverty of backward communities will be strictly banned."[106] "All foreign remittances to non-governmental agencies, social, religious or service organizations or individuals will be stopped, so that the money and material so received is not misutilized for religious conversion and other divisive conspiracies."[107]

Other Hindu websites which use an anti-conversion narrative based on the Report include Proselytism.info, HinduExistence.org, vhp.org, www. rss.org, and ChristianAggression.org.

The Report and Conversion Laws in the 21st Century

Since the Bharatiya Janata Party came to national power in the late 1990s, several attempts have been made to pass Freedom of Religion bills in various states.[108] The states that have succeeded in passing the laws are Chhattisgarh (2000),[109] Gujarat (2003),[110] Tamil Nadu (2002),[111] Himachal Pradesh (2006),[112] Rajasthan (2008), Jharkhand (2017), Uttarakhand (2018), Uttar Pradesh (2020), and Karnataka (2021).[113] Goldie observes that, "These

105. Hindu Rashtra, "Hindutva Brotherhood."

106. Hindu Rashtra, http://www.hindurashtra.org/about.php.

107. Hindu Rashtra, http://www.hindurashtra.org/about.php.

108. The states in which conversion bills had been proposed or passed but were not yet enacted: Maharashtra (1996, 2005, 2012, 2019), Rajasthan (2008) and Karnataka (2021).

109. Chhattisgarh inherited the law from Madhya Pradesh when it separated in 2000, but it passed an amendment to the Bill in 2006.

110. The dormant anti-conversion law was brought into enforcement in August 2007.

111. "The Prohibition of Forcible Conversion of Religion Ordinance" was passed in Tamil Nadu on October 5, 2002; it was repealed in 2003 due to the outcry against its perceived restriction on the freedom of religion.

112. The governor signed it into law in February 2007.

113. The Bill was passed in 2006, but it was withheld by the then state governor Pratibha Patil till 2007 and was passed to the then president Abdul J. Kalam for approbation.

laws garnered their legitimacy from the infamous *Report of the Christian Missionary Activities Enquiry Committee.*[114] The following examples show how the proposers of the conversion bills in the state legislative assemblies continue to use the Niyogi Report as an example to substantiate their appeal for the passing of bills against forcible and fraudulent conversions. On December 20, 1996, when BJP MLA Mangal Prabhat Lodha was introducing a private bill under the name of Maharashtra Dharma Swatantrya Adhiniyam (Freedom of Religion Act) in the Maharashtra Legislative Assembly, he remarked that, "It is a matter of pride to introduce this bill in the Assembly session at Nagpur which is the headquarters of the RSS. Such a bill was passed in Orissa, Madhya Pradesh and Arunachal Pradesh in the wake of the Niyogi Committee Report, and later on the Supreme Court also had approved it . . . Conversions are continuing by means of force, allurement, and use of foreign funds . . . I appeal to the Honorable Chief Minister to get this Bill passed . . . "[115] The Bill was not passed due to the lack of a majority. The Bill was proposed again in 2005 by Siddharam S. Mhetre and in 2012 by Sudhir Mungantiwar, but failed to gain support.

In the Rajasthan state assembly, the Freedom of Religion bill, known as Rajasthan Dharma Swatantrya Bill, was proposed in 2006. Although the bill was passed, it did not become law because Governor Pratibha Patil did not give her consent to it. When reintroducing the bill in the Assembly in 2008, Yogeshwar Garg, a member of BJP, cited the Niyogi Report to substantiate his argument against conversions, saying that, "the population of Christians in India was increasing."[116] He further commented in support of the bill that, "The Niyogi Commission had suggested various measures to curb the practice of conversion effected by missionaries by luring tribals . . . largescale conversions had taken place in the northeast as there was no such legislation to control it."[117]

In 2009, M. Chidananda Murthy, a former professor of Bangalore University, met with Karnataka Chief Minister B. S. Yeddyurappa of the BJP and submitted a memorandum stating that "a law may be enacted in the State of Karnataka prohibiting forcible religious conversion on the lines of law enacted in the States of Madhya Pradesh and Orissa."[118] When furnished information to justify the need for enacting such a law, he remarked that, "even earlier in the year 1956 Madhya Pradesh Government had constituted Dr. Bhavani

114. Menon, "India First."

115. The text was reproduced in Goel *Pseudo-Secularism,* 82–83.

116. *Times of India,* "Rajasthan House Okays Religion Bill."

117. *Times of India,* "Rajasthan House Okays Religion Bill."

118. Law Commission of Karnataka, Thirteenth Report, September 21, 2013, 1.

Shankar Commission to report on Christian Missionaries activities. In the light of the report of that Committee Madhya Pradesh Government enacted an Act in the year 1968 to prohibit forcible religious conversion wherein it is stated that Orissa Government has also enacted a similar law."[119] In 2012, the bill, known as "The Karnataka Dharma Swatantrya Bill, 2012," was proposed again. According to the report of Law Commission of Karnataka, it was "word to word identical with the Madhya Pradesh Dharma Swatantrya Adhiniyam, 1968 (Act No.27 of 1968) and substantially similar to Orissa Freedom of Religion Act, 1967, Arunachal Pradesh Freedom of Religion Act, 1978 and Gujarat Freedom of Religion Act, 2003."[120] The debate on the bill continued in the Karnataka state assembly until it was rejected by the majority of the Congress Party in 2014. It was finally passed in 2021.

Profiling Christians in Gujarat and Madhya Pradesh

In the context of the Hindu-Christian clashes which took place in the tribal regions of Dangs in 1998, the government of Gujarat ordered an inquiry on February 2, 1999, "to identify the Christian households in villages, the number of missionary personnel and of vehicles they own and the criminals among Christians."[121] According to a Human Rights Watch report, by the order of Chief Minister Keshubhai Patel, the office of the Gujarat Director General of Police issued a memorandum to all the district superintendents and commissioners of the Gujarat police demanding district-level information on "the total population of Christians; the location of Christian missionaries; the amounts and sources of foreign funding they received; the addresses and telephone numbers of the main leaders, the number of Hindu-Christian conflict cases registered; the number and types of vehicles and weapon-owning licenses possessed by Christian missionaries; and arrangements that had been made for their security in the wake of increasing Hindu-Christian conflict."[122]

It was evident that the state followed the pattern of the Niyogi Enquiry Committee and set a 13-point survey with questions such as "What type of trickery is being used by Christian defilement activities?"[sic] and "Which foreign countries encourage Christian missionaries?""[123] A secular minded lawyer by the name of Fali Nariman challenged the government's method of enquiry in the Gujarat High Court on the grounds that "it was

119. Law Commission of Karnataka, Thirteenth Report, September 21, 2013, 2.

120. Law Commission of Karnataka, Thirteenth Report, September 21, 2013, 12.

121. Lobo, *Globalisation*, 17.

122. https://www.hrw.org/reports/1999/indiachr/christians8-04.htm.

123. Menon, "Old Debate in a New Context."

unconstitutional to undertake such surveys outside the decennial census."[124] Soon after the circular was sent to all the police officials, "the Gujarat High Court initiated a case against the state government to ascertain the constitutional validity of the directive."[125] In response, Chief Minister Keshubhai Patel stated that "such inquiries were routine and that the information was required to provide the necessary security to members of the Christian community."[126] However, under the court's directive, the survey was halted.

In 2011, there was a similar attempt along the lines of the Niyogi Enquiry Commission by the government of Madhya Pradesh to re-study the situation of the affairs and the growth of the number of Christians in the state.[127] On March 22, 2011, the regional police stations in the state received an important notification from Police Department Headquarters in Bhopal which, according to Father Anand Muttungal, the spokesperson of the Catholic churches in M.P., "instructed all the police heads across the state to collect the details of activities of Christians as has been done in the case of criminals."[128] The notice demanded that the process of the survey should be completed within 10 days of its being received.[129] The survey questionnaire demanded that each Christian family should submit its "financial status, foreign income if any, political leanings, criminal record if any, total strength of community, break up of Protestants and Catholics, number of churches existing and upcoming, number of Christian schools and number of Christian teachers."[130] According to Muttungal, "The police officials initially approached the community leaders without any copy of the order and tried to gather such details verbally."[131] When Christian leaders approached the Director General of Police, Bhopal, they were told that the circular was not sent by the police department and were asked to ignore it.[132] According to Parvathi Menon, the Niyogi Commission of Madhya Pradesh motivates other states to institute a surveillance mechanism against Christian activities.[133]

124. Lobo, *Globalisation*, 17.

125. Human Rights Watch, "Violence in Gujarat."

126. *The Hindu,* "Circular on Christians Routine."

127. NDTV, "Is Madhya Pradesh Govt. Profiling Christians?"

128. Muttungal, "Why M.P. Govt."

129. *India Today,* "Profiling of Christians."

130. Shapoo, "Is Madhya Pradesh Govt."

131. Muttungal, "Why M.P. Govt."

132. NDTV, "Is Madhya Pradesh Govt. Profiling Christians?"

133. Menon, "Old Debate in a New Context."

THE NIYOGI REPORT AND THE SANGH PARIVAR

After carefully analyzing the Report's portrayal and criticism of Christian conversions in Madhya Pradesh, historian Bhagwan Singh Josh maintains that "the Niyogi Report ended up becoming complicit with the anti-Christian agenda of the Sangh clan."[134] Similarly, journalist Parvathi Menon's assessment is that the ideologues of the Sangh Parivar have been using the Niyogi Report as ballast for their anti-Christian arguments,[135] while John Dayal remarks that the Report "has been used by the Sangh Parivar very effectively to underpin its hate campaign against the church in general and against evangelization and missionary activity in particular."[136]

The Report and the RSS's Anti-conversion Rhetoric

As indicated in chapter four, the RSS played an indirect, yet significant, role in spawning the environment for setting up the Niyogi Enquiry Committee and for mobilizing the necessary testimonials for the making of the report against the conversion efforts of missionaries.[137] One of the reasons why the RSS kept a low profile during the time of anti-missionary agitations in the 1950s was the government's ban of the RSS in the previous years due to its communalist outlook and for the killing of Gandhi. Another reason, as pointed out by Ram Punyani, was that "its agenda is implemented through its front organizations,"[138] so that it doesn't have be in the limelight. Rajesh Joshi, a senior journalist at The Hindu Outlook, adds, "The RSS functions through its several organizations so that it could not be blamed for anything."[139]

RSS is the ideological parent of several sociocultural, religious and political Hindu organizations through which it accomplishes its various sociocultural goals, including anti-conversion campaigns and anti-Christian propaganda. Prominent organizations instituted at the instigation of the RSS were Akhil Baratiya Vidhya Parishad (1949), Vanvasi Kalyan Ashram (1952), Vidhya Bharati (1952), Bharatiya Mazdoor Sangh (1955), Vishva Hindu Parishad (1964), Bharatiya Kisan Sangh (1978), and Bharatiya Janata Party (1980). The extended family of RSS includes over forty affiliated organizations. Under the RSS's directive ideology of

---

134. Josh, "Conversions, Complicity," 106.
135. Menon, "Old Debate in a New Context."
136. Dayal's email to Manohar James dated August 8, 2014.
137. Seshadri, RSS, 74.
138. Punyani, Fascism of Sangh Parivar, 23.
139. Joshi, "Trident Speaks."

Hindutva, these organizations independently devise their strategies to implement the vision of Hindutva.

As envisioned by its founder Hedgewar, the RSS was initially reluctant to employ publicity or mass communication as he believed that publicity would undermine the character-building programs of the RSS. After the central government in 1933 declared that the RSS was a communal organization, Hedgewar changed his view and decided to publish and use affiliate newspapers to spread the word on the RSS and to avoid misinterpretation and misrepresentation of the organization by people and government.[140] After the government's ban on the RSS was lifted in 1949, the RSS began to spearhead discussions of religious issues such as cow-slaughter, indigenization of Muslims, and religious conversions, and started to articulate and publicize its vision and activities through fortnightlies such as *The Organiser* (English), *Panchjanya* (Hindi), Hindustan Samachar, and a host of other affiliate newspapers and magazines in order to tailor Hindu perceptions and opinions.

Two years before the Niyogi Committee was appointed in Madhya Pradesh, the RSS attempted to counter missionary activities in the tribal regions of Madhya Pradesh through its affiliate organization, Vanvasi Kalyan Ashram (VKA), founded in 1952. With the support of the State government and the RSS, Ramakant Keshav Deshpande founded Vanvasi Kalyan Ashram (Tribal Welfare Society). Vanvasi (or vanavasi) means forest-dwellers. Most indigenous tribal people are referred to as adivasis, meaning original or ancient dwellers. The Hindu nationalists prefer not to use the term adivasi anymore because it runs counter to the claim that Aryans are the original inhabitants of the land.[141]

Imitating Christian missionary methods, VKA established schools, hostels, and hospitals to stop conversions in the tribal regions and carried out anti-Christian propaganda, provoking disputes between Christian missionaries and adivasis, eventually leading to the appointment of the Niyogi Commission by the government of Madhya Pradesh. According to political scientist Saumya Uma, VKA was established "as an instrument to Hinduize the adivasis" through conversion and reconversion activities.[142]

Beginning with VKA, the Hinduization of tribals became an ideological project of the RSS that invigorated Sangh Parivar to set up a plethora of

---

140. Andersen, *Brotherhood in Saffron,* 114–15.

141. According to Indo-Aryan Theory, Aryans in India are believed to have migrated from Persia and settled in India in about 1,800 BC. Hindu nationalists deny that theory and argue that they are the original inhabitants of the land. Outlook India. "Adivasi vs Vanvasi." See also Jaffrelot, *Religion, Caste and Politics,* 47; Sahoo, "Religious Violence," 185.

142. Uma, *Kandhamal,* 32. See also Outlook India, "Adivasi vs Vanvasi."

organizations which focused on absorbing aboriginals and converted adivasis into the Hindu fold.[143] Prominent among these organizations are Ekal Vidyalaya, Sewa Bharati, Vivekananda Kendra, Bharat Kalyan Pratishthan, and Friends of Tribal Society. All these NGOs receive funding from India Development and Research Fund. VKA created a cult of *Hanuman* among tribals to show them that they were part of Hindu structures and to indoctrinate their minds with Hindu rituals and practices. Jaffrelot writes, "Hanuman is the devoted monkey god serving Ram as his army general in the Ramayana epic. Promoting him in the tribal land is a clever means of connecting the aboriginals to the great Hindu tradition, but at a subordinate rank. VKA made this its specialty in Madhya Pradesh where it orchestrated huge rallies of newly (re)converted aboriginals to expose them to the discourse of the movement's head ideologues and inculcate in them the proper rituals."[144]

During the Niyogi' Committee's investigation, Christian leaders openly pointed out that it was Ramakant Keshav Deshpande, the founder of VKA and a long-time follower of RSS, who caused all the trouble for missionaries and their activities in Madhya Pradesh.[145] It was evident from the Report that Deshpande himself provided large amounts of information against missionary work to the Niyogi Committee in Raigarh, Jashpur, Raipur, and Yeotmal. In addition, he mobilized tribal testimonials before the Committee.[146] Deshpande's reply to the Niyogi Committee's questionnaire runs 63 pages with about 5000 words.[147]

More than twenty years after the publication of the Report, VKA published a booklet, *Alienation of Tribals & Christian Missionaries.* The booklet used the information, assumptions, and conclusions of the Niyogi Committee regarding the proselytization of tribals by Christian missionaries.[148] Although it omitted references to the Report, its content, rhetoric, rationale, and the examples it emphasized of the Jharkhand movement, use of foreign money, missionary services, and the conversion of tribals reflect the continued influence of the Report on VKA. It has been reported that since the last quarter of the twentieth century, VKA has reconverted thousands of Christian tribals back to the Hindu fold in Madhya Pradesh.[149]

143. Outlook India, "Adivasi vs Vanvasi."

144. Jaffrelot, "India: The Politics of (Re)conversion," 207.

145. Niyogi, *Report,* 1:3; Part A, 2:19, 22.

146. Niyogi, *Report,* Part A, 2:18, 52, 128.

147. Niyogi, *Report,* Part A, 2:321–83.

148. Saxena, *Alienation of Tribals.*

149. *National Herald,* October 31, 1993.

During the early 1980s, the RSS was involved in discussions with Christian leaders and began to openly present its anti-conversion perspective, substantiating it with the Niyogi Report's findings. A first moderate dialogue between the faculty members of De Nobili College and a senior RSS office bearer, Shripaty Sastry, took place in Pune in July 1983 at the invitation of Felix Raj, the chairman of the organizing committee. Sastry presented a speech, *An exposition of the RSS view of the Relevance of Christianity in India Today,* in which he said that as an RSS man he does not hate Christ or his teachings but "the activities carried out by the church in his name are looked upon with suspicion."[150] He pointed out how Protestant missionaries in India attempted to show that "Hinduism is full of fault."[151] He also emphasized how converts are denationalized, de-Hinduized, and how they alienate themselves from Hindu culture and traditions once they are converted. He contended that for the RSS, Hindu is not a religious term as it is used only in the context of nationhood.[152] By quoting the Niyogi Report on how missionaries in the past lent money to the poor in exchange for conversions, he argued that the basic motive behind Christian social work such as schools, dispensaries, asylums, and orphanages is conversion.[153]

In the late 1990s, Gujarat experienced a high magnitude of violence against Christians in the Dangs district. For example, in 1998, during the time when the BJP ruled the state, the Hindu Jagaran Manch, along with other sister organizations of Sangh Parivar, was involved in planned attacks on Christians in Dangs, where there was bloodshed and looting and arson of churches. It was recorded that in 1998 alone, 34 churches were destroyed in Gujarat by Hindu activists.[154] As a result, the National Commission for Minorities initiated several rounds of talks between RSS Chief K.S. Sudarshan and Christian leaders of different denominations in various parts of India with the objective of bringing harmony between Christians and the opposing Hindus. On February 9, 1999, Prajna Bharati of Hyderabad, a Hindu organization, asked David Frawley, a Hindu scholar to participate in a debate with Archbishop Arulappa on "the ethics of religious conversions." In this debate, Frawley accused Christians of claiming to be exclusive guardians of truth, an attitude which creates tension for Hindus of a pluralistic

---

150. Speech produced in Chowgule, *Christianity in India,* 89.

151. Chowgule, *Christianity in India,* 89.

152. Chowgule, *Christianity in India,* 93, 98.

153. Chowgule, *Christianity in India,* 92.

154. Venkatesan, "Hate Campaign in Gujarat"; Lobo, *Globalisation,* 17; Johnstone, *Operation World,* 323.

worldview, and of seeking converts from every other religion.[155] The first meeting between Catholic Bishops and the RSS leaders was held in Delhi on August 21, 2000; the second was held between the leaders of RSS and NCCI representatives in Nagpur on September 12, 2000; the third talk was between K. S. Sudarshan and the Dinakarans of Jesus Calls, held in Delhi; the fourth in Chennai and the fifth in Kerala between RSS local leaders and Christian laity in November 2001.

Sudarshan's talk at R.S.S-Christian Perspective Meet, held on August 20, 2002, clearly indicates how the Niyogi Report continues to play a role in the RSS's understanding of Christian missions. During the meeting Sudarshan remarked that, "Conversion is the main irritant in creating a cordial relationship between the two communities [Hindu and Christian]."[156] Quoting from the Niyogi Report, he said that "it [conversion] is being carried out with a political motive."[157] "Evangelism in India appears to be a part of a uniform policy to revive Christendom for re-establishing Western supremacy and is not prompted by spiritual motives. This objective is apparently to create Christian majority pockets with a view to disrupt the solidarity of non-Christian societies. And the mass conversion of a considerable section of adivasis with ulterior motive is fraud with danger to the security of the State."[158] He argued that, "When conversion is done with a motive to just segregate a portion of the society for their imperialistic purposes that becomes the cause for concern, the cause for conflict. And therefore, we say that conversion is the main irritant."[159] Referring to the Orthodox Church, which does not actively seek conversions like Protestants and Catholics, he remarked, "We do not have any quarrel with those churches who do not subscribe to conversion."[160] Other topics in the discussion included questions on the loyalty of Christians to the country, the Christian mockery of Hindu gods and festivals, and the conversions of Dalits and weaker sections of society by means of proselytization. Most of these topics were broadly dealt with in the Niyogi Report.

155. For a full discussion on this debate, see Frawley, *How I Became a Hindu*, 144–82.

156. K. S. Sudarshan's talk was reproduced in Sudarshan, "Speech in RSS-Christian Perspective Meet," 18.

157. Sudarshan, "Speech in RSS-Christian Perspective Meet," 23.

158. Sudarshan, "Speech in RSS-Christian Perspective Meet," 18 quoting from Niyogi, *Report*, 1:131–32.

159. Sudarshan, "Speech in RSS-Christian Perspective Meet," 25.

160. Sudarshan, "Speech in RSS-Christian Perspective Meet," 25.

The Impact of the Report on Vishva Hindu Parishad (VHP)

VHP is one of the major organizations of the Sangh Parivar which shares in the ethos of Hindutva ideology and directs "all activities towards discouraging the socially alienated and economically deprived tribals from adopting Christianity, and to 'de-Christianise' those who [have] already done so."[161] In its self-understanding as an organization, VHP declares that it was the Niyogi Report which provided the impetus for the formation of VHP to unite Hindus against religious challenges and to curb conversion activities through various strategies.[162] VHP acknowledges on its website,

> The imminent cause of speed, inspiration and encouragement for the formation of Vishva Hindu Parishad was provided by the Report of Niyogi Commission appointed by the state of Madhya Pradesh in 1955[sic] to investigate the actual position of the problem of conversion of illiterate, economically weak, socially backward and untouchable segments of Hindu society like Vanavasis, Girijans and the untouchables by Christian parsons by adopting various types of improper means and methods with the help of millions of dollars received from America and other Western countries. It is through the Report of this Commission that the entire nation came to know the truth about contemptuous means and methods adopted by the Christian padres for converting these gullible sections of Hindu society. It sent shock waves throughout the country. It was for the first time that the heinous means adopted by the missionaries were analyzed on the basis of their practical applications through this Report. Their nefarious activities were not only endangering the Hindu Dharma, but also vehemently challenging the very unity and integrity of Bharat. According to the Report, the missionaries were running huge schools, hostels, orphanages, hospitals etc. with the aid of the foreign money and therefore they were forcibly converting poor, destitute and innocent Hindus to Christianity.[163]

Shivram Shankar Apte, a Maharashtrian Brahmin, who was a close associate of K. M. Munshi, joined the RSS in 1939 and started his career of *pracharak* from Tamil Nadu. After thoroughly reading the Niyogi Report, Apte, the founder of *Hindustan Samachar* news agency and a longtime

---

161. Katju, *Vishva Hindu Parishad and Indian Politics*, 27. VKA activists were also involved in planning attacks on churches in south Bihar in 1998. See Joshi, "Trident Speaks."

162. Vishva Hindu Parishad, "Inception of VHP." See also Rai, "VHP at a Glance."

163. Vishva Hindu Parishad, "Inception of VHP."

Pracharak of the RSS, was "moved to the core and he undertook an in-depth study of the problem."[164] In 1961, he wrote a series of three articles in *Kesari*, a Maharashtrian newspaper founded by Bal Gangadhar Tilak, calling Hindus worldwide to strengthen their allegiance to Hindu ideals and culture and unite them against the challenges faced by Hindus in India.[165] After a few months, Golwalkar called Apte and reminded him of his articles and encouraged him "to materialize the dream."[166] Apte seriously considered Golwalkar's advice and undertook a 10-month journey throughout the country exchanging views and notes with *Sants* (Hindu saints), sociocultural leaders, and scholars. Among the prominent Hindu leaders he met were Shankaracharya of Kanchi Kamakoti Peetham of Tamil Nadu, K. M. Munshi of Mumbai, Sant Tukdoji Maharaj of Nagpur, Chandrashekar Sashtry of Rajasthan, Supreme Court judge B. P. Sinha, politician Babu Jag Jeevan Ram, and many others.[167] He met with about 200 Hindu scholars and thinkers and exchanged letters with about 600 Hindu leaders in India and invited 150 of them to Bombay for a discussion.[168] Among those who gathered was V. G. Deshpande, who closely monitored the Niyogi Committee's investigation in Madhya Pradesh on behalf of Hindu Mahasabha.[169] It is important to note that, while thoughts of founding VHP were still vague in the minds of Hindutva leaders, "Nehru's death in May 1964, gave another boost to the Hindu right."[170] Burgeoning out of a vision to protect Hindus from religious conversions, with the motivation and cooperation of the RSS and Chinmaya mission,[171] VHP was founded on August 29, 1964 in Mumbai. Among the founding fathers that witnessed the formation of VHP were M. S. Golwalkar, K. M. Munshi, Tukdoji Maharaj, Swami Shankar Ananda, Dattamurti, Tara Singh, Giani Bhupinder Singh, Sitaramdas of Ramtek, and Secretary General of Hindu Mahasabha Shri V. G. Deshpande. Swami Chinmayananda presided over the meeting.

VHP's initial goals were to implement the vision of defending and protecting the Hindu dharma and to spread the message of Hindutva through various programs such as services, campaigns, and religious

---

164. Vishva Hindu Parishad, "Inception of VHP."

165. Jaffrelot, *Hindu Nationalist Movement in India*, 194.

166. Rai, *VHP at a Glance*.

167. A list of people he met with and a discussion of the founding of VHP can be found at http://www.hvk.org/2014/0914/84.html.

168. Rai, *VHP at a Glance*.

169. *Hitavada*, July 17, 1954.

170. Katju, *Vishva Hindu Parishad*, 1.

171. Chinmaya Mission was founded in Kerala by Swami Chinmayananda, a Kerala Brahmin.

activities. Its major goal, however, was "to check the spread of Christianity among the tribal population . . . as it had felt that the spread of Christianity among the tribal populace undermined the cultural unity of India and destroyed the ideological hegemony of Hindu beliefs."[172] Swayed by the Niyogi Committee's analysis of conversions, VHP maintains that conversions are "simple luring away of tribals through monetary means by Christian missionaries."[173] According to Manjari Katju, VHP is of the narrow perspective that, "Tribals had become easy victims for conversion to Christianity, being on the periphery of Hindu Society and divorced from knowledge of their 'Hindu background.'"[174]

In August 1964, when the Pope announced that the International Eucharist Congress would be held in Mumbai in November of that year, the Hindu Mahasabha reacted in *The Organiser* saying, "Catholicism is not merely a religion. It is a tremendous organization allied with some foreign powers . . . The large-scale conversion of tribal people in the industrial heartland of India poses a serious danger to future national security." With such a mythical imagination as painted in the Niyogi Report, Hindu nationalists were ignited with passion to resist the invasion of others into Hindu society.

What S.S. Apte, the founder and general secretary, said in the first meeting of VHP sheds light upon the task taken up by the organization. "The world has been divided into Christian, Islamic and Communist, and all these three consider the Hindu society as a very fine rich food on which to feast and fatten themselves. It is therefore necessary in this age of competition and conflict to think of, and organize, the Hindu world to save itself from the evil eyes of all the three."[175] In support of his argument, he pointed out that the Christianized Naga tribes in the northeast had arisen as an autonomist movement and demanded a separate state; a separate Nagaland was granted in 1963.[176] In the eyes of the RSS and its allies, the separation of Nagas into a Christian state was an act of denationalization prompted by Christian aggressors.[177] According to Jaffrelot, "The foundation of the VHP fulfilled the criteria of the strategy of stigmatization and emulation since it resulted from a reactivation of the majoritarian inferiority complex, namely the feeling that Christian proselytization posed a

172. Katju, *Vishva Hindu Parishad*, 12.

173. Katju, *Vishva Hindu Parishad*, 12.

174. Katju, *Vishva Hindu Parishad*, 12.

175. *The Organiser*, Diwali Special, 1964, 15, quoted in Jaffrelot, *Hindu Nationalist Movement in India*, 197.

176. Jaffrelot, *Hindu Nationalist Movement in India*, 197–98.

177. Jaffrelot, *Hindu Nationalist Movement in India*, 198.

threat to Hinduism and that close attention had to be given to imitating its techniques in order the better resist it."[178]

One of the crucial decisions made at the 1966 convention was to adopt "reversal of conversion" through programs such as *paravartan* (Homecoming) which gained new momentum. The resolution reads, "This conference of the Vishva Hindu Parishad takes note of the fact that during the past several centuries many Hindus have left the folds of their forefathers due to ignorance and helplessness and because of the pressure of violence, coercion and temptations exerted on them by the people of other faiths. The Parishad feels that a pressing need of the present time is assimilation and absorption, through reconversion of all such people who may desire, out of their own free will, to return to the faith of their forefathers."[179] VHP believes that, "Hindutva is a pre-requisite for progress in India."[180]

With the impetus received from the Niyogi report, Shivram Apte generalized that "the Church was not only converting the people but also sowing the seeds of disaffection, separatism and secessionism"[181] in northeast India. He felt that "unless conversions were curbed, the entire northeastern border populace would become Christian and threaten the unity of India."[182] He undertook a tour to Assam and started counter service programs among the tribal people there. In the following years, VHP held several conventions in various parts of India and abroad to create a sense of self-esteem in society and to promote the feeling that "we are all Hindus."[183] In the 1970s, VHP launched its forces against the so-called conversion activities of Christian missionaries in the northeast of India.[184]

Since the foremost agenda of VHP was the issue of conversion, in a meeting organized by the South Kannada district unit, VHP leaders discussed the Freedom of Religion bill to which they gave support. They said, "If the Christians started converting Hindus in the guise of social service, that would create social disharmony . . . Conversions and imperialism were respectable during a certain period in the past. But at present, just as territorial expansion was an offence so also proselytization."[185] Acting as a pressure group, VHP demanded that the central government should expel all foreign missionaries

---

178. Jaffrelot, *Hindu Nationalist Movement in India*, 196.

179. http://vhp.org/organization/org-important-resolutions-passed-by/.

180. http://vhp.org/hindutva-is-a-pre-requisite-for-progress-in-india/.

181. Rai, "VHP at a Glance."

182. Katju, *Vishva Hindu Parishad*, 13.

183. Rai, "VHP at a Glance."

184. Devadas, *Ideologies of Political Parties*, 20.

185. Swami, "Religious Conversion are Relics," 14.

from India and ban their entry forthwith.[186] It also demanded that Scheduled and other backward castes should not be given government reservation concessions after their conversion to Christianity.[187]

On February 19, 1981, in Meenakshipuram of Tamil Nadu, around 1,000 out of 1,250 Dalits had converted to Islam as a sign of protest of the denial of social equality for untouchables by upper caste people.[188] With this event of mass conversion of "untouchables" to Islam, VHP became even more vigilant of religious conversions in India. VHP, Arya Samaj, Hindu Munnani, and other Hindu organizations widely publicized against the conversions of Meenakshipuram and attempted to reconvert as many people as possible back to Hinduism.[189] While Khan mentions that there had been seven cases of actual reconversion to Hinduism in Meenakshipuram, VHP proudly claims on its website that there had been the reconversion of about 120,000.[190] As Katju mentions, the post-1983 phase of VHP demonstrated the fiery and militant characteristic of the organization.[191] In 1985, the VHP Board of Trustees unanimously agreed that "there should be a legal ban on the conversion of Hindus and that the inflow of foreign money in the name of service projects and various other social, cultural and charitable purposes should be stopped."[192] VHP rationale is that, "Swami Vivekananda, Mahatma Gandhi, Vinoba Bhave and the Niyogi Commission headed by Justice Bhavani Shankar Niyogi have condemned the conversion of Hindus to other religions. It is hence essential that a necessary legislation should be enforced to prevent conversion."[193]

Ram Punyani, a human rights activist, remarks that VHP is one of the earliest front organizations of the RSS "which came to the forefront with intensified communal agenda."[194] Within twenty years of its inception, VHP had succeeded in convincing hundreds of thousands of Hindus that Muslims and Christians are anti-national and a danger to the country, using the slogan, "the danger is from the crescent and the cross."[195]

---

186. Katju, *Vishva Hindu Parishad,* 14.

187. Hindu Vishva, December 1969/1970, 63, quoted in Katju, *Vishva Hindu Parishad,* 14.

188. *The Organiser,* (Editorial) July 5, 1981, 3.

189. Khan, *Mass-conversions of Meenakshipuram,* 159.

190. Khan, *Mass-conversions of Meenakshipuram,* 45.

191. Katju, *Vishva Hindu Parishad,* 9.

192. Katju, *Vishva Hindu Parishad,* 9.

193. Vishva Hindu Parishad, "Religious Regeneration."

194. Punyani, *Fascism of Sangh Parivar,* 29.

195. *Sunday Observer,* February 21, 1982, 5.

Media that supports the cause of Hindu nationalism tends to generalize that conversions are on the rise due to proselytizing activities of Christian evangelical groups who receive large sums of foreign money.[196] With this sort of sweeping generalization, as Varkey contends, "one gets the impression that conversion in general is a sensitive issue and looked upon with suspicion and concern."[197]

Using the rhetoric of the Niyogi Report, VHP campaigns that, "Conversion from religion means conversion of allegiance from State also,"[198] and "Conversions due to inducement and fraud are quite rampant."[199] On its website, to provide answers to 37 frequently asked questions on religious conversions, VHP mostly incorporates information from and interpretations of the Report.[200] VHP also has published pamphlets and booklets against Christian conversions basing its arguments on the Report.

Since the 1980s, the RSS, VHP, and other Sangh members have become more vigilant toward conversion activities as they were threatened by the renewed emphasis of Christian missions on the evangelization of India by 2000. Referring to a Christian meeting held in Colorado Springs, USA, in 1995, where Christian leaders from 77 countries gathered to discuss and plan a program to evangelize the world, Surendra Jain, the chief of Bajrang Dal remarked, "Unluckily India was on the top of the list"[201] of target countries. He reported that in a circular issued to missionaries called the "Mission Mandate," "it was written that 900,000 churches must be built in India by 2001."[202] Jain views such evangelistic or conversion goals as part of the international conspiracy against Hinduism or Hindus. As Sebastian Kim points out, those Christian campaigns have not only heightened tensions between the supporters of Hindutva and Christians, but also contributed to the resurgence, hostility and promotion of Hindu nationalism in India.[203]

Surendra Jain believes that the present-day plans and strategies of evangelism are not different from the 1950s when the Niyogi Committee was appointed to study missionary motives and activities. Therefore, according to Jain, the Niyogi Committee's findings, conclusions, and recommendations on missionary activities are still valid today. Jain writes,

196. Varkey, "Image of Christianity in the Newspapers," 249.

197. Varkey, "Image of Christianity in the Newspapers," 249.

198. Vishva Hindu Parishad, "Religious Regeneration."

199. Vishva Hindu Parishad, "FAQ-Religious Conversions," http://vhp.org/faq-rel/..

200. Vishva Hindu Parishad, "FAQ-Religious Conversions," http://vhp.org/faq-rel/..

201. Vishva Hindu Parishad, "Bajrang Dal."

202. Vishva Hindu Parishad, "Bajrang Dal."

203. Kim, *In Search of Identity*, 132–33.

This report exposed the misdeeds of Christian Missionaries in so much detail for the first time. This report is still relevant because they have not changed their mission or modus operandi. Moreover, they want to concentrate more on Bharat so that they can get man force to make Christianity survive in the west where they are being evaporated very fast. We have defeated them on intellectual level many times. The Report is the basis for such debates every time. Moreover, we have prepared many handbills to circulate in the masses. These, too, are based on the Report. But we are defeating them on field also. Our target is very clear. We want to bring back every Christian whose forefathers were illegally converted. We are creating the situation so that it will become impossible for illegal conversion.[204]

The Report and the Bharatiya Janata Party (BJP)

The BJP is the most prominent member of the Sangh Parivar headed by RSS. It proudly claims its ancestral connections with the RSS and walks in the foundational principles of the RSS.[205] Its guiding lights are Syama Prasad Mukherjee, Pandit Deendayal Upadhyaya, Lal Krishna Advani, and its founder, Atal Bihari Vajpayee.[206] These leaders played pivotal roles in the formation and development of the first Hindu nationalist political party, the Bharatiya Jana Sangh (BJS), which campaigned for the legal implementation of its recommendations through its manifesto.[207] Since the BJP's origins lie in BJS' political ancestry, it reflects the rhetoric of BJS' political ideology and the RSS's vision of promoting the philosophy of *Hindu Rashtra*. However, since Jana Sangh did not have much public appeal because of its fanatical use of Hindutva rhetoric, when the BJP was formed in 1980, its leaders decided to moderate its political rhetoric and values in an attempt to acquire more votes and appear as a viable alternative to the Congress Party.[208]

The BJP, which only won two seats in the parliamentary elections in 1984, multiplied its winnings with 86 seats in 1989. Less than two years later, it emerged as the leading opposition party with 120 seats. In 1996 it formed the government at the center, which lasted for only thirteen days.

204. Email correspondence of Surendra Jain with Sudhir Verma on August 19, 2014.

205. BJP, "History," http://www.bjp.org/en/about-the-party/history?u=bjp-history.

206. http://www.bjp.org/.

207. Bharatiya Jana Sangh: Party Documents, 1:82.

208. Frykenberg, "Hindu Fundamentalism," 243–44. See also Jaffrelot, *Religion, Caste and Politics*, 47.

In the 1998 parliamentary elections, the BJP attained unprecedented victory and became the first non-Congress government to rule India for a full term. During the time when BJP was burgeoning into power, L. K Advani remarked, "We are creating a nationalist force in the country . . . We are changing the nature of politics . . . "[209]

According to Partha Ghosh, who conducted a thorough research of BJP and the evolution of Hindu nationalism, the BJP used "religion and Hindu communalism to mobilize its support."[210] The BJP's advocacy for Hindu nationalism and its intolerance toward non-Hindu religions became more evident when BJP was found participating in the VHP's war against the Babri Masjid in Ayodhya, Uttar Pradesh in the early 1990s. The BJP's president, L. K. Advani, started his 10,000 km *Padyatra*-turned-*Rathyatra* from Somnath, Gujarat, to Ayodhya in Uttar Pradesh in September 1990 to educate people about the Ayodhya movement. It changed the course of BJP.[211] It not only generated communal backlash and riots in Gujarat, Karnataka, Uttar Pradesh, and Andhra Pradesh, but also "whipped up a strong Hindu fervor and increased the Party's vote bank from 85 in 1999 to 120 in the 1991 general elections."[212]

The BJP also supports and campaigns for conversion laws. The BJP president Amit Shah bragged in 2014 that, "[the] BJP is the only political party in the country that opposes forcible conversion . . . forcible conversion will be opposed at any cost."[213] BJP leaders rationalize their anti-conversion posture by taking the examples of Gandhi and the Niyogi Report. For example, in a television interview, BJP leader Narendra Modi, a member of the RSS and the former Chief Minister of Gujarat, was asked why conversions of tribals by missionaries was a problem and why they should be hindered. He replied, "If we do not know the truth, we will not be able to find an answer to the problem. What was the reason Mahatma Gandhi emphasized time and again that there should be no religious conversions in India? Mahatma Gandhi wrote articles against conversions, and raised his voice against them whenever possible. Don't we accept or obey Mahatma Gandhi's words? Just think about it! And during the time of Nehru, the Niyogi commission was appointed against conversion in Madhya Pradesh."[214] The political legacy of Narendra Modi in Gujarat was such that in 2002 the

209. Coll, "Hindu-Moslem Battles."

210. Ghosh, *BJP and the Evolution of Hindu Nationalism*, 16.

211. Jaffrelot, *Religion, Caste and Politics*, 49.

212. *India Today*, "1990–L.K. Advani's Rath Yatra."

213. *The Indian Express*, "BJP Favours Law Banning Conversion."

214. YouTube, "Exclusive: Narendra Modi."

state under his leadership experienced tumultuous communal and religious outbreaks between Hindus and Muslims. Some scholars called it a "Gujarat pogrom." It was officially reported that in the anti-Muslim violence 790 Muslims and 254 Hindus were killed, 223 more people were reported missing, and another 2,500 were injured. According to Junior Home Minister Sriprakash Jaiswal, more than 900 women were widowed and 600 children orphaned in the riots. A police officer was believed to have reported that "the Gujarat government had authorised the killing of Muslims after the riots," a charge the state government denies.[215]

During the election campaigns in 2013, the BJP leader Venkaiah Naidu made it clear to the public that the "BJP will bring an anti-conversion law to ban religious conversions in the country if it is voted to power in 2014 General Elections."[216] After winning the elections, he raised the issue of conversions in the parliament on December 11, 2014 and emphasized that by following the recommendations of the Niyogi report, Madhya Pradesh and others states had instituted anti-conversion laws.[217] Using language similar to that of the Report, he said that conversions were taking a fraudulent route and creating social tensions. At the end of his talk he demanded, "Let there be anti-conversion laws in all the states; let there be anti-conversion law at the center also."[218]

THE INFLUENCE OF THE NIYOGI REPORT
ON HINDU NATIONALIST THINKERS

Since the early 1980s, Hindutva thinkers have been involved in the intellectual argument of Hindutva discourse and the conversion dilemma. The writings of Sita Ram Goel, Arun Shourie, Ashok V. Chowgule, Kanayalal Talreja, and others indicate that, to some extent, their arguments are shaped by the Niyogi Report's assessment of conversions.

Ram Swarup Agarwal and His Superiority of Hinduism

Ram Swarup was one of the earliest in independent India to take a critical stance against Christianity, Islam and Communism. He published various works, one of which was banned by the government of India. Koenraad Elst

---

215. Human Rights Watch, "We Have No Orders to Save You."

216. *The Hindu*, 2013, quoted in Osuri, "Concern for Sovereignty," 385.

217. YouTube, "Narendra Modi Dares Opposition."

218. YouTube, "Narendra Modi Dares Opposition."

calls him "the most influential thinker in the second half of the twentieth century."[219]

He was greatly influenced by the philosophy of Sri Aurobindo. Since the late 1970s, he has turned his focus to religious issues and has attempted to provide intellectual arguments for a Hindu awakening against Christian conversions away from the channels of the Sangh Parivar.[220] Since he believed that, "The biggest problem rising India faces [is] the problem of self-alienated Hindus,"[221] he has worked hard to unite Hindus through his pen. In his works, especially *Hinduism vis-à-vis Christianity and Islam* (1982), and *Hindu View of Christianity and Islam* (1993), he criticized Islamic and Christian colonizers who used their power, trade, and religion over the centuries to subdue India. He has also written extensive studies comparing Hinduism, Islam, and Christianity.

Agarwal critiqued the spiritual value of conversion and regarded Christian proselytizing as an arrogant idea which denies God and his working in others. For him, conversion is an attack on the convert's former religion which amounts to its extinction. Quoting from Deut. 18:18–19 and Gal 1:8, he imagines that "the Bible is full of curses invoked on rivals-gods, prophets, apostles, doctrines . . . . It is not difficult to see that Christianity incarnated a new religious intolerance."[222] Listing the atrocities committed by Christians and Muslims in history, he labels these religions as "anti-human."[223] He observed that, "Christianity had its teeth knocked out in the modern West, and though it was still capable of doing considerable mischief in India, it was bound to collapse as soon as its rational review in the West became known to our people."[224]

In 1982, he founded Voice of India, a non-profit publishing house, which publishes articles and books on religious debates, particularly those that favor Hinduism over religious others and which criticize Christianity and Islam. These books are made available free through its website Voice of Dharma (voiceofdharma.org or bharatvani.org), started in 2004. The two-volume Niyogi Report, which was published as "Vindicated by Time" in 1998, has been made freely available online. Several Hindu or Hindu nationalist websites which share in Sangh's anti-conversion rhetoric have provided hyperlinks to this website providing access to the Report.

219. Elst, *Decolonizing the Hindu Mind*, 203.

220. Elst, *Decolonizing the Hindu Mind*, 122.

221. Swarup, "Hindu Renaissance."

222. Swarup, *Hindu View of Christianity and Islam*, 41.

223. Swarup, *Hindu View of Christianity and Islam*, 83.

224. Goel, *How I Became a Hindu*, 93.

Sita Ram Goel's Resistance to Christian Missions

Sita Ram Goel, Marxist-turned-Communist, became a staunch Hindu in his mid-twenties through the influence of the philosophy of Sri Aurobindo, Arya Samaj, Mahatma Gandhi, and the RSS.[225] Ram Swarup Agarwal closely mentored Goel and played a vital role in his religious thinking. Goel also spent time with some missionary friends who vainly attempted to persuade him into the Christian faith.[226] Rather, he soon after turned against missionaries' efforts toward conversions. He appeared to have generated a dislike for Christianity (which he calls "Churchianity") when a Catholic priest took him to a Christian monastery and made spiritual as well as intellectual attempts to persuade him to become a "formal" Christian or convert him into Catholicism.[227] Goel mentions meeting an anonymous Hindu convert on the Christian campus who narrated the side effects of his own conversion experience. During the time of his [convert's] illness and financial struggles, there appeared on the scene a Christian priest with a supply of medicines and other necessities. With these timely gifts, according to Goel, the Hindu young man's life was drawn to Christianity. He was eventually forced to eat beef in the fellowship of Christians which created family troubles; his wife and children left him soon after his conversion.[228]

Under the guidance of Ram Swarup, Goel became an ardent follower of Santana Dharma and regarded Hinduism as the greatest religion. In defense and promotion of Hinduism, he began to oppose Nehruism and non-Hindu religions through his writings. In late 1981, when he was sixty, he decided to devote his life to informing Hindu society about its own great heritage and about the dangers it faces.[229] He also undertook the editorship of the RSS organ, *The Organiser.*[230] He said, "I do not regard Islam and Christianity as religions at all. They are, for me, ideologies of imperialism like Nazism and Communism, legitimizing aggression by one set of people against another in the name of [a] god which gangsters masquerading as prophets have invented after their own image. I see no place

---

225. Goel, *How I Became a Hindu*, 93.

226. Goel, *How I Became a Hindu*, 46–49; See also Goel, *Jesus Christ: An Artifice for Aggression*, 1.

227. Goel, *How I Became a Hindu*, 46–49.

228. Goel, *How I Became a Hindu*, 46–49.

229. Goel, *How I Became a Hindu*, 94.

230. *Organiser* is the official magazine of RSS published in English since July 3, 1947. Its Hindi version, *Panchjanya,* began its publication on January 14, 1948 with its first editor A. B. Vajpayee.

for them in India."[231] He remarked that, "Christianity has never been a religion; its long history tells us that it has been predatory imperialism par excellence."[232] Unlike many Hindu nationalists, he hated Christ outrightly and called him "junk."[233] He said,

> It is high time for Hindus to learn that Jesus Christ symbolizes no spiritual power, or moral uprightness. He is no more than an artifice for legitimizing wanton imperialist aggression. The aggressors have found him to be highly profitable so far. By the same token, Hindus should know that Jesus means nothing but mischief for their country and culture. The West where he flourished for long, has discarded him as junk. There is no reason why Hindus should buy him. He is the type of junk that cannot be re-cycled. He can only poison the environment.[234]

Goel's opposition to Christianity seemed insignificant until a Hindu Sanyasi named Baba Madhavdas, a roaming Sadhu from Andhra Pradesh, reminded him about the Niyogi Report in 1982 and told Goel that he uses the Report as a tool to raise Hindu resistance to Christian missions.[235] Madhavdas emphatically challenged him to read it in depth and convinced him to resist missionary activities by promoting the spread of the Report.[236] Goel began to write passionate articles in periodicals like *Hinduism Today, Indian Express,* and *the Organiser* against Christianity and Islam. In the same year, Goel and Ram Swarup founded the Voice of India publishing house in New Delhi. Voice of India became an intellectual channel for the spread of anti-Christian and anti-Muslim views.

Goel first summarized the Niyogi Report in his work, *History of Hindu-Christian Encounters* in 1986. In this volume he divided the Hindu-Christian encounters into five phases: 1) the atrocities committed by Portuguese pirates, 2) the British conquest and Hindu reform movements, 3) Gandhi and Christian theology in the Indian context, 4) independence and the rift in the lute, 5) conversions and the Hindu awakening since the early 1980s. He contends that in the fourth phase, independence proved to be a boon to Christianity and provided it with new theologies of fulfillment, liberation, indigenization and dialogue that were put into action.[237] The only rifts in the lute in this phase,

231. Goel, *How I Became a Hindu,* 57.

232. Goel, *Pseudo-Secularism,* 2.

233. Goel, *Jesus Christ: An Artifice for Aggression,* 85.

234. Goel, *Jesus Christ: An Artifice for Aggression,* 85.

235. Goel, *Jesus Christ: An Artifice for Aggression,* ix.

236. Goel, *Pseudo-Secularism,* vii–xi.

237. Goel, *Pseudo-Secularism,* vii.

according to him, were K. M. Panikkar's work *Asia and Western Dominance*, the Niyogi Committee Report, and Om Prakash Tyagi's Bill on Religious Freedom.[238] Although Goel summarized the whole of the Niyogi Report in one chapter, the rest of the chapters reflect the influence of the Report on his understanding and portrayal of Christian missions.

In Chapter 17, Goel states that in the early years of independent India, Christian missions received two jolts. The first was from K. M. Panikkar's work, *Asia and Western Dominance* (1953), and the second was from the Niyogi Committee Report (1956).[239] Substantiated by the Niyogi Report's findings on Christian mission in Madhya Pradesh, Goel attempts to show how Christian missions in independent India contributed to the socio-religious tensions and disharmony. He convincingly summarizes the circumstances of the Niyogi Committee's appointment, the findings of its investigation, and its recommendations against missionaries and their activities in order to present the Report's views of the missionary enterprise as a reliable history of Christian missions in India. The themes he emphasized are Christians' separatist tendencies and their denationalized attitudes, missionaries' misuse of foreign money, the usage of schools and hospitals for the proselytization of adivasis, missionary attacks on Hindu idols, mass conversions by material inducements, and evangelism in India as part of a uniform world policy for re-establishment of Western supremacy.

In late 1986 and in 1987, Goel wrote four articles on Catholic Ashrams in *Hinduism Today* and *Indian Express* respectively, exposing contextualized, Indianized, and indigenous inculturation missionary methods as Christian marketing tricks to entice Hindus into Christianity. These writings stirred religious debates between Christian Fathers and Hindu Sadhus and fetched varied Hindu-Christian opinions in the media. Goel's articles and debates collected from *Hinduism Today* and *Indian Express* were put together as a book and published in 1988 under the title *Catholic Ashrams: Sannyasins or Swindlers.* In this book, Goel also expresses sorrow that although the Niyogi Report revealed several facts against missionary methods long ago and suggested recommendations, it has been neglected.[240]

Another work through which Goel unfolds the Niyogi Report with annotated emphasis is *Pseudo-Secularism, Christian Missions and Hindu Resistance,* published in 1998. This is a revised or expanded version of what he noted in his *History of Hindu-Christian Encounters (AD 304 to 1996),* adding to it the Report's impact on the Freedom of Religion Bill and its repercussions

238. Goel, *Pseudo-Secularism,* iv.
239. Goel, *History of Hindu-Christian Encounters,* 325.
240. Goel, *Catholic Ashrams,* 234.

on the conversion debates in the 1990s. His other books which critically view Christianity and depict it as imperialistic include *Defense of Hindu Society* and *Hindu Society under Siege (1992)*. Goel became an inspiration to many Hindutva scholars and thinkers to treat the controversial Niyogi Report as invaluable evidence in their arguments against conversions.

Arun Shourie's Anti-conversion Rhetoric

Arun Shourie, a well-known Indian journalist, Hindu nationalist thinker and BJP member, was among those who challenged Christians during the conversion debates in the 1990s. In January 1994, on the occasion of the fiftieth anniversary of the establishment of the Catholic Bishops Conference of India (CBCI), in Pune, Shourie was invited to present the Hindu perception of the work of Christian missionaries and to review the work of the Church in India.[241] His presentation was later published under the title *Missionaries in India: Continuities, Challenges, Dilemmas*, which "created a stir, particularly among the missionaries in India."[242]

Like Goel, Shourie attempts to show that conversion is an inherent problem of Christianity which poses a threat to Hindu society. According to Sebastian Kim, "The Hindu-Christian debate was intensified especially after the publication of Arun Shourie's book *Missionaries in India*, which revealed a depth of Hindu resentment toward Christian conversion that was deeply anchored in their religious understanding, which many Christian respondents had failed to recognize."[243]

Arun Shourie formed his anti-conversion thesis from the views of Swami Vivekananda, Mahatma Gandhi, and Panikkar's work, *Asia and Western Dominance*,[244] drawing upon various historical sources. He substantiates his argument with the perceptions, rhetoric, and recommendations of the M. B. Rege and M. B. Niyogi's Missionary Activities Enquiry Committee Reports.[245] He begins his line of argument by presenting England's motif of de-nationalization of Hindus through education and conversion programs. He bases his reasoning on the theory of Thomas Babington Macaulay, the British government official in India who, in 1835, said, "We must at present do our best to form a class who may be interpreters between us and the millions whom we govern; a class of persons,

---

241. Shourie, *Missionaries in India*, ix.

242. Chowgule, "Arun Shourie and the Missionaries in India."

243. Kim, *In Search of Identity*, 12.

244. Shourie, *Missionaries in India*, 4.

245. Shourie, *Harvesting Our Souls*, 54–58; *Missionaries in India*, 4–17, 41–53, 200–210. See also Kim, *In Search of Identity*, 145.

Indians in blood and color, but English in taste, in opinions, in morals, and in intellect."[246] To stress the point, Shourie also borrows the example of Sir Charles's 1838 prognosis that, "Educated in the same way, interested in the same objects, engaged in the same pursuits with ourselves, they become more English than Hindus . . ."[247]

By recounting the ill portrayal of Hinduism by foreign missionaries and their attacks on Indian culture and customs, he stressed that every missionary who was bound to spread Christianity attempted to alienate Hindus by creating a suspicion in their heads about themselves.[248] Referring to M. B. Rege's and Niyogi's Reports, he maintains that missionaries were involved in converting minors and illiterate aboriginals "who were completely incapable of comprehending the virtue of Christianity."[249] He also showed a sharp distinction between the Hindu worldview of salvation and the exclusiveness of Christianity which demands conversion of people by default. In his review of the contemporary situation of the church in India, he argued that the church still operates on the same colonial premise and believes that salvation depends on conversions.

Drawing upon selective portions of missionary history in the eighteenth and nineteenth centuries together with some contemporary examples, Shourie reemphasized Gandhi's five-fold objections to conversion: 1) Christians should give up conversions altogether; 2) They should not make the poor, illiterate, and desperate the target of their campaigns, nor offer inducements; 3) Non-Indian missionaries must return to their homelands; 4) Desist de-nationalization efforts; and 5) Live the life of Christ rather than chasing after making converts.[250] Shourie supplemented Gandhi's list with two of his own suggestions. First, if Christians want to follow their religious call to make converts, they should "persuade the people to abide by the methods of Jesus and Gandhi."[251] Second, "Conversions should be open to scrutiny,"[252] which was a suggestion taken from the Report. In his closing remarks, he urged the church to examine "calumnies" created by missionaries on Hinduism and India and to scrutinize retrospectively the present day

246. Shourie, *Missionaries in India*, x, 61.

247. Shourie, *Missionaries in India*, xi.

248. Shourie, *Missionaries in India*, 161–76.

249. Shourie, *Missionaries in India*, 24–32.

250. Shourie, *Missionaries in India*, 37–39.

251. Shourie, *Missionaries in India*, 37–39.

252. Shourie, *Missionaries in India*, 37–39.

dilemmas of the church's contextualization, localization, and liberalization of the gospel targeted to convert Hindus.[253]

There are some similarities in rhetoric between the Niyogi Report and Arun Shourie's anti-conversion debate. For example, the way he organized his argument resembles the themes, constants and allegations of the Niyogi Report against Christians in general and missionaries in particular. Shourie has relied on some of the prime historical and empirical sources of the Niyogi Report to illustrate that conversion is problematic in India.[254] While Goel often used Volume I of the Niyogi Report, which was the compilation and interpretation of the committee's investigation, Shourie selectively utilized the extracts of various historical reports found in Volume II of the Report to substantiate his arguments on the negative side of missionary activities. Emphasizing Gandhi's aversion to the conversion tactics of missionaries, Shourie claims to have found several accounts from the *Collected Works of Mahatma Gandhi* in which missionaries admitted that the aim of Christian institutions and services is "to gather a fuller harvest of converts for the Church."[255] Quoting from *Catholic Dharma Ka Pracharak,* an extract found in the Niyogi Report, Volume II, Part B, he shows that Catholic missionaries were instructed to baptize sick children and dying adults in the name of administering medicine.[256] Drawn from the extracts of the Niyogi Report, he showed how William Wilberforce and Sir Charles Trevelyan ridiculed Hindu gods and how missionaries from the sixteenth century onwards targeted tribals and depressed classes of Hindu society for evangelism.[257] He selectively relies on the Report to demonstrate how missionaries were involved in fraudulent and secessionist activities in the country.[258]

The key portions of Shourie's debate, which called for the scrutiny and cessation of conversion of Hindus, were published in various newspapers in Maharashtra[259] and received varied responses from people, especially from Christian leaders like Augustine Kanjamala[260] and Sarto Esteves.[261] Kanja-

253. Shourie, *Missionaries in India,* 179–230.

254. Shourie, *Harvesting Our Souls,* 54–58; *Missionaries in India,* 8, 109, 181–84, 201–3. See also Kim, *In Search of Identity,* 145.

255. Shourie, *Missionaries in India,* 7.

256. Shourie, *Missionaries in India,* 8.

257. Shourie, *Missionaries in India,* 181–86.

258. Shourie, *Missionaries in India,* 208–9.

259. *Maharashtra Herald,* January 29, February 5, 13, 26 and March 5, 1994; *Deccan Chronicle,* January 30, February 6, 13, 20, 27 and March 6, 1994.

260. Kanjamala wrote six articles in *Maharashtra Herald,* an English daily published from Pune on July 13, 20, 27 and August 3, 17, 24.

261. Sarto Esteves wrote two articles in *OHeraldo,* an English daily published from

mala and others accused Shourie of "flogging a dead horse by quoting from the past, and that he does not recognize the changes that have taken place, particularly since Vatican II, which was proclaimed in the 1960s."[262]

Talreja's Demand for a Constitutional Ban on Conversions

Kanaylal M. Talreja, a writer, journalist, educationist, and a staunch follower of Hindutva philosophy, has extensively relied on and reproduced redactions of the Niyogi Report in his writings[263] to ascertain that conversions are the result of missionary methods of "force, fraud, frightening, persuasion, temptation, vilification, vituperation, tortures, torments and even blood-curdling atrocities."[264] He tirelessly collected anti-Christian and anti-missionary quotes from various historical and contemporary sources and published them to show the denationalizing and subversive impact of conversions and to raise awareness among Hindus against Christianity in India.

On November 6, 1999, Pope John Paul II issued a document, *Ecclesia in Asia,* a blue print for the expansion of the Catholic faith in Asia, which calls on missionaries to fulfill their mission of witnessing Christ across cultures by means of dialogue, social service, and contextualization of contemporary realities.[265] In response, in Talreja's work, *Holy Vedas and Holy Bible,* he attempts to answer the Pope's clarion call for conversion[266] and also aims to "awaken the slumbering Hindus of Hindusthan to raise voice against the denationalizing campaign of Christian Missionaries and compel the ruling Hindu Politicians to impose ban on the proselytizing activities of the Christian Missionaries."[267] Building his argument on the rationale of the Niyogi Report, he contends that it was vague constitutional freedom which instigated Christian proselytizers to convert "millions of innocent illiterate poor Hindus to Christianity and succeeded in establishing Christendom in three states of the northeast: Nagaland, Mizoram and Meghalaya."[268] He remarks that, "the Christian missionaries misused the religious liberty accorded to them . . . "[269] By referring to various texts of the Niyogi report, he maintains

Panajim, Goa on September 8, 9, 1994.

262. Chowgule, "Arun Shourie and the Missionaries in India."

263. Talreja, *Holy Vedas and Holy Bible,* 26–36, 176; Talreja, *Appeal to Hindu Lawmakers for Constitutional Ban on Conversion of Hindus,* 144–48, 160.

264. Talreja, *Holy Vedas and Holy Bible,* 31.

265. John Paul II, "Ecclesia in Asia."

266. Talreja, *Holy Vedas and Holy Bible,* 22.

267. Talreja, *Holy Vedas and Holy Bible,* 27.

268. Talreja, *Holy Vedas and Holy Bible,* 26.

269. Talreja, *Holy Vedas and Holy Bible,* 28. He quotes from Niyogi, *Report,* 1:152.

that missionaries are prone to exploit the poor for religious conversion by offering to them loans and other inducements and eventually to affect their loyalty to nation and culture.[270] He criticizes the sea-change that a convert's personality undergoes, including his name, dress, language, script, customs, conventions, rites, rituals, food, feasts, festivals, culture, and civilization.[271] Drawing from the Report, the other claim he makes against missionaries is that missionaries are anti-national, cruel, and threatening to the security of the state.[272] He argues that had the Union Government acted quickly upon the recommendations of the Niyogi Report, Christian states like Nagaland, Mizoram, and Meghalaya would not have "posed serious threat to the integrity and security of Hindustan by resorting to Secessionism."[273]

In another work, *An Appeal to Hindu Law-makers,* he suggests the deletion of Article 370 which allots special status to Jammu Kashmir and appeals to the law-makers "to obey and implement the recommendations of Gandhiji and Justice Dr. M. B. Niyogi in *toto* and impose [a] ban on conversion of Hindus to Islam and Christianity by amending the constitution of Bharat."[274] He contends that under Article 368, the Union government has the power to abrogate any article to make the country safe and secure.[275] He feels it is necessary to maintain the integrity and solidarity of Hindus under Article 1 and to save the state from external aggression and internal rebellion under Article 355 of the constitution. His recommendations were highly praised by RSS Chief K. S. Sudarshan and a number of politicians and retired justices of the High Courts. Sahib Singh, Minister of Power, thinks that Kanayalal's work, *An Appeal to Hindu Law-makers* should be a textbook for all law-makers.[276]

Ashok V. Chowgule's Anti-conversion Argument

Ashok Chowgule, a Hindutva thinker and writer who has been actively involved with the Vishva Hindu Parishad since 1991 and who serves as trustee and working president of VHP (external), assists the RSS to protect the sociopolitical issues of Hindutva through his speeches and writing skills.[277] He believes that "Hinduism faces serious threats from the aggres-

270. Talreja, *Holy Vedas and Holy Bible*, 32–33.

271. Talreja, *Holy Vedas and Holy Bible*, 33–34.

272. Talreja, *Holy Vedas and Holy Bible*, 33–36, 176.

273. Talreja, *Appeal to Hindu Law-makers*, 145.

274. Talreja, *Appeal to Hindu Law-makers*, 160.

275. Talreja, *Appeal to Hindu Law-makers*, 112.

276. See the flap of back cover of *Appeal to Hindu Law-makers*.

277. *World Hindu News*, "Meet and Greet Event."

sive proselytizing religions, of which Christianity is one."[278] Speaking of missionary efforts of conversion, Chowgule contends that, "Conversions by fraud and inducements are the standard practice all over the world"[279] and "conversion by persuasion is a rarity."[280] Leaning on Vidiadhar S. Naipaul's analysis of conversion that, "conversion occurs when people have no idea of themselves, and have no means of understanding or retrieving their past,"[281] he contends that conversion is a violent act which destroys or erases host cultures. Following the Niyogi Report's line of argument, he maintains that, "most of the converts have been victims of threats, allurements, financial stringency, deception and persecution."[282] He questions the validity of mass conversions and the social activities of the missionary enterprise and criticizes the denationalizing features in converts. The following statement throws light on why Chowgule thinks conversion is anti-national.

> The converts were given not only a psychological affinity with the people of the Western countries but were weaned away from the national society. The language, the script, the dress, other modes of life, the feasts and the festivals, names and nomenclatures all undergo a change. It is this aspect of Christianity that has today come into conflict with nationalism and has created a strong suspicion in the minds of the national societies. That explains why conversion of a man to Christianity is not just a change in the form of worship but a change in the priority of loyalties . . . . The creation of Nagaland is a glaring example in point . . . The Nagas used foreign arms against Indian army . . . The dream is to convert Nagaland into an independent state dominated by Christian fanatics. Today, when a Christian Naga comes to Shillong he says, 'I am going to India' as if he is a non-Indian.[283]

Chowgule demands that, for harmonious and peaceful existence, "The Christians should accept that the Hindu's way of salvation is as valid as the way through Christ, and that salvation is possible in other faiths as well."[284] Through his writings and mobilization, he advocates for the judicial regulation of conversions, the expelling of foreign missionaries from India, the

278. Chowgule, *Christianity in India*, 22.

279. Chowgule, *Christianity in India*, 30.

280. Chowgule, *Christianity in India*, 90.

281. Chowgule, *Christianity in India*, 23, see also Naipaul, *Beyond Beliefs*, 1–3.

282. Chowgule, *Christianity in India*, 90.

283. Chowgule, *Christianity in India*, 93–94.

284. Chowgule, *Christianity in India*, 74.

disbanding of Western ties with Indian churches, the control of the inflow of foreign funds for the promotion of conversions in the name of social services, an independent Christianity free from church hierarchy, and the accommodation of Christian philosophy within the Hindu paradigm.[285]

285. Chowgule, *Christianity in India*, 70–78.

6

Summary and Conclusion

THE RELIGIOUS INTOLERANCE OF Hindu nationalism against Christian missions in India is embedded in the historical causes of colonialism, certain Western missionary attitudes, Hindu revitalization, and Hindutva ideology. After independence, in the 1950s, the controversial Niyogi Committee Report, which provided justification for the need to control the Christian missionary enterprise and conversion activities in Madhya Pradesh, became a reference guide for Sangh Parivar organizations to systematically stereotype, propagate against, and resist Christian conversions in India.

The Niyogi Enquiry Committee, which investigated whether Christian missionaries were converting illiterate aboriginals in Madhya Pradesh by means of force, fraud, and inducement, made logical deductions from empirical as well as historical investigations that Western Christian missionaries had attempted conversions by means of coercion, undue influence, and allurement since the European colonization of India. The Report concluded that the goal of missionaries was to reestablish Western supremacy in India through evangelization and proselytization. It further ascertained that evangelization was not prompted by spiritual motives, but rather, created Christian minority pockets in India with a view of disrupting non-Christian societies. It generalized that hospitals, schools, orphanages, and educational institutions were used as means of proselytization. It claimed that the conversion of adivasis and illiterate people is a danger to the security of the state as the converts are eventually denationalized, and therefore, proselytization activities of missionaries have to be monitored by the government.

As pointed out in chapters two and three, the Report echoed the antecedents of modern Hindu reactionary attitudes toward colonialism, nationalist consciousness, the resurgence of Hindu pride, and anxiety over imagined threats in free India. Beyond the parameters of the need of investigation of the problem, the Committee went deeper into the historical opinions of Hindu Reformation thinkers, such as Raja Ram Mohan Roy and M. K Gandhi and various anti-Christian critics to demonstrate that Christianity in general was prone to create socio-religious tensions in host countries. The Report also questioned the ethics of missionary methods and the negative portrayals and vile attacks on the religion of the majority community in India by missionaries. In the recommendations section, the Report implied that a secular state does not mean abandonment of religion, highlighting that the constitutional freedom given to citizens and non-citizens in Articles 19 through 25 are not without limitations and that restrictions may be imposed by state legislatures in the interest of the safety, security, and morality of the public.

Overall, the report suggested that government should control the influx of foreign missionaries and the inflow of foreign funds for missionary purposes; approve Christians' literature before they publish their propaganda; legally prohibit conversions sought through social services; form an overall authoritative board which would inform the government of its plans and methods of religious propaganda and methods of conversion; and enact legislation to control conversions brought about by illicit means.

Chapter five demonstrated how the report has strengthened the anti-missionary allegations among Hindu activist movements and how it has shaped their understanding of Christianity in India. It has been found that the RSS, VHP, and the BJP's perspectives and dictum of anti-conversion sentiments are prescriptively shaped by the Niyogi Committee's depiction and interpretations of missions and conversions.

The research has shown that the Report has provided impetus for fostering alterations to the constitutional definitions of individual rights of freedom of conscience, as well as showing that the Report's assessment of missions and its recommendations against missionary activities have played an influential role in the passing of Freedom of Religion Acts in various states of India. The Report has become a resource document for Sangh Parivar's stereotyping of the missionary enterprise and in its attempt to stop the spread of Christianity in India. The study has shown that advocates of Hindutva have made recensions of the Report to intensify anti-Christian propaganda and to resist Christian missions in independent India.

The Hindu nationalist perception of Christian conversions as a strategy of political conquest and a colonial appendage associated with a form of violence, as fed by the Niyogi Report, creates accelerated tensions between Christians and Sangh activists in the twenty-first century. Since the Report presented poverty as a mental disability which causes unfortunate masses to become vulnerable to religious manipulations, Hindu nationalist thinkers contend that conversion is "a mental violence," implying force and a radical take-over of people's wills. Drawing upon the thematic and theoretical framework of the Report, the member institutions of Sangh Parivar claim that as conversion meddles with the socio-religious identities of the communities, segregating them from their traditional values and cultures, it is sometimes capable of destroying an individual's innate beliefs and worldviews and therefore it is undesirable in India.

As the Sangh Parivar continues to challenge Christian missions and attack the conversion aspect of Christian missions in India, Christians cannot be silent, thinking that Hindu opposition to Christian conversions is just a convenient pretext of the Parivar to support its agenda of Hindu nationalism. Neither will Christians be able to do anything that will challenge the Hindutva framework of hostility as the phenomenon of "conversion debate," which is centered on contrasting religious worldviews and sociopolitical contexts. However, by learning the historical causes of present day religious problems between Christians and Hindu activists and by knowing each other's positions and the logical deductions of the conversion argument, challengers will be able to minimize misperceptions and misrepresentations of the other, which might eventually lead them to appreciate the multi-religious reality, the richness of diversity, and each person's dedication to his unique religious imperatives.

Appendix A

Map of India and the State of Madhya Pradesh in 1951

**Source: Niyogi Committee Report of Madhya Pradesh
on Hindu Nationalism, 1956.**

Appendix B

*Christian Centers visited by the Niyogi Committee
in Madhya Pradesh*

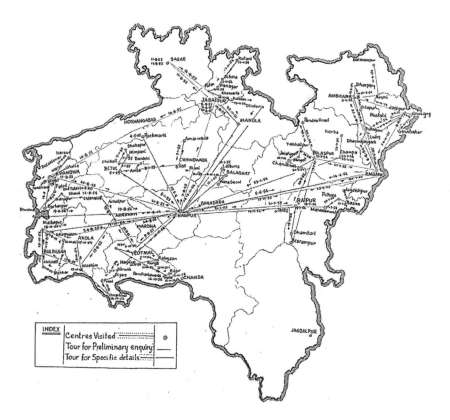

Source: Niyogi Committee Report of Madhya Pradesh
on Hindu Nationalism, 1956.

Appendix C

The Redactions and Recensions of the Niyogi Report

by Some Hindu Nationalists

1. The Niyogi Commission Report (Abridged Version)

An abridged edition of the Report, called "The Niyogi Commission Report," was published in 1956 as a joint venture of the RSS, Hindu Mahasabha and the Bharatiya Jana Sangh for inexpensive circulation among the public and for the spread of a message against Christian missionaries and their activities. It contained the Niyogi Committee's brief description of how European Christians missionaries, since the arrival of Francis Xavier, were destructive to Hindu religion, temples and Brahmins in Goa and other places in south India. This version contained extracts from Volume I of the report on the topic of how Christian missionaries have been involved in anti-national activities and fraudulent conversions since the sixteenth century. It included the conclusions and recommendations of the Niyogi Committee against Christian missions, conversion methods, and the inflow of foreign money for conversion. T.R. Vedantham not only uses the framework of the Report's assessment of missions, but also borrows a few quotes from the abridged version in his article, "Church as a Tool of Imperialism in Modern World." By referring to the Niyogi Report, Ram Swarup makes a thesis that "Christian money and missions continue to work by and large in their old style." See T.R. Vedantham, Ram Swarup and Sita Ram Goel, *"Christianity: An Imperial Ideology* (New Delhi: Voice of India, 1983).

2. Summary of the Niyogi Report on Christian Missionaries.

    A Hindu Sanyasi Baba Madhavdas from Andhra Pradesh published key extracts from Volume I as "The Summary of the Niyogi Report on Christian Missionaries," which contained the texts of Part IV of Volume I of the Report. Part IV contains the Niyogi Committee's findings about the offensive activities of missionaries and the summary of recommendations against them. According to Sita Ram Goel's account, from time to time, Madhavdas published those summaries in English and Hindi and distributed them wherever he travelled in the northern states of India, to raise opposition to Christian missions. See Sita Ram Goel, *Pseudo-Secularism, Christian Mission and Hindu Resistance* (New Delhi: Voice of India, 1998).

3. Recensions of the Niyogi Report by Hindu Nationalist Thinkers

    a. *Politics of Conversion* edited by Devendra Swarup
       (Deendayal Research Institute, 1986).

       In this 396-page volume, the authors who have contributed chapters on the issue of politics of conversion and who incline to the perspective of Niyogi Report for their anti-conversion arguments include, S. Saraswati, T. R. Vedantham, Sita Ram Goel, Ram Swarup, H.V. Seshadri, K. S. Sudarshan and S. K. Agrawal. A few of them quoted bigger portions from the Report while others utilized the framework and rationale of the Report on conversion. Goel summarizes the tricks and tactics of Christian conversion and the power of foreign money as portrayed in the Niyogi Report in his chapters titled, "Genesis and History of the Politics of Conversion and *Money-Power and Politics of Conversion,*" while T.R. Vedantham's article, "Church as a Tool of Imperialism in the Modern World" shows the bridge between imperialism and Christian missionary activities. They use the extracts of statements from both the Niyogi Commission Report (abridged version) and the original version of the Report of the Christian Missionary Activities Inquiry Committee.

    b. *Pseudo-Secularism, Christian Mission and Hindu Resistance*
       (1998, 2004) by Sita Ram Goel

       In this eighty-three-page book, Goel outlines the background which paved the way for Hindu anxiety in independent India in the 1950s, necessitating the formation of the Niyogi Committee to study missionary activities. He also reports that Hindu resistance to Christian missions had collapsed during the Freedom movement because "Gandhi has elevated Jesus to the status of spiritual giant and Christianity itself to the status of a great religion as good as Sanatana Dharma" and Nehru favored secularism, but the Niyogi Report revived Hindu resistance to Christian missions again.

He summarizes the Niyogi Report in his own way, dramatically underlining various aspects from the Report against missionary activities. For example, he says that missionaries were involved in "offering allurements of free education and other facilities to children attending their schools, adding some Christian names to their original Indian names, marriages with Christian girls, money-lending, distributing Christian literature in hospitals and offering prayers in the wages of in-door patients . . . Roman Catholic priests or preachers visiting new-born babies to give ashish (blessings) in the name of Jesus, taking sides in litigation or domestic quarrels, kidnapping of minor children and abduction of women and recruitment of labor for plantations in Assam or Andaman as a means of propagating the Christian faith among the ignorant and illiterate people." By quoting a few other statements from the Report, he highlights anti-nationalist, anti-Hindu activities, as well as political activities of missionaries and argues that "the methods of proselytization had remained the same as in days of old." In this book, Goel passionately argues for the need for India to come out of a secular mentality to control conversions and missionary activities. He also states that the anti-conversion laws in Madhya Pradesh, Orissa, and Arunachal Pradesh were the result of the Niyogi Report.

c. *History of Hindu-Christian Encounters (AD 304 to 1996)* (1986, 1996) by Sita Ram Goel

In this volume, Goel seems to use the framework of the Niyogi Report to arrange the history of Hindu reactions to Christian missions in India in a chronological order, though he only dedicates one chapter to carefully summarizing the whole Volume I of the Report under the heading of "Missions since Independence." He selectively quotes the Report at least forty-five times to substantiate his thesis that Christian missionaries have caused social tensions with Hindus in history and that Hindus have hated them across the centuries. From the report, he particularly highlights missionary involvement in the anti-national, secessionist, anti-Hindu (or offensive), and illegitimate conversion activities. He also records that conversions of the poor were achieved either by force, fraudulence or material inducement. His summarization makes it appear as if the motive of the missionary enterprise is to hurt the Hindu religion, society, and the nation as a whole. He also highlights how Indian Christians were under the cultural and economic bondage of western countries. He indicates that, had the Report's recommendations been implemented immediately, Nagaland Christians could not have demanded a separate state nor could Christian missions in independent India have spread so fast.

d. *Missionaries in India: Continuities, Changes, Dilemmas* (1994) and *Harvesting Our Souls: Missionaries, Their Design, Their Claims* (2000) by Arun Shourie

Arun Shourie picks texts from the Niyogi Report (Volume I & II) to substantiate his argument that Christian missionaries have always employed various means such as charitable, educational and financial schemes with the sole agenda of converting poor tribals and minor children. From Volume II of the Report, he reproduces some portions of text in support of anti-missionary and anti-conversion arguments. For example, he mentions that Catholic missionaries were trained to convert sick and dying children and adults in the name of administering medicine to them. He connects this example with the work of Mother Theresa as if she targeted the sick, poor, and dying for conversion. He contends that the Niyogi Report has exposed the true color of the Christian missionary motive of proselytization and reports that, "the committee encountered instance after instance which showed that the conversions had been nothing but nominal."

In *Missionaries in India,* he reproduced seven block quotes from the Niyogi Report on how Europeans missionaries achieved conversion by illegitimate methods, how they treated Hindu gods, how they forced the poor and illiterate into the church and how missionaries were at times found in criminal activities. In *Harvesting Our Souls,* on three occasions, he quotes the Report as the evidence that the Christian population is multiplied through educational endeavors, orphanages, social activities and philanthropic works in times of famine and natural calamities.

e. *Holy Vedas and Holy Bible* (2000) and *An Appeal to Hindu Law-Makers for Constitutional Ban on Conversion of Hindus* (2002) by Kanayalal M. Talreja

Talreja traces the historical events of Christian intolerance against religious others, especially Hindus, in India and presents the need for a constitutional ban on Christian conversions. By giving background to the Hindu-Christian conflicts in Madhya Pradesh in the 1950s, and by quoting various statements, conclusions and recommendations of the Niyogi Report (Volume I) against missionaries, he states that "the Union government did not pay heed to the valuable recommendations made by Justice Dr. M. B. Niyogi and continued its sinister suicidal policy of appeasement towards the religious minorities with the result that today Nagaland, Mizoram and Meghalaya are Christian majority states and the newly converted Christians, who were once Hindus, being instigated by the church, have posed a serious threat to the integrity and security of Hindusthan by resorting to secessionism." Based on the Niyogi Report's assertions, he states that Christian activities "indicated . . . nothing short of abuse of the religious liberty accorded by the constitution of India." By showing from the report the "denationalizing and subversive impact of conversion," he repeats that converts are disloyal to the nation and that evangelism is conducted in India through the impact of Western supremacy.

4. *Vindicated by Time: The Niyogi Committee Report on Christian Missionary Activities*

The two volumes of the Niyogi Report were put together and printed in one volume in 1998 under the title *Vindicated by Time*. This volume contains the original text, including the original page numbers, of the Report (cyclostyling the original print of the Report). Sita Ram Goel's book *Pseudo-secularism, Christian Missions and Hindu Resistance* was added as an introduction to the volume, making this book more impactful. Goel's summary of the report in the introduction and his emphasis on the missionaries' methods of subversion and conversion, prepare the mind of the readers and influence them to see Christian missionaries as the enemies of the land and of Hindu religion. Even if someone fails to read all 1000 pages of the Report, his introduction gives the gist of what the Niyogi Committee is all about.

Appendix D

RSS' Secret Circular Against Dalits, Christians, and Muslims

Excerpt from the Secret Circular No.411 issued by the RSS
[Source: *Saffron Fascism* by Shyam Chand, 143–44]

[. . .] Scheduled Castes and Other Backward Classes are to be recruited to the party so as to increase the volunteers to fight against the Ambedkarites and Mussalmans.

Hindutva should be preached with a vengeance among physicians and pharmacists so that, with their help, time expired [sic.] and spurious medicines might be distributed amongst the Scheduled Castes, Mussalmans and Scheduled Tribes. The newborn infants of Shudras, Anti-Shudras, Mussalmans, Christians and the like should be crippled by administering injections to them. To this end, there should be a show of blood-donation camps.

Encouragement and instigation should be carried on [sic.] more vigorously so that the womenfolk of Scheduled Castes, Mussalmans and Christians live by prostitution.

Plans should be made more fool-proof so that the people of the Scheduled Castes, Backward Classes, Musslamans and Christians, especially the Ambedkarites, become crippled by taking in [sic.] harmful eatables.

Special attention should be given to the students of Scheduled Castes and Scheduled Tribes so as to make them read the history written according to our dictates.

During riots the women of Mussalmans and Scheduled Castes should be gang-raped. Friends and acquaintances cannot be spared. The work should proceed on the Surat model.

Publication of writings against Mussalmans, Christians, Buddhists and Ambedkarites should be accelerated. Essays and writings should be published in such a way as to prove that Ashoka was opposed to the Aryans.

All literature opposed to Hindus and Brahmins are [sic.] to be destroyed. Dalits, Mussalmans, Christians and Ambedkarites should be searched out. Care should be taken to see that this literature do [sic.] not reach public places. Hindu literature is to apply [sic.] to the Backward Classes and Ambedkarites.

The demand by the Scheduled Castes and Scheduled Tribes for filling in the backlog vacancies in services shall by no means be met. Watch should be kept to see that their demands for entry and promotion in government, non-government or semi-government institutions are to be rejected and their service records are destroyed with damaging reports.

Measures should be taken to make the prejudices amongst Scheduled Castes and Backward people more deep-rooted. To this end, help must be taken from saints and ascetics.

Attacks should be started with vigour against equality, preaching communists [sic.], Ambedkarites, Islamic teachers, Christian missionaries and neighbours [?].

Assaults should be made on Ambedkar's statues with greater efforts.

Dalit and Muslim writers are to be recruited to the party and by them the essays and literature opposed to the Dalits, Ambedkarites and Mussalmans written and preached. Attention is to be paid to see that these writings are properly edited and preached [sic.].

Those opposed to Hindutva are to be murdered through false encounters. For this work the help of the police and semi-military [sic.] forces should always be taken.

Appendix E

Sangh Parivar Organizations

(Source: Wikipedia)[1]

The Sangh Parivar refers to the family of Hindu nationalist organizations which have been started by members of the Rashtriya Swayamsevak Sangh (RSS) or are inspired by its ideas. The Sangh Parivar represents the Hindu nationalist movement. Nominally, the different organizations within the Sangh Parivar run independently and have different policies and activities.

Political

1. Bharatiya Jana Sangh, a political party that existed from 1951 to 1977.

2. Bharatiya Janata Party (BJP), means, Indian People's Party

Occupational & Professional

3. Bharatiya Kisan Sangh, literally, Indian Farmers' Association

4. Bharatiya Mazdoor Sangh, literally, Indian Labour Association

5. Bharatiya Railway Sangh, a Trade Union for Railway workers

6. Fishermen's Co-op Societies

7. Samskar Bharati, Organization of artists

8. Adhivakta Parishad, Lawyers' association

9. Akhil Bharatiya Vidyarthi Parishad, literally, All India Students' Forum

10. Akhil Bharatiya Shaikshik Mahasangh, literally, All India Indian Teachers organization

1. https://en.wikipedia.org/wiki/Sangh_Parivar.

11. Akhil Bharatiya Poorva Sainik Seva Parishad, Organization of Ex-Military Servicemen.

Economic

12. Swadeshi Jagaran Manch, Nativist Awakening Front

13. Vit Salahkar Parishad, Financial consultants' association

14. Laghu Udyog Bharati, an extensive network of small industries

15. Sahkar Bharati, Organization of co-operatives

Social Services

16. Deen Dayal Shodh Sansthan, for the development of rural areas on the basis of Integral Humanism

17. Bharatiya Vikas Parishad, Organization for the development & growth of India in all fields of human endeavor

18. Vivekananda Medical Mission, Sociomedical Services

19. Seva Bharati, Organization for service of the needy

20. Sakshama, an organization working among the blind

21. Nele (a part of "Hindu Seva Pratishthana"), Home for destitute Children

22. Lok Bharti, National NGO's Front

23. Seema Suraksha Parishad, an organization working among the people of border districts

Women

24. Rashtra Sevika Samiti (National Volunteer Association for Women Shiksha Bharati, to provide education and training to underprivileged girls and women.

Religious

25. Vishva Hindu Parishad, World Hindu Council

26. Bajrang Dal, Army of Hanuman (2m)

27. Dharm Jagaran Samiti, Organization for conversion of non-Hindus to Hinduism

28. Muslim Rashtriya Manch, Organization for the improvement of Muslims

29. Rashtriya Sikh Sangat, a sociocultural organization with the aim to spread the knowledge of Gurbani to the Indian society.

30. Hindu Munnani, a religio-cultural organization based in Tamil Nadu.

Educational

31. Ekal Vidyalaya, Involved in free education and village development in rural areas and tribal villages of India.

32. Saraswati Shishu Mandir, Nursery

33. Vidya Bharati, Educational Institutes

34. Vijnana Bharati, Science Forum

Socio-Ethnic

35. Vanvasi Kalyan Ashram, Organization for the improvement of tribals

36. Anusuchit Jati-Jamati Arakshan Bachao Parishad, Organization for the improvement of Dalits

37. Bharat-Tibet Maitri Sangh, India-Tibet Friendship Association

News & Communication

38. Vishva Samvad Kendra, communication wing, spread all over India for media related work, having a team of IT professionals

39. Hindustan Samachar, a multi-lingual news agency.

Think Tanks

40. Bharatiya Vichara Kendra, General Think Tank.

41. Hindu Vivek Kendra, a resource center for the promotion of the ideology of Hindutva.

42. Vivekananda Kendra, promotion of Swami Vivekananda's ideas with Vivekananda International Foundation in New Delhi as a "Public Policy Think Tank" with 6 Centres of study.

43. India Policy Foundation, a not-for-profit Think Tank

44. Bharatiya Shikshan Mandal, a Think Tank on educational reforms.

45. India Foundation, a Think Tank

46. Akhil Bharatiya Itihas Sankalan Yojana (ABISY),

47. All-India history reform project

Overseas

48. Hindu Swayamsevak Sangh, literally, Hindu Volunteer Association—overseas wing

49. Hindu Students Council, Overseas student wing

Others

50. Samskrita Bharati, promotion of the Sanskrit language Central Hindu Military Education Society, to encourage more Hindus to join the Defence Services

51. Kreeda Bharati, Sports Organization.

Appendix F

*Text of the Pamphlet Released By
the VHP Urging Economic Boycott*

VISHVA HINDU PARISHAD (Raanip)

SATYAM SHIVAM SUNDARAM JAI SHRI RAM

WAKE UP! ARISE! THINK! ENFORCE! SAVE THE COUNTRY!
SAVE THE RELIGION!

Economic boycott is the only solution! The anti-national elements use the money earned from the Hindus to destroy us! They buy arms! They molest our sisters and daughters! The way to break the back-bone of these elements is: An economic non-cooperation movement.

Let us resolve: 1. From now on I will not buy anything from a Muslim shopkeeper! 2. I will not sell anything from my shop to such elements! 3. Neither shall I use the hotels of these anti-nationals, nor their garages! 4. I shall give my vehicles only to Hindu garages! From a needle to gold, I shall not buy anything made by Muslims, neither shall we sell them things made by us! 5. Boycott wholeheartedly films in which Muslim hero-heroines act! Throw out films produced by these anti-nationals! 6. Never work in offices of Muslims! Do not hire them! 7. Do not let them buy offices in our business premises, nor sell or hire out houses to them in our housing societies, colonies or communities. 8. I shall certainly vote, but only for him who will protect the Hindu nation. 9. I shall be alert to ensure that our sisters-daughters do not fall into the `love-trap' of Muslim boys at school-college-workplace. 10. I shall not receive any education or training from a Muslim teacher.

Such a strict economic boycott will throttle these elements! It will break their back-bone! Then it will be difficult for them to live in any corner of this country. Friends, begin this economic boycott from today! Then no

Muslim will raise his head before us! Did you read this leaflet? Then make ten photocopies of it, and distribute it to our brothers. The curse of Hanumanji be on him who does not implement this, and distribute it to others! The curse of Ramchandraji also be on him! Jai Shriram!

A true Hindu patriot.

Source: (Translated and Published by the SAHMAT Report, Gujarat 2002 and Communalism Combat Gujarat Genocide, March April 2002)

Appendix G

Freedom of Religion Acts of Orissa, Madhya Pradesh, Arunachal Pradesh, and Gujarat

THE ORISSA FREEDOM OF RELIGION ACT, 1967

Orissa Act 2 of 1968

An Act to provide for prohibition of conversion from one religion to another by the use of force or inducement or by fraudulent means and for matters incidental thereto

Be it enacted by the Legislature of the State of Orissa in the Eighteenth Year of the Republic of India, as follows:

1. Short title, extent and commencement

    a. This Act may be called the Orissa Freedom of Religion Act;. 1967.

    b. It shall extend to the whole of the state of Orissa

    c. It shall come into force at once.

2. Definitions

    In this Act unless the context otherwise requires—

    a. "conversion" means renouncing one religion and adopting another;

    b. "force" shall include a show of force or a threat of injury of any kind including threat of divine displeasure or social ex-communication;

    c. "fraud" shall include misrepresentation or any other fraudulent contrivance;

d. "inducement" shall include the offer of any gift or gratification, either in cash or in kind and shall also include the grant of any benefit, either pecuniary or otherwise;

e. "minor" means a person under eighteen years of age.

3. Prohibition of forcible conversion

No person shall convert or attempt to convert, either directly or otherwise, any person from one religious faith to another by the use force or by inducement or by any fraudulent means nor shall any person abet any such conversion.

4. Punishment for contravention of the provisions of section 3

Any person contravening the provisions contained in section 3 shall, without prejudice to any civil liability, be punishable with imprisonment of either description which may extend to one year or with fine which may extend to five thousand rupees or with both;

Provided that in case the offence is committed in respect of a minor, a woman or a person belonging to the Scheduled Castes or Scheduled Tribes the punishment shall be imprisonment to the extent of two years and fine up to ten thousand rupees.

5. Offence to be cognizable

An offence under this Act shall be cognizable and shall not be investigated by an officer below the rank of an Inspector of Police.

6. Prosecution to be made with the sanction of District Magistrate

No prosecution for an offence under this Act shall be instituted except by, or with the previous sanction of, the District Magistrate or such other authority, not below the rank of a Sub-Divisional Officer, as may be authorized by him in that behalf.

7. Power to make rules

The State Government may make rules for the purpose of carrying out the provision of this Act.

MADHYA PRADESH FREEDOM OF RELIGION ACT, 1968

ACT 27 OF 1968

An Act to provide for prohibition of conversion from one religion to another by the use of force or allurement or by fraudulent means and for matters incidental thereto.

Be it enacted by the Madhya Pradesh Legislature in the nineteenth year of the Republic of India as follows:

1. Short title, extent and commencement

    a. This Act may be called the Madhya Pradesh Dharma Swatantrya Adhiniyam [Madhya Pradesh Freedom of Religion Act], 1968.

    b. It shall extend to the whole of the State of Madhya Pradesh.

    c. It shall come into force at once.

2. Definitions

    In this Act unless the context otherwise requires:

    a. "allurement" means offer of any temptation in the form of

        i. (i) any gift or gratification either in cash or kind;

        ii. (ii) grant of any material benefit, either monetary or otherwise;

    b. "Conversion" means renouncing one religion and adopting another;

    c. "Force" shall include a show of force or threat of injury of any kind including threat of divine displeasure or social ex-communication;

    d. "fraud" shall include misrepresentation or any other fraudulent contrivance;

    e. "minor" means a person under eighteen years of age.

3. Prohibition of forcible conversion

    No person shall convert or attempt to convert, either directly or otherwise, any person from one religious faith to another by the use force or by allurement or by any fraudulent means nor shall any person abet any such conversion.

4. Punishment for contravention of the provisions of section 3

Any person contravening the provisions contained in section 3 shall, without prejudice to any civil liability be punishable with imprisonment which may extend to one year or with a fine, which may extend to five thousand rupees or with both;

Provided that in case the offence is committed in respect of a minor, a woman or a person belonging to the Scheduled Castes or Scheduled Tribes the punishment shall be imprisonment to the extent of two years and a fine up to ten thousand rupees.

5. Intimation to be given to District Magistrate with respect to conversion

a. Whoever converts any person from one religious faith to another either by performing himself the ceremony necessary for such conversion as a religious priest or by taking part directly or indirectly in such ceremony shall, within such period after the ceremony as may be prescribed, send an intimation to the District Magistrate of the district in which the ceremony has taken place of the fact of such conversion in such form as may be prescribed.

b. If any person fails with sufficient cause to comply with the provisions contained in sub-section (1), he shall be punishable with imprisonment which may extend to one year or with a fine which may extend to one thousand rupees or with both.

6. Offence to be cognizable

An offence under this Act shall be cognizable and shall not be investigated by an officer below the rank of an Inspector of Police.

7. Prosecution to be made with the sanction of District Magistrate

No prosecution for an offence under this Act shall be instituted except by, or with the previous sanction of, the District Magistrate or such other authority, not below the rank of a Sub-Divisional Officer, as may be authorized by him in that behalf.

8. Power to make rules

The State Government may make rules for the purpose of carrying out the provision of this Act.

ARUNACHAL PRADESH FREEDOM OF RELIGION ACT, 1978

Act 4 of 1978

An Act to provide for prohibition of conversion from one religious faith to any other religious faith by use of force or inducement or by fraudulent means and for matters connected therewith.

Be it enacted by the Legislative Assembly of Arunachal Pradesh in the Twenty Ninth Year of the Republic of India as follows:

1. Short title, extent and commencement

    a. This Act may be called the Arunachal Pradesh Freedom of Religion Act, 1978.

    b. It extends to the whole of the Union Territory of Arunachal Pradesh.

    c. It shall come into force at once.

2. Definitions

    In this Act, unless the context otherwise requires:

    a. "government" means the Government of the Union Territory of Arunachal Pradesh.

    b. "conversion" means renouncing one religious faith and adopting another religious faith, and "convert" shall be construed accordingly;

    c. "indigenous faith" means such religions, beliefs and practices including rites, rituals, festivals, observances, performances, abstinence, customs as have been found sanctioned, approved, performed by the indigenous communities of Arunachal Pradesh from the time these communities have been known and includes Buddhism as prevalent among Monpas, Menbas, Sherdukpens, Khambas, Khamtis and Singaphoos, Vaishnavism as practised by Noctes, Akas, and Nature worships including worships of Donyi-Polo, as prevalent among other indigenous communities of Arunachal Pradesh;

    d. "force" shall include show of force or a threat of injury of any kind including threat of divine displeasure or social excommunication;

    e. "fraud" shall include misrepresentation or any other fraudulent contrivance;

    f. "inducement" shall include the offer of any gift or gratification, either cash or in kind and shall also include the grant of any benefit, either pecuniary or otherwise.

    g. "prescribed" means prescribed under the rules;

    h. "religious faith" includes any indigenous faith.

3. Prohibition of forcible conversion

No person shall convert or attempt to convert, either directly or otherwise, any person from one religious faith to any other religious faith by the use of force or by inducement or by any fraudulent means nor shall any person abet any such conversion.

4. Punishment for contravention of the provisions of Section 3

Any person contravening the provisions contained in section 3 shall, without prejudice to any civil liability, be punishable with imprisonment to the extent of two years and fine up to ten thousand rupees.

5. Intimation of conversion to the Deputy Commissioner and punishment

    a. Whoever converts any person from his one religious faith to any other religious faith either by performing himself the ceremony necessary for such conversion as a religious priest or by taking part directly or indirectly in such ceremony shall, within such period after the ceremony as may be prescribed, send an intimation to the Deputy Commissioner of the District to which the person converted belongs, of the fact of such conversion in such form as may be prescribed.

    b. If any person fails without sufficient cause to comply with the provisions contained in sub-section (1), he shall be punished with imprisonment which may extend to one year or with fine which may extend to one thousand rupees or with both.

6. Offences cognizable

An offence under this Act shall be cognizable and shall not be investigated by an officer below the rank of an Inspector of Police.

7. Sanction for prosecution

   No prosecution for an offence under the Act shall be instituted except by or with the previous sanction of the Deputy Commissioner or such other authority, not below the rank of an Extra Assistant Commissioner as may be authorised by him in his behalf.

8. Power to make rules

   The Government may make rules for the purpose of carrying out the provisions of this Act.

GUJARAT FREEDOM OF RELIGION ACT, 2003

Gujarat Act No. 22 of 2003

An Act to provide for freedom of religion by prohibition of conversion from one religion to another by the use of force or allurement or by fraudulent means and for matters incidental thereto.

It is hereby enacted in the fifty-fourth Year of the Republic of India as follows:

1. Short title, extent and commencement

   a. This Act may be called the Gujarat Freedom of Religion Act, 2003

   b. It shall come into force on such date as the State Government may, by notification in the *Official Gazette*, appoint.

2. Definitions

   In this Act unless the context otherwise requires:

   a. "allurement" means offer of any temptation in the form of

      i. any gift or gratification either in cash or kind;

      ii. grant of any material benefit, either momentary or otherwise;

   b. 'convert' means to make one person renounce one religion and adopt another religion;

   c. "force" includes a show of force or a threat of injury of any kind including threat of divine displeasures or social ex-communication;

   d. 'fraud' shall include misrepresentation or any other fraudulent contrivance;

   e. 'minor' means a person under eighteen years of age.

3. Prohibition of forcible conversion

   No person shall convert or attempt to convert, either directly or otherwise, any person from one religious faith to another by the use force or by allurement or by any fraudulent means nor shall any person abet any such conversion.

4. Punishment for contravention of the provisions of section 3

   Whoever contravenes the provision of section 3 shall, without prejudice to any civil liability, be punished with imprisonment for a term which may extend to three years and also be liable to fine, which may extend to rupees fifty thousand:

Provided that whoever contravenes the provisions of section 3 in respect of a minor, a woman or a person belonging to Scheduled Castes or Scheduled Tribe shall be punished with imprisonment for a term which may extend to four years and also be liable to fine which may extend to rupees one lakh

5. Prior Permission to be taken from District Magistrate with respect to conversion

   a. Whoever converts any person from one religion to another either by performing any ceremony by himself for such conversion as a religious priest or takes part directly or indirectly in such ceremony shall take prior permission for such proposed conversion from the District Magistrate concerned by applying in such form as may be prescribed by rules.

   b. The person who is converted shall send intimation to the District Magistrate of the District concerned in which the ceremony has taken place of the fact of such conversion within such period and in such form as may be prescribed by rules.

   c. Whoever fails, without sufficient cause, to comply with the provisions of sub-sections (1) and (2) shall be punished with imprisonment for a term, which may extend to one year or with fine which may extend to rupee one thousand or with both.

6. Prosecution to be made with the sanction of District Magistrate

   No prosecution for an offence under this Act shall be instituted except by, or with the previous sanction of, the District Magistrate or such other authority, not below the rank of a Sub-Divisional Officer, as may be authorized by him in that behalf.

7. Offence to be cognizable

   An offence under this Act shall be cognizable and shall not be investigated by an officer below the rank of a Police Inspector.

8. Power to make rules

   a. The State Government may, by notification in the *Official Gazette,* make rules for carrying out the provisions of this Act.

b. All rules made under this section shall be laid for not less than thirty days before the State Legislature as soon as may be after they are made, and shall be subject to the rescission by the State Legislature or to such modifications as the State Legislature may make during the session in which they are so laid or the session immediately following.

c. Any rescission or modification so made by the State Legislature shall be published in the *Official Gazette*, and shall thereupon take effect.

Bibliography

Account Aid. "Accountable Issues: History of FCRA." http://www.accountaid.net/
Periodicals/AccountAble/Accountable%20List.htm.

Agrawal, S. K. "Church Goes Political in India." In *Politics of Conversion*, edited by
Devendra Swarup, 247–68. Delhi: Deendayal Research Institute, 1986.

Aghamkar, Atul Y. *Insights into Openness: Encouraging Urban Mission*. Bangalore:
SAIACS, 2000.

Aleaz, K. P. "S. K. George: A Pioneer Pluralist and Dalit Theologian." *Asian Journal of
Theology* 17 (2003) 315–40.

———. "The Theological Writings of Brahmabandhav Upadhyaya Re-Examined." *The
Indian Journal of Theology* 28 (1979) 55–77.

Ambrois, Yvon. "Hindutva's Real Agenda and Strategies." In *Hindutva: A Christian
Response*, edited by Joseph Mattam and P. Arockiadoss, 11–102. Bangalore:
Dharmaram Publications, 2002.

Anand, Dibyesh. *Hindu Nationalism in India and the Politics of Fear*. New York: Palgrave
Macmillan, 2011.

Anant, Arpita. "Anti-Conversion Laws." *The Hindu*, December 17, 2002.

Anderson, Benedict R. *Imagined Communities: Reflections on the Origin and Spread of
Nationalism*. Rev. ed. London: Verso, 1991.

Andersen, Walter K., and Shridhar D. Damle. *The Brotherhood of Saffron: The Rashtriya
Swayamsevak Sangh and Hindu Revivalism*. New Delhi: Vistaar, 1987.

Anderson, Walter. "The Rashtriya Swayamsevak Sangh, III: Participation in Politics."
Economic and Political Weekly 7 (1972) 673–82. http://www.jstor.org.ezproxy.
asburyseminary.edu/stable/4361179.

Andrews, C. F. *The Renaissance in India: Its Missionary Aspect*. London: Church
Missionary Society, 1912.

Appasamy, A. J. *The Christian Task in Independent India*. London: SPCK, 1951

Arya, Anupama. *Religion and Politics in India*. Delhi: K.K., 2001.

Aryan Voice. "What is Arya Samaj?" May 2010, 6–9. http://www.arya-samaj.org.

Asirvatham, Eddy. *Christianity in the Indian Crucible*. Calcutta: YMCA, 1957.

Athalye, D. V. *The Life of Lokamanya Tilak*. Poona: Swadeshi, 1921.

Atkins, Stephen E. *Encyclopedia of Modern Worldwide Extremists and Extremist Groups.* Westport, CT: Greenwood, 2004.

Baker, David. "Colonial Beginnings and the Indian Response: The Revolt of 1857–58 in Madhya Pradesh." *Modern Asian Studies* 25 (1991) 511–43.

Banerjee, Brojendra Nath. *Religious Conversions in India.* New Delhi: Harnam, 1982.

Barnes, R. H., et al. *Indigenous People of Asia.* Ann Arbor, MI: The Association for Asian Studies, 1995.

Baruah, Sanjib. *Critical Issues in Indian Ethnonationalism in India: A Reader.* New Delhi: Oxford University Press, 2010.

Basu, Shamita. *Religious Revivalism as Nationalist Discourse: Swami Vivekananda and New Hinduism in Nineteenth-Century Bengal.* New Delhi: Oxford University Press, 2002.

Basu, Tapan. *Khaki Shorts and Saffron Flags: A Critique of the Hindu Right.* Hyderabad: Orient Longman, 1993.

Bates, Crispin. "Race, Caste and Tribes in Central India: The Early Origins of Indian Anthropometry." Edinburgh Papers In South Asian Studies 3 (1995) 3–35.

Bates, M. Searle. *Religious Liberty: An Inquiry.* Repr. New York: Harper and Brothers, 1947.

Bauman, Chad M. "Postcolonial Anxiety and Anti-Conversion Sentiment in the Report of the Christian Missionary Activities Enquiry Committee." *Hindu Studies* 12 (2008) 181–213.

Baviskar, Amita. "Adivasis Encounter with Hindu Nationalism in MP." *Economic and Political Weekly* 40 (2005) 5105–13.

Baxter, Craig. *The Jana Sangh: A Biography of an Indian Political Party.* Philadelphia: University of Pennsylvania, 1969.

BBC News. "Gujarat Riot Death Toll Revealed." http://news.bbc.co.uk/2/hi/south_asia/4536199.stm.

Benjamin, P. N. "Prof. S. K. George: An Unknown Gandhian and an Unknown Christian."http://panavelinbenjamin.blogspot.com/2007/12/prof-skgeorge.html.

Bharatiya Janata Party. "Bharatiya Janata Party: History." http://www.bjp.org/en/about-the-party/history?u=bjp-history.

Bharatiya Jana Sangh: Party Documents [1951–1972], Volume 1. New Delhi: Bharatiya Jana Sangh, 1973.

Bhishikar, C. P. *Shri Guruji: Pioneer of a New Era.* Bangalore: Sahitya Sindhu Prakashana, 1999.

Bliss, Edwin M. *The Missionary Enterprise: A Concise History of its Objects, Methods and Extensions.* New York: Fleming Company, 1908.

Brown, Judith M. "Indian Christians and Nehru's Nation-State." In *India and the Indianness of Christianity: Essays on Understanding—Historical, Theological, and Bibliographical—In Honor of Robert Eric Frykenberg,* edited by Richard Fox Young. Michigan: Eerdmans, 2009.

———. "Who Is an Indian? Dilemmas of National Identity at the End of the British Raj in India." In *Missions, Nationalism, and the End of Empire,* edited by Brian Stanley, 111–32. Michigan: Eerdmans, 2003.

Campbell, William. *British India in its Relation to the Decline of Hindooism, and the Progress of Christianity.* London: J. Snow, 1839.

Chandra, Bipan, et al. *India's Struggle for Independence, 1857–1947.* New Delhi: Penguin, 1989.

Chethimattam, John B. *Dialogue in Indian Tradition.* Bangalore: Dharmaram College, 1969.

Cherian, M. T. *Hindutva Agenda and Minority Rights: A Christian Response.* Bangalore: Center for Contemporary Christianity, 2007.

Chitkara, M. G. *Hindutva Parivar.* New Delhi: A. P. H., 2003.

———. *Rashtriya Swayamsevak Sangh: National Upsurge.* New Delhi: APH, 2004.

———. *Sangh Pariwar.* New Delhi: A. P. H., 2003.

Chopra, Pran Nath. *A Comprehensive History of Modern India, Pt. III.* New Delhi: Sterling, 2005.

Choudhary, Valmiki, ed. *Dr. Rajendra Prasad: In the Constituent Assembly, Vol. 20.* New Delhi: Allied, 1994.

Chowgule, Ashok V. "Arun Shourie and the Missionaries in India." http://www. hindunet.org/hvk/Publications/arun.html.

———. *Christianity in India: The Hindutva Perspective.* Mumbai: Hindu Vivek Kendra, 1999.

Coelho, William. "The Niyogi Report and its Sources." In *Truth Shall Prevail: Reply to Niyogi Committee,* edited by A. Soares et al., 140–73. Bombay: Catholic Association of Bombay, 1957.

Coleridge, Henry James. *The Life and Letters of St. Francis Xavier, Vol. 1.* London: Burns and Oates, 1881.

Coll, Steve. "Hindu-Moslem Battles Sweeping India's North; Fundamentalist Fears Fuel Religious War." *The Washington Post,* January 2, 1991.

Collins Dictionary. "Evangelism." https://www.collinsdictionary.com/us/dictionary/english/evangelism#:~:text=Evangelism%20is%20the%20teaching%20of,people%20who%20are%20not%20Christians.&text=Collins!.

Comier, Jeffrey J. "Book Review: Conversi, Ethnonationalism." http://www.cjsonline.ca/reviews/ethnonationalism.html.

———. "Ethnonationalism in the Contemporary World: Walker Connor and the Study of Nationalism." Review. *Canadian Journal of Sociology Online,* July–August 2003. http://www.cjsonline.ca/reviews/ethnonationalism.html.

Conlon, Frank F. "The Polemic Process in Nineteenth-Century Maharashtra: Vishnubawa Brahmachari and Hindu Revival." In *Religious Controversies in South Asian Languages,* edited by Kenneth W. Jones, 5–26. New York: State University of New York, 1992.

Connor, Walker. *Ethnonationalism: The Quest for Understanding.* Princeton: Princeton University Press, 1994.

Constituent Assembly of India. *Supplementary Report on Fundamental Rights.* Constituent Assembly of India Debates (Proceedings)—Volume 3–20. New Delhi: Government of India, 2016.

The Constitution of India. Repr. Delhi: Ministry of Law and Justice, 2007.

Copley, Antony R. H. *Religions in Conflict: Ideology, Cultural Contact and Conversion in Late Colonial India.* Delhi: Oxford University Press, 1997.

Cornille, Catherine. "Missionary Views of Hinduism." *Journal of Hindu-Christian Studies* 21 (2008) 28–32.

De Souza, T. R. "The Portuguese in Asia and Their Church Patronage." In *Western Colonialism in Asia and Christianity,* edited by M. D. David, 11–20. Bombay: Himalaya, 1988.

———. "Goa Inquisition." http://www.vgweb.org/unethicalconversion/GoaInquisition .htm.

Dellon, M. *An Account of the Inquisition at Goa in India*. Pittsburgh: Patterson & Lambdin, 1819.

Deutsch, Karl W. *Politics and Government*. Boston: Houghton Mifflin, 1970.

Devadas, V. Henry. *Ideologies of Political Parties: A Pre-Election Study*. New Delhi: Navdin Prakashan Kendra, 1998.

Devadason, E. D. *A Study on Conversion and its Aftermath*. Madras: CLS, 1982.

Devanandan, P. D. *The Gospel and Renascent Hinduism*. London: SCM, 1959.

Dubois, Abbe J. *Description of the Character, Manners and Customs of the People of India and their Institutions, Religious and Civil*. London: Longman, 1817.

Duff, Alexander. *India and India Missions: Including the Sketches of the Gigantic System of Hinduism both in Theory and Practice*. 2nd ed. Edinburgh: John Johnstone, 1840.

Edwardes, Michael. *The Last Years of British India*. London: Cassell & Company, 1963.

Elst, Koenraad. *Decolonizing the Hindu Mind: Ideological Development of Hindu Revivalism*. New Delhi: Rupa, 2001.

———. *Negationism in India*. New Delhi: Voice of India, 1992.

Embree, Ainslie Thomas. *Utopias in Conflict: Religion and Nationalism in India*. Berkeley: University of California Press, 1990.

———, ed. *The Hindu Tradition: Readings in Oriental Thought*. New York: Modern Library, 1966.

Eshwar, Raj. *Paravartan (Homecoming): Why and How*. New Delhi: Suruchi Prakashan, 1999.

Esteves, Sarto. *Freedom to Build, Not to Destroy*. Delhi: Media, 2002.

Etymonline. "Mission." https://www.etymonline.com/word/mission.

"Exclusive: Narendra Modi on Conversion of Hindus!" https://www.youtube.com/ watch?v=wr6q1drP558.

Farquhar, J. N. *Modern Religious Movements in India*. New York: The Macmillan Company, 1919.

———. *The Crown of Hinduism*. 2nd ed. London: Oxford University Press, 1920.

Fernando, Leonard, and G. Gispert-Sauch. *Christianity in India: Two Hundred Years of Faith*. New Delhi: Penguin, 2004.

Fey, Herold E. "Report Urges Ban on Missionaries." *The Christian Century* 73 (1956).

Firth, C. B. *An Introduction to Indian Church History*. 2nd ed. New Delhi: ISPCK, 2003.

Francis, G. X. "The Background of the Niyogi Report." In *Truth Shall Prevail: Reply to Niyogi Committee Report*, edited by A. Soares et al., 109–39. Bombay: Catholic Association of Bombay, 1957.

Frawley, David. *How I Became a Hindu: My Discovery of Vedic Dharma*. New Delhi: Voice of India, 2003.

———. *The Myth of the Aryan Invasion of India*. New Delhi: Voice of India, 1994.

Frykenberg, Robert E. "Hindu Fundamentalism and the Structural Stability of India." In *Fundamentalisms and the State: Remaking Polities, Economies and Militance*, edited by M. E. Marty and R. S. Appleby, 233–55. Chicago: The University of Chicago Press, 1993.

———. "Hindutva and the Aftermath of Ayodhya: Dangers of Political Religion and Religious Nationalism." In *Nationalism and Hindutva: A Christian Response:*

Papers From the 10Th CMS Consultation, edited by Mark T. B. Laing. New Delhi: ISPCK, 2005.

———. "The Concept of 'Majority' as a Devilish Force in the Politics of Modern India." *The Journal of Commonwealth and Comparative Politics* 25 (1987) 267–74.

Frykenberg, Robert E., and Alaine M. Low. *Christians and Missionaries in India: India: Cross-Cultural Communication Since 1500*. Grand Rapids: Eerdmans, 2003.

Fuller, Bampfylde. *The Empire of India*. London: Pitman, 1913.

Gandhi, M. K. *Christian Missions*. Allahabad: Navajivan, 1941.

———. *God is Truth*. Ahmedabad: Navajivan, n.d.

———. *Hindu Dharma*. Ahmedabad: Navajivan, 1950.

———. "Interview to a Missionary Nurse." *Harijan*, May 11, 1935.

———. *Truth is God*. Edited by R. K. Prabhu. Ahmedabad: Navajivan, 1987.

———. *Young India*. N.d: n.d., 1924.

Ghosh, Partha S. *BJP and the Evolution of Hindu Nationalism from Periphery to Center*. New Delhi: Manohar, 1999.

Gier, Nicholas F. *The Origins of Religious Violence: An Asian Perspective*. Maryland: Lexington, 2014.

Goel, Sita Ram. *Catholic Ashrams: Sannyasins or Swindlers?* New Delhi: Voice of India, 1987.

———. *Hindu Society Under Siege*. New Delhi: Voice of India, 1981. http://voiceofdharma.org/books/hsus/ch3.htm.

———. *Hindu Temples: What Happened to Them, Vol. I*. New Delhi: Voice of India, 2016.

———. *History of Hindu-Christian Encounters (AD 304 to 1996)*. New Delhi: Voice of India, 1996.

———. *How I Became a Hindu*. New Delhi: Voice of India, 1982.

———. *Jesus Christ: An Artifice for Aggression*. New Delhi: Voice of India, 1994.

———. *Pseudo-Secularism, Christian Missions and Hindu Resistance*. Repr. New Delhi: Voice of India, 2004.

———. *The Story of Islamic Imperialism in India*. New Delhi: Voice of India, 1982.

Goel, Sita Ram, and M. B Niyogi. *Vindicated by Time: The Niyogi Committee Report on Christian Missionary Activities*. New Delhi: Voice of India, 1998.

Goheen, Michael W. *A Light to the Nations: The Missional Church and The Biblical Story*. Grand Rapids: Baker Academic, 2011.

Gold, Daniel. "Organized Hinduisms: From Vedic Truth to Hindu Nation." In *Fundamentalisms Observed, Volume I*, edited by Martin E. Marty and R. Scott Appleby, 531–93. Chicago: University of Chicago Press, 1991.

Golwalkar, Guruji. "Sangh Parivar | Shri Golwalkar Guruji." http://www.golwalkarguruji.org/shri-guruji/homage-to-a-patriarch/sangh-parivar

Golwalkar, Madhav Sadashiv. *Bunch of Thoughts*. 4th ed. Bangalore: Sahitya Sindhu Prakashana, 2011.

———. *We Or Our Nationhood Defined*. Nagpur: Bharat, 1939. http://hinduebooks.blogspot.com.

———. *Why Hindu Rashtra?* Bangalore: Kesari, 1962.

Gopal, S. *Selected Works of Jawaharlal Nehru, Vol. 18*. New Delhi: Oxford University Press, 1952.

Gould, William. *Religion and Conflict in Modern South Asia*. Cambridge: Cambridge University Press, 2012.

Government of India. "Indian Constitution." *National Portal of India*. http://india.gov. in/my-government/constitution-india.

Government of Madhya Pradesh. *State History Committee: Political and Military Department Compilation*. Sub-file No. 93 of 1944. Nagpur, n.d.

Grim, Brian J., and Roger Finke. *The Price of Freedom Denied: Religious Persecution and Conflict in the Twenty-First Century*. New York: Cambridge University Press, 2011.

The Guardian (Madras). "The Nazis or Hinduism." April 16, 1936.

Guha, Ramachandra. "The Guru of Hate." *The Hindu*, 2006.

Gujarat Riots. "Gujarat Carnage 2002: The Hard Facts." http://www.gujarat-riots.com/ hatespeechBJPRSS.htm.

Gurumurthy, S., and Anju Prasar. "Conversion and Anti-Conversion in India." *Transnational Identity Investments*, Review Report, 2006.

Hansen, Thomas Blom. *The Saffron Wave: Democracy and Hindu Nationalism in Modern India*. Princeton: Princeton University Press, 1999.

Hasan, Zoya. *Forging Identities: Gender, Communities, and the State in India*. Boulder, CO: Westview, 1994.

Hedlund, Roger. "Hindus and Christians for 2000 Years." *Global Missiology* 2 (2008) 1–10. http://ojs.globalmissiology.org/index.php/english/article/view/245/687.

Hiebert, Paul G. "Missiological Issues in the Encounter with Emerging Hinduism." *Missiology: An International Review* 28 (2000) 47–63.

Herdenia, L. S. "Debating Religious Conversions | Millennium Post." http://www. millenniumpost.in/NewsContent.aspx?NID=33733.

Hermanns, M. *Hinduism and Tribal Culture: An Anthropological Verdict on the Niyogi Report*. Bombay: K. L. Fernandes, 1957.

The Hindu. "Circular on Christians Routine: Gujarat CM." February 12, 1999.

The Hindu Outlook 19 (July 18, 1955).

Hindu Janajagruti Samiti. "'The Eleventh Commandment: 'Thou Shall Not Convert'— Hindu Janajagruti Samiti." *Hindu Janajagruti Samiti*. http://www.hindujagruti. org/news/27495.html.

———. "What Was the Main Cause of Religious Conversions In Bharat During Past Centuries? | Hindu Janajagruti Samiti." http://www.hindujagruti.org/hindu-issues/ religious-conversion/15793-html.

Hindu Rashtra. "Hindutva Brotherhood—Soldiers of Hindutva." http://www. hindurashtra.org/statements.php.

Hindustan Samachar. "Christian Missionaries." May 7, 1954.

———. "Summary of the Recommendations of the Niyogi Committee Report." http:// www.hvk.org/publications/faq/quest31.html.

The Hindustan Times. "Missionary Activities: Govt. Stand Clarified." May 5, 1954.

The Hitavada. "Activities of Missionaries: Govt. Measures Under Consideration." September 1, 1953.

———. "Activities of Missionaries: Govt. Measures Under Consideration."1953.

———. "American Aid." July 20, 1954.

———. "Anti-National Tendencies." July 20, 1954.

———. "Christian Tribals Forced to Sign Anti-Missionary Documents: Disclosure at C. Y. M. Symposium." August 3, 1954

———. "Foreign Missionaries in Nagpur: Dr. N. B. Khare to Lead Morcha." July 22, 1954.

———. "Inquiry into Missionaries' Complaints: MP Govt. Appoints Three Man Committee." 1953.

———. "Niyogi Committee Proceedings: Maha Sabha Deputes Observers." July 17, 1954.

———. "Probe into Missionary Activities: Enquiry Committee Records Oral Statements." July 20, 1954.

———. "RSS Rally at Raipur: Golwalkar's address." January 22, 1953.

———. "Christian Missionaries Active in Chhattisgarh." 1954.

———. "Inquiry into Missionaries' Complaints: M. P. Govt. Appoints Three-Man Committee." May 19, 1953.

Hooton, W. S. *The Missionary Campaign: Its Principles, Methods, and Problems.* London: Longmans, 1912.

Hudson, D. Dennis. "Arumuga Navalar and the Hindu Renaissance among the Tamils." In *Religious Controversies in South Asian Languages,* edited by Kenneth W. Jones, 27–51. New York: State University of New York, 1992.

Humans Rights Watch. "We Have No Orders to Save You." https://www.hrw.org/reports/2002/india/India0402-05.htm.

———. "Violence in Gujarat." https://www.hrw.org/reports/1999/indiachr/christians8-04.htm.

Inboden, William. "Religious Freedom and National Security." http://www.hoover.org/research/religious-freedom-and-national-security.

India Today. "1990-L.K. Advanis Rath Yatra: Chariot of Fire." http://indiatoday.intoday.in/story/1990-L.K.+Advani's+rath+yatra:+Chariot+of+fire/1/76389.html.

———. "Profiling of Christians In MP Stopped, Probe Ordered." http://indiatoday.intoday.in/story/madhya-pradesh-police-orders-survey-of-christians-in-state/1/135313.html.

The Indian Express. "BJP Favours Law Banning Conversion: Amit Shah." http://indianexpress.com/article/india/politics/bjp-against-forcible-conversions-says-amit-shah/.

"Is Madhya Pradesh Govt. Profiling Christians?" https://www.youtube.com/watch?v=aNO-Kjuy2ps.https://www.youtube.com/watch?v=aNO-Kjuy2ps.

Jaffrelot, Christophe. *Hindu Nationalism: A Reader.* Princeton: Princeton University Press, 2007.

———. *The Hindu Nationalist Movement in India.* New York: Columbia University Press, 1996.

———. "India: The Politics of (Re)conversion to Hinduism of Christian Aboriginals." In *Annual Review of the Sociology of Religion, Volume 2: Religion and Politics,* edited by Patrick Michel and Enzo Pace, 197–215. 1st ed. Boston: Brill, 2011.

———. *Religion, Caste, and Politics in India.* New York: Columbia University Press, 2011.

———, ed. *The Sangh Parivar: A Reader.* New Delhi: Oxford University Press, 2005.

Jain, Girilal. *The Hindu Phenomenon.* New Delhi: UBSPD, 1994.

Jain, P. C. *Christianity, Ideology and Social Change among Tribals: A Case Study of Bhils of Rajasthan.* New Delhi: Rawat, 1995.

Jalal, Ayesha. *Self and Sovereignty: Individual and Community in South Asian Islam since 1850.* London: Routledge, 2000.

Jean-Francois, Mayer. "Conflicts over Proselytism: An Overview and Comparative Perspective." In *Proselytization Revisited: Right Talk, Free Markets and Culture Wars*, edited by Rosalind Hackett, 35–52. London: Equinox, 2008.

Jeevan Lal Kapur Commission Report on Gandhi's Killing. 8 vols. https://archive.org/details/JeevanlalKapoorCommissionReport.

Jethmalani, Ram. "Hindutva is A Secular Way of Life." http://www.sunday-guardian.com/analysis/hindutva-is-a-secular-way-of-life.

Jhangiani, Motilal A. *Jana Sangh and Swatantra: A Profile of the Rightists Parties in India*. Bombay: Manaktalas, 1967.

John Paul II, Pope. "Ecclesia in Asia (November 6, 1999)." http://w2.vatican.va/content/john-paul-ii/en/apost_exhortations/documents/hf_jp-ii_exh_06111999_ecclesia-in-asia.html.

Johnstone, Patrick, and Jason Mandryk. *Operation World: When we Pray God Works: 21st Century Edition*. 6th ed. Cumbria: UK: Paternoster Lifestyle, 2001.

Jois, M. Rama. *Supreme Court Judgement on "Hindutva," A Way of Life*. 3rd ed. New Delhi: Suruchi Prakashan, 2013.

Jones, E. Stanley. "Evangelism in India." Manuscript. Wilmore, 1953. Papers of E Stanley Jones. Asbury Theological Seminary, B. L. Fisher Library. ACC 2000–007, File 18:40.

———. "Missionaries in India." Papers of E. Stanley Jones, ARC 2000–007, Box 15 of 62, File 15:7.

Jones, Kenneth W. *Arya Dharma: Hindu Consciousness in 19th Century Punjab*. California: University of California, 1976.

Josh, Bhagwan. "Conversions, Complicity and the State in Post-Independence India." In *Christianity and The State in Asia: Complicity and Conflict*, edited by Julius Bautista and Francis Khek Gee Lim, 97–114. New York: Routledge, 2009.

Joshi, L. T., ed. *"Shraddheya."* *Tarun Bharat*. Special edition, July, Nagpur, 1996.

Joshi, Rajesh. "The Trident Speaks." *Outlook* February 8, 1999. http://www.outlookindia.com/article/the-trident-speaks/206951.

Jowett, Garth, and Victoria O'Donnell. *Propaganda and Persuasion*. 4th ed. Thousand Oaks, CA: Sage, 2006.

Karandikar, V. R. *Architects of RSS*. Pune: Snehal Prakashan, 2009.

Katju, Manjari. "The Understanding of Freedom in Hindutva." *Social Scientist* 39 (2011) 3–22.

———. *Vishva Hindu Parishad and Indian Politics*. Hyderabad: Orient Longman, 2003.

Kaye, John William. *Christianity in India: An Historical Narrative*. London: Smith, Elder, 1859.

———. *History of the Indian Mutiny of 1857–8*. London: W. H. Allen, 1880.

Keer, Dhananjay. *Veer Savarkar*. Bombay: Popular Prakashan, 1988.

Kelkar, Sanjeev. *Lost Years of the RSS*. New Delhi: SAGE, 2011.

Khan, Mumtaz Ali. *Mass-Conversions of Meenakshipuram: A Sociological Enquiry*. Madras: CLS, 1983.

Khare, Narayan Bhaskar. "Militarising of Hindudom." *The Hindu Outlook*, November 8, 1953.

Kim, Sebastian C. H. *In Search of Identity: Debates on Religious Conversion in India*. New Delhi: Oxford University Press, 2003.

Kinnvall, Catarina. "Globalization and Religious Nationalism: Self, Identity, and the Search for Ontological Security." *Political Psychology* 25 (2016) 741–67.

Kopf, David. *The Brahmo Samaj and the Shaping of the Modern Indian Mind.* Princeton: Princeton University Press, 1979.

Koschorke, Klaus, et al. *A History of Christianity in Asia, Africa, and Latin America, 1450–1990.* Grand Rapids: Eerdmans, 2007.

Kraft, Charles. *Culture, Communication and Christianity: A Selection of Writings by Charles H. Kraft.* California: William Carey Library, 2001.

Kuruvachira, J. "Indian Christians and the Independence Movement." *Mission Today* 8 (2006) 355.

Lal Chand, R. B. *Self-Abnegation in Politics.* Lahore: Central Hindu Yuvak Sabha, 1938.

Lederle, Matthew. *Philosophical Trends in Modern Maharashtra.* Bombay: Popular Prakashan, 1976.

Lexology. "Overview of the Foreign Contribution Regulation Act in India | Lexology." http://www.lexology.com/library/detail.aspx?g=f86ace93-2a47-4ed0-a88a-d54912e1c0e0.

Liebau, Heike. *Cultural Encounters in India: The Local Co-workers of the Tranquebar Mission, 18th to 19th Centuries.* Translated by Rekha V. Rajan. New Delhi: Social Science Press, 2013.

Lilly, William Samuel. *India and Its Problems.* London: Sands, 1902.

Lincoln, Abraham. *The Literary Works of Abraham Lincoln.* Edited by Carl Van Doren. New York: The Limited Editions Club, 1942.

Lipner, Julius. "On 'Hindutva' And a 'Hindu-Catholic,' With a Moral for our Times." *Journal of Hindu-Christian Studies* 5 (1992) 1–8.

Lobo, Lancy. *Globalisation, Hindu Nationalism, and Christians in India.* Jaipur: Rawat, 2002.

Lok Sabha Debates, Part 2, Vol. 9. New Delhi: Government of India, 1954.

Louis, Prakash. *The Emerging Hindutva Force.* New Delhi: Indian Social Institute, 2000.

Madhya Pradesh Gazette. "The Madhya Pradesh Dharma Swatantrya Adhiniyam, 1968." Act No. 27 of 1968. Extraordinary, October 21, 1968.

Majhi, Anita Srivastava. *Tribal Culture, Continuity, and Change: A Study of Bhils in Rajasthan.* New Delhi: Mittal, 2010.

Majumdar, R. C. *History of the Freedom Movement in India, Vol. I.* Calcutta: Firma KL Mukhopadhyay, 1975.

———. *History of the Freedom Movement in India, Vol. II.* 2nd ed. Calcutta: K.L. Mukhopadhyay, 1971.

Malhotra, Bimal. *Reform, Reaction and Nationalism in Western India (1885–1907).* Mumbai: Himalaya, 2000.

Malik, Sameer. "Voices of Hindutva: Creating and Exploiting Religious Binaries." *Interreligious Dialogue* 1 (2009). http://irstudies.org/?s=Sameer+Malik&x=0&y=0.

Malkani, K. R. *The RSS Story.* New Delhi: Impex India, 1980.

Mander, Harsh. "Incursions of Hindutva—Times of India." http://timesofindia.indiatimes.com/edit-page/incursions-of-hindutva/articleshow/1362402.cms.

Marshman, J. C. *Life and Times of Carey, Marshman, Ward.* London: Longman, 1859.

Mathew, C. V. *The Saffron Mission: A Historical Analysis of Modern Hindu Missionary Ideologies and Practices.* New Delhi: ISPCK, 1999.

Mattam, Joseph, and Reuben Gabriel. *In the Shadow of the Cross: Christians and Minorities in India Encounter Hostility.* Mumbai: St. Pauls, 2002.

Mayhew, Arthur. *Christianity and the Government of India.* London: Faber & Gwyer Ltd, 1929.

——. *Christianity in India*. Delhi: Gian, 1988.

McPhee, Arthur G. *The Road to Delhi: Bishop Pickett Remembered 1890–1981*. Bangalore: SAIACS, 2005.

Meera, Meera. "Arya Samaj and Caste System: A Study of the Impact of the Arya Samaj in the United Provinces." *IOSR Journal of Humanities and Social Science* 19 (2014) 68–72.

Mehta, Piarey Lal. *Constitutional Protection to Scheduled Tribes in India*. Delhi: H.K. , 1991.

Melanchthon, Monica. "Persecution of Indian Christians." *A Journal of Theology* 41 (2002) 103–13.

Menon, Nivedita. "India First and the BJP Anti-Conversion Platform: Goldie Osuri." http://kafila.org/2013/10/12/india-first-and-the-bjp-anti-conversion-platform-goldie-osuri.

Menon, Parvathi. "An Old Debate in a New Context." http://www.frontline.in/static/html/fl1608/16080380.htm.

Mill, James. *The History of British India, Vol. I*. London: James Madden and Co., 1840.

Mills, Kenneth, and Anthony Grafton, eds. *Conversion: Old Worlds and New*. Rochester, NY: University of Rochester Press, 2003.

Mishra, Dwarka Prasad. *The History of the Freedom Movement in Madhya Pradesh*. Nagpur: Government Printing, 1956.

Misra, Amalendu. "The Missionary Position: Christianity and Politics of Religious Conversion in India." *Nationalism and Ethnic Politics* 17 (2011) 361–81.

Mitter, Partha. *Much Maligned Monsters: A History of European Reactions to Indian Art*. Oxford: Clarendon, 1977.

Moffett, Samuel Hugh. *A History of Christianity in Asia, Vol. II: 1500 To 1900*. Maryknoll NY: Orbis, 1998.

Moon, Vasant. *Growing up Untouchable in India: A Dalit Autobiography*. Lanham, MD: Rowman & Littlefield, 2000.

Morris, Jan. *Heaven's Command: An Imperial Progress*. London: Faber and Faber, 1974.

Mozoomdar, P. C. *The Faith and Progress of the Brahmo Somaj*. Calcutta: Calcutta Central, 1882.

——. *Will the Brahmo Somaj Last?* Calcutta: The Brotherhood, 1913.

Mukerji, N. C. "Communalism of the Niyogi Report." In *Voice of Truth: A Topical Symposium*, M. Ruthnaswami, et al., 38–45. Allahabad: O. M. Thomas, 1957.

Mukul, Akshaya. "RSS Officially Disowns Golwalkar's Book—Times of India." *The Times of India*. http://timesofindia.indiatimes.com/india/RSS-officially-disowns-Golwalkars-book/articleshow/1443606.cms.

Muttungal, Anand. "Why M.P. Govt. Seeks Christians'Antecedents?" http://www.franand.com/Page.aspx?AID=122.

Nag, Udayan. "RSS Body Dharam Jagran Samiti Sets Fixed Rates for Converting Muslims, Christians Into Hindus." *International Business Times, India Edition*. http://www.ibtimes.co.in/rss-body-dharam-jagran-samiti-sets-fixed-rates-converting-muslims-christians-into-hindus-616924.

Naidu, Venkayya. "Narendra Modi Dares Opposition to Support Anti-Conversion Law." https://www.youtube.com/watch?v=BFT6eHv3DOg.

Naipaul, V. S. *Beyond Beliefs: Islamic Excursions among the Converted People*. London: Little Brown & Co., 1998.

Nandy, Ashis. "The Fear of Gandhi: Nathuram Godse and His Successors." *The Times of India*, 1994.

———. *The Intimate Enemy: Loss and Recovery of Self Under Colonialism*. Delhi: Oxford, 1983.

"Narendra Modi Dares Opposition to Support Anti-Conversion Law." https://www.youtube.com/watch?v=BFT6eHv3DOg.

NCCI. "Minutes of the Meeting of the Executive Committee of the NCCI." *National Christian Council of India and Pakistan Review*, February 25–27, 1959.

———. "Proceedings of the Thirteenth Meeting of the National Christian Council of India." *National Christian Council of India Review*, 1956.

NDTV. "Is Madhya Pradesh Govt. Profiling Christians?" April 14, 2011. https://www.youtube.com/watch?v=aNO-Kjuy2ps.

Nehru, Jawaharlal. *The Discovery of India*. New York: John Day, 1945.

Neill, Stephen. *A History of Christian Missions*. 2nd ed. Harmondsworth, England: Penguin, 1986.

———. *A History of Christianity in India: The Beginning to AD 1707*. Cambridge: Cambridge University Press, 1984.

Nelson, Richard Alan. *A Chronology and Glossary of Propaganda in the United States*. Westport, CT: Greenwood, 1996.

The New Indian Express. "SC's Seven-Judge Bench to Revisit Hindutva Judgement." http://www.newindianexpress.com/nation/SCs-Seven-judge-Bench-to-Revisit-Hindutva-Judgement/2014/02/02/article2033912.ece.

Niyogi, M. Bhavani Shankar. *Report of the Christian Missionary Activities Enquiry Committee, Volume I*. Nagpur: Government Printing, 1956.

———. *Report of the Christian Missionary Activities Enquiry Committee, Volume II*. Nagpur: Government Printing, 1956.

Noorani, A. C. "BJP: Child of RSS and Heir to Hindu Mahasabha." *Mainstream Weekly*, July 27, 1991.

Nussbaum, Martha Craven. *The Clash Within: Democracy, Religious Violence, and India's Future*. Cambridge: Belknap Press of Harvard University Press, 2007.

Oddie, Geoffrey A. *Imagined Hinduism: British Protestant Missionary Constructions of Hinduism*. New Delhi: Sage, 2006.

Oommen, T. K. "Religious Nationalism and Democratic Polity: The Indian Case." *Sociology of Religion* 55 (1994) 455–72. http://www.jstor.org/stable/3711982.

Orissa Gazette. "The Orissa Freedom of Religion Act, 1968, Orissa Act 2 of 1968." Extra Ordinary, January 11, 1968.

Osuri, Goldie. *Religious Freedom in India: Sovereignty and (Anti) Conversion*. New York: Routledge, 2013.

———. "The Concern for Sovereignty in the Politics of Anti-Conversion" *Religion Compass* 7/9 (2013) 385.

Outlook India. "Adivasi vs Vanvasi: The Hinduization of Tribals in India." November 20, 2002. http://www.outlookindia.com/article/adivasi-vs-vanvasi-the-hinduization-of-tribals-in-india/217974.

Offord Dictionary. "Oxford Dictionaries—Dictionary, Thesaurus, & Grammar." http://www.oxforddictionaries.com.

Pachpore, Virag. *The Indian Church?* Nagpur: BDHRR & DI, 2001.

———. "A Peep into the History of Anti-Conversion Laws." http://www.newsbharati.com/Encyc/2013/7/17/A-peep-into-the-history-of-anti-conversion-laws.

Pachuau, Lalsangkima. "A Clash of Mass Movements? Christian Missions and the Gandhian Nationalist Movement in India." *Transformation* 31 (2014) 157–74.

———. "Ecumenical Church and Religious Conversion: A Historical-Theological Study with Special Reference to India." *Mission Studies* 17 (2001) 181–201.

———. *Ethnic Identity and Christianity: A Socio-Historical and Missiological Study of Christianity in Northeast India with Special Reference to Mizoram.* Frankfurt: Peter Lang, 2002.

———. "Nationhood in Conflict: Ethnonationalism and Political Nationalism in Northeast India." In *Nationalism and Hindutva: A Christian Response: Papers From the 10th CMS Consultation,* edited by Mark T. B. Laing, 53–66. New Delhi: ISPCK, 2016.

Page, Melvin E. *Colonialism: An International Social, Cultural, and Political Encyclopedia, Vol. 3.* 1st ed. Santa Barbara, CA: ABC-CLIO, 2003.

Pal, Bipin Chandra. *The Brahmo Samaj and the Battle for Swaraj in India.* Calcutta: Devaprosad Mitra, 1926.

Panadan, Davis. "Anti-Conversion Laws: A Fraud on the Constitution and Democracy of India." *Journal of Dharma* 35 (2010) 131–41.

Panicker, P. L. John. *Gandhi on Pluralism and Communalism.* Delhi: Indian Society for Promoting Christian Knowledge, 2006.

Panikkar, K. M. *Asia and Western Dominance. A Survey of the Vasco da Gama Epoch Of Asian History, 1498–1945. [With Maps.].* London: George Allen & Unwin, 1959.

———. *Hinduism and the Modern World.* Allahabad: Kitabistan, 1938.

———. *Malabar and the Portuguese.* New Delhi: Voice of India, 1997.

———. *A Survey of Indian History.* Calcutta: Asia, 1954.

Parekh, Manilal C. *Christian Proselytism in India: A Great and Growing Menace.* Rajkot: The Author, Harmony House, 1947.

———. *The Brahma Samaj: A Short History.* Rajkot: Oriental Christ House, 1929.

Pattanaik, D. D. "The Swadeshi Movement: Culmination of Cultural Nationalism." *Orissa Review* (2005) 9–16.

Pearson, Hugh. *Memoirs of the Life and Correspondence of the Reverend Christian Frederick Swartz, Vol. II.* London: Hatchard, 1835.

Pickett, Jarrell Waskom. *Christian Mass Movements in India.* New York: Abingdon Press, 1933.

Pickett, Jarrell Waskom, et al. *Christian Missions in Mid India: A Study of Nine Areas with Special Reference to Mass Movements.* Jubbulpore, India: Mission, 1938.

Pillay, T. Ponnambalam. "Life History of Arumuga Navalar." http://www.shaivam.org/english/sen-arumuga-navalar.htm.

Plattner, Felix Alfred. *The Catholic Church in India: Yesterday and Today.* Allahabad: St. Paul, 1964.

Ponnumuthan, Selvister. *The Spirituality of Basic Ecclesial Communities in the Socio-Religious Context of Trivandrum/Kerala, India.* Rome: Gregorian University Press, 1996.

Pothacamury, Thomas. *The Church in Independent India.* New York: Maryknoll, 1956.

Prasad, Rajendra. *India Divided.* 3rd ed. Bombay: Hind Kitabs, 1947.

Prasad, Rajendra, and Valmiki Chaudhari. *Dr. Rajendra Prasad: Correspondence and Select Documents.* New Delhi: Allied, 1994.

Prasad De, Krishna. *Religious Freedom Under the Indian Constitution.* Calcutta: Ajanta Printers, 1977.

Priolkar, Anant Kakba. *The Terrible Tribunal for the East: The Goa Inquisition*. New Delhi: Voice of India, 1998.

Puniyani, Ram. *Fascism of Sangh Parivar*. Delhi: Media House, 2000.

———. "M.S. Golwalkar: Conceptualizing Hindutva Fascism." http://www.countercurrents.org/comm-puniyani100306.htm.

Puntambekar, S. V. "Vishnu Bawa Brahmachari, (1825–1871)—An Utopian Socialist." *The Indian Journal of Political Science* 6 (1945) 154–61.

Puri, Geeta. *Bharatiya Jana Sangh: Organization and Ideology*. New Delhi: Sterling, 1980.

Radhakrishnan, S. *East and West: Some Reflections*. New York: Harper, 1956.

Rai, Champat. "VHP at a Glance." http://www.hvk.org/2014/0914/84.html.

Rai, Lajpat. *The Arya Samaj: An Account of its Origin, Doctrines, and Activities, With a Biographical Sketch of the Founder*. London: Longmans, 1915.

Raj, Ebe Sunder, et al. *Divide to Rule: Communal attacks on Christians in India during 1997–2000*. Chennai: Bharat Jyoti, 2000.

Raj, Sunder. *The Confusion Called Conversion*. New Delhi: TRACI, 1986.

Ramaseshan, Radhika. "Cabinet to Discuss Bajrang, VHP Ban." http://www.telegraphindia.com/1081005/jsp/nation/story_9930126.jsp.

Richter, Julius. *A History of Christian Missions in India*. New York: Fleming H. Revell Company, 1908.

Robson, John. *Hinduism and its Relations to Christianity*. Edinburgh: Oliphant Anderson, 1893.

Rolland, Romain. *Dayananda and Arya Samaj*. New Delhi: Sarvadeshik Arya Pratinidhi Sabha, 2006.

Roy, Arundhati. "Fascism's Firm Footprint in India." http://www.ratical.org/co-globalize/AR093002.pdf.

Roy, Raja Rammohun. "The Brahmunical Magazine of the Missionary and the Brahmun Being a Vindication of the Hindoo Religion against the Attacks of Christian Missionaries." In *The English Works of Raja Rammohun Roy*, edited by Jogendra Chunder Ghose, 143–98. Allahabad: The Panini Office, 1906.

R.S.S.–Christian Perspective Meet. Kottayam: Indian Institute of Christian Studies, 2002.

Ruthnaswami, M. "Obsessions of the Niyogi Committee." In *Voice of Truth: A Topical Symposium*, edited by M. Ruthnaswamy et al., 46–51. Allahabad: O. M. Thomas, 1957.

Ruthnaswamy, M., et al. *Voice of Truth: A Topical Symposium*. Allahabad: O. M. Thomas, 1957.

Rutherfurd, John. *Missionary Pioneers in India*. Edinburgh: Andrew Elliot, 1896.

Sahoo, Sarbeswar. "Religious Violence and the 'Developmental State' in Rajasthan." In *Perspectives on Violence and Othering in India*, edited by R. C. Tripathi and Purnima Singh, 175–95. New Delhi: Springer, 2016.

Saldanha, Julian. *Conversion and Indian Civil Law*. Bangalore: Theological Publications in India, 1981.

Samadder, Radhikaranjan. "Marxist: History of Armed Revolution—Lotus and Dagger—Aurobindo Ghose (Contd-9)." http://radhikaranjanmarxist.blogspot.com/2011/10/lotus-and-dagger-aurobindo-ghose.html.

Sanyasi, Shraddhananda. *Hindu Sanghatan—Saviour of the Dying Race*. Delhi: Arjun, 1926.

Saraswati, S. "British Policy towards Religion in India." In *Politics of Conversion* edited by Devendra Swarup, 101–10. New Delhi: Deendayal Research Institute, 1986.

Sarma, D. S. *Renascent Hinduism.* Bombay: Bharatiya Vidya Bhavan, 1966.

Sastri, Sivanatha. *History of the Brahmo Samaj.* Calcutta: R. Chatterjee, 1911.

Satyavrata, Ivan M. *God Has Not Left Himself Without Witness.* Oregon: Regnum, 2011.

Savarkar, V. D. *Hindu Rashtra Darshan* (A Collection of the Presidential Speeches Delivered from the Hindu Mahasabha Platform). Bombay: Laxman Ganesh Khare, 1949.

———. *Hindutva.* Nagpur: V.V. Kelkar, 1923.

———. *The Indian War of Independence of 1857.* Bombay: Sethani Kampani, 1905.

Savarkar.org. "Essentials of Hindutva." http://www.savarkar.org/en/hindutva-hindu-nationalism/essentials-hindutva.

Saxena, Surya Narayan. *Alienation of Tribals and Christian Missionaries.* Bombay: Bharatiya Vsanvasi Kalyan Ashram, n.d.

Schmidlin, Joseph. *Catholic Mission History.* Techny, IL: Mission, S.V.D., 1933.

Schurhammer, Georg, and Joseph Costelloe. *Francis Xavier: His Life, His Times: India, 1541–1544.* Rome: Jesuit Historical Institute, 1982.

Seamands, J. T. "The Present-Day Environment of Christian Missions." Unpublished article. Papers of J. T. Seamands-Printed material. Asbury Theological Seminary, B. L. Fisher Library. Wilmore, n.d.

Sen, Surendra Nath. *Eighteen Fifty-Seven.* Calcutta: Publications Division, Government of India, 1957.

Servin, Oscar. *Annotations on the Niyogi Report Relating to Raigarh and Surguja.* Nagpur: Pushpa, 1957.

Seshadri, H. V. *RSS, A Vision in Action.* 2nd ed. Bangalore, India: Sahitya Sindhu Prakashana, 2012.

Shapoo, Rubina Khan. "Is Madhya Pradesh Govt. Profiling Christians?" https://www.youtube.com/watch?v=aNO-Kjuy2ps.

Sharma, Arvind. "Christian Proselytization: A Hindu Perspective." *Missiology: An International Review* 33 (2005) 425–34.

———. *Hinduism as a Missionary Religion.* Albany: State University of New York Press, 2011.

Sharma, Jyotirmaya. *Hindutva: Exploring the Idea of Hindu Nationalism.* New Delhi: Viking, 2003.

Sharma, Prabha. "Bharatiya Jana Sangh: The Development of a Political Party in India." MA diss., Kansas State University, 1969.

Shaw, Graham. "An Initiative that Backfired." *The Hindu.* http://www.thehindu.com/books/an-initiative-that-backfired/article5534044.ece.

Shourie, Arun. *Harvesting Our Souls.* New Delhi: ASA, 2000.

———. *Missionaries in India: Continuities, Changes and Dilemmas.* New Delhi: ASA, 1994.

———. "The 'Roman Brahmin.'" http://arunshourie.bharatvani.org/articles/roman.htm.

Shukla, I. K. *Hindutva: An Autopsy of Fascism as a Theoterrorist Cult and Other Essays.* New Delhi: Media, 2003.

Smith, Anthony D. *National Identity.* Reno: University of Nevada Press, 1991.

Smith, Donald Eugene. *India as a Secular State.* Princeton: Princeton University Press, 1963.

Smith, George. *The Conversion of India: From Pantaenus to the Present Time A. D. 193–1893*. New York: Fleming H. Revell, 1894.

———. *The Life of William Carey: Shoemaker and Missionary*. Edinburgh: R. & R. Clark, 1885. http://www.wmcarey.edu/carey/gsmith/smith.htm.

Singh, Raja. "Bhagwa Dwaj | Raja Singh—BJP MLA—Goshamahal, Hyderabad." http://www.trajasingh.com/hindutva/our-culture-values/bhagwa-dwaj/.

Soares, Aloysius. "Conversion—Means and Ends." In *Truth Shall Prevail: Reply to Niyogi Committee*, A. Soares et al., 1–106. Bombay: Catholic Association of Bombay, 1957.

Sontheimer, Gunther, and Hermann Kulke, eds. *Hinduism Reconsidered*. Heidelberg: South Asia Institute, 1989.

Srivastava, A. R. N. *Essentials of Cultural Anthropology*. New Delhi: PHI Learning Pvt. Ltd, 2013.

Srivastava, Piyush. "We Will Free India of Muslims and Christians by 2021." https://www.dailymail.co.uk/indiahome/indianews/article-2879597/We-free-India-Muslims-Christians-2021-DJS-leader-vows-continue-ghar-wapsi-plans-restore-Hindu-glory.html.

Stahnke, Tad. "The Right to Engage in Religious Persuasion." In *Facilitating Freedom of Religion on Belief: A Deskbook*, edited by T. Lindholm et al., 619–50. The Hague: Konninklijke Brill NV, 2004.

Stanislaus, L. "A Christian Response to Hindutva." In *Nationalism and Hindutva: A Christian Response*, edited by Mark T. B. Laing, 177–203. New Delhi: ISPCK, 2005.

Stanley, Brian. *The History of Baptist Missionary Society 1792–1992*. Edinburg: T. & T. Clark, 1992.

———. "Winning the World: Carey and the Modern Missionary Movement." *Christian History | Learn the History of Christianity and the Church*. http://www.christianitytoday.com/history/issues/issue-9/winning-world-carey-and-modern-missionary-movement.html.

Strickland, William. *The Jesuit in India: Addressed to all Who are Interested in the Foreign Missions*. London: Burns & Lambert, 1952.

Stromberg, Peter. *Language and Self-Transformation: A Study of the Christian Narrative*. Cambridge: Cambridge University Press, 1993.

Studdert-Kennedy, Gerald. *British Christians, Indian Nationalists, and the Raj*. Delhi: Oxford University Press, 1991.

Sudarshan, K.S. "Speech in RSS-Christian Perspective Meet." In *RSS-Christian Perspective Meet*, 18–38. Kottayam: Indian Institute of Christian Studies, 2003.

Sunder Raj, Ebe, et al. *Divide to Rule*. Chennai: Bharat Jyoti, 2000.

Swami, Pejawar. "Religious Conversion are Relics of Imperialist Days." *Organizer* (May 27, 1974) 14.

Swami, Praveen, and Anupama Katakam. "Malegaon: the Road to Perdition." *The Hindu*. http://www.thehindu.com/todays-paper/tp-opinion/article3072855.ece.

Swarup, Devendra, ed. *Politics of Conversion*. Delhi: Deendayal Research Institute, 1986.

Swarup, Ram. "Hindu Renaissance." *Organizer*, October 12, 1995.

———. *Hindu View of Christianity and Islam*. New Delhi: Voice of India, 1992.

Sweetman, Will. "Prehistory of Orientalism: Colonialism and the Textual Basis for Bartholomaus Ziegenbalg's Account of Hinduism." *New Zealand Journal of Asian Studies* 6 (2004) 12–38.

Sweetman, Will, and Aditya Malik, eds. *Hinduism in India: Modern and Contemporary Movements.* New Delhi: SAGE, 2016.

Talreja, Kanayalal M. *An Appeal to Law-Makers for Constitutional Ban on Conversion of Hindus.* New Delhi: Rashtriya Chetana Sangathan, 2002.

———. *Holy Vedas and Holy Bible: A Comparative Study.* New Delhi: Rashtriya Chetana Sangathan, 2000.

Tennent, Timothy C. *Building Christianity on Indian Foundations: The Legacy of Brahmabhandav Upadyay.* Delhi: ISPCK, 2000.

Thaliath, Joseph. "An Improper Choice." In *Voice of Truth: A Topical Symposium,* edited by M. Ruthnaswamy et al., 34–37. Allahabad: O. M. Thomas, 1957.

Thomas, Abraham Vazhayil. *Christians in Secular India.* Rutherford: Fairleigh Dickinson University Press, 1974.

Thomas, K. T. *RSS-Christian Perspective Meet 20th August, 2002.* Kottayam: Indian Institute of Christian Studies, 2003.

Thomas, Mathew. "Christian Missions in the Pluralistic Context of India—The Relevance of Gandhian Approach." PhD thesis, Mahatma Gandhi University, 2002.

Thomas, O. M. "Christian-Baiting in Madhya Pradesh." In *Voice of Truth: A Topical Symposium,* edited by M. Ruthnaswamy et al., 24–33. Allahabad: O. M. Thomas, 1957.

———. "A Critique of the Niyogi Report." In *Voice of Truth: A Topical Symposium,* edited by M. Ruthnaswamy et al. Allahabad: O. M. Thomas, 1957.

Thursby, Gene. R. *Hindu-Muslim Relations in British India: A Study of Controversy, Conflict and Communal Movements in North India 1923–1928.* Netherlands: E. J. Brill, 1975.

Tiedemann, R. G. "Indigenous Agency, Religious Protectorates, and Chinese Interests: The Expansion of Christianity in Nineteenth-Century China." In *Converting Colonialism: Visions and Realities in Mission History, 1706–1914,* edited by Dana L. Robert, 206–41. Grand Rapids: Eerdmans, 2008.

The Times of India. "Rajasthan House Okays Religion Bill—India—The Times of India." http://timesofindia.indiatimes.com/India/Rajasthan_House_okays_Religion_Bill/rssarticleshow/2885975.cms.

Tiwary, Deeptiman. "VHP Defends Attack on Haryana Church, Calls 1857 'Communal War'—Times of India." *The Times of India.* http://timesofindia.indiatimes.com/india/VHP-defends-attack-on-Haryana-church-calls-1857-communal-war/articleshow/46590892.cms.

United Nations. "The Universal Declaration of Human Rights | United Nations." http://www.un.org/en/universal-declaration-human-rights/.

Uma, Saumya, and Vrinda Grover. *Kandhamal.* New Delhi: Multiple Action Research Group, 2010.

Varkey, S. A. C. "The Image of Christianity in the Newspapers." *Indian Missiological Review* 9 (1987).

Varma, V. P. *The Political Philosophy of Sri Aurobindo.* New Delhi: Motilal Banarsidass, 1990.

Vedantham, T. R. "Church as a Tool of Imperialism in the World." In *Politics of Conversion,* edited by Devendra Swarup, 71–80. New Delhi: Deendayal Research Institute, 1986.

Vedhamanickam, PrabhuSingh. "Serving Under the Saffron Shadow: Hindu Nationalism, Violence and Christianity in Gujarat, India." PhD diss., Asbury Theological Seminary, Wilmore, 2008.

Veer, Peter van der. *Religious Nationalism: Hindus and Muslims in India.* Berkeley, CA: University of California Press, 1994.

Venkatesan, V. "A Hate Campaign in Gujarat." http://www.frontline.in/static/html/fl1602/16021070.htm.

Vishva Hindu Parishad. "Bajrang Dal | Vishva Hindu Parishad | Official Website." http://vhp.org/vhp-glance/youth/dim1-bajrang-dal/.

———. "Inception of VHP | Vishva Hindu Parishad | Official Website." http://vhp.org/organization/org-inception-of-vhp/.

———. "Religious Regeneration: The Only Solution to Various National Problems." http://vhp.org/vhp-glance/dimensions/dharm-prasar/religious-regeneration-the-only-solution-to-various-national-problems/.

———. "Who Is A Hindu? | Vishwa Hindu Parishad of America." https://www.vhp-america.org/aboutus/who-is-a-hindu.

Viswanathan, Gauri. "Literacy and Conversion in the Discourse of Hindu Nationalism." *Race and Class* 42 (2000).

———. "Literacy in the Eye of India's Conversion Storm." In *Conversion: Old Worlds and New,* edited by Kenneth Mills and Anthony Grafton. New York: University of Rochester, 2003.

Wallace, Anthony F. C. "Revitalization Movements." *American Anthropologist* 58 (1956) 264–81.

Ward, William. *A View of the History, Literature and Religion of the Hindoos: Including a minute Description of their Manners and Customs and Translations from their Principal works.* 2nd ed. Serampore: Mission, 1815.

Webster, John C. B. *The Christian Community and Change in Nineteenth Century North India.* Delhi: Macmillan Co. of India, 1976.

Wolpert, Stanley A. *A New History of India.* 3rd ed. New York: Oxford University Press, 1989.

World Hindu News. "Meet & Greet Event: Shri Ashok Chowgule | President—External, VHP-Norwalk, CA." http://worldhindunews.com/2013111112109/to-meet-greet-event-shri-ashok-chowgule-president-external-vhp/.

Wyche, Susan, et al. "Historical Analysis: Using the Past to Design the Future." In *UbiComp 2006: Ubiquitous Computing,* edited by Paul Dourish and Adrian Friday, 35–51. Berlin: Springer, 2006.

Young, Richard F., and Jonathon A. Seitz. *Asia in the Making of Christianity: Conversion, Agency and Indigeneity, 1600S to the Present.* Leiden and Boston: Brill, 2013.

Zachariah, Aleyamma. *Modern Religious and Secular Movements in India.* Bangalore, India: Theological Book Trust, 1994.

Zavos, John. *The Emergence of Hindu Nationalism in India.* New Delhi: Oxford University Press, 2000.

Index of Significant People

Subject Index